The MIS:Press *Slackware* Series

CONFIGURATION AND INSTALLATION
Third Edition

PATRICK VOLKERDING
KEVIN REICHARD
ERIC FOSTER-JOHNSON

MIS: PRESS

A Subsidiary of
Henry Holt and Co., Inc.

**A Subsidiary of
Henry Holt and Co., Inc.**

Copyright © 1997 by Patrick J. Volkerding, Kevin Reichard, and Eric Foster-Johnson
A Subsidiary of Henry Holt and Company, Inc.
115 West 18th Street
New York, New York 10011
http://www.mispress.com

Printing History

First Edition—1996

Second Edition—1996

Third Edition—1997

Library of Congress Cataloging-in-Publication Data

```
Volkerding, Patrick.
    LINUX configuration and installation / by Patrick Volkerding,
Kevin Reichard, Eric Foster-Johnson. -- 3rd ed.
        p.    cm.

    ISBN 1-55828-566-0

    1. Linux.  2. Operating systems (Computers) I. Reichard, Kevin.
II. Johnson, Eric F.   III. Title.
QA76.76.063V64  1997
005.4'469--dc21                                97-19183
                                               CIP
```

Printed in the United States of America.

10 9 8 7 6 5 4 3 2 1

Associate Publisher: Paul Farrell   **Managing Editor:** Shari Chappell

Editor: Laura Lewin   **Copy Edit Manager:** Karen Tongish

Production Editor: Kitty May

For Sean

The MIS:Press *Slackware* Series

Linux Programming
Patrick Volkerding, Eric F. Johnson, Kevin Reichard

The Linux Database
Fred Butzen, Dorothy Forbes

The Linux Internet Server
Kevin Reichard

Linux in Plain English
Patrick Volkerding, Kevin Reichard

Contents

Chapter 3: Installing and Configuring XFree86 . . .111

Section II: Using Linux

Section III: Linux Communications and Networking

Chapter 7: Linux and Telecommunications 383

Section IV: Linux Programming

Introduction

Welcome to Linux

Welcome to the Linux operating system and the third edition of *Linux Installation and Configuration*! Whether you are looking for a version of UNIX that you can run on an inexpensive PC or are just totally disgusted with the antics of Microsoft et al. when it comes to operating systems, we think you'll get a lot out of this book.

In these pages, you'll be guided through a Linux installation and configuration process from beginning to end. You'll also learn about the many unique tools offered by the Linux operating system, as well how to use these tools in a variety of situations.

What is Linux?

Linux (pronounced *lih-nux*) is a 32-bit operating system designed for use on Intel 80386 (or better) PCs. Technically, Linux is a UNIX workalike, which means that it responds to standard UNIX commands and will run UNIX programs. You might see some references elsewhere to Linux as a UNIX clone, but that's not strictly correct. (If it were a UNIX clone, Linux would be a lot more expensive than it is, due to the additional overhead of licensing fees.)

Linux began life as the project of a single man, Linus Torvalds (then a student at the University of Finland at Helsinki), who wanted his own alternative to another UNIX alternative—namely, the Minix operating system. He designed Linux to be similar to Minix (the original Minix filesystem was incorporated into Linux), yet more stable and freely available.

For a long time Linux was an operating system under development, as many beta versions of Linux circulated throughout the computer world—mostly distributed through the Internet world. Version 0.2 was released to the world in the middle of 1991; in 1994, version 1.0 was finally released. A ready and willing group of volunteers helped Torvalds finish Linux; additionally, these volunteers (including one of the authors of this book, Patrick Volkerding) helped create the add-on software that helps make Linux so popular. The CD-ROMs that accompany this book are based on Linux 2.0.

Linux, as an operating system, is actually rather trim and fit. You could install Linux from a three-disk set (the *a* series, which you'll learn about in Chapter 2). So why do you need two CD-ROMs, filled to the brim with bits and bytes? Because the core Linux operating system, as such, doesn't do much more than offer a command line and respond to the core UNIX commands. You'll need the additional software—ranging from utilities like **diff** from the Free Software Foundation to compilers and editors. Because this additional software is different from distribution to distribution (on the accompanying CD-ROMs, you're using the highly regarded Slackware distribution), there are differences between Linuxes (Linuci? Linuces?) available on the market. (For example, the installation program—so critical for many users—is unique to Slackware.) And Linux features its own graphical interface, based on the X Window System.

This leads us to one essential truth about Linux (something also true about UNIX): Linux is a series of tools. You use one tool to do one thing, another tool to perform another function. As a set of tools, the Slackware distribution is more than just Linux.

What Makes Slackware Linux Special?

Why use Linux? The following features make Linux special in the operating system world:

- **Linux is an alternative to the commercial operating system world.** There's something to be said for striking a blow against the Empire. Linux is the result of many hours of volunteer workers who believed that a grass-roots approach to software development was a more harmonic approach than commercial offerings. Whether you buy into this ethos is up to you, but you cannot help but be impressed that such an outstanding computer operating system, rich in complexity and features, is the work of so many.

- **Linux is built for the Internet and networking.** The Internet is all the rage, and the Linux world is part of the hubbub. Linux probably wouldn't be where it is today without the Internet, as hundreds of volunteers have collaborated via the Internet, shipping source code and program files from machine to machine. In addition, Linux can be used right out of the box for Internet and networking; there's no need to buy additional software. All you need to do is configure what you have.

- **Linux is completely open.** You get the source code for the Linux operating system on an accompanying CD-ROM. If you want to make changes to the operating system, you can do so. If you want a driver for your oddball peripheral, you can write it yourself or con someone else into writing it for you.

Why Should You Use Linux?

Because it runs UNIX programs—most notably through compiling original source code written for the many UNIX variants around the world—Linux is the ideal platform for many potential users:

- Users who want to learn more about the UNIX operating system and the X Window System.
- Internet surfers who want a powerful platform for cruising the Net.
- System administrators who want an alternative to expensive UNIX workstations, either in their workplace or at home.
- Programmers who want a cheap home or small-business platform for developing software that can be used on other, more powerful UNIX systems.

There are many features to Linux that you should find attractive:

- **You've already paid for it.** By purchasing this book, you've purchased a full implementation of Linux, complete with scads of useful programs.
- **Linux follows standards**. For the most part, Linux and its tools follow various standards, such as POSIX compliance. As a programming platform, Linux can be used to develop and test code for a wide variety of platforms.
- **Linux can be used for most of your everyday needs**. True, Linux lacks the wide range of applications found in the PC world. However, for most of your daily tasks (particularly if you want to use Linux for programming or the Internet), the accompanying CD-ROMs contain enough tools to satisfy most of your needs.
- **Linux runs binaries created on other PC versions of UNIX.** The new iBCS capability allows you to run a program that was compiled for another Intel-based PC, including SCO UNIX and FreeBSD.

Will Linux replace more popular operating systems, like MS/PC-DOS and Windows? That depends on your needs. For many basic computing tasks—word processing, spreadsheets, telecommunications—Linux and the Slackware distribution are a perfectly adequate alternative to other

PC operating systems. As a development platform, Linux is more than adequate. Because Linux is freely available, it attracts the attention of many programmers and developers who release their software to the computing community—meaning that there's a decent selection of software in the computing world, even beyond what's available on the CD-ROMs with this book. The one drawback to Linux—which, admittedly, is a major drawback—is the lack of robust applications for everyday use. True, you can do work with **emacs** and **groff** for document creation, but this process is awkward at best. Given the track record of the UNIX industry and the robust growth enjoyed by Linux, you can expect to see many more applications down the road.

Of course, this isn't to say that you won't use the applications on the CD-ROMs with this book. For many, the use of Linux as an Internet tool will alone be worth the price of the book. Programmers who want to code for other UNIX and X Window platforms will also find this book and its CD-ROMs extremely useful.

Linux, Slackware, and This Book

This book isn't a general primer on the Linux operating system. Instead, we've decided to focus on the version of Linux included on the accompanying CD-ROMs. We made this decision because the world of Linux is very wide and varied, and despite what some people think, there *are* differences among Linux distributions.

If you own another Linux distribution, there will be things in this book that apply to your distribution (particularly in Chapter 4 and beyond). However, be warned that we're sticking to the Slackware distribution of Linux for the particulars in this book.

What is Slackware Compared to Linux?

Linux, as distributed by the many good people who work on it, is actually quite a limited piece of software. Essentially, it's the three-disk set beginning with *a* that make up the true core of the operating system.

The Slackware distribution of Linux builds on this core with utilities, programming libraries, and ports of other UNIX and X Window programs, under a unified whole. Many of the setup utilities on the CD-ROMs, for example, are unique to the Slackware distribution of Linux. These things make the Slackware distribution unique.

Differences between This Book and the First Edition

The first edition of this book sold phenomenally well—much better, quite frankly, than we anticipated. It quickly spawned a group of Linux wannabes who really didn't know the operating system but could license Linux from another source and pawn it off as an authentic guide to Linux.

But this sort of approach, quite honestly, isn't in the true spirit of Linux. As a whole, Linux owes a lot to the many volunteers who make it work and help others use it. We've bought into this ethos; Slackware Linux is available at no charge via the Internet. And, as a bonus, we've managed to keep the cost of this book affordable (less than other commercial implementations of Linux) while at the same time offering two CD-ROMs containing a slew of Linux software. The second CD-ROM contains the work of many other software programmers, and if you find their work to be useful in your work, we strongly recommend that you send along a contribution to reward their efforts.

So, what else distinguishes this book from the first and second editions? Well, Linux has changed, and so has the Slackware implementation. On a user level, you'll notice that the operating system is generally more stable, and the X Window implementation is easier to configure and much less cranky to tweak. More tools have been added to the core Slackware Linux distribution on the first CD-ROM. Programmers will appreciate the new data formats that cut down on the size of executable files and the new tools that allow Motif programs to be run without an actual OSF/Motif license from the Open Software Foundation. Several security tools have been added, as well as an updated version on XFree86.

In short, if you've been a Linux user, you'll have reasons both to upgrade your version of Linux and to review the new information presented in this book. Linux is a dynamic, ever-changing operating system, and it's always fun to keep track of the latest and greatest.

The Free Software Foundation

Many of the utilities and programs contained in this distribution of Linux (and most other Linux distributions) come from the Free Software Foundation (FSF) or are licensed under the general terms of the Free Software Foundation. Because so many of the utilities are connected with the FSF, we urge you to check out the group (via its many Usenet newsgroups) and to read through its general license, which is contained along with its programs (for example, **emacs** gives you an option to read through the general license). For more information about the Free Software Foundation, write:

Free Software Foundation
675 Massachusetts Avenue
Cambridge, MA 02139
(617) 876-3296 (voice)
(617) 492-9057 (fax)

gnu@prep.ai.mit.edu

Resources on the CD-ROMs

We've included two CD-ROMs with this book. A full implementation of the Linux operating system can be found on the first CD-ROM. This includes a rather robust set of UNIX utilities and a complete implementation of the X Window System. In addition, we've included a set of documents, called the *Linux HOW-TOS*, in the **docs** directory. These are text files that examine a portion of the Linux operating system in great detail. Occasionally, we will refer to these documents in the course of this book.

The second CD-ROM contains software, software, software. Most of the software contained on the second CD-ROM is already compiled for Slackware Linux, but when appropriate we've included source code so you can compile the software for use on your own system. We present the software "as is" (that is, directly from the authors via the Internet), and there's no way we can support it. Almost all of the software has files that contain information about contacting the authors, and that's where you should turn if you have problems with the software. Also, some of the authors ask for a contribution if you find their software useful, and we *strongly* urge you to send one.

Conventions Used in the Book

To make this book more usable, we've incorporated a few formatting conventions that should make it easier for you to find what you need. These include the following icons:

The Note icon indicates something that you should pay special attention to.

The Warning icon warns you about actions that could be hazardous to the health of your computer or your Linux installation.

The CD-ROMs icon refers to items found on the accompanying CD-ROMs, such as the aforementioned **HOWTO** files.

In addition, we've used some specific formatting commands in the text:

- **Bold** type refers to a command
- *Italic* type refers to a new concept
- **Monospaced** type refers to a command line entered directly at a prompt and ending with the **Enter** key, as in the following:

```
gilbert:/ elvis
```

How to Reach the Authors

You're free to drop us a line via electronic mail at: reichard@mr.net.

However, we must warn you that we promise no further guidance to Linux than what's printed in this book. Among the three of us, we receive a lot of electronic mail, and at times it's impossible to keep up with it. Please don't assume that this electronic-mail address will bring you instant help.

Section I

Linux Installation and Configuration

Welcome to your brave new journey with the Linux operating system! This section covers the installation and configuration of Linux.

Chapter 1 is an overview of the Linux operating system It explains the components and other facts you'll need to know about Linux before installation. If you're not a past or present Linux user, you'll want to read this chapter carefully.

Chapter 2 guides you through a Linux installation from beginning to end. In many ways, installing Linux is one of the more daunting tasks you'll face; Linux runs rather smoothly once it's installed and configured correctly. Again, this is a chapter you'll want to follow very closely.

Chapter 3 covers the installation, configuration, and basic usage of XFree86, the implementation of the X Window System designed for PC-based Unices.

Linux and PC Hardware

This chapter covers:

- The hardware needs of Linux
- PC configuration requirements
- Processor needs
- RAM needs
- Supported hard drives
- Supported SCSI cards
- Supported network cards
- Supported mice
- Supported CD-ROM drives
- Linux and laptops

Preparing for Linux

An ounce of preparation is worth a pound of cure, goes the old (and clichéd, some would say) saying. However, there's a kernel of truth to the old saying—particularly when it comes to installing and configuring Linux.

Before you rush into a half-baked and ill-conceived Linux installation, there are a few things you should do, mostly relating to your PC's setup and configuration. In this chapter, we'll tell you if your PC is capable of efficiently running Linux and point out some potential problem areas. This should be handy if you're thinking about installing Linux on an existing machine or if you're considering the purchase of a new computer (laptop or desktop) for the express purpose of running Linux. In the next chapter, we'll run through a typical Linux installation.

NOTE

We're PC-centric in our attitudes toward Linux. Linux was developed for use on PCs, and the vast majority of Linux users work on PCs. The version of Linux on the accompanying CD-ROM is designed for a PC platform.

However, there have been attempts to move Linux to non-PC hardware platforms—some of which have been quite successful. Appendix A lists the Linux ports to other platforms and ways to get more information about them.

Preparing Your PC for Linux

Like all PC-based Unices (including SCO UNIX and BSD), Linux is pretty fussy about the hardware it runs on. By *fussy*, we mean that Linux does a lot of interacting directly with PC hardware. DOS, by comparison, is a very forgiving operating system, pretty much able to run and function on almost any PC. It will ignore some small flaws in the PC architecture.

Linux, however, will expose those flaws. As a PC UNIX, Linux interacts *very* closely with the PC hardware, writing directly to the various PC components. If there's a problem with your PC—however small—Linux will find it. The problem is somewhat lessened if you're using brand-name equipment; remember (as mentioned in the Introduction) that Linux is a product of a virtual army of volunteers, and they're like everyone else when it comes to computer equipment—if half a million people bought a particular PC model from Compaq, chances are good that a Linux developer (or two) will be among the half-million buyers. This is how hardware gets supported under Linux; the most devoted users make sure Linux works well on their systems. It's certain that someone out there will have experience with Linux on popular hardware—it's less likely that someone out there will have experience on your spanking-new computer from NoNameClone Corp. in the strip mall on the outskirts of town.

If you do buy a PC from NoNameClone Corp., this puts an additional burden on you, as you'll need to know more about your PC than you ever thought. The ideal situation, of course, would be if you didn't actually own a PC yet and you were putting one together expressly to run Linux. (This is the way we approached it, in one instance.) A bad situation is if you bought a no-name clone from a local vendor and had no idea about its components. The worst situation is if you bought a no-name clone and were a UNIX workstation user, fairly ignorant of the quirks surrounding the PC architecture. A middling situation is if you bought a clone from the likes of a CompUSA or Best Buy and had decent documentation regarding the components.

Because we don't live in an ideal world, we'll assume you know little about your PC and need a primer on its components. We'll run down both the minimal and ideal Linux PC configurations and then give a compatibility list.

NOTE   When buying a PC, the temptation is to spend as little as possible or to try to squeeze by with lesser or inferior components. We understand the need to live on a budget—we certainly don't have thousands of dollars worth of computer equipment sitting around our home offices. But there comes a point when you need to make the necessary investment if you want to run Linux effectively. Too often we see people complaining in the Usenet newsgroups that Linux doesn't run properly on their PCs or that XFree86 won't run in higher resolutions on their unsupported graphics cards. You can avoid this by either taking an inventory of your PC before installing Linux (which may mean actually taking off the cover and physically poking through the components) or making sure a new PC meets the compatibility guidelines. Either action is a real pain, we admit; but by spending some time up front, you'll avoid many problems later in the installation and configuration process. You may be pleased with yourself after saving some cash buying a new graphics card from NoNameClone Corp., but in the end you're better off paying a little more for hardware that's been thoroughly tested by the huge number of existing Linux users.

Table 1.1 lists the minimum and ideal configuration guidelines for Linux.

Table 1.1 Linux PC Configuration Guidelines

PC Component	Minimum	Ideal
Processor	Intel 80386 or equivalent	Pentium is ideal (power, power, power!); i486 works fine, as do Intel clones
RAM	4MB (8MB for running X Window)	16MB
Graphics card	VGA graphics	SVGA graphics; card explicitly supported by XFree86
Hard drive	125MB	500MB or more
Bus	Anything but MCA	Anything but MCA
CD-ROM	Double-speed drive	Quadruple-speed drive
Mouse	Microsoft, Logitech, or compatible	Microsoft, Logitech, or compatible
Network card	None	Supported model (if networking)

If you're not sure about your particular hardware setup and Linux compatibility, check out the **Hardware Compatibility-HOWTO** (see Appendix A for details).

Watch out for hardware advertised as "plug-and-play." Most of this hardware is extremely difficult to use with Linux, although it can be done by first booting DOS and then "warm booting" into Linux with Loadbin. Some experimental kernel patches and a plug-and-play configuration tool are included in Slackware, but in general, if you can avoid plug-and-play devices (at least until   Linux support improves) you'll be better off.

The Core Components

In the rest of this chapter, we'll run down the various PC components and warn you about any potential downfalls if you want to use Linux. In addition, you'll want to check out Chapter 3 for a discussion of supported graphics cards—support that becomes vitally important if you're looking to run XFree86 (the implementation of the X Window System) with Linux.

In this section, we'll begin with a rundown of the basic components of your computer: bus, processor, and so on.

Bus

Linux runs on all the major bus architectures—ISA, VLB, PCI, EISA—except for the nonstandard Micro Channel Architecture, found on most IBM PS/2 models. (Not every IBM PC features an MCA bus, luckily; the ValuePoint and PS/1 models feature an industry-standard ISA bus.)

Processor

Linux needs at least an Intel 80386-based processor in order to run efficiently. Don't bother with a 80286-based PC. If you've got an older PC sitting in the closet and you think it might be neat to recycle by using Linux, leave it there, donate it to your local charity, or give it to the kids to bang on. It won't be useful in your Linux adventure.

Basically, any PC built around the Intel 80386 or better (including the i486, and Pentium, and chips from AMD and Cyrix) is capable of running Linux. If there is no math coprocessor (which may be an issue in older 80386-based PCs), Linux has built-in FPU emulation.

A Few CPU Problems

There are a few reported instances of Linux conflicting with a CPU or math coprocessor:

- Some AMD 486DX CPUs may hang in very specific situations, a problem that's not unique to Linux. If this happens to you, contact your PC vendor and get a replacement chip.

- Some older math coprocessors from Cyrix, IIT, and ULSI (the Math*Co series) have problems with the FSAVE and FRSTOR instructions, which may cause problems with Linux. Again, you can get a replacement chip from your PC vendor.

RAM

Random-access memory is one of those sticky issues when it comes to the PC. If you're a workstation user, you're probably used to working with scads of RAM. (Then again, most workstation users have someone else footing the bill, as the costs of that RAM can add up rather quickly.) In theory, it would be great to work with scads of RAM on a PC. Linux, like any 32-bit operating system, loves to work with as much RAM as possible.

In the real world, however, there are bills to pay, and the reality is that RAM is one of the most expensive parts of a PC, both upon initial purchase and if you ever want to upgrade. If you're a workstation user, you'll want to read through the following section, which explains RAM and the PC; if you're a PC user and are comfortable in your knowledge of RAM, you can skip to the following section.

The PC and RAM

If you buy a PC these days and aren't too attentive to details, you can easily end up with a PC that has 8 megabytes (MB) of RAM, as this is a popular figure with packages offered by the likes of CompUSA, Best Buy, and Computer City. In this day and age, 8MB isn't a whole lot of memory, even when running Microsoft Windows, MS-DOS, and memory-hungry applications. It becomes even more confining when running Linux.

This selection from the Slackware FAQ should illustrate problems associated with low memory:

Q: I can't get anything to work at all! What's the deal?

A: If you seem to suffer catastrophic failure (!), then check the file **FILE_LIST** on *ftp.cdrom.com* in **/pub/linux/ slackware** against the contents of your disks and make sure you're not missing any files.

Also, I've noticed that most of the reports of kernel panics and system hangs have come from people with 4MB. If you're running into these types of problems I'd suggest forking over the $$$ for 4 more megs. I have 8 MB of RAM and never have crashes. (Well, only when I really push my luck.) If you don't want to do that, then go through your **/etc/rc.d/rc.*** files and get rid of any daemons you don't use, like **cron**, **lpd**, or **selection**.

If you've got 4MB and you're getting "virtual memory exceeded in new" warnings, make sure you set up and activate a swap partition before running setup. If you're really hard up on memory, you can boot a rootdisk using **editroot** instead of one of the usual boot kernels. This will mount the floppy in the root drive, and you'll have to install from the other drive or from the hard drive. You will also not be able to create any kind of boot disk, so you'll have to install LILO and take your chances. I suggest using this approach only if a swapfile will not work.

Linux will boot and run on a PC with 4MB of RAM. However, you'll be running into memory constraints very quickly, and chances are that you won't be able to run the X Window System at all. In fact, 8MB is barely enough to run X and Linux. We used the combo on an 8MB machine, and the results weren't too encouraging; in fact, we were strongly encouraged to ramp up to 16MB of RAM right away.

This is why we recommend you upgrade and buy as much RAM as you can afford. Before you do so, you should know how today's PCs handle RAM and how you can buy it.

Almost every new PC supports Single Inline Memory Modules, or SIMMs. Additionally, almost every new PC has four SIMM slots on the motherboard, and most SIMMs are sold in multiples of two or four—1MB, 2MB, 4MB, or 8MB. The less memory on a SIMM, the cheaper the SIMM.

If you bought a PC with only 4MB of RAM, you probably ran into a situation where there were four 1MB SIMMs installed in the four motherboard slots. When you upgrade your PC's RAM, these 1MB

SIMMs will be relatively worthless, unless you bought a PC from a vendor that allows you to trade in old RAM when buying new RAM. (The trade-in price depends on the vendor. Typically, you'll get a credit for half the price of the old RAM when trading it in, provided you bought a PC from a vendor that assembles its own PCs. We've dealt with some cloners that give you full credit on the old RAM when trading it in, provided the PC was bought within the last year.) The same would be true if you bought a system with 8MB of RAM, and the SIMM slots were filled with 2MB SIMMs.

The best-case scenario is if you have a PC and only half of the SIMM slots are filled; in our case, we lucked into purchasing an 8MB PC that had 4MB SIMMs. (Contrary to popular belief, not every PC needs all the SIMM slots filled in order to function properly.) In this case, we needed to buy two more 4MB SIMMs to stick in the empty slots, bringing the total to 16MB.

Depending on the motherboard configuration, you may have to play with the SIMMs and their order in the slots. In the case of the 8MB PC with two more SIMMS added, we needed to stagger the SIMMs (old SIMM, new SIMM, old SIMM, new SIMM) before the system would recognize all 16MB of RAM. Normally this isn't something that's documented, so you might need to call the customer-support line for your PC manufacturer for advice when adding new SIMMs.

EDO RAM is all the rage these days on new PCs. Basically, EDO RAM is faster than conventional RAM, but like everything else in the computer world, you pay a little extra for the privilege of speed.

Therefore, the issue becomes whether it's worth the extra money to buy EDO RAM instead of conventional RAM (provided, of course, that the base price of a PC doesn't already feature EDO RAM; several large computer companies, such as Dell, have already started featuring EDO RAM in all of their configurations). Our experience is that it's worth the extra money. We've not run into a situation where the price of upgrading to EDO was too exorbitant, and the increase in performance was worth the slight increase in price.

Slackware Linux doesn't care whether you're using EDO RAM or conventional RAM.

Graphics Card

Dealing with a graphics card has been one of the most problematic areas of Linux—or rather, of XFree86, which serves as the X Window System graphical interface to Linux. XFree86 deals directly with the graphics card and must know everything about the card in a configuration file (such as the amount of RAM it has, the chipset it features, and what modes it supports), putting more stress on you than the average software. Chapter 3 details how to configure XFree86, and in almost every respect this will be the most daunting task you will face as a budding Linux user.

Controllers

If you're a DOS/Windows user, you're probably not too tuned into what sort of controller your computer features, because DOS and Windows are pretty tolerant of almost any PC controller.

This isn't the case with Linux, which works directly with a PC controller and thus needs to really support it. In this next section, we'll run down the controllers supported by Slackware Linux. There's a domino effect to the controller compatibility: if Linux doesn't recognize the controller, it won't recognize anything connected to the controller. And most of us have many goodies connected to the controller, including hard drives, CD-ROM drives, and scanners.

Hard-Drive Controllers

Unlike most PC-based Unices, Linux isn't too fussy about the hard disk or hard disks it supports; basically, if a hard disk is supported by a PC's BIOS, it will work fine under Linux. This goes for IDE, EIDE, MFM, RLL, ESDI (with controllers that emulate the ST-506 interface, that is), and most SCSI interfaces. In fact, the following Enhanced IDE (EIDE) interfaces are explicitly supported, even on systems with up to two IDE interfaces and up to four hard drives and/or CD-ROM drives:

- CMD-640
- DTC 2278D
- Intel Triton (82371FB) IDE (with busmaster DMA)
- FGI/Holtek HT-6560B
- RZ1000

If you're using a hard disk with an MFM, ESDI, or RLL controller, you'll need to use the **ext2f** file system format when installing Linux.

Regarding how large a hard drive you'll need—as always, the bigger the better. A full installation of Linux takes up a little less than 275MB, but you can do quite well in 100MB (40MB if you don't install the X Window System) if you're careful about what you install.

The price of hard disks has been falling rapidly, so many people will be able to afford 1-gigabyte drives. This is a good thing, of course; we recently noticed 1.2-gigabyte IDE drives advertised for less than $300. (SCSI hard drives, of course, cost a little more.)

However, if you buy one of these mondo IDE hard drives, you'll need to do a few things before you install Linux on them—or rather, *not* do a few things. MS-DOS can't handle such large drives (in their infinite wisdom, the designers of MS-DOS placed a cylinder limit on DOS, and newer hard drives exceed that 1023-cylinder limit), so most manufacturers, such as Conner and Western Digital, ship disk-management software (such as Ontrack's Disk Manager) that allow MS-DOS to deal with large hard drives. *Don't install this software.* A program like Disk Manager is designed to work only with MS-DOS or a variant, not Linux or another operating system.

Instead, change your PC's BIOS per the directions found in the hard-disk documentation. Then, using the steps detailed in Chapter 2, use the DOS FDISK utility to partition the hard drive into two smaller partitions that can be seen by both DOS and Linux.

However, there's still a chance you could experience some problems. For example, the **Hardware Compatibility-HOWTO** reports that some Conner CFP1060S drives may have problems with Linux when using the ext2fs file system. The symptoms are inode errors during e2fsck and corrupt file systems. Conner has released a firmware upgrade to fix this problem (call 1-800-4CONNER), but you'll need the microcode version (found on the drive label, **9WA1.6x**) before Conner can help you.

In addition, certain Micropolis drives have problems with Adaptec and BusLogic cards. In these situations, contact the drive manufacturers for firmware upgrades.

SCSI Controllers

In theory, you shouldn't have any problems with a SCSI card, because all SCSI cards are written to exacting technical specifications.

If you believe that, we have some swampland in Florida for you.

The fact is that SCSI cards are not all alike, and you can't assume that because you have a SCSI controller on your PC, you'll be able to use Linux with no sweat. Most low-end SCSI controllers were designed to interface with a CD-ROM drive, not necessarily a hard drive or another SCSI device.

These SCSI controllers are explicitly supported under Linux: AMI Fast Disk VLB/EISA (BusLogic-compatible); Adaptec AVA-1505/1515 (ISA) (Adaptec 152x-compatible); Adaptec AHA-1510/152x (ISA) (AIC-6260/6360); Adaptec AHA-154x (ISA) (all models); Adaptec AHA-174x (EISA) (in enhanced mode); Adaptec AHA-274x (EISA)/284x (VLB) (AIC-7770); Adaptec AHA-2940/3940 (PCI) (AIC-7870); Always IN2000; BusLogic (ISA/EISA/VLB/PCI) (all models); DPT PM2001, PM2012A (EATA-PIO); DPT Smartcache (EATA-DMA) (ISA/EISA/PCI) (all models); DTC 329x (EISA) (Adaptec 154x-compatible); Future Domain TMC-16x0, TMC-3260 (PCI); Future Domain TMC-8xx, TMC-950; Media Vision Pro Audio Spectrum 16 SCSI (ISA); NCR 5380 generic cards; NCR 53c400 (Trantor T130B) (use generic NCR 5380 SCSI support); NCR 53c406a (Acculogic ISApport/Media Vision Premium 3D SCSI); NCR 53c7x0, 53c8x0 (PCI); Qlogic/Control Concepts SCSI/IDE (FAS408) (ISA/VLB); Seagate ST-01/ST-02 (ISA); SoundBlaster 16 SCSI-2 (Adaptec 152x compatible) (ISA); Trantor T128/T128F/T228 (ISA); UltraStor 14F (ISA), 24F (EISA), 34F (VLB); and Western Digital WD7000 SCSI.

In addition, there are some SCSI controllers that can be used under Linux only after patches have been added to an installed system. These controllers and the Internet locations of the patches are listed in Table 1.2.

Table 1.2 SCSI Controllers Needing Patches and the Internet Locations

Controller	Internet address
AMD AM53C974, AM79C974 (PCI) (Compaq, HP, Zeos onboard SCSI)	ftp://sunsite.unc.edu/pub/Linux/kernel/patches/scsi/AM53C 974-0.3.tgz
Adaptec ACB-40xx SCSI- MFM/RLL bridgeboard	ftp://sunsite.unc.edu/pub/Linux/kernel/patches/scsi/adaptec- 40XX.tar.gz
Always Technologies AL-500	ftp://sunsite.unc.edu/pub/Linux/kernel/patches/scsi/al500- 0.2.tar.gz
BusLogic (ISA/EISA/VLB/PCI)	ftp://ftp.dandelion.com/BusLogic-1.0-beta.tar.gz
Iomega PC2/2B	ftp://sunsite.unc.edu/pub/Linux/kernel/patches/scsi/iomega _pc2-1.1.x.tar.gz
Qlogic (ISP1020) (PCI)	ftp://sunsite.unc.edu/pub/Linux/kernel/patches/scsi/isp1020- 0.5.gz
Ricoh GSI-8	ftp://tsx-11.mit.edu/pub/linux/ALPHA/scsi/gsi8.tar.gz

Parallel-port SCSI adapters (popular among laptop users) and DTC boards (327x, 328x) that are not Adaptec-compatible are not supported by Linux.

The SCSI device must support block sizes of 256, 512, or 1024 bytes. Other block sizes will not work. (Use the **MODE SELECT SCSI** command to change the block size.)

If you're having trouble with SCSI and Linux, you'll want to read the **SCSI- HOWTO** on the CD-ROM. See Appendix A for more details on this resource.

However, be warned that you may need to play around with various SCSI cards, as you'll see from this excerpt from the Slackware FAQ:

```
Q: Why the $%#@! isn't my UltraStor SCSI detected? It works under DOS!
A: Set the I/O address to 0x340 instead to 0x330.
```

For any hardware that doesn't work, a good rule is to try playing around with the IRQ and I/O settings on it to see what happens. If your system is up and running and you're having problems with a CD-ROM or tape or something like this, you can always look around for the driver source in **/usr/src/linux/drivers...** really, it won't bite! Often, the source contains important documentation, such as the default IRQ settings for that type of device and the major number for the entry in **/dev**. Also, try other boot kernels and see if that helps.

 A discussion of IRQs and interrupts can be found later in this chapter.

Support for SCSI should extend to tape drives (as you'll learn in the section entitled "Tape Drives," later in this chapter).

Floppy Drive

The Linux installation process assumes that you'll be creating a bootdisk and a rootdisk for use on a high-density drive. Because larger 1.2MB drives have all but disappeared from daily use, the accompanying CD-ROM contains drivers only for the 1.44MB, 3.5-inch floppies that most computers use for drive **A:**.

Tape Drives

Any tape drive that works from the SCSI connector, such as the QIC-20, should be fine under Linux (in other words, if your SCSI card works, so should the tape drive). In these cases, you'll need to make sure that drives of both fixed and variable lengths have blocks smaller than the driver buffer length (set to 32k in the distribution sources). In addition, Linux works pretty well with other tape drives that are connected via floppy controller, like QIC-117, QIC-40/80, and QIC-3010/3020 (QIC-WIDE) drives.

Other tape drives using the floppy controller, including Colorado FC-10/FC-20, Mountain Mach-2, and Iomega Tape Controller II, should work, but you may have to grab a patch from *ftp://sunsite.unc.edu/ pub/Linux/ kernel/tapes*.

There are several unsupported tape drives, including Emerald and Tecmar QIC-02 tape controller cards, drives that connect to the parallel port (like the Colorado Trakker), some high-speed tape controllers (Colorado TC-15), the Irwin AX250L/Accutrak 250 (which are not QIC-80 compatible), the IBM Internal Tape Backup Unit (which is not QIC-80 compatible), and the COREtape Light.

For further information, check out **FTAPE-HOWTO**.

CD-ROM

You can use a SCSI-based CD-ROM for Linux, or you can use one of the many CD-ROM/sound board combinations from the likes of Creative Labs. If you use a SCSI CD-ROM with a block size of 512 or 2048 bytes, you'll be fine as long as Linux recognizes the SCSI card; Linux works directly with the SCSI card and not necessarily directly with the CD-ROM. Pretty much any EIDE (ATAPI) CD-ROM drive should work, and there's explicit support for the following drives: Aztech CDA268, Orchid CDS-3110, Okano/Wearnes CDD-110, Conrad TXC, GoldStar R420, LMS Philips CM 206, Mitsumi, Optics Storage Dolphin 8000AT, Sanyo H94A, Sony CDU31A/CDU33A, Sony CDU-535/CDU-531, Teac CD-55A SuperQuad, and the variety of drives that fall under the Creative Labs label and are used in Sound Blaster Pro bundles— Matsushita/Panasonic, Creative Labs, Longshine, and Kotobuki.

You'll need patches to use the following CD-ROM drives: LMS/Philips CM 205/225/202 (*ftp://sunsite.unc.edu/pub/Linux/kernel/ patches/cdrom/lmscd0.3d.tar.gz*), Mitsumi FX001D/F (alternate drivers can be found at *ftp://ftp.gwdg.de//pub/linux/cdrom/drivers/mitsumi/mcdx-1.0a.tar.gz*), NEC CDR-35D (*ftp://sunsite.unc.edu/pub/Linux/kernel /patches/cdrom/linux-neccdr35d.patch*), and Sony SCSI multisession CD-XA (*ftp://tsx-11.mit.edu/pub/linux/patches/sony-multi-0.00.tar.gz*).

Again, watch out for "plug-and-play" soundcards—they don't work well with Linux. If you have an IDE/ATAPI CD-ROM drive connected to a plug-and-play soundcard and Linux doesn't detect it, try connecting it to the IDE connector on your motherboard (or I/O card) instead. If that doesn't work, try moving the jumpers on the back. (Remember the original settings just in case.)

We've received some complaints about the CD-ROM drives used in Gateway 2000 PCs, and there are have been reports in the trade press about some models that don't do what's advertised, whether it be compatibility with another CD-ROM type or the speed. You may want to do some research if you own a Gateway and have some problems with the CD-ROM drive.

Linux supports the ISO-9660 file system, the Rock Ridge Extensions, and the PhotoCD (XA) format.

Not every Sound Blaster features a proprietary interface, as some versions are based on a SCSI architecture. You'll need to know what specific Sound Blaster board you're using before you sit down for your Linux installation.

Here's another selection from the Slackware FAQ regarding Sound Blaster boards:

Q: I see my Sound Blaster/Panasonic CD-ROM detected at boot, but I can't install from it or mount it. What's going on?

A: Try setting the drive's ID to 0. This is expected by the install disks. There should be a jumper on the back of the drive that sets this—just move it to the leftmost position.

Removable Drives

As is the case with all SCSI controllers, any removable drive connected to a working SCSI controller should work, including optical (MO), WORM, floptical, Bernoulli, Zip, SyQuest, and other PD drives.

If you're using a parallel-port Zip drive, you can grab a patch from *ftp://gear.torque.net/pub/* and see if it works.

Linux supports both 512 and 1024 bytes/sector disks.

I/O Controllers

Any standard serial/parallel/joystick/combo card can be used with Linux, including those sporting 8250, 16450, 16550, and 16550A UARTs. Cards that support nonstandard IRQs (such as an IRQ of 9) can be used.

Outward Connectivity

UNIX was written with the express purpose of linking computers. Therefore, it's no surprise that Linux puts a premium on outward connectivity. This begins at a very basic level with network cards and expands to other telephone-based connectivity tools, such as modems and ISDN cards. This section covers all such devices.

Network Cards

If you're planning on using Linux on a network, you'll need a networking card. (If you're not planning on using Linux on the network, you won't need a card.) Other PC Unices require the presence of a network card to run (even on a single-user installation), but Linux is not one of them.

The following Ethernet cards have been tested and are supported under Linux: 3Com 3C501, 3C503, 3C505, 3C507, 3C509/3C509B (ISA)/3C579 (EISA); AMD LANCE (79C960)/PCnet-ISA/PCI (AT1500, HP J2405A, NE1500/NE2100); AT&T GIS WaveLAN; Allied Telesis

AT1700; Ansel Communications AC3200 EISA; Apricot Xen-II; Cabletron E21xx; DEC DE425 (EISA) / DE434/DE435 (PCI); DEC DEPCA and EtherWORKS; HP PCLAN (27245 and 27xxx series); HP PCLAN PLUS (27247B and 27252A); HP 10/100VG PCLAN (ISA/EISA/PCI); Intel EtherExpress; Intel EtherExpress Pro; NE2000/NE1000 (not all clones work, however); New Media Ethernet; Racal-Interlan NI5210 (i82586 Ethernet chip); Racal-Interlan NI6510 (am7990 lance chip) (this board doesn't work if your computer has more than 16MB of RAM); PureData PDUC8028, PDI8023; SEEQ 8005; SMC Ultra; Schneider & Koch G16; Western Digital WD80x3; and Zenith Z-Note/IBM ThinkPad 300 built-in adapter. The following pocket and portable adapters have been tested and will work with Linux: AT-Lan-Tec/RealTek parallel port adapter and D-Link DE600/DE620 parallel port adapter. The following methods can be used to connect to a network: SLIP/CSLIP/PPP (serial port); EQL (serial IP load balancing); and PLIP (parallel port) using a bidirectional cable.

In addition, Linux works with all ARCnet cards and the IBM Tropic chipset Token Ring cards. Finally, Linux will work with the following amateur radio (AX.25) cards: Ottawa PI/PI2 and most generic 8530-based HDLC boards.

The following line appears in the **HARDWARE-HOWTO** regarding the 3Com 3C501:"avoid like the plague."

WARNING

In addition, Linux will work with the following Ethernet cards once you go out and grab patches from the Internet. 3Com Demon Ethercards (3C592, 3C597 (100 mbps)) (EISA), with the patch at *http://cesdis.gsfc.nasa.gov/linux/drivers/vortex.html*; 3Com Vortex Ethercards (3C590, 3C595 (100 mbps)) (PCI), with the patch at *http://cesdis.gsfc.nasa.gov/linux/drivers/vortex.html*; DEC 21040/21140 Tulip, with a patch at *http://cesdis.gsfc.nasa.gov/linux/drivers/tulip.html*; SMC PCI EtherPower 10/100, with a patch at *http://cesdis.gsfc. nasa.gov/linux/drivers/tulip.html*; and the HP J2585 (PCI) and HP J2573 (ISA) (ATT2MDx1 / 100VG), with a patch at *http://cesdis1.gsfc.nasa. gov:80/linux/drivers/100vg.html*.

Dealing with a network card is like dealing with any other Linux hardware peripheral: you need to make sure it's not conflicting with other PC hardware. Note the following from the Slackware FAQ:

Q. I also have an SMC card. I could only get mine to work on IRQ 3 or 4.

A. There might be a way to work around the problem, but I haven't had time to go looking for it. I don't know what happened but today when I rebooted my machine after power shutdown, the Ethernet card suddenly started working. I only changed the base address options in the drivers file to look for 0x2a0 address.

Xircom adapters (PCMCIA and parallel port) are not supported.

Multiport Controllers

Linux supports many multiport controllers. They fall into two groups: intelligent controllers and nonintelligent controllers. Supported nonintelligent controllers are: AST FourPort and clones (4 port); Accent Async-4 (4 port); Arnet Multiport-8 (8 port); Bell Technologies HUB6 (6 port); Boca BB-1004, 1008 (4, 8 port), with no DTR, DSR, and CD; Boca BB-2016 (16 port); Boca IO/AT66 (6 port); Boca IO 2by4 (4 serial/2 parallel, uses 5 IRQs); Computone ValuePort (4, 6, 8 port) (AST FourPort-compatible); DigiBoard PC/X (4, 8, 16 port); Comtrol Hostess 550 (4, 8 port); PC-COMM 4-port (4 port); SIIG I/O Expander 4S (4 port, uses 4 IRQs); STB 4-COM (4 port); Twincom ACI/550; and Usenet Serial Board II (4 port). These nonintelligent controllers usually come in two varieties:

- The first uses standard port addresses and four IRQs.
- The second is AST FourPort-compatible and uses a selectable block of addresses and a single IRQ. (Addresses and IRQs are set using the setserial utility.)

Linux supports the following intelligent multiport controllers: Cyclades Cyclom-8Y/16Y (8, 16 port) (ISA/PCI); Stallion EasyIO (ISA)/ EasyConnection 8/32 (ISA/MCA); and Stallion EasyConnection 8/64 and ONboard (ISA/EISA/MCA)/Brumby/Stallion (ISA).

In addition, Table 1.3 lists multiport controllers that Linux will recognize after patches have been downloaded from the Internet and installed.

Table 1.3 Multiport Controllers and the Patch Locations

Controller	Internet Address
Comtrol RocketPort (8/16/32 port)	ftp://tsx-11.mit.edu/pub/linux/packages/ comtrol/
DigiBoard PC/Xe (ISA) and PC/Xi (EISA)	ftp://ftp.digibd.com/drivers/linux/
Moxa C218 (8 port) / C320 (8/16/24/32 expandable)	ftp://ftp.moxa.com.tw/drivers/c-218-320/linux/
Specialix SIO/XIO (modular, 4 to 32 ports)	ftp://sunsite.unc.edu/pub/Linux/kernel/patches/serial/sidrv0_5.taz

Modems

Again, if a modem works under DOS, it should work under Linux—whether it is internal or external. When you install Linux, you'll need to specify the location of the modem (serial port 1, 2, 3, or 4). This also goes for PCMCIA modems.

You'll need fax software to take advantage of a fax modem. Some fax modems require special programs: the Digicom Connection 96+/14.4+ needs a DSP code downloading program (which can be found at *ftp://sunsite.unc.edu/pub/Linux/system/Serial/smdl-linux.1.02.tar.gz*), and the ZyXEL U-1496 series needs ZyXEL 1.4, a modem/fax/voice control program (which can be found at *ftp://sunsite.unc.edu/pub/Linux/system/ Serial/ZyXEL-1.4.tar.gz*).

ISDN Cards

ISDN cards fall under the category of either direct-link devices to the Internet or replacements for standard modems or network cards. If you're using an ISDN card to emulate a modem or network card, you should have no problem. However, if you're using ISDN to connect to the Internet, you'll need to install some patches. Table 1.4 lists the ISDN devices that Linux will recognize, followed by an Internet location for the appropriate patch.

Table 1.4 ISDN Devices and the Patches that Love Them

ISDN Device	Internet Patch Location
3Com Sonix Arpeggio	ftp://sunsite.unc.edu/pub/Linux/kernel/patches/network/sonix.tgz
Combinet EVERYWARE 000 ISDN	ftp://sunsite.unc.edu/pub/Linux/patches/network/combinet1000isdn-1.02.tar.gz
Diehl SCOM card	ftp://sunsite.unc.edu/pub/Linux/kernel/patches/network/isdndrv-0.1.1.tar.gz
ICN ISDN / Teles ISDN Creatix AVM ISDN cards	ftp://ftp.franken.de/pub/isdn4linux/
German ISDN (1TR6) and Euro-ISDN	ftp://ftp.uni-stuttgart.de/pub/unix/systems/linux/isdn/

If you want more information on using Linux and ISDN devices, point your Web browser to *http://www.ix.de/ix/linux/linux-isdn.html*.

ATM Network Adapters

Work has been done on the Efficient Networks ENI155P-MF 155 Mbps ATM adapter. You can grab a driver and description of the process from *http://lrcwww.epfl.ch/linux-atm/*.

Frame Relay Cards

Work has been done on a driver for the Sangoma S502 56K Frame Relay card. You can grab a copy from *ftp://ftp.sovereign.org/pub/wan/fr/*.

Other Devices

These days, it's hard to buy a PC that's not gussied up with a slew of additional components, such as sound boards and network cards. In this section, we'll run down the most popular of the add-ons and other miscellaneous components.

Sound Boards

Linux supports a wide range of sound cards, including: 6850 UART MIDI; Adlib (OPL2); Audio Excell DSP16; Aztech Sound Galaxy NX Pro; cards based on the Crystal CS4232 (plug-and-play); ECHO-PSS cards (Orchid SoundWave32, Cardinal DSP16); Ensoniq SoundScape; Gravis Ultrasound; Gravis Ultrasound 16-bit sampling daughterboard; Gravis Ultrasound MAX; Logitech SoundMan Games (SBPro, 44kHz stereo support); Logitech SoundMan Wave (Jazz16/OPL4); Logitech SoundMan 16 (PAS-16 compatible); MPU-401 MIDI; MediaTriX AudioTriX Pro; Media Vision Premium 3D (Jazz16); Media Vision Pro Sonic 16 (Jazz); Media Vision Pro Audio Spectrum 16; Microsoft Sound System (AD1848); OAK OTI-601D cards (Mozart); OPTi 82C928/82C929 cards (MAD16/MAD16 Pro); Sound Blaster; Sound Blaster Pro; Sound Blaster 16 (not plug-and-play!); Turtle Beach Wavefront cards (Maui, Tropez); and Wave Blaster (and other daughterboards).

In addition, the following sound boards can be coaxed into working under Linux, provided you install the proper patches and drivers (which can be found at the accompanying Internet addresses): MPU-401 MIDI (*ftp://sunsite.unc.edu/pub/Linux/kernel/sound/mpu401-0.2.tar.gz*); PC speaker/parallel-port DAC (*ftp://ftp.informatik.hu-berlin.de/pub/os/linux/hu-sound/*); and Turtle Beach MultiSound/Tahiti/Monterey (*ftp://ftp.cs.colorado.edu/users/mccreary/archive/tbeach/multisound/*).

Not every feature on every sound board is supported, however. The ASP chip on Sound Blaster 16 series and AWE32 is not supported, and neither is the AWE32's onboard E-mu MIDI synthesizer.

Also, the Sound Blaster 16 with DSP 4.11 and 4.12 has a hardware bug that causes hung/stuck notes when playing MIDI and digital audio at the same time.

Why would you use a sound board and Linux? Well, Doom works much better when there's sounds of agony to accompany the splattering bits of blood and brain tissue. In addition, there's a new breed of Internet audio software that's actually supported for use under Linux. Some of it's actually pretty cool, such as the Real Audio real-time audio decoder. We'll be covering sound, Linux, and the Internet throughout the course of this book.

Mouse and Joystick

We've used various mice with Linux, mostly under the auspices of the X Window System. Basically, if you use a serial mouse with Linux, you'll just be telling the system to look to a specific serial port for the mouse. (You'll learn this in Chapter 2 and the Linux installation.) The same goes for trackballs and joysticks that run off a serial port. The following mouse models are explicitly supported under Linux: Microsoft serial mouse, Mouse Systems serial mouse, Logitech Mouseman serial mouse, Logitech serial mouse, ATI XL Inport busmouse, C&T 82C710 (QuickPort; used on Toshiba, TI Travelmate laptops), Microsoft busmouse, Logitech busmouse, and the PS/2 (auxiliary device) mouse.

To use other mouse models, you'll need to grab a patch. These would include the Sejin J-mouse (the patch is at *ftp://sunsite.unc.edu/pub/ Linux/kernel/patches/console/jmouse.1.1.70-jmouse. tar.gz*) and MultiMouse, which uses multiple mouse devices as a single mouse (the patch is at *ftp://sunsite.unc.edu/pub/ Linux/system/Misc/MultiMouse-1.0.tgz*).

If your joystick doesn't work, you may want to check out one of the joystick drivers at *ftp://sunsite.unc.edu/pub/Linux/kernel/patches/console/joystick-0.7.3.tgz* or *ftp://sunsite.unc.edu/pub/Linux/kernel/patches/console/joyfixed.tgz*.

In addition, touchpads that emulate a mouse (like the Alps Glidepoint) should work if they precisely emulate a supported mouse.

Printers

Essentially any printer connected to a parallel or serial port that works under DOS should work under Linux. During the installation, you'll be asked to specify which port contains the printer. There are special programs that enhance the basic printing capabilities: HP LaserJet 4 users can grab free-lj4, a printing modes control program, at *ftp://sunsite.unc.edu/pub/Linux/system/Printing/free-lj4-1.1p1.tar.gz*, while those using the BiTronics parallel port interface can grab a program at *ftp://sunsite.unc.edu/pub/Linux/kernel/misc/bt-ALPHA-0.0.1.tar.gz*.

The issue becomes a little dicier when dealing with XFree86 and Ghostscript, the utility used to create and print PostScript documents. Ghostscript allows you to print PostScript-formatted documents on non-PostScript printers; much of the UNIX documentation that flows down the pike is formatted with PostScript, and this capability is very handy. Ghostscript supports the following printers: Apple Imagewriter; C. Itoh M8510; Canon BubbleJet BJ10e, BJ200, LBP-8II, and LIPS III; DEC LA50/70/75/75plus, LN03, and LJ250; Epson 9 pin, 24 pin, LQ series, Stylus, and AP3250; HP 2563B, DesignJet 650C, DeskJet/Plus/500, DeskJet 500C/520C/550C/1200C color, LaserJet/Plus/II/III/4, and PaintJet/XL/XL300 color; IBM Jetprinter color and Proprinter; Imagen ImPress; Mitsubishi CP50 color; NEC P6/P6+/P60; Okidata MicroLine 182; Ricoh 4081; SPARCprinter; StarJet 48 inkjet printer; Tektronix 4693d color 2/4/8 bit and 4695/4696 inkjet plotter; and Xerox XES printers (2700, 3700, 4045, etc.). Those using the Canon BJC600 and Epson ESC/P color printers can grab a printer program at *ftp://petole.imag.fr/pub/ postscript/*.

 Ghostscript will be covered in much more detail in Chapter 5.

Scanners

Slackware Linux right out of the box doesn't support any scanners. However, several folks have contributed scanner drivers and programs to the Linux community, and there may be a program available on the Internet for your particular scanner. (Be warned that some of the products listed here are commercial products.) Scanners with support software available include: A4 Tech AC 4096 (*ftp://ftp.informatik.hu-berlin.de/pub/local/linux/ac4096.tgz*), Epson GT6000 (*ftp://sunsite.unc.edu/pub/Linux/apps/graphics/scanners/ppic0.5.tar.gz*), Genius GS-B105G (*ftp://tsx-11.mit.edu/pub/linux/ALPHA/scanner/gs105-0.0.1.tar.gz*), Genius

GeniScan GS4500 handheld scanner (*ftp://tsx-11.mit.edu/pub/linux/ ALPHA/scanner/gs4500-1.3.tar.gz*), HP ScanJet and ScanJet Plus (*ftp://ftp.ctrl-c.liu.se/unix/linux/wingel/*), HP ScanJet II series SCSI (*ftp://sunsite.unc.edu/pub/Linux/apps/graphics/scanners/hpscanpbm- 0.3a.tar.gz*), HP ScanJet family (including ScanJet 3c) (*http://www. tummy.com/xvscan/*), Logitech Scanman 32/256 (*ftp://tsx-11.mit.edu/ pub/linux/ALPHA/scanner/logiscan-0.0.2.tar.gz*), Mustek M105 handheld scanner with GI1904 interface (*ftp://tsx-11.mit.edu/pub/linux/ ALPHA/scanner/scan-driver-0.1.8.tar.gz*), Mustek Paragon 6000CX (*ftp://sunsite.unc.edu/pub/Linux/apps/graphics/scanners/muscan-1.1.5.taz*), and Nikon Coolscan SCSI 35mm film scanner (*ftp://sunsite.unc .edu/pub/Linux/apps/graphics/scanners/*).

Video-Capture Boards

Slackware Linux doesn't support any video-capture boards right out of the box. To use such a board, you'll need to make sure that the board has a driver, and then go out and grab that driver from the Internet. Boards with Linux drivers available are: FAST Screen Machine II (*ftp://sunsite. unc.edu/pub/Linux/apps/video/ScreenMachineII.1.2.tgz*), ImageNation Cortex I (*ftp://sunsite.unc.edu/pub/Linux/apps/video/cortex. drv.0.1.tgz*), ImageNation CX100 (*ftp://sunsite.unc. edu/pub/Linux/apps/video/cxdrv-0.1beta.tar.gz*), Pro Movie Studio (*ftp://sunsite.unc.edu/pub/Linux/apps/video/PMS-grabber.2.0.tgz*), Quanta WinVision video capture card (*ftp://sunsite.unc.edu/pub/Linux /apps/video/fgrabber-1.0.tgz*), Video Blaster/Rombo Media Pro+ (*ftp://sunsite.unc.edu/pub/Linux/apps/video/vid _src.gz*), and VT1500 TV cards (*ftp://sunsite.unc.edu/pub/Linux/apps/video/vt 1500-1.0.5.tar.gz*).

Uninterruptible Power Systems

Slackware Linux doesn't support UPSes right out of the box, but there are drivers available for APC SmartUPS (*ftp://sunsite.unc.edu/pub/ Linux/system/UPS/apcd-0.1.tar.gz*) and general UPSes with RS-232 monitoring port (known as the "unipower" package) (*ftp://sunsite. unc.edu/pub/Linux/system/UPS/unipower-1.0.0.tgz*). Others have managed to interface Linux with other UPSes; for more details, check out the **UPS-HOWTO,** on the accompanying CD-ROM.

Data-Acquisition Equipment

Hardware used for data acquisition is not explicitly supported in Slackware Linux, but you can grab software from the Linux Lab Project (*ftp://koala.chemie.fu-berlin.de/pub/linux/LINUX-LAB/*) to learn about supporting the following devices: Analog Devices RTI-800/815 ADC/DAC board, CED 1401, DBCC CAMAC, IEEE-488 (GPIB, HPIB) boards, Keithley DAS-1200, and National Instruments AT-MIO-16F / Lab-PC+.

Miscellaneous

If a device is connected to the SCSI card and Linux has no problems with the SCSI card, then you should have no problems with the device. This would include most CDR, WORM, optical, and floptical drives. Additionally, we've not heard complains with proprietary drives from the likes of SyQuest and Bernoulli.

In addition, there are other miscellaneous devices that are definitely not supported by Slackware Linux but that have drivers available on the Internet. Our favorite is a driver for the Mattel Powerglove (*ftp://sunsite.unc.edu/pub/Linux/apps/linux-powerglove.tgz*); why mess with a simple mouse when you can grab Linux by the throat to make it work? Other miscellaneous device drivers include support for the AIMS Labs RadioTrack FM radio card (*ftp://sunsite.unc.edu/pub/Linux/apps/sound/radiotrack-1.1.tgz*), Maralu chip-card reader/writer (*ftp://ftp.thp.uni-koeln.de/pub/linux/chip/*), Reveal FM Radio card (*ftp://magoo.uwsuper.edu/pub/fm-radio/*), and Videotext cards (*ftp://sunsite. unc.edu/pub/Linux/apps/video/videoteXt-0.5.tar.gz*).

Dealing with Some Specific Systems

The guidelines so far in this chapter pertain to components. However, the Linux community has found that some specific PC configurations have posed some challenges.

David Ludwig (*davidl@hal-pc.org*) has been compiling a list of user experiences with specific hardware configurations at *http://www.hal-pc.org/~ davidl/linux/ desktop.config.html*. This list is quite long and getting longer, so if you're curious about someone else's experiences with your computer, you may want to check out this database. Be warned, however, that many of the respondents to the survey just list generic information, not the names of specific models.

Compaq Deskpro XL

If you're into PC hardware at all—and you probably are, if you've gotten this far—you'll recognize how odd the configuration for the Compaq Deskpro XL series is: a PCI/EISA bus system with an onboard AMD SCSI/ethernetchip (AMD79C974), a Microsoft Sound System–compatible audio system built around an AD1847, and a QVision 2000 graphics card with a Matrox Atlas chip and a Cirrus Logic PX2085 Ramdac.

Unfortunately, the Deskpro XL series was pretty popular. Be warned that you may need to jump through some hoops to get Linux up and running; those who have done it say that you can pretty much forget about any sound support, and you may run into additional problems during installation.

Because these details can be rather technical, we're not going to describe them here, but we are including the appropriate **HOWTO** on the CD-ROM. You can check for an updated **HOWTO** at *http://www-c724.uibk.ac.at/XL/*.

Linux on Laptops

Generally speaking, Linux should run fine on most laptops with enough horsepower—that is, the newer breed of 486- and Pentium-based laptops on the market, decked out with at least 8MB of RAM. However, you may not be able to get the full functionality of the laptop when running Linux; for example, most laptops feature proprietary power-management and graphics capabilities that Linux simply can't use. In these cases, you'll lose the advanced power management, and you'll need to run Linux and XFree86 in a lower graphics mode (VGA or SuperVGA).

If you've spent any time at all in the laptop world, however, you know that each laptop model tends to be a little different when it comes to hardware and assorted gewgaws. The Linux world has found that some laptop models present challenges when it comes to installation and configuration. In this section, we'll run down some of the more popular laptop models and the challenges faced when using Linux on them. Also, Table 1.5 lists (in abbreviated form) the results of the Linux Laptop Survey, where users from around the world reported on laptops that successfully ran Linux.

The Linux Laptop Home Page (*http://www.cs.utexas.edu/users/kharker/linux-laptop/*) contains additional information on laptops and Linux, including many additional sites that contain information about specific laptop models beyond what is covered here. Some of the information here is gleaned from that Web site, courtesy of Kenneth E. Harker (*kharker@cs.utexas.edu*), and some is from our personal experiences. If you own a laptop and want to know more about using Linux on it, the Linux Laptop Home Page is really the place to start.

An alternative source of information is the Linux on Portables Web site, found at *http://queequeg.ifa.hawaii.edu/linux/portables.html*.

Many laptop users are using parallel-port SCSI adapters. However, most of these adapters are not yet supported by Linux. (Only the parallel-SCSI adapter for the Iomega ZIP drive is supported.)

In Table 1.5, we list whether the laptop has power conservation that works with Linux. This isn't necessarily APM; it could be proprietary hardware routines written into the laptop's BIOS.

Table 1.5 The Condensed Results of the Linux Laptop Survey, as of April 1997

Laptop Make and Model	CPU	Max battery	Power Cons.?	Notes
AcerNote 350	Pentium/100	2 hours	Yes	NE200 Ethernet, modem work; APM does not
AMS PN325	486/66	2 hours	Yes	None
AMS SoundPro	486/50	3 hours	Yes	X is balky
AMS TravelPro 5300	486/66	1.5-2 hours	Yes	PCMCIA IC-card Ethernet works
AMS TravelPro 5366	486/66	1 hour	n/a	None
ARM TS30A	486DX4/100	2.5-3 hours	Yes	PCMCIA PreMax 14.4 modem works
AST Advantage! Explorer	486sx/25	2-3 hours	Yes	None
AST PowerExec 4/25	486sx/25	n/a	yes	PCMCIA D-link works; PCMCIA Intel 1440 does not
AST PowerExec	486/33SL	2-3 hours	Yes	None
AT&T Globalyst 200S	486DX4/75	2 hours	Yes	PCMCIA works
AT&T Globalyst 250	486DX4/100	2 hours	Yes	Microphone works
Austin Active Color	486/66	2 hours	Yes	PCMCIA D-Link DE-650 works
Austin 33MHz Mono (Arima)	486/33	3 hours	Yes	Internal modem works
Austin DX66-2 (Arima)	486/66	2 hours*	Yes	None
Austin/IPC (Arima) 466D	486/66	n/a	Yes	None
BIT DU33	486/33	3.5 hours	n/a	None
BIT FR-800	486/66	2 hours	Yes	None
Canon Innova Subnotebook #10	486sx/33	1.5 hours	No	None
Caravene AV-B5NT	486sx/25	2 hours	Yes	None
Chicony NB5	486/66	1 hour	Yes	PCMCIA SCSI, Ethernet, modem work
Chicony NoteBook 9800	486/66	2 hours	Yes	Intel 14.4 DataFax runs after some tweaking
Compaq Aero 4/33C	486sx/33	2-3 hours	Yes	See later

Laptop Make and Model	CPU	Max battery	Power Cons.?	Notes
Compaq Concerto 4/33	486/33	3.5 hours	Yes	Pen does not work w/Linux; see later for a fix
Compaq Contura 4/25	486sx/25	4 hours	Yes	See later
Compaq Contura 4/25cx	486SL/25	under 2 hours	No	Trackball does not work; see later
Compaq Contura 430C	486DX4-100	2 hours	Yes	None
Compaq 4/25 Lite	486SL/25	4 hours	Yes	None
Compaq LTE Elite 4/75 CX	486DX4XL/75	2-8 hours	Yes	None
Compaq LTE 5280	Pentium	n/a	n/a	None
Compat TS37 (Wang)	486sx/25	2 hours	n/a	X not tested
Compudyne SubNote 4SL/25	486SL/25	3 hours	Yes	AT-LAN-TEK(ATP) parallel worked
Databyte 486SLC	486SLC/25	4 hours	No	None
DECpc 425 SL/e	486SL/25	3.5 hours	Yes	None
DECpc 433SLC premium (AST)	486/33 SLC	2 hours	Yes	PCMCIA ethernet card works
Dell 320N+	386sx/20	3.5 hours	No	PCMCIA D-Link 600 works
Dell Latitude 433C	486sx/33	1 hour	No	None
Dell Latitude XP 4100cx	486DX4/100	3 hours	Yes	PCMCIA Ethernet, modem (using SLIP) work
DUAL	486sx/25	2.5 hrs	No	None
DUAL SKD-4000	486/66	1 hour	No	None
EPS Technologies Apex	Pentium/133	1.5 hours	Yes	None
Epson 700	Cyrix DX33	2.5 hours	Yes	Linksys ne2000 combo card works
Epson Direct Endeavor NT-500	486DX4/75	1 hour	Yes	None
Epson NB-SL/25	386SL/25	n/a	Yes	None
Epson VN575ST	Pentium/75	1 hour	n/a	None
Escom Paradigma SX33	486sx/33	2 hours	Yes	Sound card does not work
Escom Notebook 90	Pentium/90	1.5 hours	Yes	None
FOSA 9200M	486DX/66	1 hour	Yes	Hardware extras don't work with Linux
Gateway 2000 ColorBook	486sx/33	1.25-1.75 hours	Yes	None
Gateway 2000 HandBook	486sx/25	1 hour	No	None

Laptop Make and Model	CPU	Max battery	Power Cons.?	Notes
Gateway 2000 HandBook	486DX/40	1-1.5 hours	Yes	PCMCIA D-link 600 works
Gateway 2000 HandBook	486SL/40	2-2.5 hours	Yes	None
Gateway 2000 Liberty	486DX4/100	3 hours	Yes	None
Gateway Solo	Pentium/150	2.5 hours	Yes	CD-ROM included
GRiD 1450SX	386sx/16	n/a	Yes	X will not run if less than 3MB of RAM
GRiD 1550SX	386sx/20	1 hour	Yes	None
GRiD 1660	386sx/20	1.5 hours	Yes	PCMCIA D-link 600 works
Highscreen 486 SLC 33	Cyrix 486/33	2-3 hours	Yes	Quirks with X
Highscreen Blue Note	486DX2/66	2 hours	Yes	Problems with X on dual-scan monitor, but not external monitor
Hyperdata Expor CD100	486DX4/100	4 hours	Yes	Some problems with Ethernet cards; other PCMCIA cards work fine
IBM L40SX	386sx/20	n/a	n/a	None
IBM PS/Note 425	486SL/25	2.5 hours	Yes	None
IBM ThinkPad 340CSE	486SL/50	3 hours	Yes	See later
IBM ThinkPad 350	486SL/25	3 hours	Yes	Megahertz PCMCIA modem works; see later
IBM ThinkPad 365 CSD	486DX4/75	3-6 hours	Yes	None
IBM ThinkPad 500	486SLC/50	2 hours	Yes	None
IBM ThinkPad 701C	486DX4/75	2.5 hours	Yes	IBM PCMCIA Ethernet
IBM ThinkPad 750 (Mono)	486/33	6 hours	Yes	IBM Ethernet PCMCIA, Intel 14.4 modem work; see later
IBM ThinkPad 750CS	486SL/33	3 hours	Yes	PCMCIA D-Link 650, Megahertz modem, IBM modem all work; X server needs fixes; see later

Laptop Make and Model	CPU	Max battery	Power Cons.?	Notes
IBM ThinkPad 755C	486DX4/75	3 hour +	Yes	See later
Innovace 620px	Pentium/75	n/a	n/a	None
INSI EchoBook	486DX2/50	2-2.5 hours	Yes	PCMCIA D-Link 650 works
INSI EchoBook	486DX4/75	2-3 hours	Yes	PCMCIA D-Link 650 works
IPC P5	486sx/25	2 hours +	Yes	None
IPC Porta-PC P5E-486/DSTN	486DX4/100	3 hours	Yes	None
Jetta Jetbook	Cyrix 486/3333	1 hour	Yes	None
Lion NB 8500	486DX4-S/100	2 hours	Yes	None
MacPerson Scriba	486DX2/66	3.5-4 hours	Yes	None
Magnavox Metalis SX/16	386sx/16	1 hour	Yes	Conflicts with power management
Midwest Micro Elite	486sx/25	2 hours	Yes	None
Midwest Micro Elite	486slc/33	2 hours	n/a	None
Midwest Micro Ultra	486sx/25	3 hours	Yes	PCMCIA D-Link via parallel port
Midwest Micro Elite	486DX2/66MHZ	2 hours	Yes	3Com Etherlink III, modem, EXP Thinfax 14400 work
Midwest Micro Soundbook	486DX4/100	2 hours	Yes	PCMCIA D-Link 650 works
Midwest Micro Soundbook P-90	Pentium/90	1.75-2 hours	Yes	None
NEC Ultralite Versa E	486/50	2 hours	n/a	PCMCIA D-link works
NEC Ultralite Versa E w/docking	486/50	2 hours	n/a	Docking works
NEC Ultralite Versa 33C	486SL/33	3.5-5 hours	yes	Battery life measured with second battery in place of floppy; Megahertz XJ144 PCMCIA modem works
NEC Ultralite Versa S/33D	486sx/33	1.5 hours	Yes	See later
NEC Versa 4000C	Pentium/75	2.5 hours	Yes	3Com EtherLink III PCMCIA works
NEC Versa 6030X	Pentium/133	2.1 hours	Yes	None
NoteBook 3500	486sx/25	1.5 hours	No	No external monitor
Notestar NP-743D	486DX2/66	1.5 hours	Yes	PCMCIA D-Link 650 works

Laptop Make and Model	CPU	Max battery	Power Cons.?	Notes
Olivetti Philos 33	386sx/20	8 hours	Yes	None
Paccomp	486DX2/66	3 hours	Yes	PCMCIA works
Panasonic CF-25	Pentium/133	1.5 hours	Yes	PCMCIA works
Prostar 9200	486DX4/100	3 hours	Yes	3c589B PCMCIA card works
SagerNP943	486/33	2 hours	Yes	PCMCIA D- Link, modem work
Sager NP7500	486sx/33	2.5 hours	Yes	None
Sager NP7600	Pentium 90	2 hours	Yes	PET-105 (RPTI EP400 Ethernet) 10Base2 and 10BaseT; 28k fax modem all work
Sager NP8600	Pentium/75	1.5 hours	Yes	PCMCIA modem works
Sager NP9200	486DX4/100	1.5-2 hours	Yes	None
Samsung 800	Pentium/90	2 hours	Yes	None
Samsung 800C	Pentium/75	3 hours	Yes	None
SDK 4000	486SX/33	2 hours	Yes	NE2100-compatible Ethernet,modem; power-management doesn't work
SDK 4000 III Extended version	486DX2/66	2 hours	n/a	PCMCIA didn't work
SEH DesignCD	Pentium/100	1.5 hours	Yes	None
Siemens Nixdorf PCD 4 ND	486DX4/75	2.5 hours	Yes	None
Sharp PC-8650	486/33	n/a	Yes	Internal fax modem works
SNI PCD-4NE	486SX-SL/33	2-3 hours	Yes	None
Tadpole P1000	Pentium 100	1.5 hours	Yes	None
Targa	486DX2/66	2-3 hours	Yes	None
TI Travelmate 4000E	486/50	1.25 hours	No	None
TI Travelmate Win4000	486DX2/50	1.5 hours	No	None
TI Travelmate 4000M	486DX4/100	1 hour	Yes	AHA1510 adapter is slow
TI TravelMate 5000	Pentium/75	5-8 hours	No	PCMCIA Ethernet (IBM CreditCard Adapter) works

Laptop Make and Model	CPU	Max battery	Power Cons.?	Notes
TI TravelMate 5100	Pentium/90	4-5 hours	Yes	Ethernet, modem work
Toshiba Dynabook GT475	486DX/75	3 hours	Yes	PCMCIA Ethernet works; PCMCIA CD-ROM, APM does not
Toshiba T700CS	Pentium/120	3 hours	Yes	CD-ROM works
Toshiba T1800	386sx/16	2 hours	n/a	None
Toshiba T1900C	486sx/20	1.5 hours	n/a	None
Toshiba T1910	486sx/33	2.5 hours	Yes	X does not work
Toshiba T1950 (mono)	486/20	3.5 hours	Yes	None
Toshiba T1950CT/200	486/40	2 hours	Yes	None
Toshiba Satellite T2100	486DX2/50	3 hours +	Yes	X not tested
Toshiba Satellite T2135CS	486DX4/75	2-3 hours	Yes	Linksys PCMCIA Ethercard works
Toshiba T2200SX	386/25	n/a	Yes	None
Toshiba T3100SX/40	386sx/16	1.5 hours	n/a	Only X in mono tested
Toshiba T3200SXC	386sx	n/a	No	X runs only in mono
Toshiba T3400	486SL/33	5 hours	No	PCMCIA cards work
Toshiba T4400SX	486sx/20	2 hours	Yes	None
Toshiba T4400SX	486sx/33	n/a	Yes	X not tested
Toshiba T4600 (mono)	486SL/33	5 hours	Yes	X not tested
Toshiba T4600	486SL/33	2 hours	Yes	PCMCIA: Linksys Ethernet, Megahertz XJ1144 14.4 fax modem work
Toshiba T4600C	486SL/33	3 hours	Yes	Lacks PCMCIA support
Toshiba T4700	486/33 SL	4 hours	n/a	None
Toshiba T5200/100	386sx/20	2 hours	n/a	None
Total Peripherals NBD486	486sx/25	4 hours	Yes	Problems with X
Twinhead Slim 484	486/33	2 hours	Yes	De620 (parallel-port adapter) works
Tulip NB	386sx/16	1 hour	n/a	X not tested
Vobis ModuleNote	486DX2/66	2 hours	Yes	X not tested

Laptop Make and Model	CPU	Max battery	Power Cons.?	Notes
WinBook	486DX2/50	2 hours	Yes	None
WinBook XP	486/100	2 hours	Yes	CD-ROM works
Zenith SuperSport SX	386sx/16	n/a	n/a	None
Zenith Z*Lite	486SL/25	2 hours	Yes	None
Zenith Z-Note 425-Inc	486SL/25	2.5 hours	Yes	Driver available for built-in Ethernet
Zenith Z-Star 433VL	486SX/33	n/a	Yes	None
Zeos Contenda 386 Subnotebook	486/25	3 hours	Yes	PCMCIA D-Link DE600 works; Linksys PE-EEP pocket adapter did not

*Respondents to the survey reported battery lives ranging from 1.5 hours to 3 hours

Other Specific Models

Just because Linux will run on a given laptop doesn't mean that you can take full advantage of the laptop's hardware features. Many dedicated Linux users have taken the challenge of making Linux work on their quirky laptops, and they've been gracious enough to share their solutions with the rest of the Linux community. We'll briefly run down some specific laptop models and how Linux was made to work on them. If there's a FAQ mentioned here, we've included it on the accompanying CD-ROMs.

NOTE

You can't extrapolate from the specific models presented here. The laptop world isn't known for consistency among product lines, and what may be true of a specific model may not be true for that model's second cousin. Use the information presented here *only* for the specific model, unless the information explicitly covers a wide range of models (as is the case with the IBM ThinkPad information).

AST 900N

Basically, there are no major challenges with installing Linux on this laptop model, but there are some pitfalls. A **HOWTO** on installing Linux on the AST 900N is included on the CD-ROM.

Compaq Concerto

The Compaq Concerto features a pen device, not a mouse. Linux doesn't recognize the pen device, but Dr. Joseph J. Pfeiffer Jr. has posted a driver at his Web site (*http://www.cs.nmsu.edu/~pfeiffer/*).

Compaq Contura Aero

The Compaq Contura Aero is a very popular and very inexpensive laptop model, but it poses many challenges to the Linux user—so many that an entire FAQ has been devoted to making Linux work on one. Issues range from making the PCMCIA floppy work to making specific function keys respond. Ali Albayrak and Harald T. Alvestrand have put together a FAQ and posted it to *http://domen.uninett.no/~hta/linux/aero-faq.html*.

Dell Latitude XPi

You'll definitely want to do some homework before installing Linux on a Dell Latitude XPi, because it contains some quirky hardware configurations. Larry Meadows (*lfm@pgroup.com*) has detailed his experiences and posted it to the Web (*http://www.cs.utexas.edu/users /kharker/linux-laptop/latitude.xpi.html*), and it's included on the accompanying CD-ROM.

HP Omnibooks

Two brave souls have tried to install Linux on two popular Hewlett-Packard subnotebooks: the Omnibook 600 and 5000. They report that it can be done ("Linux cannot be installed in the obvious way, and not every peripheral works under Linux [at least not so far]. However, the dark rumors that have spread across the Net are unwarranted: all the critical components work nicely. Some of the Omnibook's limitations might be fixed with further hacking and others can be worked around"), but it takes a lot of effort and tweaking." Their **HOWTOs** are on the accompanying CD-ROM; you can also find them at *http://www.cs.uiowa.edu/~mfleck/vision-html/omnibook.html* and *http://www.ens.fr/~dicosmo/Linux/OmniBook5000.html*.

IBM ThinkPad

Despite the ThinkPad's reputation for being a quirky machine, Linux installs and runs pretty smoothly on this line of IBM laptops (all things considered). However, the ease of installation and the actual installation details themselves differ by model, and you can run into some problems if you're unfamiliar with your ThinkPad and the intricacies of both Linux and X Window/XFree86.

You can find excellent FAQs on the subject of Linux and IBM ThinkPads at *http://peipa.essex.ac.uk/tp-linux/tp-linux.html*, *http://reality. sgi.com/mende/linuxTP701/index.html*, and *http://www.iusd.iupui.edu/~ henslelf/thinkpad/index.html*.

NEC Versa

Linux installs without a hitch on the NEC Versa laptop, but X needs some tweaking. For more details, check out *http://www.santafe.edu:80/~nelson/ versa-linux/*.

Tadpole P1000

Tadpole Technology makes a series of SPARC- and PC-compatible laptops. The P1000 series of laptops are based on the Intel Pentium processor. They've been tested to work with Linux, but there are a slew of installation and configuration details to wade through. You can find them at *http://www.tadpole.com/Support/online/linux.html*.

TI Travelmate 5100

A Web site at *http://www.wri.com/~cwikla/ti5100.html* details how to install Linux, including how to make Linux peacefully coexist with Windows 95.

Toshiba T400CDT

Most of the information about this Toshiba model covers X Window configuration and some power-management routines. You can see for yourself at *http://terra.mpikg-teltow.mpg.de/~burger/T400CDT-Linux.html*.

PCMCIA and Laptops

A separate package, Card Services, is used for PCMCIA support on laptops; this package is included on the accompanying CD-ROM. We'll cover the topic in more depth in Chapter 2 (including the installation of Card Services), but for now, all you need to know is that all the common PCMCIA controllers (including those built around chips from Databook, Intel, Cirrus, Ricoh, Vadem, and VLSI), as well as custom controllers found in IBM and Toshiba laptops, are supported. In addition, the **PCMCIA-HOWTO** reports that the package is used on desktop computer systems with PCMCIA card adapters.

Be warned that the Motorola 6AHC05GA controller used in some Hyundai laptops and the proprietary controller used in Hewlett-Packard Omnibook 600 subnotebooks are not supported.

Learning About PC Hardware

You've probably noticed references in this chapter to things like interrupts and IRQ settings. If you're a PC hack, you know what these nasty things mean. If you're not a PC hack—you are in for a rude awakening.

Simply put, the PC architecture assigns addresses to peripheral devices. If these addresses conflict, you have problems. Some peripherals, such as network cards, need to be set to specific addresses, while others don't.

Our goal here isn't to turn you into a hardware hack (and, quite honestly, discussions of interrupts and IRQ settings really depress us), so we suggest checking into a more specifically angled PC hardware book like Jim Aspinwall's *IRQ, DMA & I/O* (MIS:PRESS). PC hardware doesn't have to be intimidating, but you should be prepared for a high level of detail if you start messing around with the innards of your personal computer, especially if you're a UNIX hack who doesn't know much about PCs in general. For your convenience, we list several good books on PC hardware in Appendix A.

Summary

This chapter outlined the hardware requirements for running Linux. Linux actually runs on a wide assortment of PC hardware, which tends to be unusual for PC UNIX. Still, there are many places where you may be tripped up by an oddball or misadvertised component, bringing your nascent Linux experience to a screeching halt. The point of this chapter was to highlight any potential problem areas and to give you some guidance if you're thinking about buying a new or used computer expressly for Linux and want to know what hardware to purchase.

In the next chapter, we'll cover a typical Linux installation from beginning to end.

Installing Linux

This chapter covers:

- Preparing your PC for Linux
- Creating new partitions under DOS
- Creating new partitions under Linux
- Creating your bootdisk and rootdisk
- Booting Linux for installation
- Installing from the **setup** command
- Selecting the software to install
- Booting Linux with **Loadlin**
- Logging in the virgin Linux system
- Setting up additional users
- Adding hardware drivers with kernel modules
- Shutting down Linux

Before You Install Linux

Now that you have the perfect PC for running Linux, it's time to prepare for the installation. No, you can't just install Linux from the accompanying CD-ROMs; you must first configure your hard drive and create boot floppies. Neither step is particularly difficult. Here, we'll cover how to create boot floppies for booting Linux, followed by a discussion of preparing your hard drive for the Linux installation. The actual installation process is:

- Create boot and root floppies
- Prepare your hard drive for installation
- Boot Linux from boot and root floppies
- Install Linux from the CD-ROM

In the following steps, we're assuming you already have an Intel-based PC up and running with the MS-DOS operating system, with the CD-ROM drive installed correctly, because you'll need to copy some files from the CD-ROM onto your hard drive. (On a PC, you'll need to install special drivers to use the CD-ROM drive; these drivers ship with the CD-ROM drive.) This doesn't need to be the PC on which you plan to install Linux—it just needs to be a PC with a DOS command line and access to the CD-ROM drive.

The procedures in this chapter are closely tied to the installation and configuration routines found on the accompanying CD-ROMs. Other distributions of Linux are not exactly the same. If you're using a distribution of Linux other than the Slackware distribution on the accompanying CD-ROMs, you can still follow along, keeping in mind that your exact steps may differ.

Creating Boot and Root Floppies

Your first steps will be to create two floppy disks used to boot Linux: the boot and root diskettes. The *boot diskette* is the diskette used (as the name implies) to boot the PC, while the *root diskette* contains a set of Linux commands (actually, a complete mini-Linux system). Creating these disks is probably the best way to install Linux, although it is possible to install Linux without using any floppy disks using **LOADLIN.EXE**, a DOS program that loads Linux from an MS-DOS prompt. We'll cover this option a little later, but unless your floppy disk doesn't work under Linux it is recommended that you install using a bootdisk and a rootdisk.

Your next step is to determine which bootdisk and rootdisk images you'll be using and writing the images onto formatted floppy disks. Because selecting the disk images to use (especially the bootdisk) can be a relatively large task, it warrants its own section.

Choosing Bootdisk and Rootdisk Images

Linux needs to know a lot about your PC's hardware, and that knowledge begins the second you boot the system. That's why you need to put some thought into selecting your bootdisk and rootdisk images.

Before we go any further, we should explain what *bootdisk* and *rootdisk images* are. Linux needs to boot from floppies initially, and it needs to know what sort of hardware it's working with. When you boot Linux for the first time, the information is contained on the bootdisk and rootdisk. To create a bootdisk and a rootdisk, you need to select the proper image. You'll then use the **RAWRITE.EXE** utility to copy the image byte-for-byte to the diskette.

How do you select the proper image? The first step is to determine the disk size of your drive **A:**, which you boot the system from. If you're using a 3.5-inch disk drive as **A:**, you'll need to grab an image from the **bootdsks.144** directory. (This is so labeled because the capacity of a 3.5-inch high-density floppy is 1.44 megabytes.) If you're using a 5.25-inch disk drive to boot from, you'll need to grab an image from the **bootdsks.12** directory. (This is so labeled because the capacity of a 5.25-inch high-density floppy is 1.2 megabytes.)

If you look inside either directory, you'll see a list of filenames ending in **.I** (for *IDE*) or **.S** (for *SCSI*). (The filenames are the same in both directories; it doesn't matter from this point which directory you grab the image from.) Each image supports a different set of hardware; a list of the files and supported hardware is in Tables 2.1 (for IDE bootdisks) and 2.2 (for SCSI bootdisks).

Table 2.1 Linux IDE Bootdisks and Supported Hardware

Filename	Supported Hardware
aztech.i	CD-ROM drives: Aztech CDA268-01A, Orchid CD-3110, Okano/Wearnes CDD110, Conrad TXC, CyCDROM CR520, CR540
bare.i	IDE hard-drive only
bareapm.i	IDE hard-drive plus advanced power management BIOS support (for laptops).
barepnp.i	IDE hard-drive plus experimental plug-and-play BIOS support.
cdu31a.i	Sony CDU31/33a CD-ROM
cdu535.i	Sony CDU531/535 CD-ROM
cm206.i	Philips/LMS cm206 CD-ROM with cm260 adapter card
fat32.i	Like bare.i, with experimental FAT32 support.
goldstar.i	Goldstar R420 CD-ROM (sometimes sold in a Reveal Multimedia Kit)
mcd.i	Non-IDE Mitsumi CD-ROM
mcdx.i	Improved non-IDE Mitsumi CD-ROM support
net.i	Ethernet support
optics.i	Optics Storage 8000 AT CD-ROM (know as the "Dolphin" drive)
sanyo.i	Sanyo CDR-H94A CD-ROM
sbpcd.i	Matsushita, Kotobuki, Panasonic, Creative Labs (SoundBlaster), Longshine, and TEAC non-IDE CD-ROM
xt.i	MFM hard drive

All IDE bootdisks support IDE hard drives and CD-ROM drives, plus additional support listed in table.

Table 2.2 Linux SCSI Bootdisks and Support Hardware

Filename	Supported Hardware
7000fast.s	Western Digital 7000FASST SCSI
advansys.s	AdvanSys SCSI support
aha152x.s	Adaptec 152x SCSI
aha1542.s	Adaptec 1542 SCSI

Filename	Supported Hardware
aha1740.s	Adaptec 1740 SCSI
aha2x4x.s	Adaptec AIC7xxx SCSI (including AHA-274x, AHA-2842, AHA-2940, AHA-2940W, AHA-2940U, AHA-2940UW, AHA-2944D, AHA-2944WD, AHA-3940, AHA-3940W, AHA-3985, AHA-3985W)
am53c974.s	AMD AM53/79C974 SCSI
aztech.s	All supported SCSI controllers, plus CD-ROM support for Aztech CDA268-01A, Orchid CD-3110, Okano/Wearnes CDD110, Conrad TXC, CyCDROM CR520, CR540
buslogic.s	Buslogic MultiMaster SCSI
cdu31a.s	All supported SCSI controllers, plus CD-ROM support for Sony CDU31/33a
cdu535.s	All supported SCSI controllers, plus CD-ROM support for Sony CDU531/535
cm206.s	All supported SCSI controllers, plus Philips/LMS cm206 CD-ROM with cm260 adapter card
dtc3280.s	DTC (Data Technology Corp.) 3180/3280 SCSI
eata_dma.s	DPT EATA-DMA SCSI (boards such as PM2011, PM2021, PM2041, PM3021, PM2012B, PM2022, PM2122, PM2322, PM2042, PM3122, PM3222, PM3332, PM2024, PM2124, PM2044, PM2144, PM3224, PM3334)
eata_isa.s	DPT EATA-ISA/EISA SCSI support (boards such as PM2011B/9X, PM2021A/9X, PM2012A, PM2012B, PM2022A/9X, PM2122A/9X, PM2322A/9X)
eata_pio.s	DPT EATA-PIO SCSI (PM2001 and PM2012A)
fat32.s	Like scsi.s, but with experimental FAT32 support.
fdomain.s	Future Domain TMC-16x0 SCSI
goldstar.s	All supported SCSI controllers, plus Goldstar R420 CD-ROM (sometimes sold in a Reveal Multimedia Kit)
in2000.s	Always IN2000 SCSI
iomega.s	IOMEGA PPA3 parallel-port SCSI (also supports parallel-port version of the ZIP drive)
mcd.s	All supported SCSI controllers, plus standard non-IDE Mitsumi CD-ROM

Continued...

Filename	Supported Hardware
mcdx.s	All supported SCSI controllers, plus enhanced non-IDE Mitsumi CD-ROM
n53c406a.s	NCR 53c406a SCSI
n_5380.s	NCR 5380 and 53c400 SCSI
n_53c7xx.s	NCR 53c7xx, 53c8xx SCSI (most NCR PCI SCSI controllers use this driver)
optics.s	All supported SCSI controllers, plus support for the Optics Storage 8000 AT CD-ROM (the "Dolphin" drive)
pas16.s	Pro Audio Spectrum/Studio 16 SCSI
qlog_fas.s	ISA/VLB/PCMCIA Qlogic FastSCSI! (also supports Control Concepts SCSI cards based on the Qlogic FASXXX chip)
qlog_isp.s	Supports all Qlogic PCI SCSI controllers, except the PCI-basic, which is supported by the AMD SCSI driver
sanyo.s	All supported SCSI controllers, plus Sanyo CDR-H94A CD-ROM
sbpcd.s	All supported SCSI controllers, plus Matsushita, Kotobuki, Panasonic, Creative Labs (SoundBlaster), Longshine, and TEAC non-IDE CD-ROMs
scsi.s	All supported SCSI controllers.
scsipnp.s	All supported SCSI controllers, plus experimental plug-and-play card support.
scsinet.s	All supported SCSI controllers, plus full Ethernet
seagate.s	Seagate ST01/ST02 and Future Domain TMC-885/950 SCSI
trantor.s	Trantor T128/T128F/T228 SCSI
ultrastr.s	UltraStor 14F, 24F, and 34F SCSI
ustor14f.s	UltraStor 14F and 34F SCSI

All SCSI bootdisks feature full IDE hard-drive and CD-ROM support, plus additional drivers listed in table.

NOTE All of these images support UMSDOS, if you prefer this method of installation. UMSDOS will be covered later in this chapter in the section, "Should You Use UMSDOS?"

You'll need one of the images listed to get Linux started on your system so that you can install it. Because of the possibility of collisions between the various Linux drivers, several bootkernel disk images are provided. You should use the one with the least drivers possible to maximize your chances of success. All of these disks support UMSDOS.

At first glance, Tables 2.1 and 2.2 can be a little confusing. To clear things up, Table 2.3 contains a handy little guide where you can match installation medium and hard disk format to the preferred image (in **bold**).

Table 2.3 Chart for Choosing Bootdisk Images

Installation Medium	IDE Destination	SCSI Destination	MFM Destination
Hard drive	**bare.i**	Use a SCSI controller bootdisk from the list following the table.	**xt.i**
SCSI CD-ROM	Use a SCSI controller bootdisk from the list following the table.	Use a SCSI controller bootdisk from the list following the table	-
IDE/ATAPI CDROM	**bare.i**	Use a SCSI controller bootdisk from the list following the table.	
Aztech, Orchid, Okano, Wearnes, Conrad, CyCD ROM non-IDE CD-ROM	**aztech.i**	**aztech.s**	
Sony CDU31a, Sony CDU33a CD-ROM	**cdu31a.i**	**cdu31a.s**	
Sony CDU531, Sony CDU535 CD-ROM	**cdu535.i**	**cdu535.s**	
Philips/LMS cm206 CD-ROM	**cm206.i**	**cm206.s**	
Goldstar R420 CD-ROM	**goldstar.i**	**goldstar.s**	
Mitsumi non-IDE CD-ROM	**mcdx.i, mcd.i**	**mcdx.s, mcd.i**	
Optics Storage 8000 AT CD-ROM ("Dolphin")	**optics.i**	**optics.s**	
Sanyo CDR-H94A CD-ROM	**sanyo.i**	**sanyo.s**	

Installation Medium	IDE Destination	SCSI Destination	MFM Destination
Matsushita, Kotobuki, Panasonic, Creative Labs (SoundBlaster), Longshine, and TEAC non-IDE CD-ROM	sbpcd.i	sbpcd.s	
NFS	net.i	scsinet.i	
Tape	bare.i (for floppy tape); for SCSI tape, use a SCSI controller bootdisk from the list following the table	Use a SCSI controller bootdisk from the list following the table	xt.i (for floppy tape)

The SCSI controller bootdisks are:

7000fast.s, advansys.s, aha152x.s, aha1542.s, aha1740.s, aha2x4x.s, am53c974.s, buslogic.s, dtc3280.s, eata_dma.s, eata_isa.s, eata_pio.s, fdomain.s, in2000.s, iomega.s, n53c406a.s, n_5380.s, n_53c7xx.s, pas16.s, qlog_fas.s, qlog_isp.s, seagate.s, trantor.s, ultrastr.s, ustor14f.s

Choosing the Proper Rootdisk Image

After selecting the proper bootdisk, you'll need to select the proper rootdisk. The selections are more limited, so you won't have to put much work into this selection. The rootdisks are stored in the **ROOTDSKS** directory and will work with either 3.5-inch or 5.25-inch high-density diskettes.

Your rootdisk image selections are listed in Table 2.4.

Table 2.4 Rootdisk Selections

Filename	Purpose
COLOR.GZ	This image contains a full-screen color install program and should be considered the default rootdisk image. This version of the install system has some known bugs, however; in particular, it is not forgiving of extra keystrokes entered between screens. This is probably the file you'll want to use.
UMSDOS.GZ	This is similar to the color disk, but it installs using UMSDOS, a filesystem that allows you to install Linux into a directory on an existing MS-DOS partition. This filesystem is not as fast as a native Linux filesystem, but it works, and you don't have to repartition your hard drive.

Filename	Purpose
TEXT.GZ	This is a text-based version of the install program derived from scripts used in previous Slackware releases.
TAPE.GZ	This image is designed to support installation from tape. See the section "Installing from Tape" later in this chapter.
PCMCIA.GZ	Similiar to the color disk, but used for installing on a laptop's internal hard drive through a PCMCIA card (SCSI, ethernet, or CD_ROM drive).

NOTE You'll notice that these filenames end with the **.GZ** extension; this indicates that the files have been compressed with GNU **zip**. Some older distributions of Linux required that the files be decompressed prior to use, but this is not necessary anymore. The kernel on the bootdisk will detect that the rootdisk is compressed and will automatically decompress the disk as it is loaded into RAM. This allows the use of a 1.44MB uncompressed image size for both 1.44MB and 1.2MB floppy drives.

Most users will use the **COLOR.GZ** rootdisk image.

Should You Use UMSDOS?

The UMSDOS filesystem allows you to install Linux in an MS-DOS directory on an existing DOS partition. The advantage of this is that you won't need to reformat or repartition your existing system. There are two disadvantages to using this system, however.

First, the UMSDOS system is somewhat slower than a native Linux filesystem. This is especially true of machines with 8 megabytes of memory or less—UMSDOS is virtually unusable on a 4MB machine. The second disadvantage of UMSDOS has to do with a shortcoming of the MS-DOS FAT filesystem. MS-DOS allocates space for files in units called *clusters*. A cluster is usually 4K or 8K in size. This means that the smallest file that can be created on a UMSDOS filesystem takes up a full cluster (4096+ bytes), even if the file is much smaller. Linux contains many such small files, including symbolic links and device entries. As a result, installing with UMSDOS may require more drive space than installing with a native Linux filesystem.

Now that you've chosen your bootdisk and rootdisk images, it's time to actually create the bootdisk and rootdisk.

Creating the Diskettes

For this step, you'll need two high-density diskettes. It doesn't matter what's on the diskettes, but they must be formatted. Be warned that this process will completely wipe out anything currently stored on the diskettes. You might also wish to format a third high-density floppy disk at this time for the installation program to use later when it's preparing your system bootdisk.

As you'll recall from an earlier note, the images for the rootdisks do not need to be decompressed; the kernel will automatically decompress them as they are loaded into memory.

In these examples, we'll be using the **BARE.I** and **COLOR.GZ** images. If you're using a different set of images, just substitute those filenames instead.

The procedures in this section do not need to be done on the computer you're planning to use as your Linux workstation. You can create the files on a different PC or even use a UNIX workstation to create the floppies. On a UNIX workstation the **dd** command is used to write an image to the floppy drive. When using **dd** on Suns, and possibly on some other UNIX workstations, you must provide an approximate block size. Here's an example:

```
dd if=bare.i of=/dev/(rdfd0, rdf0c, fd0, or whatever) obs=18k
```

Now it's time to make your bootdisk. First, move into the **bootdisks.144** (or **bootdisks.12** if you use a 1.2MB floppy drive) directory on your Slackware CD-ROM.

Assuming your CD-ROM drive has the drive letter **E:** assigned to it, you'd move into the directory like this:

```
C:\> E:
    E:\> CD BOOTDSKS.144
E:\BOOTDSKS.144>
```

Now you'll actually create the bootdisk. Put the eventual bootdisk diskette in drive **A:** and type the following command:

```
E:\> RAWRITE BARE.I A:
```

This will use the **RAWRITE** command (there's a copy of this in each of the **BOOTDSKS** and **ROOTDSKS** directories) to copy the **BARE.I** disk image to the **A:** floppy drive. As it writes, **RAWRITE** will give you a status report. After it's finished writing the bootdisk, remove the disk from the drive and put it aside.

Then insert another formatted high-density floppy and use the same procedure to write the rootdisk. In this case, you'll need to move into the **ROOTDSKS** directory and write the **COLOR.GZ** image using **RAWRITE**:

```
E:\BOOTDSKS.144> cd \ROOTDSKS
E:\ROOTDSKS> RAWRITE COLOR.GZ A:
```

There's really not a lot to the **RAWRITE** command; the only things that could trip you up would be if you're not using a high-density diskette or if the diskette is flawed.

Preparing Your Hard Drive for Linux

Now that you've created your boot diskettes, it's time to prepare your hard drive for Linux. In order to install Linux, you must create a Linux partition on your hard drive. You should also consider creating a DOS partition on your hard drive in addition to the Linux partition—a step that's not necessary, but one that we follow for many reasons (which we'll explain later).

 If you're a UNIX workstation user, you're not going to be familiar with some of the concepts and operations we describe here. If, after reading this section, you're still a little fuzzy about the IBM PC and its many quirks, you may want to head to your local bookstore and purchase a good guide to the PC.

Intel-based PCs have the ability to divide a hard drive into *partitions*. This is why you may have several different drive letters (**C:**, **D:**, **E:**), even though you have only one physical hard drive. (This dates from early versions of MS-DOS, which lacked the ability to recognize hard disk partitions larger than 33 megabytes. MS-DOS 4.0 was the first version to do away with this restriction.) The ability to create partitions also yields a bonus (as far as a Linux user is concerned): You can install different operating systems on a hard drive, and these different operating systems won't conflict. As a matter of fact, they can coexist quite nicely; you can configure Linux to give you a choice of operating systems when you boot your PC, and you can access DOS-formatted partitions from within Linux. Linux is relatively good about coexisting with other operating systems—primarily, DOS, Windows, Windows 95, and OS/2. Linux requires at least one partition for itself.

You must physically create partitions, as Intel-based PCs need to know what type of operating system is residing on a portion of the hard drive. If you've purchased your PC from a clone vendor or superstore and started using it immediately, chances are that you've treated the hard disk as one contiguous drive, without partitioning it into smaller drives. In a perfect world, of course. you're installing Linux on a brand-new system, and there's little of importance currently installed on your hard disk. This is the route we try to follow, because there's little chance of doing damage to anything important.

However, if you've been using your PC for a while, you've probably accumulated software, data files, and configurations that you're loathe to give up. In this case, you'll want to retain as much of the DOS configuration as possible while making room for Linux. There are two routes you can take:

- Using the **FIPS** utility to partition the hard drive without (theoretically) destroying the existing data.

- Backing up the DOS data, creating the new Linux and DOS partitions, and then reinstalling the backup. (This is our preferred method.) You'll need to make sure that the new partition is large enough to contain all the data from the old DOS partition, of course.

In either case, you'll want to first make a backup of your hard disk, on either floppy disks or some tape-based medium (Bernoulli drive, SyQuest tape, DAT tape). Depending on your system configuration, you'll either want to back up everything or just those directories that can't easily be reinstalled from floppy or CD-ROM. (We find that a system cleansing is good every once in a while, so we tend to back up data and irreplaceable configuration files but reinstall applications from scratch.) Yes, we know backing up your hard drive is a pain (and we probably don't do it as often as we should), but you should make a backup every time you do something to your hard drive that has the potential to destroy data.

Using FIPS to Divide Your Hard Drive

After you make your backup, you'll need to decide which route to take. The **FIPS** utility described earlier is stored in **install fips** on the first accompanying CD-ROM as **FIPS.EXE**; the guide to using **FIPS** is stored in the same location in **FIPS.DOC**. (If you plan on using the **FIPS** utility, we *strongly* advise you to read this file a couple of times, as it contains far more information and detail than is given here.)

Basically, **FIPS** works by creating a new partition on the physical end of the hard drive. Before the **FIPS** utility does this, you must first *defragment* your hard drive. A word about how a PC's hard drive stores data is in order here.

When a PC writes to a hard disk, it writes to clusters on the disk. Generally speaking, this writing is done sequentially; the first clusters appear at the physical beginning of the disk. As you use the system, you inevitably write more and more to the hard drive, and you probably delete some data as well. As you delete the data, the clusters it occupied are freed; at the same time, new data is written to the end of the disk. Any hard disk that's been in use for a while will have data scattered throughout the physical drive. (This is why hard drives slow down when they fill with data; the drive head must physically hop around the drive to retrieve scattered data.)

When you defragment your hard drive, you're replacing the freed clusters at the beginning of the drive with data from the end of the drive. While not purely sequential, your data is all crammed at the beginning of the hard drive. This improves disk performance—because your data is physically closer together, the drive head spends less time retrieving data that was scattered in the past.

Newer versions of MS-DOS, and PC-DOS, (that is, versions 6.0 and better) contain a defragmenting utility. (Check your operating system documentation for specifics, as the utilities differ.) If you're using an older version of MS-DOS, you'll need to use a general-purpose utility package (such as the Norton Utilities or PC Tools Deluxe) to defragment your hard drive.

The **FIPS** utility takes advantage of the fact that the data is crammed at the beginning of the hard drive. It allows you to create a point past the end of the DOS data to begin the new Linux partition (if you use this method, remember to leave room for more data in the DOS partition!).

We're not going to spend a lot of time on **FIPS** here, because the documentation on the accompanying CD-ROM more than adequately explains how **FIPS** works, its limitations, and the exact procedures for dividing a hard drive. The only caveat we offer is that you should know a little about how PCs deal with hard drive partitions before using **FIPS**; if you're a PC neophyte, we suggest you follow the steps detailed in the next section.

FIPS will not work with OS/2. The details are contained in the **FIPS.DOC** file. You should run **FIPS** from DOS rather than from a multitasking environment like Windows or DESQview. FIPS will also not work with FAT32, a new filesystem Microsoft has included in some newer Windows95 systems. If you're unlucky enough to have this, you'll either have to erase your DOS partition to make room for Linux, or add a new hard drive.

Using DOS Utilities to Divide Your Hard Drive

The second method to prepare your hard drive for Linux involves various DOS utilities, which you'll use to create new partitions and configure a floppy diskette you can use to boot your PC with DOS.

The first step involves creating a DOS boot diskette. (You've already created a Linux boot diskette; the two are different.) This is a rather simple procedure, involving the following command line:

```
C:> format /s A:
```

where **A:** is your boot drive. This command formats a floppy disk and adds the system files (**COMMAND.COM** and hidden files **IO.SYS** and **MSDOS.SYS**) needed to boot DOS from the floppy. If you install a DOS partition, booting from this diskette will give you access to that partition (which will appear as drive **C:**). It will *not*, however, give you access to the CD-ROM until you install the CD-ROM drivers on the DOS boot diskette.

When you installed OS/2, it should have directed you to create an emergency boot floppy. You may need this diskette if something goes wrong in the installation.

After doing this, you'll need to copy some additional utilities to the floppy. You'll need to be fairly selective about what files you copy to the floppy, because the sum of all DOS **.EXE** and **.COM** files (essentially, the utility files) in a typical DOS installation won't fit on a floppy disk. You'll need to copy the **FDISK.EXE** and **FORMAT.COM** files to the floppy drive with the following command lines:

```
C:> copy \DOS\FDISK.EXE A:
        1 file(s) copied


C:> copy \DOS\FORMAT.COM A:
        1 file(s) copied
```

You may also want to copy onto a floppy the files that restore your system backup, if you used operating system utilities to create the backup. Check your documentation for the specific files; they differ between operating systems.

What are FDISK and FORMAT?

We've told you to copy **FDISK.EXE** and **FORMAT.COM** onto the floppy for future use, we should take some time to explain what they do.

FDISK.EXE is the program that creates MS-DOS partitions. Every operating system has a program that does something similar (you'll use the Linux **fdisk** command later in this process). You'll need to use the partitioning software specific to the operating system; for example, you can't use **FDISK** to create Linux or OS/2 partitions. **FDISK.EXE** works very simply: You delete an existing partition or partitions, and you create new partitions in their place.

Creating a partition merely leaves a portion of your hard disk devoted to the particular operating system. After you've used **FDISK.EXE** to create a new DOS partition, you'll use the **FORMAT.COM** program to format that partition for use under MS-DOS. If you don't format the MS-DOS partition, the operating system won't be able to recognize it.

Using the DOS FDISK Utility

Now that you've created the system backup and a boot diskette, it's time to destroy the data on your hard drive with the **FDISK** utility. Destroy? Yup. The act of creating new partitions is by definition a destructive act. You must destroy the existing partitions and the records of the data contained therein in order to create the new partitions.

You can use **FDISK** if your system has more than one hard drive. In this case, you'll want to make sure that you're working on the correct hard drive. **FDISK** does not use the normal DOS drive representations (**C:, D:, E:,** etc.); rather, **FDISK** uses numerals, such as *1* or *2*.

Begin by booting your PC from the floppy disk you created in the previous section. This "vanilla" boot will ask for today's date and time (ignore both; they don't matter) and then give you the following command line:

```
A>
```

You're now ready to run the DOS **FDISK** utility:

```
A> fdisk
```

There are no command-line parameters to **FDISK**.

The program loads and displays something like the screen shown in Figure 2.1.

```
MS-DOS Version 5.00
Fixed Disk Setup Program
(C) Copyright Microsoft 1983 - 1991


                        FDISK OPTIONS


Current fixed disk drive: 1


Choose one of the following:


1. Create DOS partition or Logical DOS Drive
2. Set active partition
3. Delete partition or Logical DOS Drive
4. Display partition information




Enter choice: [1]



Press Esc to exit FDISK
```

Figure 2.1 The opening screen to the **FDISK** utility.

The figures is this section are for a specific version of MS-DOS, 5.00. However, most versions of MS-DOS follow the conventions shown and explained here. If the choices on your system aren't exactly like the choices here, read through them carefully and use the similar choice. Remember: You are essentially deleting a partition and creating a new one in this procedure.

At this point you'll need to delete the existing partition, so you'll choose **3**. (If you're not sure about the existing partitions on your disk—or whether you're even working on the correct disk if you have more than one—select **4**.)

When using the **FDISK** utility, you'll see references to primary and extended partitions, as well as to logical drives. Here an explanation:

- The *primary partition* is the partition containing the files (**IO.SYS, MSDOS.SYS,** and **COMMAND.COM**) needed to boot MS-DOS. In essence, this is your C: drive. The primary partition cannot be divided into other logical drives.

- The extended partition or partitions do not contain these boot files. An extended partition can exist as its own logical drive (such as D: or E:) or be divided into additional logical drives.

- The *logical drive* is the portion of a partition assigned a drive letter. For example, an extended partition can be divided into up to 23 logical drives (**A:** and **B:** are reserved for floppies, and **C:** is reserved for the primary partition, leaving 23 letters).

Additionally, the *non-DOS partition* is for another operating system, such as Linux.

Chances are that you won't need to deal with more than a primary drive or an extended drive.

After selecting **3**, you'll see the screen shown in Figure 2.2.

What you do at this point depends on how your hard drive has been configured. If you have primary and extended partitions, delete them. If you have only a primary drive, delete it. **FDISK** will confirm that you do indeed want to delete a partition. This is your last chance to chicken out and check the DOS partition one more time before actually wiping it out.

After deleting a partition, you'll need to create a new DOS partition—a choice that's listed in Figure 2.1 as option **1**. After choosing **1**, you'll be shown a screen like that in Figure 2.3.

```
              Delete DOS Partition or Logical DOS Drive


Current fixed disk drive: 1


Choose one of the following:


1. Delete Primary DOS Partition
2. Delete Extended DOS Partition
3. Delete Logical DOS Drive(s) in the Extended DOS Partition
4. Delete Non-DOS Partition




Enter choice: [ ]




Press Esc to return to FDISK Options
```

Figure 2.2 The delete screen for **FDISK**.

```
              Create DOS Partition or Logical DOS Drive


Current fixed disk drive: 1


Choose one of the following:


1. Create Primary DOS Partition
2. Create Extended DOS Partition
3. Create Logical DOS Drive(s) in the Extended DOS Partition




Enter choice: [1]




Press Esc to return to FDISK Options
```

Figure 2.3 Creating a new partition with **FDISK**.

Of course, you'll want to create a new primary partition; this is the partition that will be used for DOS.

The next thing you'll need to decide is how much of the hard drive to devote to DOS. There are no hard-and-fast rules concerning partition sizes. Obviously, you'll first need to think about how much of a priority Linux is—if you plan on running Linux a lot, you should give it a lot of hard disk space. If you plan on using it as much as DOS, you should equalize the two installations somewhat, keeping in mind that Linux will require far more hard disk space than DOS. And if you plan on using Microsoft Windows along with DOS and Linux, you should assume that Windows will take up as much hard disk space as it can get.

Our only advice: Don't be stingy when it comes to Linux hard disk allocation, and remember that Linux applications tend to eat up a *lot* of disk space. It's not unusual to run across freely available binaries on the Internet that are more than a megabyte (such as the popular Web browser NCSA Mosaic for X Window), and in time these applications add up. If you're really careful during installation and you install only the applications you need, you can keep a Linux installation down to 100 megabytes or so. Realistically, however, by the time you include everything worth having, you'll be up to 275 megabytes or so. If you only have a 325MB hard disk, you'll obviously need to keep the DOS partition to 10 or so megabytes.

Don't bother with any other partitions—at least for Linux usage. You probably won't want to create a logical DOS drive; if you do, you can't use it for a Linux installation, as all Linux partitions must be created through Linux later in the installation process.

After deciding how much hard disk space to give to DOS, you'll want to exit **FDISK**. Go ahead and make the DOS partition active (this means that you can boot from it later, which you'll want to do; you can have multiple partitions able to boot).

After quitting **FDISK**, reboot the system, leaving the DOS diskette in drive **A:**. You'll now want to format drive **C:**—at least the DOS portion of it—with the DOS **FORMAT** command:

```
A> FORMAT /S C:
```

This command formats the DOS partition with the core of the operating system (the **COMMAND.COM, IO.SYS,** and **MSDOS.SYS** files). The **FORMAT** command makes sure that you want to go ahead with the format (this is to make sure that DOS neophytes don't accidentally format a partition that contains valuable information); answer in the affirmative when asked if you want to proceed with the format.

 You can use any version of DOS for these steps, as long as it's DOS 4.0 or better. DOS doesn't care if you format the hard drive with one version of DOS and install another version later.

NOTE

Now that you've prepared the DOS side of your hard disk (and after looking back you realize that it's a lot easier than the extended verbiage in the previous sections made it seem), it's time to boot Linux.

FDISK and OS/2

When preparing a PC for use with OS/2 and Linux, you'll need to use a slightly different route for preparing your hard drive.

OS/2 has trouble with partitions not originally created with *its* **FDISK** utility. Therefore, you must start by partitioning your hard disk with the OS/2 **FDISK** utility (keeping in mind that OS/2 needs more than 35 megabytes of hard disk space to run). Then you must create the Linux partition with the OS/2 **FDISK** utility—marked as another OS/2 partition—and make that a potential boot partition using OS/2's Boot Manager. (OS/2 gives you the ability to select a boot partition every time you boot the PC.)

You'll then boot your PC with the instructions given next. However, later in the process you'll do something a little different when it comes to the Linux **fdisk** command (which we'll cover at that point in the installation process).

Booting Linux with the Bootdisk

Obviously, you boot Linux with the bootdisk you prepared earlier. Put it in your boot drive and restart your PC with a cold or warm boot (it doesn't matter).

Initially your PC will do the things that it normally does when it boots, such as check the memory and run through the BIOS. However, the word *LILO* will appear on your screen, followed by a full screen that begins with the line:

```
Welcome to the Slackware Linux 3.2.0 bootkernel disk!
```

You'll also see some verbiage about passing parameters along to the kernel; most users won't need to pass along any additional parameters.

The exceptions are some IBM PS/1, ValuePoint, and ThinkPad users, as Linux will not recognize the hard disks used by these machines. These IBM computers don't store the hard disk information in the CMOS, which is checked by Linux upon booting up. Because Linux lacks this information, it assumes there's no hard drive present. You must pass along the hard disk geometry at this point.

If you are using one of these machines, you cannot use the **bare** bootdisk; instead, you should use **scsi**. When you boot using this bootdisk, you should press down the left **Shift** key, which gives you a menu where you can specify the geometry of the hard disk. Where do you get this information? From the drive's installation guide or by checking the machine's internal setup.

Most users will be able to press the **Enter** key and proceed to load the Linux RAM disk.

There are some cases where *LILO* appears on the screen and the system hangs or rows of *0*s and *1*s cascade down the screen. In these cases, you are probably using the wrong bootdisk for your PC. The first thing to do is to create a few alternate bootdisks and try them; if the problem persists, scan the Usenet newsgroups and the FTP archives (see Appendix A for details) to make sure that your PC and its peripherals are indeed supported by Linux.

The bootdisk runs through your system hardware, noting which hard drives and peripherals are present and scouting out other salient details about your PC. It's at this point that Linux discovers any problems with your PC, and if you have problems installing or using Linux, it's a place you'll want to check. (The same information is displayed and gathered every time you boot.)

If there are no problems, you can put in your rootdisk and press **Enter**. A core of the Linux operating system is then copied to the RAM disk, which then gives you access to some Linux commands, including the important **fdisk** command. The installation process instructs you to login the Linux system as *root*:

```
slackware login : root
```

There will be no password required.

If you're asked for a password, it means you don't have enough memory to install.

Before you proceed, carefully look through the instructions on the screen. There are a few notes that may apply to your specific computing situation.

Linux and Hard Disk Names

After logging in, you'll want to directly run the **fdisk** command (ignoring what the screen instructions say about the **setup** command). The **fdisk** command assumes that the first IDE drive is the default drive. If you plan on installing Linux on another drive, you'll need to specify that on the command line. Table 2.5 lists the hard disk device names.

Table 2.5 Linux Hard Disk Device Names

Name	Meaning
/dev/hda	First IDE hard drive
/dev/hdb	Second IDE hard drive
/dev/sda	First SCSI hard drive
/dev/sdb	Second SCSI hard drive
/dev/fd0	First floppy drive (**A:**)
/dev/fd1	Second floppy drive (**B:**)

Note the pattern in Table 2.5? In addition, Linux allows you to specify the partitions in the device names. For example, the first primary partition on the first IDE drive would be known as **/dev/hda1**, the second primary partition on the first IDE drive would be known as **/dev/hda2**, and so on. If you're installing logical partitions, the first logical partition would appear as **/dev/hda5**, the second logical partition would appear as **/dev/hda6**, and so on.

The files representing these devices will end up in the directory **/dev**.

To run **fdisk** on the second SCSI hard drive, you'd use the following command line:

```
# fdisk /dev/sdb
```

Most of you (most PCs are sold with IDE drives) will be told that Linux is using the first hard drive as the default. When you press **m** for a list of options, you'll see the following listing:

```
Command action
   a   toggle a bootable flag
   c   toggle the dos compatibility flag
   d   delete a partition
```

```
l    list known partition types
m    print this menu
n    add a new partition
p    print the partition table
q    quit without saving changes
t    change a partition's system id
u    change display/entry units
v    verify the partition table
w    write table to disk and exit
x    extra functionality (experts only)
```

There are really only three options you'll ever use, unless you run into some esoteric configurations:

- **d**, which deletes a current partition. This will work on non-Linux partitions.
- **n**, which creates a new partition.
- **p**, which prints a rundown of the current partition table. This will list non-Linux partitions as well.

WARNING

Linux allows you to make your hard disk configuration (and *any* configuration) as complex as you want it to be. Our philosophy is to keep it as simple as possible; unless you have a real need for multiple partitions and the like, just keep to the basics—a DOS partition, a Linux partition, and perhaps a partition for an additional operating system (like OS/2) if you like.

Some argue that by creating multiple Linux partitions, you'll be able to recover more easily if something happens to the boot partition. (Damage to one partition doesn't automatically mean that all the partitions are damaged.) However, if you're making frequent backups of important files (mostly data and configuration files), you'll have a more reliable setup. If there's damage to the PC's File Allocation Table (FAT), you'll have problems with *all* your partitions.

If you select **p**, you'll see the following:

```
    Device Boot  Begin   Start    End  Blocks   Id  System
  /dev/hda1    *      1       1     63   20762+   4  DOS 16-bit (32M)
```

This is the DOS partition you created in the previous sections.

Before you actually create the Linux partition, you should decide if you want to install a swap partition.

Linux and a Swap Disk

If you are using a PC with 4 megabytes of RAM, you may want to set up a *swap partition*. This partition is treated by the system as extended RAM; if you run low on memory (and with 4 megabytes of RAM, you're guaranteed to), Linux can treat this hard disk section as RAM, or *virtual memory*. You'll take a performance hit, as a hard disk will always be slower than real RAM, and you'll have the joy of watching your hard disk churn furiously when you try to use a few applications. However, a swap partition can be used *only* for swap space by Linux; it can't be used for any other storage. Therefore, you need to weigh your RAM needs versus your hard disk storage needs, keeping in mind that Linux should have as much hard disk territory for storage as possible.

You may also want to consider a swap partition if you have more than 4 megabytes of RAM. We've found that XFree86 is a little tight when running under only 8 megabytes of RAM, and some swap space can't hurt, especially if you have a very large hard disk. (XFree86 won't tell you that it's low on RAM; it will simply refuse to do anything, such as failing to load an application.) Some Linux experts recommend that you have 16 megabytes of virtual memory. If you have only 8 megabytes of RAM, this would mean that you would want to set up at least an 8MB swap partition.

If you do want to create a swap partition, read on. If you don't, you can skip to the next section, "Creating the Main Linux Partition."

Your first move is to create a swap partition with the **fdisk** command. You'll need to decide how large to make this partition. That will depend on how much free space you think you can give up on your hard drive. For the purposes of this chapter, we'll devote 10 megabytes to swap space.

Run the **fdisk** command and choose the **n** option, for creating a new partition. You'll see the following:

```
Command action
   e    extended
   p    primary partition (1-4)
```

Type **p**, and enter the partition number. If you've already installed a DOS or OS/2 partition, you'll need to select the number **2**, as partition number 1 is already is use:

```
Partition number (1-4): 2
```

You'll then be asked where to place the partition and how large to make it. Generally speaking, you'll want to place the partition immediately after the previous partition:

```
First cylinder (64-1010): 64
```

Your numbers will undoubtedly be different. The point here is that **fdisk** automatically lists the first unassigned cylinder here (in this case, it was cylinder *64*), and you should go with that number.

You'll then be asked how large you want to make the partition:

```
Last cylinder or +size or +sizeM or +sizeK (64-1010): +10M
```

Because we're not into figuring out how many cylinders or kilobytes it would take to make up 10 megabytes, we use the easy way out and specify 10 megabytes directly as **+10M**.

This won't apply to most users, but Linux doesn't do very well if it's installed as a boot partition on cylinder 1023 or above. (This occurs with very large hard drives—1 gigabyte or larger.) This has nothing to do with Linux, but rather with the limitations in the PC's BIOS. Thus, you should avoid installing the Linux boot partition on a partition containing this cylinder or higher.

Fdisk then creates the partition. To make sure that everything went correctly, type **p** to see a list of the current partitions:

```
Device Boot  Begin  Start  End  Blocks  Id  System
/dev/hda1    *    1      1     63   20762+   4  DOS 16-bit (32M)
/dev/hda2         63     64    95   10560   83  Linux native
```

The number of blocks listed here will be handy when you actually make this partition a swap partition. Jot it down.

Fdisk then gives you its command prompt; type **w** and exit.

You may notice that the hard disk is pretty quiet when you're making all these changes to the partition. The **fdisk** command doesn't make its changes until you type the **w** command to exit. You can make all the changes you want and change your mind many times, but until you type **w**, it won't matter.

You'll then want to use the **mkswap** command to make the partition a swap partition. The command line is quite simple: You list the partition you want to make a swap partition (remembering that Linux lists partitions as **/dev/hda1**, **/dev/hda2**, and so on) and the size of the partition *in blocks*. The command line would look like the following:

```
# mkswap -c /dev/hda2 10560
```

We told you the number of blocks would come in handy!

The *-c* option checks for bad blocks on the partition. If **mkswap** returns any errors, you can ignore them, as Linux already knows of their existence and will ignore them.

After creating the swap partition, you'll need to activate it with a command line like:

```
#  swapon /dev/hda2
```

Finally, you need to tell the filesystem that **/dev/hda2** is indeed a swap partition, again using the **fdisk** command. In this instance, you'll need to change the *type* of the partition. When you created this partition, it was set up as a Linux native partition. However, Linux needs to explicitly know that this is a swap partition, so you need to change the type with the **t** command:

```
Partition number (1-4): 2
Hex code (type L to list codes): 82
```

Linux supports a wide range of partition types, as you'd see if you typed **L**. However, you can take our word for it; *82* is the proper hex code. (You don't need to know every single hex code; there's little reason for you to know that *8* is the hex code for *AIX* or that *75* is the hex code for *PC/IX*.)

Quit **fdisk** using **w**, making sure that your changes are written to disk. It will take a few seconds for this to happen.

You're now ready to create your main Linux partition.

Creating the Main Linux Partition

Most of you will want to designate the remainder of the hard drive as the Linux partition, so that's the assumption made in the remainder of this chapter. With *Command (m for help):* on your screen, select **n** for new partition. You'll see the following:

```
Command action
   e   extended
   p   primary partition (1-4)
```

Type **p**, and enter the partition number. If you've already installed a DOS or OS/2 partition, you'll need to select the number **2**, as partition number 1 is already is use:

```
Partition number (1-4): 2
```

If you've already installed a swap partition, you'll need to designate this partition as **3**.

You'll then be asked where to place the partition and how large to make it. Generally speaking, you'll want to place the partition immediately after the previous partition:

```
First cylinder (64-1010): 64
```

Your numbers will undoubtedly be different. The point here is that **fdisk** automatically lists the first unassigned cylinder here (in this case, it was cylinder *64*), and you should go with that number.

You'll then be asked how large you want to make the partition:

```
Last cylinder or +size or +sizeM or +sizeK (64-1010): 1010
```

Since Linux gives us the number of the last cylinder (*1010*), we'll go with that. There are no advantages to creating more than one Linux partition, unless you're using a *very* large hard drive (larger than 4 gigabytes).

This won't apply to most users, but Linux doesn't do very well if it's installed as a boot partition on cylinder 1023 or above. (This occurs with very large hard drives—1 gigabyte or larger.) This has nothing to do with Linux, but rather with the limitations in the PC's BIOS. Subsequently, you should avoid installing the Linux boot partition on a partition containing this cylinder or higher.

Finally, you'll want to make sure that this is a Linux boot partition so you can boot from the hard disk in the future via LILO. The **t** command toggles whether or not you want to use a partition as a boot partition. Type **t**, and then specify this partition (**2**) as the partition you want to boot from.

Fdisk will then ask for a command. You'll need to make sure your changes are recorded, so select **w**, which writes the partition table to disk and then exits **fdisk**. After this is done, Linux gives you a command prompt (#) again. It's now time to run the **setup** program.

OS/2 Partitions and the Linux Fdisk Command

If you've used the OS/2 **FDISK** command to create your Linux partition, now is the time to change the partition from an OS/2 partition to a Linux partition.

With the Linux **fdisk** command, you can change the current status of partitions by changing the tag. Using the Linux **fdisk**, you'll change the tag of the OS/2 partition to a Linux native partition. In this instance, you'll need to change the type of the partition. When you created this partition, it was set up as an OS/2 partition. However, Linux needs to know that this is a Linux partition, so you need to change the type with the **t** command:

```
Partition number (1-4): 2
Hex code (type L to list codes): 83
```

Linux supports a wide range of partition types, as you'd see if you typed **L**. However, you can take our word for it; *83* is the proper hex code for a Linux native partition.

Quit **fdisk** using **w**, making sure that your changes are written to disk. It will take a few seconds for this to happen.

Installing Linux from the Setup Program

Now comes the fun part: actually installing Linux. For this, you'll run the **setup** command from a command line:

```
# setup
```

You'll then see a menu with the following choices:

```
HELP          Read the Slackware Setup Help file

KEYMAP        Remap your keyboard if you're not using a US one

MAKE TAGS     Experts may customize tagfiles to preselect files

ADDSWAP       Set up your swap partition(s)

TARGET        Set up your target partition

SOURCE        Select source media

DISK SETS     Decide which disk sets you wish to install

INSTALL       Install selected disk sets

CONFIGURE     Reconfigure your Linux system

EXIT          Exit Slackware Linux Setup
```

You should first look through the help file, which is listed first. Some of the steps presented therein may assist you in the Linux installation process.

To move through the selections in this menu, you use the cursor (arrow) keys or type the first letter in each line (such as **H** for *help*).

Basically, the installation from CD-ROM is pretty simple. It follows these steps:

- Set up swap space for Linux.
- Tell Linux where you want it to be installed.
- Select the source for the files needed to install Linux (in most. cases, this will be the CD-ROM).
- Select the software you want to install.
- Actually install the software.
- Configure the installed software.

Each of these steps will be covered in its own section.

Before you get started on the installation steps, you should know that the Slackware distribution of Linux supports many different keymaps for different languages and setups. If you want access to another language—say, German—or another keyboard layout—such as the Dvorak keyboard—you should select **Keymap** from the Setup menu.

Setting up the Swap Space

As you've probably guessed by now, a lot of Linux installation involves an actual installation and then additional steps, telling Linux about the installation. This is certainly true if you've installed a swap partition. (If you have not, you can skip this step.) You've already installed the partition, made it active, and changed its type to a Linux swap partition. You again need to tell Linux about this partition. However, you don't need to format this partition, as you've already done so with the **mkswap** command.

Selecting the Target for Linux

This selection should be rather simple: You'll want to install to the Linux partition you set up earlier in this chapter. When you select **Target** from the Setup menu, you'll automatically be presented with this partition. This section covers the choices you'll make; for the most part, you'll want to go with the default choices.

Formatting the Linux partition is the next step. You'll want to format the Linux partition for a new installation; however, if you're using the **setup** program to upgrade from a previous installation, you won't want to format the Linux partition.

Choosing inode density is next. Again, you'll want to go with the default, unless you have Linux experience and know that the default won't help you.

After the hard disk chugs and formats the Linux partition, you'll be asked if you want to make a DOS or OS/2 partition visible (or, more technically speaking, *mounted*) from Linux—assuming that you've created such a partition. Making this partition visible won't affect Linux performance, nor will it eat away at the size of the Linux partition. Because you may find it handy to move files via the DOS or OS/2 partition, you probably will want to make this partition visible. You'll be asked to provide a name for the drive; the name doesn't really matter, so we use **dos** or **dosc**. When you run the **ls** command later in your Linux usage, you'll see **dos** or **dosc** listed as just another directory, and the files within will appear as Linux files.

Selecting the Source for Linux

You have five choices for where you want to install Linux from:

- hard drive partition
- floppy disks
- NFS
- premounted directory
- CD-ROM

Because you've bought this book, we'll assume you want to use the accompanying CD-ROMs for installation. However, other installation methods will be discussed later in this chapter.

There may be cases where DOS sees a CD-ROM drive with no problems but Linux cannot. In these cases you won't necessarily know about this problem until you try to install Linux from the CD-ROM and are told that the CD-ROM drive does not exist. In this case, there are two ways to go: Search for a Linux bootkernel that supports your CD-ROM or use DOS to copy the installation files to a hard drive partition. The first option was discussed earlier in this chapter; the second option will be discussed later in this chapter.

The **setup** program then gives you a set of choices about the CD-ROM you're installing from. The choices are straightforward; if you're using a Sony or SoundBlaster CD-ROM interface, you certainly would have known about it before now (you would have needed the proper bootdisk to get to this point), so there are no surprises on this menu.

Should You Keep Some Stuff on the CD-ROM?

For those of you with smaller hard drives, Slackware gives you the option of doing a partial install, leaving some of the program files on the CD-ROM and running it from there. The advantage, of course, is that you keep hard disk space free that normally would be devoted to Linux. The disadvantages come in the form of speed—accessing your CD-ROM drive is slower than accessing your hard drive—and in tying up your CD-ROM drive with Slackware. Our recommendation, of course, is to install everything to your hard drive; this offers the best performance overall, and it's the easiest system to maintain.

However, Slackware does offer an alternative that uses the CD-ROM, as **slaktest** links **/usr** to **/cdrom/live/usr** and runs everything from the CD-ROM. This yields a Linux hard disk installation of 10 megabytes or so. The disadvantage, of course, is that you'll need to completely reinstall Linux if you decide to upgrade your system.

If it sounds like we're a little negative about the idea of running Linux off of the CD-ROM, it's because we are. If you're careful about installation, you can easily install only the parts of Linux you're really going to use. And by running partially from the CD-ROM, you're sacrificing both speed and flexibility.

If you're doing a normal install, choose the **slakware** selection.

Choosing the Disk Sets to Install

Now comes the fun part: choosing the software you want to install.

True to its roots as a diskette-based operating system, Linux divides software into *disk sets*. Each disk set is uniquely named and corresponds to a specific part of the operating system. For example, the *A* series contains the core of Linux, and its installation is mandatory.

The **setup** program divides disk sets and the software within into mandatory and optional installations. Some of the elements of Linux, such as the aforementioned *A* series, is mandatory. Other installations, such as terminal packages, are optional. During the installation process, Linux will automatically install the mandatory packages and will prompt you before installing the optional packages.

There is a way to override this, as will be explained later in this section.

During the initial menu entitled *Series Selection*, you'll be presented with a list of the disk sets and a short explanation of what is contained on them. Generally speaking, you won't want to install *all* the disk sets, as there are some disk sets that overlap and their coexistence on the hard drive is not wise (particularly when it comes to development tools). In addition, you don't want to waste the hard disk space needed for a full installation—will you really need three or four text editors, multiple text-formatting packages, and a slew of fonts you will never use? Choose the software you think you're likely to use. You can always run the **setup** program again and install additional disk sets in the future.

Technically speaking, all that's needed for a minimal installation of Linux is the *A* disk set.

The full set of disk sets is listed in Table 2.6.

Table 2.6 A Full List of the Linux Disk Sets

Series	Purpose
A	The base system; if you install only this disk set, you'll have enough to get up and running and have **elvis** and comm programs available.
AP	Various applications and add-ons, such as the online manual (**man**) pages, **groff**, **ispell**, **term** (and many TCP/IP programs ported to **term**), **joe**, **jed**, **jove**, **ghostscript**, **sc**, **bc**, **ftape** support, and the **quota** utilities.
D	Program development; GCC/G++/Objective C 2.7.2.1, **make** (GNU and BSD), **byacc** and GNU **bison**, **flex**, the 5.4.23 C libraries, **gdb**, kernel source for Linux 2.0.x. **SVGAlib**, **ncurses**, **clisp**, **f2c**, **p2c**, **m4**, **perl**, **rcs**, and **dll** tools.
E	GNU **emacs** 19.31.
F	A collection of FAQs and other documentation.
K	Source code for the Linux 2.0.x kernel.
N	Networking; TCP/IP, UUCP, **mailx**, **dip**, PPP, **deliver**, **elm**, **pine**, BSD **sendmail**, **cnews**, **nn**, **tin**, **trn**, and **inn**.
T	teTeX release 0.4 (teTex is Thomas Esser's Tex distribution for Linux.)
TCL	Tcl, Tk, TclX; A port of the major Tcl packages to Linux, including shared library support.
X	The base XFree86 3.2 system, with **libXpm**, **fvwm** 1.23b, and **xlock** added.
XAP	X applications: X11 **ghostscript**, **libgr13**, **seyon**, **workman**, **xfilemanager**, **xv** 3.01, GNU **chess** and **xboard**, **xfm** 1.3, **ghostview**, **gnuplot**, **xpaint**, **xfractint**, **fvwm-95-2**, and various X games.
XD	X11 server link kit, static libraries, and PEX support.
XV	Xview 3.2p1-X11R6; XView libraries, and the Open Look virtual and nonvirtual window managers for XFree86 3.2.
Y	Games; the BSD games collection, Tetris for terminals, and Sasteroids.

Mark the disk sets you want to install by pressing the **SpaceBar**.

You'll then be asked whether you want to use the default tagfiles or create your own. When a piece of software is installed, it's said to be *tagged*. By using the default tagfiles, you are installing software deemed to be mandatory, while the system prompts you before installing packages that aren't mandatory. Again, your best move is to go with the default unless you've had experience with custom tagfiles and know exactly what you want to install.

At this point there's an option to install everything. Don't do this, unless you've designated a small group of disk sets to be installed and know that you do indeed want to install everything.

Linux will begin the installation. It will tell you what's being installed, including mandatory packages. When it comes to a nonmandatory piece of software, it will stop and ask if you do indeed want to install the software. (It also differentiates between software, noting if the installation is recommended—which means you really should install it—or optional.) An added bonus during this process is that **setup** will tell you how much disk space the nonmandatory software will use (alas, there's no overall reckoning of how much space the entire installation will use). Use the cursor keys to move between the **Yes** and **No** choices, and use **Enter** to move on.

We're not going to list every piece of software that can be installed; you can make most of these decisions on your own. However, there are some things to note as the disk sets are installed:

- Linux will install a kernel best suited for your PC configuration; most of the precompiled kernels should meet the needs of most users. However, during the installation process, you'll be asked about installing various kernels that are not applicable to your PC configuration. In fact, one of the first disk sets includes support for a Linux kernel lacking SCSI support. Because the **setup** program doesn't know anything about your hardware, it will ask if you want to install this kernel. In most cases, you'll want to install the kernel from your bootdisk—**setup** gives you this option once all the packages are installed.

- During the installation process you'll be asked whether you want to install a package called **gpm**, which manages the mouse for Linux running in character mode. This package can cause conflicts with the X Window System and its mouse control, so if you planning on using X, you shouldn't install this software. (However, if you don't plan on using X, you should install **gpm**, because it allows you to better use the Midnight Commander, a useful text-based disk utility.)

- There are many text editors available in the Linux disk sets, including **emacs** and **vi** clones called **elvis** and **vim**. These should meet your needs; if you're tight on space, you can avoid the other text editors, such as **jove** and **joe**. (Not that we're saying anything bad about **jove** or **joe**, mind you.)

- You'll be asked about alternate shells, including **zsh**, **ash**, and **tcsh**. The default Linux shell is **bash** (Bourne Again shell), and most users—especially beginners—will find that it works well. However, you may find that one of the alternate shells better fits your needs or works more like a shell you've used in the past. Because the shells don't take up much disk space, go ahead and install them all.

- If you install the GNU C compiler, you also need to install **binutils**, **libc**, and the **linuxinc** package (this contains the include file from the Linux kernel source). Some of these packages are tagged *mandatory* by the Linux **setup** program; the warning applies if you use your own tagfiles.)

- The version of **emacs** that's initially installed from the CD-ROM was compiled with the assumption that it would be running under the X Window System. If you don't plan on using X, be sure to install the **emac_nox** package, which doesn't contain the X Window support and can be run in character mode. It's also smaller and will save some disk space.

- If you install the **x** series of disk sets, you'll be asked about the chipset used in your graphics card, as there are some X Window servers tailored to specific chipsets. If you're not sure which chipset you have, don't respond to any specific chipsets and install the SuperVGA or VGA X server; you can always change this when you install XFree86 (as described in Chapter 3).

- Some of the older applications require some older libraries to run, and at some point you'll be asked about including those libraries. You should install them.

- Generally speaking, you should install as many fonts as possible.

Being a Good Linux Citizen

As you install the disk sets, you'll occasionally see a message pointing out that Linux is installing unregistered software. This means that the UNIX freeware is being included as a service, and it's up to you to pay a registration fee. (The best example of this is **xv**, an outstanding graphics program from John Bradley.) As a good Linux citizen, you'll want to check through the online-manual pages or **README** documents associated with these programs and register the software.

Dealing with Errors

Although it is a very infrequent occurrence, you may experience an error message or two when installing Linux from the disk sets. One of the errors may be *Device Full*, which means that you've filled your hard drive. Slackware, however, will continue to attempt to install software, even if the disk is full.

To end the installation program, either hit the **Esc** key a few times or type **Ctrl-C**.

Configuring the Installed Software

There are two main tasks involved after the Linux disk sets are installed: configuring XFree86 and setting up boot options.

Installing a Kernel

The first Linux configuration task is to install a Linux kernel on your hard drive. It's possible that you've already installed a kernel from the *A* series (there are two kernels on the *A* series, an IDE and a SCSI generic kernel), but in most cases it is preferable to replace this kernel with the one you've used to install. That way, there won't be any surprises when you reboot; you've installed a kernel that you know works on your machine.

To do this, select the **bootdisk** option on the Kernel Installation menu. You'll be asked to reinsert your installation bootdisk, and the kernel will be copied from it onto your hard drive. Other options on this menu include installing a kernel from a DOS floppy or from the Slackware CD-ROM drive. If you know exactly which kernel you need, you can try one of these options. You should be aware that installing the wrong kernel here can leave Linux unbootable, requiring you to use your bootdisk or **Loadlin** to start the system.

When you install a kernel from this menu, all it does is put the kernel file onto your root Linux partition as **/vmlinuz**. Until you make a system bootdisk from it or install LILO, your system is not ready to boot. So, you'll want to make a system bootdisk from the next menu.

Creating a Boot Floppy

Linux will boot from either a floppy drive or a hard drive. However, it's recommended that you set up the means to boot either way; that way, if you have hardware problems, you can always boot the system from a floppy drive. Hence, the request from the **setup** program to create a boot floppy. This floppy can be used to boot Linux at any point. This will be handy should you experience some hard disk problems or screw up your hard disk so severely that the system won't load.

If you don't create a boot floppy at this time, you can always do so later. The topic is covered in some depth in Chapter 6.

Configuring the Modem

If you're planning on using a modem for connecting to online systems or to a TCP/IP network via SLIP or PPP, you need to configure the modem. Essentially, this involves just telling Linux exactly what serial port the modem is connected to. The first serial port on a PC is called *com1*, and under Linux parlance this becomes *cua0*; the second serial port on a PC is called *com2*, and under Linux parlance this becomes *cua1*; and so on. (Note the numbering difference; UNIX likes to start things at *0*, and PCs prefer to start things at *1*.)

After you set up the mouse, you'll be asked to set the speed for the modem. The choices (*38400, 19200,* et al.) are pretty clear.

If you're using a modem and the speed isn't represented on the menu, use the next-fastest speed. For example, to properly configure a 28800-bps modem, you'd choose **38400**.

Configuring the Mouse

You'll want to use a mouse if you're using the X Window System, and this menu allows you to set up the proper mouse. For newer PCs, setting up a mouse isn't a hassle at all because they usually contain a serial port for that purpose. All you need to do is tell Linux what kind of mouse you're using and its location (if you're using a serial mouse, you'll need to specify where the mouse is connected), and then move on from there.

Configuring LILO

LILO is the Linux Loader, and it's used to boot Linux from the hard disk. It can also be used to boot additional operating systems (like OS/2 and MS-DOS) from the hard disk.

NOTE   LILO is a tool best left to Linux veterans. If you've used LILO before, go ahead and follow these directions to install it. However, if you're a Linux newbie and don't feel up to the task of a challenging configuration, it's best for you to skip LILO.

LILO works with a configuration file that's generated automatically through this Setup program. Your first move will be to start the process, then mark any operating systems you want to appear in this configuration file. Because you want Linux to be able to boot, you'll want to begin by specifying Linux. After that, you can designate another operating system (MS-DOS or OS/2) as a possible boot option. You'll want to specify Linux first, however, so it appears first in the configuration file. When you're finished running through these queries, you'll end up with a file that looks like this:

```
# LILO configuration file
# generated by 'liloconfig'
#
# Start LILO global section
boot = /dev/hda
#compact        # faster, but won't work on all systems.
delay = 50
vga = normal    # force sane state
ramdisk = 0     # paranoia setting
```

```
# End LILO global section
# Linux bootable partition config begins
image = /vmlinuz
  root = /dev/hda2
  label = Linux
  read-only # Non-UMSDOS filesystems should be mounted read-only
for checking
# Linux bootable partition config ends
# DOS bootable partition config begins
other = /dev/hda1
  label = DOS
  table = /dev/hda
# DOS bootable partition config ends
```

This file is stored as **/etc/lilo.conf**.

You'll also be asked about how long to wait before loading Linux. LILO is pretty handy, in that it lets you specify a period of time (5 seconds or 30 seconds) between when LILO loads and when the first operating system is loaded. (In the **/etc/lilo.conf** file, this appears as the numeral *50* if you chose 5 seconds, and *300* if you chose 30 seconds.) This gives you time to specify another operating system to boot, should you want to boot DOS or OS/2 instead of Linux. This is done by pressing the left **Shift** key after LILO loads; you will see the following prompt:

```
boot:
```

If you specify DOS, DOS will boot from the DOS partition (provided, of course, that you've marked this partition as a boot partition). Pressing the **Tab** key gives you a list of options.

If you're using OS/2's Boot Manager, you may want to use that for the primary boot loader and use LILO to boot Linux.

Miscellaneous Installation Notes

At this time you can configure your Linux box for use on the network. However, because this is an advanced subject, we'll skip it for now and revisit it in Chapter 8.

There might be other configuration options presented to you, depending on what you installed (for example, if you installed **sendmail**, there will be a query regarding its installation). Again, these tend to be advanced topics, so we'll revisit them throughout the course of this book.

Now that the installation is finished, it's time to actually run Linux. Before we get to that point, however, we'll discuss some alternate installation methods.

Other Installation Methods

You may run into situations where you are able to access a CD-ROM drive from DOS but not from Linux's installation process. (This will happen if a SCSI card is not supported by Linux but there are drivers available for DOS or OS/2.) If this occurs, you can still use the accompanying CD-ROM for installation, but you'll need to copy the files to your hard drive, floppy disks, or a tape drive. All three types of installation are explained here.

Installing from Hard Drive

This installation method involves moving installation files from the CD-ROM to a DOS hard disk partition and installing from there. This must be a straight DOS partition, not altered via a disk-doubling technology such as the disk doubler in MS-DOS 6.x or Stacker.

You'll need to replicate the file structure from the CD-ROM on the DOS partition, keeping intact the many subdirectories (**A1**, **A2**, and so on).

When you run the **setup** program and specify the source of the installation files, you'll choose a hard disk partition instead of a CD-ROM.

Installing from 3.25-Inch Floppy Disks

The disk sets contained on the CD-ROM can be copied directly to DOS-formatted diskettes. (You'll end up with a slew of diskettes, of course.) For each disk, make an MS-DOS format disk and copy the proper files to it. Then, when you run the **setup** program, you can specify that you're installing from diskettes and not from another source.

The **00index.txt** files are added by the FTP server; you don't need those.

Installing from 5.25-Inch Floppy Disks

Linux prefers to be installed from a 3.5-inch disk drive. However, it is possible to install on a machine that has only a 5.25-inch drive. This isn't as easy as installing from a 3.5-inch drive, but if you install off of your hard drive it may actually be easier.

The first three disks of Slackware Linux, the *A* disks, should all fit within a 1.2MB diskette. To install them, you'll need a boot kernel and a rootdisk. To make the boot-kernel disk, copy the boot kernel of your choice to a floppy using the UNIX command **dd** or **RAWRITE.EXE**. To make the rootdisk, write **color.gz**, **text.gz**, **umsdos.gz**, or **tape.gz** to a floppy in the same way. (These are in **/ROOTDSKS**.)

Use the boot-kernel disk to boot the rootdisk, and then install from there. This will load the ramdisk. Once you have the *slackware:* prompt you can remove the disk from your machine and continue with the installation.

Once you've got the base system installed, you can install the rest of the disks by downloading them on to your hard drive and installing them from there. Disk series other than *A* won't fit onto 1.2MB disks.

Installing from Tape

The **TAPE.GZ** rootdisk file can be used to install Slackware96 from tape. This has been tested on a Colorado Jumbo 250, but it should work for most floppy tape and SCSI tape drives. To do this, you'll need to know a little about UNIX and its filesystem.

Any of the boot-kernel disks will work for floppy tape support. If you're installing from a SCSI drive, make sure you use a boot kernel with SCSI support.

You need to have a blank MS-DOS formatted disk ready to store the install scripts and installation defaults. The installation uses two tape passes—one to read these files from the tape and the second to do the actual installation. Once you've written the files from the first tape pass to your floppy, you won't need to scan those files again if you install from the same tape in the future.

The tape must be written in GNU **tar** format (or in a compatible block size with some other **tar**). This is the command that would write out the tape, assuming you're sitting in a directory set up like **/pub/linux/slackware** on **ftp.cdrom.com**:

```
tar cv {a?,ap?,d?,d1?,e?,f?,k?,n?,t?,tcl?,x?,x1?,xap?,xd?,xv?,y?}/*
```

This ensures that the files are written to the tape in the proper order.

You must set your TAPE variable first, like these lines in the **.profile** file under **bash**:

```
TAPE=/dev/nrft0
export TAPE
```

Unlike installing from floppy disks, you don't need to install all the ***.tgz** files, or even all the directories. The only requirement is that **base.tgz** be the first package (***tgz** file) written to the tape.

This method isn't fully guaranteed to work.

Installing When RAM is Very Tight

Installation can be tricky on a machine with 4 megabytes or less of RAM. Here are a few tricks that can be helpful if you run into problems. (Some of the symptoms of low memory might include system hangs while booting the bootdisk; root password required on the rootdisk; and an inability to run **fdisk** or **mkswap**.)

It's still possible to install Linux in this situation by avoiding the use of a ramdisk during installation. Normally the entire rootdisk image is loaded into memory before installation begins; this uses 1440K of RAM, a sizable chunk on a machine with only 4096K (and probably less available) in the first place. To save this memory for Linux, you'll need to prepare a decompressed rootdisk and use it to install.

First, you'll want to prepare a directory for the various files you'll need to decompress the rootdisk image and write it to a floppy. Under DOS, create a directory with the **MKDIR** command. The name of the directory doesn't matter; in the following examples we've arbitrarily chosen **SLACK** as the name of the directory:

```
C:> MKDIR SLACK
```

You'll then want to copy the appropriate files from the CD-ROM to the **SLACK** directory. We'll start with **GZIP.EXE** (needed to decompress the image file) and **RAWRITE.EXE** (needed to write the decompressed image to floppy disk). In the following example, we assume the CD-ROM drive is represented by the drive letter **E:**. If your drive uses a different letter, use that instead.

```
C:> COPY E:\INSTALL\GZIP.EXE C:\SLACK
C:> COPY E:\INSTALL\RAWRITE.EXE C:\SLACK
```

Next, select an appropriate rootdisk image from the **E:\ROOTDSKS** directory on the CD-ROM and copy it to the **C:\SLACK** directory. In this example we'll use the **COLOR.GZ** image:

```
C:> COPY E:\ROOTDSKS\COLOR.GZ C:\SLACK
```

Now we need to use **GZIP.EXE** to decompress the image. Execute these commands to change into the **SLACK** directory and decompress the rootdisk image:

```
C:> CD \SLACK
C:\SLACK> GZIP -D COLOR.GZ
```

Once **GZIP** has done its thing, the **COLOR.GZ** file will be replaced in the **C:\SLACK** directory by the uncompressed version, named **COLOR**. To write this to a diskette, insert a formatted 3.5-inch floppy disk in your **A:** drive and use the **RAWRITE** command to dump the image to disk:

```
C:\SLACK> RAWRITE COLOR A:
```

If your 3.5-inch drive is on **B:**, use this command instead:

```
C:\SLACK> RAWRITE COLOR B:
```

Now you're ready to boot the install disk. Assuming you've selected and created a bootdisk already (if not, see the previous section explaining this), put the bootdisk in your **A:** drive and reboot. When the disk starts, you'll see a welcome message and a screenful of information, as well as a

```
boot:
```

prompt at the bottom of the screen. You'll need to enter some information at this prompt to tell the kernel where to mount your rootdisk. If you have a 3.5-inch floppy drive on **B:**, great—you'll want to use that for the rootdisk. If not, you'll have to manages with the rootdisk in your boot drive. With the rootdisk in the boot drive you won't be able to install from floppy disks or make a bootdisk at the end of the installation process, because the disk will be "mounted" in the boot drive and cannot be removed (no matter what the screen tells you) until the machine is rebooted. Here's the command to enter at the *boot:* prompt to use an uncompressed rootdisk in your **A:** drive:

```
boot: mount root=/dev/fd0 ramdisk=0
```

If you have the rootdisk in your **B:** drive, insert the rootdisk in **B:**, and enter this command instead:

```
boot: mount root=/dev/fd1 ramdisk=0
```

The kernel will now boot. If you're using drive **A:** for your rootdisk, you'll be prompted to exchange the disks and hit **Enter**. Once you've done this, the rootdisk will start loading, eventually giving you a login prompt. From here, you can install Linux. A word of caution: If you're using this method to install with the rootdisk in drive **A:**, you cannot remove the rootdisk from your drive until the machine has been shut down. As a result, you'll be unable to install your bootdisk kernel or make a system bootdisk when configuring your system, and you will need to have a different method of initially starting your machine. A simple way to boot your machine is to use the installation bootdisk with a slightly different command at the *boot:* prompt. If, for example, you installed Linux on **/dev/hda2**, you can start Linux with this command on the bootdisk's *boot:* prompt:

```
boot: mount root=/dev/hda2 ramdisk=0 ro
```

This will boot Linux on **/dev/hda2**, with no ramdisk, read-only. If you use UMSDOS, you'll want to boot your system in read-write mode, like this:

```
boot: mount root=/dev/hda2 ramdisk=0 rw
```

Once your machine is up and running, you can switch to a different kernel if you like, using one of the choices in the **\KERNELS** directory on the CD-ROM, or compile your own from the kernel source in **/usr/src/linux**. This will provide optimal performance, because it won't contain any unnecessary drivers.

Booting Linux from DOS Using Loadlin

Loadlin is a handy utility for Linux users that also run MS-DOS or Windows 95. Using **Loadlin**, you can start Linux from a DOS prompt or set up an icon in Windows 95 that allows you to switch to Linux. **Loadlin** is also probably the safest way to launch Linux from your hard drive, because it doesn't require messing with the partition table at all— you just boot DOS normally and then use the **LOADLIN.EXE** command to start Linux when you need it.

To use **Loadlin**, you'll need to install it on your DOS drive. To do this, you'll need to use an unzip program, such as **UNZIP.EXE** or **PKUNZIP. EXE**; most DOS users will already have copies of these. Assuming your Slackware CD is on drive **E:** and you want to put **Loadlin** on drive **C:**, unzip the file like this:

```
C:\> PKUNZIP -d E:\KERNELS\LODLIN16.ZIP
```

The *-d* flag tells the command to preserve the directory structure found in the zip archive. This will create a **C:\LOADLIN** directory on your machine containing a number of files.

The next step is to pick an appropriate kernel from a subdirectory under **\KERNELS** on the CD-ROM. The **\BOOTDSKS.144 \WHICH.ONE** document might be helpful in making your selection. The actual kernel file will be named **ZIMAGE** or **BZIMAGE**; this is what you'll want to copy into your **C:\LOADLIN** directory.

For this example, we'll use the kernel in the **E:\KERNELS\BARE.I** directory:

```
C:\> CD LOADLIN
C:\LOADLIN> COPY E:\KERNELS\BARE.I\ZIMAGE .
```

Now we have everything we need to start a Linux system. To do that, you need to know the following things:

- The device name of the Linux partition you intend to boot (such as **/dev/hda2**)
- The path and filename of the Linux kernel you plan to use (such as **C:\LOADLIN\ZIMAGE**)
- Whether the partition should be mounted read-only (as in the case of a native Linux partition, so it can do safe filesystem checking at boot time) or read-write (needed by UMSDOS, which does not check filesystems at boot)

This information is fed to the **LOADLIN.EXE** program, which in turn loads Linux into memory and boots it. Here's an example:

```
C:\LOADLIN> LOADLIN C:\LOADLIN\ZIMAGE ROOT=/dev/hda2 RO
```

This loads the Linux kernel and boots the **/dev/hda2** partition in read-only (RO) mode. If you're using UMSDOS, you'd replace the *RO* with *RW* to use read-write mode instead.

Some DOS drivers interfere with **Loadlin**, in particular the emm386 driver for expanded memory. If this happens, you'll have to remove the driver from your **CONFIG.SYS** file and try again. Also, **Loadlin** will not run directly under Windows 95, although you can still set up an icon for it that first switches your computer into DOS mode. (In other words, the process is to start a DOS session under Windows 95 and then launch **Loadlin**. We'll explain further in the next section.)

If all goes well, your machine should switch to Linux. If you'd like to automate the process further, edit the **LINUX.BAT** file in your **C:\LOADLIN** directory. Then copy **LINUX.BAT** into your **C:\DOS** directory, and you'll be able to switch to Linux from DOS by simply typing **LINUX** at a prompt.

Adding a Linux Icon to Windows 95

For users running Windows 95, it can be handy to set up a shortcut to start Linux from the Windows desktop. Once you've installed **Loadlin** and configured your **LINUX.BAT** file, it's a simple matter to add an icon that starts **LINUX.BAT**. Here's how it's done:

1. Click on the Windows Desktop with your right mouse button. Under New, select **Shortcut**.
2. Windows 95 will display a Create Shortcut dialog box, asking for the command line used to start the program. Type the location of your **LINUX.BAT** file into the box and hit **Enter**. For example:

   ```
   C:\LOADLIN\LINUX.BAT
   ```

3. Next, Windows will want a title for the program. The default of *Linux* should be just fine, but you can enter whatever you like.
4. Now you'll need to select an icon. Again, you can pick whatever you like. (We use the first-aid kit icon—Linux to the rescue!)

Now you'll see the new **Linux** icon appear on the desktop. It's not quite ready to go yet, however; as you recall, **Loadlin** will not run directly under Windows 95, so we need to adjust the properties to force the program to run in real MS-DOS mode:

1. Click on the **Linux** icon with your right mouse button, and select **Properties** from the menu.
2. Click the **Program** tab.
3. Click the **Advanced...** button.
4. Select the checkbox for **MS-DOS mode** and then hit the **OK** button.
5. Hit the main dialog box's **OK** button, and your **Linux** icon is ready to use.

Using Loadlin to Install Linux without Floppies

It's rare, but in some cases (especially with laptops, it seems) a machine's floppy controller doesn't work correctly with Linux, and the boot/rootdisks don't load correctly. If that happens on your machine, you'll be happy to know that **Loadlin** has a new feature that allows you to use it to load an installation rootdisk.

First, you'll need to install **Loadlin** as described before, unzipping the **lodlin16.zip** file on your **C:** drive:

```
C:\> PKUNZIP -d E:\KERNELS\LODLIN16.ZIP
```

Next, choose a kernel from under the CD-ROM's **\KERNELS** directory and install it in your **C:\LOADLIN** directory. In this example we'll use a kernel from the **E:\KERNELS\BARE.I** directory:

```
C:\> COPY E:\KERNELS\BARE.I\ZIMAGE C:\LOADLIN
```

Now you'll need to copy a rootdisk image such as **COLOR.GZ** into your **LOADLIN** directory:

```
C:\> COPY E:\ROOTDSKS\COLOR.GZ C:\LOADLIN
```

Now you're all set to use **Loadlin** to start the installation process. Change into the **LOADLIN** directory and use **Loadlin** to load the Linux kernel and your rootdisk image:

```
C:\> CD LOADLIN
C:\LOADLIN> LOADLIN ZIMAGE ROOT=/dev/ram RW INITRD=COLOR.GZ
```

This will boot Linux and give you a login prompt. From here you can login and proceed to install Linux as usual.

Recompiling a Kernel

Most Linux users will find that the precompiled kernels that come on the accompanying CD-ROMs should work for them; PC hardware is becoming reasonably standard, and if you paid any attention at all to

Chapter 1, you'll have a hardware configuration that optimizes Linux installation and usage.

However, on the remote chance you need to recompile your kernel (whether directed to in a Linux HOW-TO or through the advice from an expert on the Usenet; this will happen if you're using an unsupported SCSI CD-ROM, bus mouse, or sound card), here's how to do so:

0. If you haven't installed the C compiler and kernel source, do that.

1. Use the boot-kernel disk you installed with to start your machine. At the *LILO:* prompt, enter:

```
LILO: mount root=/dev/hda1
```

   assuming that **/dev/hda1** is your Linux partition. (This is the assumption made through the rest of this section.) If not, enter your Linux partition instead. After this, ignore any error messages as the system starts up.

2. Log in as **root**, and recompile the kernel with these steps:

```
cd /usr/src/linux
make config
```

At this point you'll choose your drivers. Repeat step 3 until you are satisfied with your choices.

If you are using LILO, the following will build and install the new kernel:

```
make dep ; make clean ; make zlilo
rdev -R /vmlinuz 1
```

If you are using a bootdisk, the following commands will build the kernel and create a new bootdisk for your machine:

```
make dep ; make clean ; make zImage
rdev -R zImage 1
rdev -v zImage -1
rdev zImage /dev/hda1
fdformat /dev/fd0u1440
```

```
cat zImage > /dev/fd0
```

You'll need to place a clean floppy disk into your drive before the **fdformat** command.

You should now have a Linux kernel that can make full use of all supported hardware installed in your machine. Reboot and try it out.

Upgrading from a Previous Version of Linux

If you're using an older version of Slackware and you want to upgrade to the version on the accompanying CD-ROMs, you can do so without going through the agony of a full installation.

The new versions of **pkgtool** (a package maintenance tool developed for the Slackware distribution) should provide a clean upgrade path from earlier versions of Slackware. Because **pkgtool** can now remove packages from your hard drive while running on a self-contained Linux filesystem loaded into a ramdisk, it can remove *any* files from your system, including ones, such as the shell, shared libraries, init, and other crucial system files, that were difficult or impossible to remove while running on the hard drive.

NOTE

Upgrading through this method is probably more trouble than it's worth. For example, several commonly reported bugs are caused by improper upgrading—mixing disks from different versions of the distribution and/or failing to remove old packages first. We need to face the fact that things haven't quite settled down yet, and until they do it's not always possible to foresee differences in filesystem structure, daemons, utilities, and so on that can lead to problems with the system.

The *correct* and best way to upgrade to a new distribution version is to back up everything you want saved and then reinstall from scratch. This is especially true for the *A* and *N* series disks. If you do upgrade packages from one of those disksets, you should seriously consider which packages from the other one might be related somehow and install those too. Again, it can be tricky to know just which packages are related, given the overall complexity of the Linux system. That's why, unless you *really* know what you're doing, there is a substantial risk of screwing up a system while attempting to upgrade it.

Here's how you'd upgrade to a newer version of Slackware from any previous version that supports package information files in **/var/adm/packages**. (If your system puts these files elsewhere, you might still be able to do this by creating a symbolic link from the package information directory to **/var/adm/packages**.) The steps are as follows:

1. Back up important files, or take your chances. Odds are you'll come through OK. However, there are two important exceptions to this rule. The first (and most obvious) is when a package overwrites a file you meant to keep with a new one. The second, and possibly more serious, situation is when the system needs to replace an existing file with a symbolic link. It will replace the file, whether it's a simple file, a file with a file permission of 444, or a directory filled with other subdirectories, each containing part of your doctoral dissertation. So, be careful.

2. Make a list of the packages you plan to replace.

3. Use a boot-kernel disk to boot one of the root/install disks. Log in as **root**.

4. Mount your root Linux partitions under **/mnt** while logged into the install disk. The method used here differs, depending on what filesystem you're using for Linux. For example, to mount an *ext2fs* partition, use

   ```
   mount /dev/hda1 /mnt -t ext2
   ```

   Replace **/dev/hda1** with the name of your root partition.

   If you're using UMSDOS (the system that allows you to install onto an existing MS-DOS filesystem), use this command:

   ```
   mount /dev/hda1 /mnt -t umsdos
   ```

   If you've got other partitions that are part of your Linux filesystem, mount them after you've mounted that root partition. The method is the same; for example, here's how you'd mount an *ext2fs* /*usr* partition:

   ```
   mount /dev/hda2 /mnt/usr -t ext2
   ```

5. Once the partition has been mounted, you need to activate swap space if the system has less than 8 megabytes of RAM. (If you

have 8 or more megabytes of RAM, you may go on to step 6.)

You may use either a swap partition or a swapfile. To get a quick listing of your partition information, you can always type **fdisk -l**. Doing this on a typical machine provides the following information:

```
Disk /dev/hda: 15 heads, 17 sectors, 1001 cylinders
Units = cylinders of 255 * 512 bytes

   Device Boot  Begin  Start   End  Blocks  Id  System
 /dev/hda1          10     10    90  10327+   1  DOS 12-bit FAT
 /dev/hda2          91     91  1000  116025   5  Extended
 /dev/hda3    *      1      1     9    1139   a  OPUS
 /dev/hda5    *     91     91  1000  116016+  6  DOS 16-bit >=32M

Disk /dev/hdb: 16 heads, 31 sectors, 967 cylinders
Units = cylinders of 496 * 512 bytes

   Device Boot  Begin  Start   End  Blocks   Id  System
 /dev/hdb1    *      1      1   921  228392+   6  DOS 16-bit >=32M
 /dev/hdb2         922    922   966   11160   82  Linux swap
```

From this display, you can see that **/dev/hdb2** has been designated as the Linux swap partition. If the partition has not been previously prepared with **mkswap**, here's how that would be done:

```
mkswap /dev/hdb2 11160
```

To activate the swap partition, you would type:

```
swapon /dev/hdb2
```

6. Remove the packages. To do this, type **pkgtool** and select the option **Remove installed packages**. You'll be given a list of packages that you've installed—just select the packages that you plan to replace.

   If you're using one of the full-color versions of **pkgtool**, select the packages to remove by moving up and down through the list with **+** and **-** and selecting packages to remove with the **Spacebar**.

Once you've selected all the packages you want to remove, hit **Enter** to remove them.

If you're using one of the tty-based versions of **pkgtool**, you'll have to type in the names of the packages you wish to remove. Separate each name with a space. Don't worry about how long the line is—just keep typing in the names until you've entered them all, and then hit **Enter** to remove them.

That's it! Now you've cleaned up the old packages and you're ready to install the new ones. Type **setup** at a command line and install the new packages as normal.

Although it never hurts to play it safe and remove all packages from the bootdisk, almost all of them can be removed using **pkgtool** from your hard drive. The *A* series is the important exception here.

Booting the System

After Linux has been installed, go ahead and reboot. If you've installed LILO, you'll see it appear after the PC runs through its BIOS check. As Linux boots, you'll see a long Linux-related diagnostic, as Linux checks the system and makes sure everything is where it's supposed to be. For the most part, you can ignore any errors messages you see here (such as a proclamation that the name of the machine *darkstar* does not appear to be supported). After all the diagnostics, you'll finally be presented with a command prompt:

```
Welcome to Linux 2.0.29.
darkstar login:
```

If you installed networking capabilities when you installed Slackware96, you were asked the name of your machine. This name should appear in the place of *darkstar*.

Because there are no users on the system, you'll login as the root user, so go ahead and type in **root** as the login. There will be no prompting for a password.

The *root user* is the supreme being on a UNIX system. Most of the traditional security tools within the UNIX operating system don't apply to the root user—when logged in as **root**, you can do just about anything. It's generally not a good idea to use the UNIX system as the root user, however; the proscribed practice is to set up your own account and then save the root login only for those times when you're performing system administration.

After you're logged in, you'll see the following command prompt:

```
darkstar:~#
```

A *command prompt* is where you enter commands into the UNIX system. Your first commands will be to change your machine name and to set up a user account for yourself.

Adding Users

Your first action as the Linux supreme being is to set up an account for your daily usage. To do this, type the following at the command prompt:

```
darkstar:~# adduser
Login name for new user (8 characters or less) []: kevinr
```

The **adduser** command does exactly what it says: adds a new user to the system. In the previous example, the user *kevinr* has been added to the system. After specifying the username, you'll be asked additional information about the preferences of that user. Unless you're familiar with Linux, you'll want to stick with the defaults for now. (The defaults will be listed in brackets. Wherever there's a default, you can go ahead and hit the **Enter** key instead of typing in the default selection. In our example, we'll type in the defaults.) The entire sequence will look something like this:

```
User id for kevinr [defaults to next avaliable]:
Initial group for kevinr [users]: users
Additional groups for kevinr []:
kevinr's home directory [/home/kevinr]: /home/kevinr

kevinr's shell [/bin/bash]: /bin/bash
kevnir's account expiry date (MM/DD/YY) []:
OK, I'm about to make a new account. Here's what you entered so far.

New login name: kevinr
New UID: [Next available]
Initial group: users
Additional groups: [none]
Home directory: /home/kevinr
Shell: bin/bash
Expiry date: [no expiration]


This is it...if you want to bail out, hit Control-C.
Otherwise, press ENTER and go ahead and make the new account.

Making new account:

Changing the user information for kevinr
Enter the new value, or press return for the default


        Full Name []: Kevin Reichard
        Room Number []:
        Work Phone []:
        Home Phone []:
        Other []:


Changing password for kevinr
Enter the new password (minimum of 5, maximum of 8 characters)
Please use a combination of upper and lower case letters and numbers.
```

```
New password: <new password1>
Re-enter new password: <new password1>
Password changed.
Done...
```

If you're not planning on using Linux for anything but a single-user operating system, you don't need to worry about things like group ID and UID (which is short for *user ID*). And even if you do plan on using Linux on a network, you can change these parameters later.

Additionally, you probably noticed that the name *darkstar* appears as the name of your machine. You probably don't want to leave this as the name of your machine, so you should change it right off the bat. This name is contained in the file **/etc/HOSTNAME**, and the default is **darkstar.frop.org**. To change it, you'll use a text editor (in the example, we'll use **vi**) and edit this file. To load the **vi** text editor and the **/etc/HOSTNAME** file, use the following command line:

```
darkstar:~# vi /etc/HOSTNAME
```

You'll see a screen like the one in Figure 2.4.

Figure 2.4 Editing the **/etc/HOSTNAME** file.

You may have to make further changes if you're on a TCP/IP network. For now, you can change the name to anything you'd like.

You'll want to edit this file, changing *darkstar.frop.org* to whatever you'd like. If you've never used the **vi** or **elvis** text editor, skip ahead to Chapter 4 for a short tutorial.

If your system is configured properly, you should have the following directories in your root directory:

bin/	dev/	home/	mnt/	sbin/	var/
boot/	dos/	lib/	proc/	tmp/	
cdrom/	etc/	lost+found/	root/	usr/	

If you've installed Slackware from the CD-ROM, and then the system refuses to see the drive when you reboot, you'll need to install a new kernel or add the support through loadable kernel modules.

Using Kernel Modules

The kernels used in Slackware are designed to support the hardware needed to get Linux installed. Once you've installed and rebooted your system, you may find that your kernel lacks support for some of your hardware, such as a CD-ROM drive or Ethernet card. In this case, there are a couple of ways you can add this support. The traditional way would be to compile a custom Linux kernel that includes drivers for all your hardware. This requires that you have the Linux source code and C compiler installed and that you know exactly which options need to be compiled into your kernel. In short, compiling a custom kernel can be a rather difficult task for Linux beginners.

Kernel modules to the rescue! If you've installed device drivers before on MS-DOS, you'll probably find this a familiar way of adding support—just think of the module configuration file **/etc/rc.d/rc. modules** as being the Linux counterpart of DOS's **CONFIG.SYS** file. To add support for new hardware, you need to edit the file and uncomment the lines that load the needed support. As an example, let's look at the section of the file used to load CD-ROM support, as shown in Figure 2.5.

```
# These modules add CD-ROM drive support. Most of these drivers will probe
# for the I/O address and IRQ of the drive automatically if the parameters
# to configure them are omitted. Typically the I/O address will be specified
# in hexadecimal, e.g.: cm206=0x300,11
#
#/sbin/modprobe aztcd aztcd=<I/O address>
#/sbin/modprobe cdu31a cdu31a_port=<I/O address> cdu31a_irq=<interrupt>
#/sbin/modprobe cm206 cm206=<I/O address>,<IRQ>
#/sbin/modprobe gscd gscd=<I/O address>
#/sbin/modprobe mcd mcd=<I/O address>,<IRQ>
#/sbin/modprobe mcdx mcdx=<I/O address>,<IRQ>
#/sbin/modprobe optcd optcd=<I/O address>
# Below, this last number is "1" for SoundBlaster Pro card, or "0" for a clone.
#/sbin/modprobe sbpcd sbpcd=<I/O address>,1
#/sbin/modprobe sonycd535 sonycd535=<I/O address>
#/sbin/modprobe sjcd sjcd=<I/O address>
```

Figure 2.5 A section of the **/etc/rc.d/rc.modules** file.

You'll notice that each of the lines starts with #. In most Linux configuration files, any line beginning with # is ignored, much like lines in DOS configuration files that begin with REM. To activate support for one of these devices, you'll need to remove the # from the beginning of the line and edit the line to include any extra information about your hardware needed by the kernel module. For example, if your machine needs support for a SoundBlaster CD-ROM drive on port 0x300, you'd need to edit the line for **sbpcd** support so that it looks like this:

```
/sbin/modprobe sbpcd sbpcd=0x300,1
```

Then, the next time you boot your machine, the **sbpcd** module will be loaded, and you'll be able to use your drive. Drivers for nearly every device supported by Linux can be added in a similar fashion.

If you use kernel modules and decide later to upgrade your kernel, you'll need to upgrade your kernel modules as well. When configuring the kernel, select **M** instead of **Y** to build selected drivers as kernel modules instead of building them into the kernel. Once you've compiled your kernel with:

```
make dep ; make clean ; make zImage
```

you can compile and install the kernel modules with the command:

```
make modules ; make modules_install
```

The modules will be installed in a directory named for the running kernel—if you're running Linux 2.0.0, you'll find them under **/lib/modules/2.0.0**.

Looking for Help

Most UNIX systems have an online-manual page system, and Linux is no exception. You can use the **man** command to summon information about specific commands:

```
darkstar:~# man man
```

Online-manual pages aren't organized by topic; they're organized by specific command.

There are other informational sources included with the Linux operating system. They'll be discussed in Chapter 5.

Shutting Linux Down

Like any good UNIX, Linux responds to the **shutdown** command. You'll need to provide it with a command-like parameter and an amount of time to wait before actually shutting the system down. This may seem odd if you're used to working alone on a PC, but the **shutdown** command is usually saved for serious shutdowns, as most UNIX installations support many users and rarely shutdown. In fact, you must be logged in as **root** in order to use the **shutdown** command. Use the following command line:

```
$ shutdown -r now
```

This shuts down the system immediately.

 Don't just turn off the power to turn off a Linux system. This can cause damage to important files.

An alternative method of shutting down Linux is the old tried-and-true PC **Ctrl-Alt-Del** sequence, which is used to reboot a system. When running Linux, this sequence performs the same functions as **shutdown -r now**. When the PC cycles to reboot, simply turn it off. Despite what others may claim, this is a perfectly acceptable way to shutdown a Linux system.

What to Do if Things Go Wrong

For the most part, installation of Linux from the accompanying CD-ROMs is a pretty straightforward proposition, and you shouldn't have many problems. However, there may be some cases when you run into problems when you reboot the Linux system after installation. These problems may include:

- You're told that the system is out of memory. You'll probably run into this problem if you're operating with 4 megabytes of RAM or less.
- Your system hangs when you first run Linux. In these situations, you'll want to watch the screen closely for error messages. Sometimes Linux will be seeking a device at a specific address (say, a CD-ROM drive) and instead find a network card. In these situations, Linux will hang. You'll need to tell Linux to look for the device at the address on your system, which requires that you send an option line to Linux upon bootup. This is a situation that's covered in the many documents included on the CD-ROMs.

Other Configuration Procedures

Now that you've got Linux basically installed and running, you can take the time to set up some system peripherals. These include printers, sound cards, and (for laptop users) PCMCIA devices.

Setting Up a Printer

When you installed Slackware, you were asked about the location of your printer. This information was translated into the UNIX equivalent; a printer on the first parallel port is assigned a device name of **/dev/lp0**. Similarly, if you're using a serial printer (which, thank goodness, are getting rarer and rarer), it will probably be assigned a device name of **/dev/ttyS1**.

This simple configuration means that you can immediately print ASCII characters, with the Linux system treating your printer like a simple line printer. Printing is actually a more involved process than you might think. We'll cover printing in Chapter 4, but you should be aware right now that printing in Linux involves the following steps:

- When your computer boots, the **lpd** daemon runs, looking at the **/etc/printcap** to see what printer you're using; the process continues to run throughout your Linux computing session.
- When you print a document with **lpr**, the **lpd** command actually handles the print job.
- To change anything in the printing process (like when you want to kill or suspend print jobs), the **lpc** and **lprm** commands are used to talk with the **lpd** daemon.

Obviously, you'll want to make sure that **/etc/printcap** contains correct information about your printer. When you look at it in a text editor like **elvis** or **emacs**, you'll see that all the lines are commented out with # characters. Most popular printers are listed in this file (such as HP LaserJets), and if you uncomment out the lines specific to your printer, you should be able to use it.

It's important to get this information correct, because Linux printers that aren't configured properly have a tendency to suffer from the "staircase effect," where lines are staggered at the beginning:

```
We hate the staircase effect.
        It makes our documents look really stupid.
             And it makes it hard for us to do our work properly.
                  In fact, we find that we don't print things out
     when our printer is misconfigured.
```

More information about printing in Linux can be found on the first CD-ROM, in the **PRINTING-HOWTO**.

Setting Up a Sound Card

As installed, Slackware includes no support for the sound component of sound boards. Yet many of you installed kernels that supported sound boards, like the **sbpcd** kernel used for systems with a CD-ROM attached to the sound board. What gives?

When you install one of these kernels, you're actually making sure that the *CD-ROM* attached to the sound board will work, not the sound board itself. To actually use one of these sound boards, you'll need to recompile a kernel that supports a sound board.

Why would you do this? Well, maybe you're a dedicated Internet surfer and you want to be able to use the RealAudio streaming-audio player on your machine (yes, there *is* a Linux version; check out *http://www.realaudio.com*). Or maybe you're a dedicated gamesperson and you want to experience the audio gore of DOOM. Or maybe you want to play musical CDs using some of the tools we discuss in Chapter 4.

To add sound support, you'll want to recompile a Linux kernel specific to your needs, a process we explained earlier in the section entitled "Recompiling a Kernel." In step 2 of that process, you'll be asked to specify components that you'll need. There will be a line in that process requiring a positive response from you:

```
Sound card support (CONFIG_SOUND) [M/n/y/?]
```

You'll answer **y** (for *yes*).

After that process is completed, another configuration script will be run, going through a list of sound cards and asking you to specify your sound card. The questions are very specific; you'll be asked about every sound board listed in Chapter 1, so be patient and wait for your sound board to be listed.

Be careful about sound cards that are advertised as being "compatible" with popular sound cards, such as the SoundBlaster from Creative Labs. *Compatibility* can mean two different things: One level of compatibility means that the hardware is exactly the same as a popular model, while the other means that a computer can be tricked, usually with special drivers, to think that it's using a clone instead of the popular model. In the second case, these special drivers run under DOS or Windows and will be worthless under Linux.

After saying **yes** to a specific sound card, you may be asked about your sound card and where it's actually found on the computer system, meaning the I/O address, IRQ, and DMA. (If you don't know this, you better start reading the documentation.) You may also be asked to supply a file used to initialize the card; this information will be incorporated into the kernel. These files should be found on installation diskettes that ship with your sound card.

After you recompile the kernel and reboot the machine, you'll want to make sure that the sound card installed properly. When the new kernel boots, there should be a line or two pertaining to the sound card; if these lines pass through, then the system at least recognized that the card was present. (This is also your first indication that there's a problem; bad configuration information will cause an error message.) You can also check the file **/dev/sndstat** to see if a sound card installed and the **/proc/devices** to see that the following device line is installed:

```
25 sound
```

More detailed information can be found in the **SOUND-HOWTO** on the first CD-ROM.

If you're using **Loadlin** and first booting DOS (where the sound card is already installed), you may find that your sound board works without any additional customization. Test the board before reinstalling a kernel.

Working with PCMCIA Devices

The Slackware installation prompts you for the installation of PCMCIA devices with Card Services. This will save you many steps that are best avoided, such as the recompilation of a kernel.

In fact, one of the nicest things about Card Services is that it's relatively painless (thanks to David Hinds for all his work on this) after you've installed a kernel. During the boot process, Card Services will avoid hardware conflicts and work with a wide range of PCMCIA devices automatically. The trick, of course, is to use a PCMCIA device that generally conforms to PCMCIA standards. In our experience, most new hardware conforms to these standards, but some older laptops were rather liberal as to their interpretation of PCMCIA support.

If your PCMCIA device doesn't work, you'll need to look through the excellent **PCMCIA-HOWTO** on the first CD-ROM for information about recompiling a new kernel and adding support.

Working with a UPS

Slackware supports uninterruptible power supplies, or *UPSes*. This support is rather easy to implement. First you get a UPS, hook it up to your PC, and then run a Linux daemon called **powerd** that monitors the power situation and shuts down the system if necessary. (It will also halt the shutdown if the power appears in time.)

For more information, check out the **man** page for the **powerd** command and the **UPS-HOWTO** on the first CD-ROM.

Adaptive Technologies and Linux

After the Americans with Disabilities Act (ADA) was passed, the corporate world was forced to use adaptive technologies to open the workplace to all qualified workers. Linux supports a number of ways to implement adaptive technologies. Some involve changing the settings on existing Linux tools, while others involve special software tools, like **xzoom**, used to magnify a portion of the screen, and **emacspeak**, used to read the contents of a document in **emacs** (both of which we've included on the second CD-ROM).

More information about adaptive technologies can be found in the **ADAPTIVE-HOWTO** document on the first CD-ROM.

Using Linux with Ham Radio

Amazingly enough, Linux is one of the few operating systems that will work smoothly with ham radio. (Think of ham radio as an airborne precursor to the Internet, if you're unfamiliar with the concept.) You'll want to check out the **AV25-HOWTO** (found on the first CD-ROM) for more information.

Making Linux Work with Your Language

Us English-speakers assume that the rest of the world speaks English (you probably do, to some extent at least, if you've gotten this far). However, if you're not a native English-speaker and want to adapt Linux for your own language, you may want to check out the many HOWTOs on the first CD-ROM.

Languages covered in specific HOWTOs include: Cyrillic (used in Russia), Danish, Finnish, German, Hebrew, Polish, and Portuguese.

Summary

This chapter covered Linux installation and configuration. Basically, the process is:

- Create boot and root floppies.
- Prepare your hard drive for installation with DOS utilities.
- Boot Linux from boot and root floppies.
- Prepare your hard drive for installation with Linux utilities.
- Install Linux from the CD-ROM.

None of these steps is exceptionally complicated; if you're attentive at all to detail, you'll have no problem following the steps detailed here.

The chapter ended with a few of the basic commands you'll need after installing Linux, such as **adduser** and **shutdown**.

The next chapter introduces XFree86, a version of the X Window System optimized for PCs and compatibles.

Installing and Configuring XFree86

This chapter covers:

The X Window System

Simply put, the X Window System, or just X, provides graphics on UNIX. (It's never called X Windows; to call it X Windows is a sign of ignorance.) Although X runs on many more operating systems than UNIX, such as Windows NT, Windows, MacOS, and DOS, X is by far the *de facto* graphics system on UNIX. As such, X tends to be confusing for anyone with experience in the personal computer world.

Because X tends to confuse, this chapter starts with an overview of both the X Window System and X on Linux. If you're experienced with X in general, jump ahead to the section covering X on Linux for a rundown of how X differs on Linux. After that, we tackle the toughest part of X: installing and configuring it for your hardware. We've all been lulled by the ubiquitous PC hardware and assume that because Microsoft Windows runs with just about every graphics card, so should Linux. Linux does to an extent, but you pay a price in added complexity.

The X Window System began life as an academic exercise at the Massachusetts Institute of Technology's Project Athena. The goal was to link a motley crew of disparate workstations from various vendors. Instead of providing the link at the operating-system level, the decision was made to create a C-based graphical windowing layer that could exist with any operating system. And so the X Window System was born.

Now under the supervision of the not-for-profit X Consortium Inc., the X Window System is made available to the computing public at large, which has engendered its widespread adoption in the UNIX world. Virtually every UNIX vendor supports X on some level. The popular interfaces CDE/Motif and OpenWindows, as well as the Common Desktop Environment (CDE), are based directly on X.

X on the Network

True to its UNIX roots, the X Window System runs graphics with multiple processes. The main process, simply called **X**, is the X server itself. The server deals with local requests (thus its usage on a single-user Linux workstation) and TCP/IP-based network requests. Because of this networking capability, it's possible to run an X application on one workstation and display the results of the application on another workstation. You could, for example, save your local computing resources for something important while running Doom on your boss's workstation and displaying the game on yours. You get to play the game; your boss's system provides the CPU horsepower.

The X server controls the monitor, keyboard, and mouse and allows graphics applications—called X *clients*—to create windows and draw into them. On the face of it, this seems so basic that it shouldn't require any explanation. But, as is true of most of UNIX, X takes a simple concept and makes it difficult. You benefit from the complexity of X, but it can make it tough to get going.

The X server process is the only process allowed to draw dots on the screen or track the mouse. X application programs then connect to the X server via an interprocess communication link, usually some form of TCP/IP network socket (see Chapter 8 for more on networking). Because X uses a network link, programs running on other machines connected by a network can display on your workstation.

Many programs can connect to the same X server at the same time, allowing you to run multiple applications on the same screen—again, a basic fact you've probably taken for granted. One of these X applications you run must be a window manager. (Technically, you don't *have* to run a window manager, but it makes things difficult if you don't.)

The Window Manager

Unlike the Macintosh and Windows environments, X makes the window manager a separate process. In fact, a window manager is merely an X application program, although it's a special application. By separating the windowing system from the window manager, you are free to run any window manager that suits your needs. The main purpose of a window manager is to control how you move and resize windows on your Linux display. The window manager also creates the titlebar at the top of your application windows.

The key concept if you're new to X is that the window manager—not the application—owns the window's titlebar. This is really odd if you come from the Windows or Macintosh worlds. To show this, we'll run the same X application, **xman** (which displays UNIX online manuals—a very useful program, indeed), under different window managers.

The **fvwm** window manager provides a vaguely Motif-like look for the window titlebars, as we show in Figure 3.1.

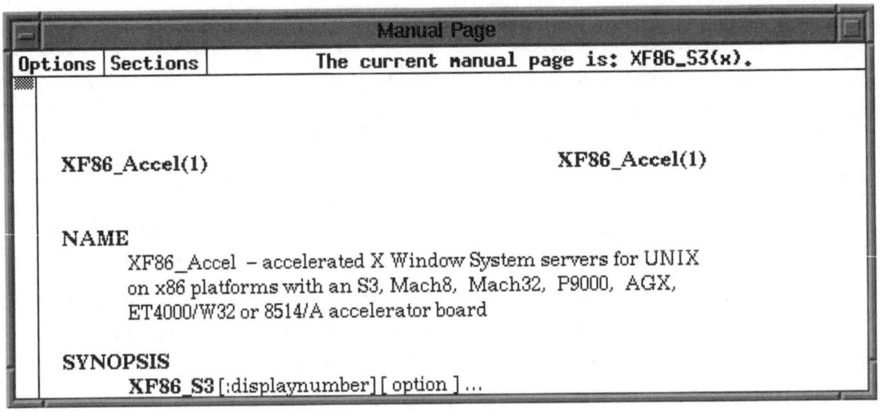

Figure 3.1 Xman running under the **fvwm** window manager.

If we switch to **olwm**, we see an Open Look visual display, as shown in Figure 3.2.

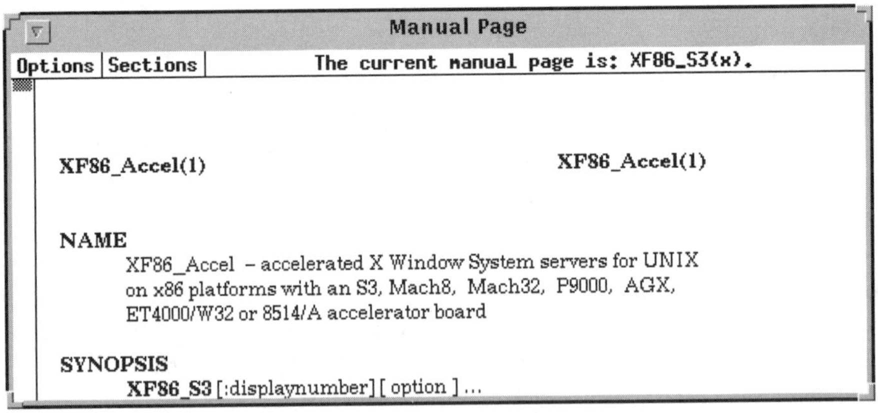

Figure 3.2 Xman running under the **olwm** window manager.

If we switch yet again, to **twm**, we see yet another look for the titlebar of the application, as shown in Figure 3.3.

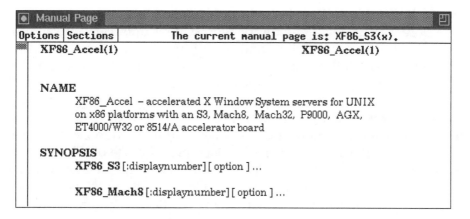

Figure 3.3 Xman running under the **twm** window manager.

With all three window managers, the **xman** program itself looks the same; it's only the window-manager-controlled titlebar that's different.

X also follows the policy of providing the means to do neat things—the *mechanism*—without making any decisions about what is good for the user—the *policy*. This mechanism without policy approach has led to a great deal of innovation in the X and UNIX worlds, but at a price of difficult-to-configure, poorly done interfaces across the board. Slackware Linux comes with a number of window managers, including those listed in Table 3.1, and we've taken the liberty of adding a few free window managers to the second CD-ROM. (Unless noted otherwise, all the window managers here are part of the core Slackware Linux distribution.) You're free to choose the window manager you desire and change at any time.

Table 3.1 Linux Window Managers

Window Manager	Description
bwm	Bowman Window Manager, used to provide a Nextstep-type interface, which we included on the second CD-ROM
fvwm	The most common window manager, presenting a Motif-like look
fvwm95	An add-on to **fvwm** that makes it look like Windows 95, which we included on the second CD-ROM
twm	The bared-boned Tab Window Manager
olwm	Open Look Window Manager, from Sun Microsystems
olvwm	A virtual-screen version of **olwm**

Most commercial UNIX systems run **mwm**, the Motif window manager, or a close variant. You'll find this on workstations from Hewlett-Packard, SCO, IBM, Silicon Graphics, and even Sun Microsystems (with the Common Desktop Environment). Because **mwm** (and the rest of Motif, including the programming libraries) is a commercial product, you won't see **mwm** on Linux unless you purchase it separately (see Appendix A for details). Because something so fundamental to most UNIX systems remains different on Linux, this may make getting used to Linux harder, especially if you work on other UNIX systems. Because of this common problem, we'll show you how to configure **fvwm**, the default window manager on Linux, to look and act more like the Motif window manager, to help make you feel at home on Linux. See the section on "Toward a Motif-Like Look and Feel" later in this chapter for the details.

X on Linux

X is very hardware-dependent. In the UNIX workstation world, you don't see many problems with this, because the UNIX vendors maintain tight control over the hardware and do the hard work of supporting X for that hardware.

The PC realm, though, is different. You have zillions of vendors and a huge number of combinations of various graphics cards, monitors, buses, even lowly mice. So, as we'll repeat again and again, you need to know the intimate details of your hardware in order to get the X Window System up and running. If you're used to the UNIX workstation world, this will come as a rude surprise. If you've already charted Chapters 1 and 2 of this book, it will less of a surprise.

X on Linux is actually in the form of XFree86, a public project devoted to bringing X Window to PC-based Unices. While there are some changes between a straight X Window System installation on a workstation and XFree86, you probably won't notice these differences.

How XFree86 Works

Remember that X is both the X server (also named **X**) and a number of X application programs (also called *clients*). To get X going, you must first start the X server and then start a number of X applications. Almost always, one of these X applications will be a window manager.

To start X, you must first login your Linux system, such as in the following:

```
Welcome to Linux 2.0.29
yonsen login:
Password:
```

Once you login and get the Linux shell prompt, you can start X with the **startx** script:

```
yonsen~#: startx
```

This assumes that XFree86 has been configured correctly for your Linux installation, a process we'll go over in a bit.

The **startx** script runs a program called **xinit**, which starts up the X server, **/usr/X11R6/bin/X** (you may be more familiar with **/usr/bin/X** on most other UNIX systems), and looks for a file named **.xinitrc** (note the leading dot) in your home directory. The **.xinitrc** file is a shell script that launches all the X applications you want. For example, our **.xinitrc** file launches a number of instances of the **xterm** program, which provides a shell window, and the rounded clock called **oclock**, as shown in Figure 3.4.

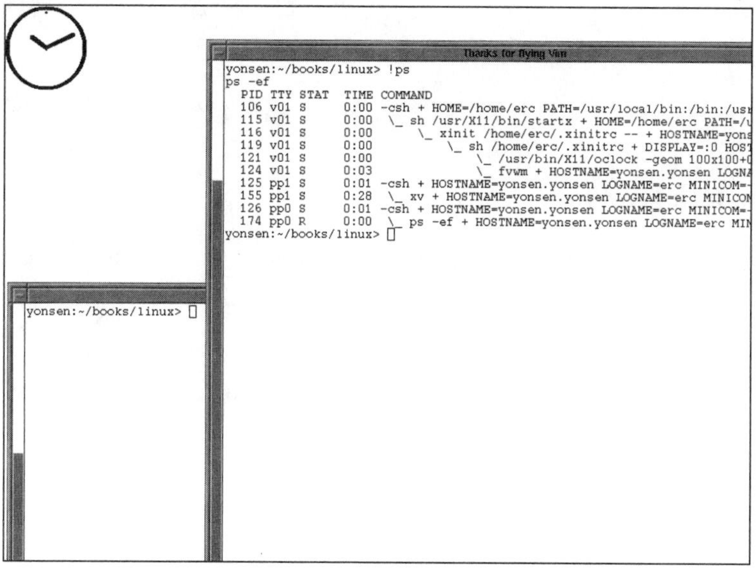

Figure 3.4 A typical X environment started from the **.xinitrc** file.

Before any of these programs is launched, though, the X server must be started, a task also handled by **xinit**.

The X server looks for the XFree86 configuration file—the most critical file for X on your system. This file, usually named **XF86Config** and stored in **/usr/X11R6/lib/X11** (symbolically linked to **/var/X11R6/lib**), is a specially formatted file that tells XFree86 about your system's hardware.

The hardest part about installing XFree86 on your system will be in fleshing out this file. There are tools that help, but the process is still dangerous and fraught with error.

The **XF86Config** file contains six sections, each of which describes some part of your system to the X server. We list these sections in Table 3.2.

Table 3.2 Sections in the **XF86Config** File

Section	Usage
Files	Tells where font and RGB files are located
ServerFlags	Special X server flags like DontZap, which turns off the **Ctrl-Alt-Backspace** sequence that aborts the X server
Keyboard	What kind of keyboard you have
Pointer	Information on your mouse
Monitor	Excruciating details about your monitor
Device	Graphics card
Screen	Combined card and monitor

Installing XFree86

To install and properly set up XFree86, a scary task under the best of conditions, you need to go through the following steps:

- Determine your system configuration.
- Set up the proper X server for your graphics card.
- Fill out the **XF86Config** file.
- Test that you can run X.
- Tune your **XF86Config** file.

We'll cover all these steps in the rest of this chapter.

Virtually all of XFree86—including the version with the Slackware Linux on the accompanying CD-ROMs—installs into the **/usr/X11R6** directory. Note that many other directories, such as **/usr/bin/X11** and **/usr/lib/X11**, will be symbolic links into locations in **/usr/X11R6**.

If you installed Linux and XFree86 from the accompanying CD-ROM, all the files are in the right place.

If you picked up an update to XFree86 from the Internet, then you'll likely need to unpack the collected files. Check the **README** file that was in the same directory as the XFree86 files you grabbed. Most likely, the files are compressed **tar** archives. For example, if you see a file like **X312bin.tar.gz**, you know that this file was compressed with GNU zip (**.gz**) from a tar file (**.tar**). To extract this file, use the following commands:

```
mv X312bin.tar.gz /usr/X11R6
cd /usr/X11R6
gunzip X312bin.tar.gz
tar xvof X312bin.tar
```

The first two commands move the **XFree86** file (and your current working directory) to the **/usr/X11R6** directory, where Linux expects X files to be located.

Especially if you acquired XFree86 over the Internet, you must untar any XFree86 archives as the root user. Otherwise, you'll find that XFree86 does not install properly.

If you load XFree86 from the Slackware CD-ROM and use Slackware's installation program, you shouldn't have any problems.

Setting Up XFree86

Because there's so much variety in PC graphics hardware and because doing something wrong can actually destroy your hardware (in theory, anyway; we're rather credulous of tales of exploding monitors and such), XFree86 ships in a mode that prevents you from running X. This fact strikes us as bizarre, but setting up X is probably the hardest thing you have to do to get Linux up and running.

Before you start setting up XFree86, track down every piece of documentation that came with your monitor and graphics card. You'll need to know some obscure values about your monitor, such as the horizontal and vertical frequency ranges.

If you can't find any of this information, you may want to pop open the machine and check the text written on your graphics card—there's often a lot of useful information there. Even if this fails and you can't find out anything about your graphics card, you still have a chance to run X. If your graphics card can support standard Super VGA, you should be able to use the example **XF86Config** file that comes with XFree86.

We list the graphics cards supported by XFree86 in Tables 3.3 and 3.4. Table 3.3 lists the accelerated chipsets and Table 3.4 the Super VGA chipsets.

Table 3.3 Accelerated Cards and Chipsets Supported by XFree86

Type	Chips and Cards
8514/A	8514/A and true clones
ATI	Mach8, Mach32, Mach64
Cirrus	CLGD5420, CLGD5422, CLGD5424, CLGD5426, CLGD5428, CLGD5429, CLGD5430, CLGD5434
IBM	XGA-2
IIT	AGX-014, AGX-015, AGX-016
Oak Tech.	OTI087
S3	86C911, 86C924, 86C801, 86C805, 86C805i, 86C928, 86C864, 86C964, 86C732, 86C764, 86C868, 86C968
Tseng	ET4000/W32, ET4000/W32i, ET4000/W32p
Weitek	P9000
Western Digital	WD90C31, WD90C33

The Cirrus, Oak, and Western Digital cards are supported in the Super VGA server, **XF86_SVGA**. The other types each have their own X server.

The Super VGA server, **XF86_SVGA**, supports a whole range of graphics cards and chipsets, which are listed in Table 3.4.

Table 3.4 Super VGA Chipsets Supported by the **XF86_SVGA** Server

Vendor	Chipsets
ARK Logic	ARK1000PV, ARK2000PV
ATI	18800, 18800-1, 28800-2, 28800-4, 28800-5, 28800-6, 68800-3, 68800-6, 68800AX, 68800LX, 88800CX, 88800
Advance Logic	ALG2101, ALG2228, ALG2301, ALG2302, ALG2308, ALG2401
Chips & Technology	65520, 65530, 65540, 65545
Cirrus Logic	CLGD5420, CLGD5422, CLGD5424, CLGD5426, CLGD5428, CLGD5429, CLGD5430, CLGD5434, CLGD6205, CLGD6215, CLGD6225, CLGD6235, CLGD6410, CLGD6412, CLGD6420, CLGD6440
Compaq	AVGA
Genoa	GVGA
MX	MX68000, MX680010
NCR	77C22, 77C22E, 77C22E+
Oak	OTI067, OTI077, OTI087
RealTek	RTG3106
Tseng	ET3000, ET4000AX, ET4000/W32
Western Digital/Paradise	PVGA1
Western Digital	WD90C00, WD90C10, WD90C11, WD90C24, WD90C24A, WD90C30, WD90C31, WD90C33
Trident	TVGA8800CS, TVGA8900B, TVGA8900C, TVGA8900CL, TVGA9000, TVGA9000i, TVGA9100B, TVGA9200CX, TVGA9320, TVGA9400CX, TVGA9420
Video 7/Headland Technologies	HT216-32

Each release of XFree86 supports more and more cards. If your card or chipset isn't listed here, don't give up hope. You may need to get a new release of XFree86, though. (When this book was written, the most recent release of XFree86 was 3.2, and that's the version on the accompanying CD-ROM.)

To see which chipset your graphics card uses, you'll need to look in the documentation that came with your graphics card.

You'll need about 50MB of disk space for XFree86, and you should have at least 16MB of RAM to run X effectively. You can launch X and perform some basic functions with 8MB of RAM, but you'll soon run into some performance problems with limited RAM. To compound matters, you won't be told that you're running low on RAM; your chosen X window manager will simply fail to respond to your commands.

Once you've determined your system configuration, the next step is to set up the proper X server for your graphics card. XFree86 ships with a number of X servers, each compiled with drivers for a certain type of graphics card or chipset. Each of these X server executables usually starts with **XF86_** and ends with the type of cards supported. For example, the **XF86_SVGA** X server is built with support for standard Super VGA chipsets. **XF86_S3** is the X server for S3-based graphics cards.

You'll need to know which chipset your graphics card has and then figure out which X server to use. We list the X servers in Table 3.5.

Table 3.5 XFree86 X Servers

Filename	For Chipsets
XF86_8514	8514/A and true clones
XF86_AGX	IIT AGX-014, AGX-015, AGX-016
XF86_Mach8	ATI Mach8
XF86_Mach32	ATI Mach32
XF86_Mach64	ATI Mach64
XF86_Mono	Monochrome VGA, also Hercules, Hyundai HGC1280, Sigma LaserView, Visa, and Apollo monochrome cards
XF86_P9000	Weitek P9000
XF86_S3	S3-based cards
XF86_S3V	S3 VIRGE-based cards
XF86_SVGA	Super VGA
XF86_VGA16	16-color VGA server
XF86_W32	Tseng ET4000/W32, ET4000/W32i, ET4000/W32p

The reason you have to know which X server to use is that the wrong server at best won't work and at worst may damage your system.

XFree86 is set up to run only one X server, the program named **X** and stored in **/usr/X11R6/bin**. Because of this, you need to link the X server you chose earlier to the file named **X**. The following command, when run as root user, links the S3 X server we use to the standard named **X**:

```
ln -sf /usr/X11R6/bin/XF86_S3 /usr/X11R6/bin/X
```

All the XFree86 files are stored in **/usr/X11R6**, but there are many links to other parts of the filesystem. For example, **/usr/bin/X1** is linked to **/usr/X11R6/bin**, where the X binaries really reside. The Slackware installation should have taken care of these links for you.

Now you have the proper X server set up to run when you start X. The next step is to tell XFree86 about your hardware in even more detail by filling out the infamous **XF86Config** file.

Setting Up the XF86Config File

The **XF86Config** file, located in **/usr/lib/X11** (really a link to **/usr/X11R6/lib/X11**), is read when the X server starts up; it describes your graphics hardware and other configuration options for XFree86.

When you've gotten to this step, there are two routes you can take. You can set up a generic **XF86Config** file for Super VGA graphics, or you can tune the **XF86Config** file for your particular card. We'll cover both routes in this chapter. We strongly advise you to configure the **XF86Config** file for your graphics card. Unfortunately, this has proven (in our experience) to be the most daunting task under Linux. Nothing else has been this difficult. So be warned—dangerous waters lie ahead.

The main reason this is a difficult task is that virtually all graphics-card vendors write device drivers for Microsoft Windows, but virtually none write drivers for Linux. Because of this, you're left with the task of setting up your system to run with the graphics card.

Hardware, Hardware, Hardware

We keep repeating the mantra that you need to know your system's hardware inside and out. If you know your hardware, you can get the most out of X. If you don't, you run the danger of destroying your system.

Yes, we'll repeat that: Making a mistake in your X configuration can result in damaged hardware.

Unless you're independently wealthy, this should cause you to pause for a moment. Take advantage of the time and go dig up all the documentation on your mouse, monitor, and graphics card. This can be hard. On a system that's a few years old, you may not be able to find everything. On a new system, your computer case may be full of no-name, off-brand hardware and the documentation may tell you nothing of value.

We've found that some newer systems just tell you the amount of video RAM and how to run DOS terminate-and-stay-resident (TSR) programs to configure the card, which is not very useful for a non-BIOS operating system like Linux. Let's face it: the vast majority of PC users run DOS and Microsoft Windows, not Linux. As one of the few pioneers, your task is harder. Try examining the original boxes the system came in. On at least one of our prepackaged systems, we found more technical information about the graphics card (especially the chipset) on the box than in all the printed manuals that came with the system.

Laptops and X

If your hardware includes a laptop computer, you may be able to run X on it. Many others have taken the time to configure X on a wide range of laptops. If you have a ThinkPad laptop, for example, there's a wealth of information specific to Linux on the World Wide Web at URL *http://peipa.essex.ac.uk/tp-linux/tp-linux.html*.

This Web page is available on the CD-ROMs in the **/docs** directory.

This Web page also contains a number of X configuration files for various ThinkPad models.

You are likely to have problems with the ThinkPad 700, 720, and any other MCA-architecture machines, as Linux does not yet support MCA. The Linux Laptop Home Page (http://www.cs.utexas.edu/users/kharker/linux-laptop/) has a lot of information about setting up X with laptops.

WARNING

If you have a model 760, you may have problems with the latest editions of XFree86. See the Linux Notebook Web page at URL *http://www.castle.net/X-notebook/index_linux.html*. Because versions of X change rapidly, this problem may already be fixed.

Some of the key bits of information you want to discover about your system are listed in Table 3.6.

Table 3.6 Information You Need to Know about Your System

Aspect	What You Need to Know
Card	Vendor and model, of course
Card	Chipset, such as S3
Card	Amount of video RAM, such as 1 or 2MB
Card	RAMDAC, if one is used, such as ATT20C490
Monitor	Bandwidth in megahertz (MHz), such as 25.2
Monitor	Horizontal Sync range, such as 31.5–64.3 kilohertz (kHz)
Monitor	Vertical refresh range, such as 55–120 Hertz (Hz)
Mouse	Serial or parallel? If serial, which serial port it's connected to
Mouse	Vendor and model, such as Logitech Firstmouse

Note that some of the more obscure details, such as the RAMDAC, may be described for you in the XFree86 documentation. XFree86 comes with a description of a number of graphics cards and monitors. If you're lucky, you can pull some of these values directly from the XFree86 documentation into your **XF86Config** file, the master file that describes your hardware to X.

Normally located in **/usr/X11R6/lib/X11**, the **XF86Config** file is an ASCII text file, formatted in a special way that the XFree86 X server understands. By default, XFree86 searches for this file in a number of directories, in the following order:

> **/etc/XF86Config**
>
> **<*Xroot*>/lib/X11/XF86Config.hostname**
>
> **<*Xroot*>/lib/X11/XF86Config**

The <*Xroot*> is shorthand for the top-level X directory. In Slackware Linux, this is **/usr/X11R6**. Previous to release 6 of X11 (hence the X11R6), XFree86's top directory was **/usr/X386**.

You can create the **XF86Config** file with a text editor such as **vi** or **emacs**. In most cases, though, you'll want to copy an example file to avoid entering the whole thing. Under Slackware, this example file is named **XF86Config.eg**. While this example is not ready to go, you can get a lot of useful information out of it. (See the section on Super VGA.)

In the **XF86Config** file, each section follows the same basic pattern:

```
Section "SectionName"
   data entry...

   ...

EndSection
```

The # acts as a comment character, which is very useful in documenting the odd syntax in the **XF86Config** file.

In the next sections of this chapter, we'll cover these six sections in depth and show how you can automate part of the process by using a program called **xf86config**.

Never use someone else's **XF86Config** file. And don't use the examples we provide verbatim. Always configure X for *your* hardware. Wrong data in the file may cause X to damage your hardware.

Automating the Configuration Process

For a number of years, various programs have attempted to automate the difficult creation of **XF86Config** files. So far, though, all have failed miserably for us—that is, until the most recent versions and a program called **xf86config**. For the first time, **xf86config** seems to create a workable **XF86Config** file, and we don't even have any odd hardware.

Before running **xf86config**, read over each of the following sections which describe the various parts of the **XF86Config** file that the **xf86config** program will be filling in. By having a greater understanding of the **XF86Config** file, your success rate with the **xf86config** program will be much greater.

Because of this, we'll discuss each of the six sections and then cover using **xf86config**.

Setting Up Paths in the Configuration File

The Files section is by far the easiest to set up in your **XF86Config** file. That's because just about everybody has the same paths. In the Files section, you need to tell X where the RGB (Red-Green-Blue) color database file is kept and where the fonts are located. Because both should go in standard locations, you can simply use the following section in your **XF86Config** file (in fact, the sample version already comes this way):

```
Section "Files"
    RgbPath     "/usr/X11R6/lib/X11/rgb"
    FontPath    "/usr/X11R6/lib/X11/fonts/misc/"
    FontPath    "/usr/X11R6/lib/X11/fonts/Type1/"
    FontPath    "/usr/X11R6/lib/X11/fonts/Speedo/"
    FontPath    "/usr/X11R6/lib/X11/fonts/75dpi/"
    FontPath    "/usr/X11R6/lib/X11/fonts/100dpi/"
EndSection
```

This Files section tells XFree86 that your RGB database is located in **/usr/X11R6/lib/X11/** and that the fonts are located in **/usr/X11R6/lib/X11/fonts/**. These are the standard locations for both. One tricky thing to note is that you may not have loaded all the font directories (we recommend you do, though). Because of this, you should check the **/usr/X11R6/lib/X11/fonts/** directory:

```
$ ls /usr/X11R6/lib/X11/fonts/
100dpi/  75dpi/  PEX/    Speedo/  Type1/  misc/
```

On our system, we have all the directories listed and a **PEX** directory for PEX fonts (you can ignore this for now; see Appendix B for more on PEX, the 3D extension to X). What you should do is delete any entries in the **XF86Config** file if you don't have the corresponding font directory. For example, if you did not load the 100-dots-per-inch fonts (the **100dpi**) directory, then your Files section should look like:

```
Section "Files"
    RgbPath     "/usr/X11R6/lib/X11/rgb"
    FontPath    "/usr/X11R6/lib/X11/fonts/misc/"
    FontPath    "/usr/X11R6/lib/X11/fonts/Type1/"
    FontPath    "/usr/X11R6/lib/X11/fonts/Speedo/"
    FontPath    "/usr/X11R6/lib/X11/fonts/75dpi/"
EndSection
```

We removed the entry for 100dpi fonts.

When running **xf86config**, you should say you do not intend to use the X font server, even if you'd like to. If the font server isn't running before you start X, then your system may lock up. We found it's much easier to split the problem. First, get X up and running. Then, configure the X font server (which provides scaled fonts). You may have to go back and edit the **XF86Config** file, but that's a lot easier than having your system lock up.

Configuring the ServerFlags Section

After the Files section comes the ServerFlags section. Again, you rarely have to do much with this. In fact, we normally have everything commented out in this section. The main options you can set here are listed in Table 3.7.

Table 3.7 Server Flags Options

Option	Meaning
NoTrapSignals	Core dumps X when a signal arrives; useful for debugging
DontZap	Disables **Ctrl-Alt-Backspace**
DontZoom	Disables switching between graphics modes

Most of these flags work backwards. If you uncomment the entry, it turns the feature off. By default, we comment out (leaving on) the two "don't" features. We also comment out (leaving off) the NoTrapSignals option.

We like being able to kill an errant X server by simply holding down **Ctrl-Alt-Backspace**, so we always comment out DontZap. If you turn on DontZap, you are disabling this feature.

DontZoom disables the keyboard sequences that allow you to switch between graphics modes. We find this switching to be essential in testing our **XF86Config** files, so we always leave this feature on by commenting it out in the **XF86Config** file.

Our ServerFlags section, with everything commented out, looks like:

```
Section "ServerFlags"
#     NoTrapSignals
#     DontZap
#     DontZoom
EndSection
```

Just like in UNIX shell scripts, the # character marks a comment line in the **XF86Config** file.

Configuring the Keyboard Section

The Keyboard section allows you to set up a number of options about your keyboard, which we list in Table 3.8.

Table 3.8 Options in the Keyboard Section

Option	Usage
Protocol	Standard (the default) or Xqueue
AutoRepeat delay rate	Sets up the keyboard auto-repeat delay and rate
ServerNumLock	Asks X server to handle **NumLock** internally
LeftAlt key	Overrides default for left **Alt** key (**Meta**)
RightAlt key	Overrides default for right **Alt** key (**Meta**)
ScrollLock key	Overrides default for **ScrollLock** key (**Compose**)
RightCtl key	Overrides default for right **Ctrl** key (**Control**)
XLeds	Allows programs to use LEDs, rather than keyboard
VTSysReq	Uses **Alt-SysRq-Fn** to switch to virtual terminals
VTInit command	Runs command passed to **/bin/sh -c**, when X server starts up and has opened its virtual terminal

You almost never want to run the Xqueue protocol, which uses a UNIX SVR3 or SVR4 event queue driver. With Linux, skip this option.

With X11 Release 6, X finally handles the **NumLock** key properly. You probably don't need to worry about the ServerNumLock protocol unless you have older applications that prove to be a problem.

For the key-mapping overrides, you can set each to one of the following values:

- Compose
- Control
- Meta
- ModeShift
- ModeLock
- ScrollLock

This is probably more than you want to know about your keyboard. See the online-manual page for **XF86Config** for more information on this.

Virtual Terminals

Linux supports virtual terminals. A *virtual terminal* is a pseudo-tty UNIX terminal connected to your screen. X uses up one virtual terminal, but you may often have many more.

Each virtual terminal takes over your entire display and presents a traditional UNIX textual terminal, much like what you see when you login. A special key sequence allows you to change between virtual terminals. When you do this, the screen gets cleared and you see the next virtual terminal.

The magic key sequence to change to a virtual terminal is **Alt-*Fn***, where *Fn* is one of your keyboard's function keys, such as **F1**. But watch out: In X, the magic key sequence to change to a virtual terminal is not **Alt-*Fn***, but rather is **Ctrl-Alt-*Fn***. The discrepancy occurs because most window managers capture all **Alt-*Fn*** keys.

Most laptops have a special **Fn** key that's used to provide a second set of functions to the keyboard function keys. The **Fn** key on a laptop keyboard should not be confused with the *Fn* notation used here.

A virtual terminal is not very worthwhile when you have a whole screen with multiple **xterm** terminal windows. The X environment allows you to use the font of your choice, provides a great many lines, supports a scrollbar, and copies and pastes—none of which the virtual terminals do. So, we only rarely use a virtual terminal.

But there's one place where a virtual terminal comes in handy: if your X display gets locked up, you can often switch to another virtual terminal and kill off all the X processes.

The VTSysReq option in Table 3.8 allows you to use **Alt-SysReq-*Fn*** instead of the default **Ctrl-Alt-*Fn***.

Putting this all together, our Keyboard section follows:

```
Section "Keyboard"
    Protocol    "Standard"
```

```
#    Protocol    "Xqueue"
     AutoRepeat  500 5
#    ServerNumLock
#    Xleds       1 2 3
     LeftAlt     Meta
     RightAlt    ModeShift
#    RightCtl    Compose
#    ScrollLock  ModeLock
EndSection
```

Note that we comment out most of it.

Configuring the Pointer Section

The mouse—called *pointer* in X terminology—is rather easy to set up, but you must watch out for some tricks. The main reason for this is that many vendors' mice (e.g., Logitech) are set up to emulate other vendors' mice, most notably Microsoft mice. Because of this, you may have to lie about your mouse.

For example, one of our test systems uses a serial Logitech Firstmouse. This mouse was designed by Logitech to emulate the Microsoft serial mouse. What's odd is that the Logitech mouse has three buttons (a very good thing for X, as most X programs expect three-button mice), while the Microsoft serial mouse sports only two buttons.

When we configure the **XF86Config** file, we claim our Logitech mouse is really a Microsoft mouse (the other common choice for Logitech mice is to claim that they are Mouseman mice).

The two key things you must specify for your Pointer section is what kind of mouse, e.g., Microsoft, and what port, if it's a serial mouse.

With this, our Pointer section is rather short:

```
Section "Pointer"
    Protocol     "Microsoft"
    Device       "/dev/ttyS0"
EndSection
```

Be sure to put in the type of mouse you have and the device it is connected to, rather than merely copying our configuration.

The protocol must be one of the options listed in Table 3.9.

Table 3.9 Pointer Protocols

Protocol
BusMouse
Logitech
Microsoft
MMSeries
Mouseman
MouseSystems
PS/2
MMHitTab
Xqueue
OSMouse

For Logitech mice, you'll most likely use BusMouse (if a bus mouse); for serial mice, you'll probably use the Microsoft or Mouseman protocols, rather than the more obvious Logitech protocol. If your mouse is connected to a PS/2 port, use the PS/2 protocol. (If you're using a newer system from a mass merchandiser like Dell, check the mouse port. Many newer systems feature PS/2 mouse ports, but they're not always called PS/2 ports; for example, Dell calls it a mouse port.)

The Xqueue protocol is only used if you set that up for the keyboard, too. We don't advise using this. The OSMouse is only for SCO UNIX, not for Linux.

In our case, the mouse is connected to serial port number one, often called *com1* in the DOS lexicon. In true UNIX tradition, however, Linux starts counting serial ports with 0. To specify our mouse is connected to com1, we use a device name of **/dev/ttyS0**, the Linux device file for this port. We list commonly used ports in Table 3.10.

Table 3.10 Commonly Used Serial Ports in Linux

Port	Device File Name in Linux
com1	/dev/ttyS0
com2	/dev/ttyS1
com3	/dev/ttyS2
com4	/dev/ttyS3

Your system may also have the **/dev/mouse** device file set up for the mouse port. No matter what device file you choose, the device must exist beforehand. (On our system, **/dev/mouse** is a link to **/dev/ttyS0**.)

The bus mouse device files are listed in Table 3.11.

Table 3.11 Bus mouse Device Names

Device	Usage
/dev/atibm	ATI bus mouse
/dev/logibm	Logitech bus mouse
/dev/inportbm	Microsoft bus mouse
/dev/psaux	PS/2 or Quickport mice

Note that except for the **/dev/psaux** PS/2 mice, all the bus mice should use a protocol of *busmouse*.

There are a few more options for the Pointer section, but you're normally better off leaving them alone. (We know; we were curious and we managed to mess things up.)

We list the other Pointer options in Table 3.12.

We generally don't set the baud rate. When we tried to, the mouse didn't work. If you do this, it is one time where the **Ctrl-Alt-Backspace** zapping sequence comes in handy.

For best results in X, you want to have a three-button mouse. Many X programs assume such a mouse.

Table 3.12 Other Pointer Section Options

Option	Usage
BaudRate rate	Specifies the baud rate for the serial mouse
Emulate3Buttons	Allows a two-button mouse to act like a three-button mouse; the third button is emulated by pressing both at once
ChordMiddle	Fixes a problem with some Logitech Mouseman mice
SampleRate rate	Fixes a problem with some Logitech mice
ClearDTR	May be required by dual-protocol mice in MouseSystems protocol mode
ClearRTS	May be required by dual-protocol mice in MouseSystems protocol mode

Configuring the Monitor Section

The Monitor section describes your monitor to X. You can define a number of monitors in the **XF86Config** file, as each Monitor section is named. The Screen section (discussed later) then connects a monitor to a video card. For example, the following abbreviated entry defines our NEC MultiSync XE17 monitor:

```
Section "Monitor"
Identifier  "NEC MultiSync XE17"
VendorName  "NEC"
ModelName   "MultiSync 4FGe"
HorizSync   31.5 - 64.3
VertRefresh 55-120
# Modes from the NEC MultiSync 4FGe monitor, a close monitor.
ModeLine "640x480"  31  640  680  704  832 480 489 492 520
ModeLine "800x600"  50  800  864  976 1040 600 637 643 666
ModeLine "1024x768" 81 1024 1068 1204 1324 768 776 782 807
EndSection
```

For each monitor, you need to define the items listed in Table 3.13.

Table 3.13 Monitor Data

Item	Usage
Identifier string	Used to identify the monitor later
VendorName string	Used for your reference
ModelName string	Used for your reference
Bandwidth bandwidth	The bandwidth for the monitor, in MHz
HorizSync range	Horizontal sync frequencies, in kHz
VertRefresh range	Vertical refresh range, in Hz
Gamma value	Gamma correction value for your monitor
Modeline values	A single resolution mode

The identifier is a string used to refer to the monitor later. You can define more than one monitor in the **XF86Config** file.

The HorizSync range describes the horizontal sync frequencies for your monitor. It can be a set of comma-separated values or a range separated by a dash, such as 42-65, for multisync monitors. You should get this value from your monitor documentation (where you'll find most of the key information needed here).

The format for a Modeline is:

```
Modeline "name" horizontal-values vertical values
```

For example, the following sets up a standard VGA mode:

```
# 640x400 @ 70 Hz, 31.5 kHz hsync
Modeline "640x400"  25.175 640   664   760   800    400   409   411   450
```

There can be a whole set of modeline values. You can get this from the **probeonly** mode of X or from documentation that comes with XFree86. Some of the relevant documentation is listed in Table 3.14.

Table 3.14 Video-Mode Documentation with XFree86

File	Usage
VideoModes.doc	Explains—in excruciating detail—how to calculate modes
modeDB.txt	Database of modelines for monitors
Monitors	Database of modelines for monitors

All these files are located in **/usr/X11R6/lib/X11/doc**. An example entry from the Monitors file follows:

```
#Date: Sat, 17 Sep 1994 00:50:57 -0400
#From: Erik Nygren <nygren@mit.edu>
Section "Monitor"
  Identifier "NEC MultiSync 4FGe"
  VendorName "NEC"
  ModelName "MultiSync 4FGe"
  BandWidth 80Mhz          #\
  HorizSync 27-62KHz        #> from monitor documentation
  VertRefresh 55-90Hz      #/
  ModeLine "640x480"   31   640   680   704   832 480 489 492 520
  ModeLine "800x600"   50   800   864   976 1040 600 637 643 666
  ModeLine "1024x768"  81 1024 1068 1204 1324 768 776 782 807
EndSection
```

One of the monitors we have, an NEC MultiSync XE17, was not in either the **modeDB.txt** or **Monitors** file. We found the closest monitor in the listing, an NEC MultiSync 4FGe, and experimented with those Modelines. Calculating the Modelines yourself is a real pain, so you want to find a monitor or a close facsimile in the **Monitors** or **modeDB.txt** files.

Having said that, be careful about using Modelines for other monitors. You can destroy your monitor if you're not careful.

Configuring the Graphics Card Section

The Device section describes your graphics card to X. For example, a standard Super VGA device appears as the following:

```
# Standard VGA Device:
Device
    Identifier   "Generic VGA"    VendorName   "Unknown"
    BoardName    "Unknown"
    Chipset      "generic"
#   VideoRam     256
#   Clocks       25.2 28.3
EndSection
```

A more detailed device section, for an Actix S3 accelerated card, follows:

```
# Device configured by xf86config:
Section "Device"
Identifier   "Actix GE32+ 2MB"
VendorName   "Actix"
BoardName    "GraphicsENGINE Ultra"
#VideoRam     1024
#Option "dac_8_bit"
Ramdac       "att20c490"
Clocks       25 28 40 72 50 77 36 45 90 120 80 32 110 65 75 95
EndSection
```

Of these options, the clocks are the hardest to fill in. One option is to try X in **probeonly** mode to fill in the details. You can also look in a file called **AccelCards** in **/usr/X11R6/lib/X11/doc** for more information on accelerated chipsets and cards. An entry from the **AccelCards** file follows:

```
Card Vendor            : Actix
Card Model             : GraphicsEngine32 Plus
Card Bus (ISA/EISA/VLB) : ISA
Chipset                : S3 86C801
```

```
Video Memory            : 2048k
Memory Type (DRAM/VRAM) : DRAM
Memory Speed            : 45ns
Clock Chip              : Avasem AV9194-11
Programmable? (Y/N)     : No
Number of clocks        : 16
Clocks                  : 25.175 28.322 40.0 0.0 50.0 77.0 36.0 44.9
Clocks (cont)           : 130.0 120.0 80.0 31.5 110.0 65.0 75.0 95.0
Option Flags            :
RAMDAC                  : AT&T 20C490-11
Submitter               : David E. Wexelblat <dwex@xfree86.org>
Last Edit Date          : Sept 25, 1993
```

You can convert the Clocks lines into the proper syntax for the **XF86Config** file by placing the same values in order in a line (or lines) starting with Clocks in the Device section:

```
Clocks 25.175 28.322 40.0 0.0 50.0 77.0 36.0 44.9
Clocks 130.0 120.0 80.0 31.5 110.0 65.0 75.0 95.0
```

Be sure to put all the clock values in the original order.

Combining the Graphics Card with the Monitor to Make a Working X Setup

The Screen section connects a monitor with a graphics card. Your **XF86Config** file may have multiple Devices and Monitors defined. It is the Screen section that connects the two.

A complicated Screen section can look something like:

```
Section "Screen"
   Driver      "accel"
   Device      "Actix GE32+ 2MB"
```

```
Monitor      "NEC MultiSync XE17"
Subsection "Display"
   Depth        8
   Modes        "1024x768" "800x600" "640x480"
   ViewPort     0 0
   Virtual      1024 768
EndSubsection
Subsection "Display"
   Depth        16
   Modes        "640x480" "800x600"
   ViewPort     0 0
   Virtual      800 600
EndSubsection
Subsection "Display"
   Depth        32
   Modes        "640x400"
   ViewPort     0 0
   Virtual      640 400
EndSubsection
EndSection
```

Note that the Screen section uses the monitor and device identifiers we entered earlier. This is essential to connect the screen to the proper monitor and card.

The Driver tells what kind of X server you're using; the choices are Accel, SVGA, VGA16, VGA2, or Mono. In almost all cases, you'll use *SVGA* for Super VGA cards (and the **XF86_SVGA** X server) or *Accel* for any accelerated chipset and X server, such as the **XF86_S3** server we mentioned in the last chapter.

Each Display subsection covers the modes available at a particular depth. (A depth of eight specifies eight planes for color, or 256 maximum colors.) The Modes used refer back to the Modelines for the monitor that we defined earlier.

Virtual Screens

The Virtual line allows you to define a virtual screen that is larger than the number of pixels supported by your monitor. The X server will automatically scroll the display when the mouse hits the end. If you like this effect (we don't), then set the Virtual resolution to something larger than your monitor allows, such as:

```
Virtual 1152 900
```

This virtual setting creates a traditional Sun Microsystems resolution. This is useful if you need to run older programs that were designed with Sun systems in mind and want to grab more than the default 1024-by-768 screen area available on most PCs.

The ViewPort line tells where the X server should start up. For example, a ViewPort of 0,0 tells X that when it starts up, it should display position 0,0 in the upper-left-hand corner (which is what you'd expect on X). If you'd rather start in the middle (an unlikely option), you can change this.

The **fvwm** window manager supports a different kind of virtual screen. Don't mix the two types of virtual screen or you'll likely have trouble.

Running the Xf86config Program

Now that we've gone over the contents of the **XF86Config** file, we can run the **xf86config** program, or, if you'd prefer, fill in the file by hand. We recommend using **xf86config** and then checking the **XF86Config** file it builds by hand. The **xf86config** program isn't flawless and needs careful supervision.

When you run **xf86config**, you should not be in the **/usr/X11R6/lib/X11** directory. Instead, put an **XF86Config** file in a directory in your user account and try copying it later to **/usr/X11R6/lib/X11**.

As the program starts up, it will start asking a lot of questions. The **xf86config** program will prompt you for a lot of the values necessary for the **XF86Config** file, such as type of mouse, your desires for the keyboard, and monitor frequencies. When you're done, **xf86config** will write out the data into a file named **XF86Config** in the current directory. (This is why you don't want to be in **/usr/lib/X11**, which is a symbolic link to **/usr/X11R6/lib/X11**, when you run this program.)

Once the **xf86config** program finishes, you should carefully examine the **XF86Config** file it generates. This file will still be incomplete, because you haven't probed for the clocks yet. Edit the **XF86Config** file. If it looks OK, then, as the root user, copy the file to **/usr/X11R6/lib/X11**, but be sure to back up any existing **XF86Config** file first.

Now you're ready to try **X** in **probeonly** mode.

Probing for Dot Clocks

The XFree86 X server has a special **probeonly** mode that outputs values from the **XF86Config** file and values it detects. You need to run X in this mode to see if things are going to work and to see if it detects any problems.

Run the command line:

```
X -probeonly
```

when your system has no extra load on it. Stop any unneeded programs before running this, as any extra system load may influence the timings X obtains.

The following command runs X in **probeonly** mode and sends the output to the file named **/tmp/x.values**:

```
X -probeonly > /tmp/x.values 2>&1
```

Be sure to run **X** from the console. Don't try to run **X** if you're already running **X**.

If you have some dot clocks in the **XF86Config** file, then **X -probeonly** won't try to detect new ones. Because of this, the first time you run X this way, you should comment out the clocks in your **XF86Config** file. After you run X in **probeonly** mode, you can add the clocks to the **XF86Config** file and try it again, seeing if things still seem to work.

You can then look at the file **/tmp/x.values**, which should contain something like the following:

```
XFree86 Version 3.1.1 / X Window System
(protocol Version 11, revision 0, vendor release 6000)
Operating System: Linux
Configured drivers:
  S3: accelerated server for S3 graphics adapters (Patchlevel 0)
      mmio_928, s3_generic
(using VT number 7)


XF86Config: /usr/X11R6/lib/X11/XF86Config
(**) stands for supplied, (-) stands for probed/default values
(**) Mouse: type: Microsoft, device: /dev/ttyS0, baudrate: 1200
(**) S3: Graphics device ID: "Actix GE32+ 2MB"
(**) S3: Monitor ID: "NEC MultiSync XE17"
(**) FontPath set to
"/usr/X11R6/lib/X11/fonts/misc/,/usr/X11R6/lib/X11/fonts/Type1/,/u
sr/X11R6/lib/X11/fonts/Speedo/,/usr/X11R6/lib/X11/fonts/75dpi/,/us
r/X11R6/lib/X11/fonts/100dpi/"
(-) S3: card type: ISA
(-) S3: chipset:   928, rev E or above
(-) S3: chipset driver: mmio_928
(**) S3: videoram:  1024k
(**) S3: Ramdac type: att20c490
(-) S3: Ramdac speed: 110
(-) S3: clocks: 25.24 28.32 39.99  0.00 50.13 77.02 37.35 44.89
(-) S3: clocks: 90.11 119.98 80.30 31.50 110.16 65.08 75.17 94.68
(-) S3: Maximum allowed dot-clock: 110.000 MHz
(**) S3: Mode "1024x768": mode clock =  81.000, clock used =  80.300
(**) S3: Mode "800x600": mode clock =  50.000, clock used =  50.130
(**) S3: Mode "640x480": mode clock =  31.000, clock used =  31.500
(-) S3: Using 6 bits per RGB value
(**) S3: Virtual resolution set to 1024x768
```

Note that many of these values come from our **XF86Config** file.

Now, add the clocks to the Device section of your **XF86Config** file. Note that each time we ran **X -probeonly**, it returned slightly different clock values. For example, in this run, we got the following clock values (formatted for the **XF86Config** file):

```
Clocks  25.24  28.32  39.99   0.00  50.13  77.02  37.35  44.89
Clocks  90.11 119.98  80.30  31.50 110.16  65.08  75.17  94.68
```

From the **AccelCards** file, we found these clocks—close, but not exact:

```
Clocks 25 28 40 72 50 77 36 45
Clocks 90 120 80 32 110 65 75 95
```

Testing Your Configuration

Now you're ready to start X and see if things work. Type in the following command and see if things start up:

```
startx
```

The **startx** shell script is the official way to start X from a user account.

Starting X

The **startx** script runs the **xinit** program, which does two things: runs the X server (the program named **X**) and then runs the commands in the **.xinitrc** file in your home directory. These commands should set up the X applications you want launched on startup. If there's no **.xinitrc** file in your home directory, then **xinit** runs a default script. The system default **.xinitrc** file is **/usr/lib/X11/xinit/xinitrc.fvwm** (no dot).

The best way to start out with X is—once you verify your **XF86Config** file—to copy the system **.xinitrc** into your home directory and then edit this file. Most of the **.xinitrc** file comes from the standard XFree86 installation for Linux; it looks for certain files, few of which will actually exist, and it executes programs using those files it finds. The section at the end is where you'll set up the X applications you want started when X starts.

In our case, we use **xsetroot** to change the screen's background color and then launch **oclock**, a rounded clock, the **fvwm** window manager, and two **xterms**. No matter what, you need a window manager program, to control the display. The default window manager on Linux is called **fvwm** (see Figure 3.1) and you'll find it highly customizable.

X quits when the last program in the **.xinitrc** (system or local) stops. Often, this last program is preceded by an **exec** statement. When you quit this last program, X stops and you're back at the console. In our case, we use **fvwm** as this last—key—process, because you need a window manager running during your entire X session, making **fvwm** a natural for this last process.

All our customizations to the **.xinitrc** file fit into a few simple lines:

```
# Start X applications
xsetroot -solid bisque3
/usr/bin/X11/oclock -geom 100x100+0+6    &
/usr/bin/X11/xterm -ls -geom 80x24+3+372 &
/usr/bin/X11/xterm -ls -geom 80x48+264+13 &
exec fvwm
```

The full **.xinitrc** file will look something like the following:

```
#!/bin/sh
userresources=$HOME/.Xresources
usermodmap=$HOME/.Xmodmap
sysresources=/usr/X11R6/lib/X11/xinit/.Xresources
sysmodmap=/usr/X11R6/lib/X11/xinit/.Xmodmap

# merge in defaults and keymaps

if [ -f $sysresources ]; then
    xrdb -merge $sysresources
fi

if [ -f $sysmodmap ]; then
    xmodmap $sysmodmap
fi

if [ -f $userresources ]; then
    xrdb -merge $userresources
fi

if [ -f $usermodmap ]; then
```

```
        xmodmap $usermodmap
fi

# start some nice programs
xsetroot -solid SteelBlue

# Changed lines are below.
xterm -geom 80x32+264+0 -ls &
xterm -geom 80x32+0+250 -ls &
oclock -geom -7-7 &
exec fvwm
```

If you don't set up a **.xinitrc** file and there is no system one, the default behavior is to create a single **xterm** window in the top-left corner of the screen. This **xterm** then becomes the key process, even if you later launch a window manager. When this **xterm** exits, X exits.

Chances are you can start with the above file and customize it to your needs later.

Stopping X

To stop X in the no **.xinitrc** file configuration, you need to find the **xterm** window that started out in the upper-left corner (you might have moved it) and exit it. You'll soon be out of X and back to the boring old terminal mode.

If you use a **.xinitrc** file, simply exit the window manager to exit X. Normally, you can exit the window manager from a menu called up by placing the mouse over an empty area of the screen and holding down the leftmost mouse button. If this doesn't work, try any and all mouse buttons.

Tuning Your Modes

It's likely that the default mode in the **XF86Config** file will specify a 640-by-480 resolution. Chances are your hardware supports much higher resolutions. While running X, you can press **Ctrl-Alt-Keypad-+** to switch to the next mode in the **XF86Config** file.

This is very useful, because the way X comes up may not look like a normal screen. If this is the case, try switching modes to see if things get better.

You can also change the **XF86Config** file to start up in the best mode. Look for the Screen section in your **XF86Config** file. You'll want to change the modes line from something like:

```
Modes "640x480" "800x600" "1024x768"
```

to

```
Modes "1024x768" "800x600" "640x480"
```

Note that we merely put the best mode first. This makes XFree86 start up in 1024-by-768-pixel-resolution mode, a much nicer display mode, especially for X. Before doing this, though, make sure that all graphics modes work by using **Ctrl-Alt-Keypad-+** while X is running. Ensure that each change results in a valid display.

VGA to the Rescue

If all the preceding methods have failed, you may want to fall back on VGA, just to get X up and running. This is presuming, of course, that you don't have a plain old Super VGA card, for which the Super VGA modes would be most appropriate. Instead, the theory is that if you can't get your super-duper card to run X in its super-duper accelerated mode, maybe you can get it running in plain old VGA. Most PC graphics boards support the VGA modes, so this method, while it won't take advantage of the power of your graphics card, may at least allow you to run X if you can't so far.

In the next section, we'll show how to get a generic VGA file built. This step is usually much quicker than getting the file properly built for your graphics hardware.

 Setting up XFree86 incorrectly can harm your system hardware, so watch out.

Using the Default Super VGA

In this section, we discuss using the sample Super VGA **XF86Config** file that comes with XFree86. You should always set up the **XF86Config** file for your exact hardware configuration. We only mention this technique because setting up X can prove to be nearly impossible. It is always best to set up X for your hardware. Remember, you were warned.

The first thing to do is find the example **XF86Config** file that comes with XFree86. This file, usually named **XF86Config.eg** and stored in **/usr/X11R6/lib/X11**, has the default mode for a 640-by-480-pixel Super VGA device. Most PC graphics boards support this mode, so you might be in luck.

Copy the **XF86Config.eg** file and edit it. You'll need to add the data about your mouse and monitor. In fact, the more you can fill in, the better. When you're done, you can copy this file to **XF86Config** and start up X. If you do use the Super VGA example file, you must use this X server. (Unless you have an Accel screen section set up, none of the accelerated X servers will work.)

Remember that running X this way may damage your hardware (don't say we didn't warn you). The only reason you want to run in a lower-resolution mode is if all else fails.

Again, it's best to configure X for *your* hardware. Only try the Super VGA mode if you have a card for which all else fails (unless, of course, your graphics card is a Super VGA card and the **XF86_SVGA** program is the appropriate X server).

If you're still having problems with X, you may want to look for extra help on the Internet.

Making the Most of X

By now, you should have X up and running. Even so, with only a window manager and a few shell windows (**xterms**), you haven't seen much at all about what X can do for you and how to configure X more to your liking.

Setting Up Your X Account

Depending on your preferences, there are different programs you may want to set up in your X environment. If you're new to UNIX, you may want to run a file manager program such as **xfm**, as shown in Figure 3.5.

If you're more familiar with UNIX, you'll probably want to run a number of shell windows with the program called **xterm**. **xterm** presents a UNIX shell in a window but allows you to specify the number of lines, the fonts, and the colors used. You can also copy and paste between **xterm** windows, a handy feat with long, complicated UNIX command lines. (See the section on **xterm** later for more on this handy application.)

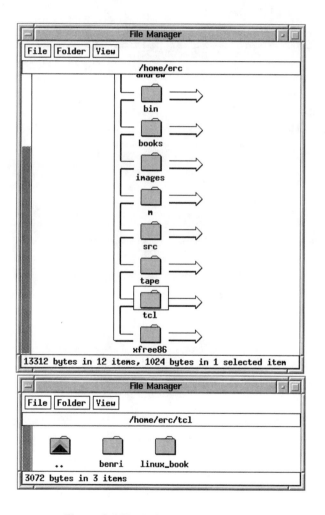

Figure 3.5 The X file manager in action.

Configuring the Xterm Program

The **xterm** program is probably the most popular X program. It seems kind of funny to run a shell window program, which is what **xterm** is, in a fancy graphical environment. But we're still running X on top of Linux and we still need access to the UNIX environment.

Figure 3.6 shows **xterm**.

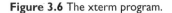

```
┌─────────────────────────────────────────────────────────────────────┐
│                      VIM - /usr/X11R6/INSTALL                         │
├─────────────────────────────────────────────────────────────────────┤
│Installation instructions for XFree86[TM] 3.1.1 Linux distribution [1/28/95]│
│-----------------------------------------------------------------------│
│                                                                       │
│                                                                       │
│Introduction                                                           │
│------------                                                           │
│            This is the Linux binary distribution of XFree86 release 3.1.1.│
│Please read this document carefully before installation, and the included│
│doc package for detailed configuration information.                    │
│                                                                       │
│Requirements                                                           │
│------------                                                           │
│            Linux 1.0, 1.1.X, or later                                 │
│            libc-4.5.26, or newer                                      │
│            libm-4.5.26, or newer                                      │
│            ld.so-1.4.3, or newer                                      │
│            shadow-3.3.2 (if using xdm-shdw)                           │
│                                                                       │
│            This distribution was tested using Linux 1.1.54 and should work│
│without problems on all versions 1.0, 1.1.X and later. Kernel networking│
│support is required, although each server will work without TCP support│
│(using the "partial network" option). In order to use the XShm extension,│
│kernel shared memory support is required. All serial and bus mice detected│
│by the 1.1.54 kernel are supported by the servers.                     │
│                                                                       │
│Contents                                                               │
│--------                                                               │
│            The distribution is composed of the following parts:       │
│                                                                       │
│            name          req/opt description                          │
│            X3118514.tgz   R[1]   Server for 8514-based boards.         │
│            X311AGX.tgz    R[1]   Server for AGX-based boards.          │
│            X311Ma32.tgz   R[1]   Server for Mach32-based boards.       │
│            X311Ma64.tgz   R[1]   Server for Mach64-based boards.       │
│            X311Ma8.tgz    R[1]   Server for Mach8-based boards.        │
│            X311Mono.tgz   R[1]   Server for monochrome video modes.    │
│            X311P9K.tgz    R[1]   Server for P9000-based boards.        │
│            X311S3.tgz     R[1]   Server for S3-based boards.           │
│            X311SVGA.tgz   R[1]   Server for Super VGA-based boards.     │
│            X311VGA.tgz    R[1]   Server for VGA/EGA-based boards.       │
│            X311W32.tgz    R[1]   Server for ET4000/W32-based boards.    │
│            X311bin.tgz    R      The rest of the X11R6 binaries.        │
│            X311cfg.tgz    R      Configuration files.                   │
└─────────────────────────────────────────────────────────────────────┘
```

Figure 3.6 The xterm program.

The neatest things about **xterm** are that you can:

- Run multiple shell windows (**xterms**) at once.
- Control the size of each **xterm** window.
- Control the fonts and colors used by the **xterm** program.
- Copy and paste between **xterm** windows and other X programs.
- Use a scrollbar to view program output that has scrolled by.

Even though it's called **xterm**, the program isn't really a terminal emulator; it provides you with a UNIX shell window.

Controlling the Size of the Xterm Window

The simplest way to control the size of an **xterm** window is through the *-geometry* command-line parameter:

```
gilbert:/$ xterm -geometry WidthxHeight &
```

With this parameter, the *Width* is the number of characters wide, almost always 80, and the *Height* is the number of lines to use. We find that 40 is a good number (the default is 24 lines).

Just about every X program supports the *-geometry* command-line parameter, but virtually every X program treats the *-geometry* command-line parameter differently from **xterm** (**xterm** is the main exception, in other words). While you specify the width and height in terms of characters with **xterm**, just about every other X program treats the *-geometry* as the size in pixels. This is important to note if you create some really small windows.

For example, the command to start **xterm** with 80 columns (the default) and 40 lines is:

```
$ xterm -geometry 80x40 &
```

With the *-geometry* command-line parameter you can also specify the starting location in pixels. The full syntax is:

```
-geometry WidthxHeight+X+Y
```

In this case, *X* and *Y* specify the location of the upper-left corner of the program's window in pixels. In X, the origin is also in the upper-left corner of the screen, so the following command creates an **xterm** window offset 10 pixels (in both *X* and *Y*) from the upper-left corner:

```
gilbert:/$ xterm -geometry 80x40+10+10 &
```

You can skip the size (*width* and *height*) or the location (*x* and *y*). The following are all valid commands:

```
gilbert:/$ xterm -geometry 80x40 &
gilbert:/$ xterm -geometry +10+10 &
gilbert:/$ xterm &
```

Setting Up a Scrollbar for Xterm

By default, **xterm** does not provide for a scrollbar, although one is available. You can use the *-sb* command-line parameter:

```
gilbert:/$ xterm -sb &
```

This creates a scrollbar in the **xterm** window (usually on the left side).

The **xterm** scrollbar is kind of tricky. Use the middle mouse button to move to the position you want. The right mouse button (assuming you have a three-button mouse) moves back, while the left mouse button moves forward. We almost always just use the middle mouse button.

In addition to the *-sb* command-line parameter, you can request a scrollbar for **xterm** in an X resource file.

X Resource Files

Another topic under X that is different from the Windows and Macintosh environments is *resource files*. You'll find that X resource files are either the savior or bane of your existence. Like the Windows and Macintosh systems, resource files on X allow you to customize fonts, colors, and text messages, all without access to the application's source code.

This concept is great. You can tell an application to use a more readable font, you can get rid of garish colors, you can even write Finnish messages in place of all the English ones, or you can fix up the English messages to something more to your liking.

X resource files provide a powerful mechanism to customize just about every X application. There are many locations—both within a resource file and on disk—to which you can place these resources files. Because many options conflict, it's easy to get lost in all the details.

Stripped to its basics, an X resource file is an ASCII text file that specifies some option for a program or programs. Each line of the resource file specifies a resource to set and its value. For example, you can specify in an X resource file that all **xterm** programs should start up with the scrollbar turned on, which we'll show how to do soon. You can also control fonts, colors, and a lot of the text displayed by most X programs.

To set up the scrollbar commands for **xterm** in a resource file, create a file named **XTerm** (note the capitalization) in your home directory. Both the file name, **XTerm**, and the location (your home directory) are essential. Put in the following lines:

```
XTerm*scrollBar: True
XTerm*saveLines: 1000
```

These X resource commands tell **xterm** to use a scrollbar and to save 1000 lines in its scroll buffer. Save this file and start another **xterm** program. You should see a scrollbar.

For more on X resource files, see the book list in Appendix A.

Controlling Fonts and Colors

Like most options, you can control **xterm**'s choice of fonts and colors from both command-line parameters and X resource files. What we usually do is set up the options we always want in an X resource file and then use the command-line parameters only for options we rarely need.

Normally, we're happy with **xterm**'s color defaults: black text on a white background. It's the font we'd like to change. By default, **xterm** uses the font named *fixed*, a fixed-character-size font (as opposed to a proportional font). We find this font far too small, so we'd like to use a larger one.

For setting the font, you can use the **-font** command-line parameter or set the font resource. To do the latter, you can add the following line to the **XTerm** file you created:

```
XTerm*font: -*-courier-medium-r-normal--14-140-75-75-m-90-*
```

This sets up a much more pleasing (to our eyes at least) and larger font for **xterm**.

To get a list of the available fonts, use the program **xlsfonts**, which will present you with a huge list. For **xterm**, you want a fixed-width font. The Courier fonts typically are fixed-width, as are the Lucida typewriter fonts. In the very long font names, the fixed-width fonts should have an *m* or *c*, as shown here, after the two 75s:

```
-adobe-courier-medium-r-normal--14-140-75-75-m-90-iso8859-1
```

As usual, to test this, save the **XTerm** file and start another **xterm** program.

For our **XTerm** file, we set the following resources:

```
!
!     XTerm resource file
!
XTerm*foreground:  black
XTerm*cursorColor: black
XTerm*background:  white
XTerm*scrollBar:   True
XTerm*saveLines:   1000
XTerm*font: -*-courier-medium-r-normal--14-140-75-75-m-90-*
```

Lines beginning with an exclamation mark (!) are comments. We list the most-used **xterm** command-line parameters in Table 3.15.

Table 3.15 Commonly Used Xterm Command-Line Parameters

Parameter	Meaning
-bg *color*	Sets background color; defaults to white
-cr *color*	Sets color of text cursor; defaults to black
-display *hostname*:0	Sets name of X display to which to connect
-e *program* [*args*]	Runs program instead of shell
-fg *color*	Sets foreground color; defaults to black
-fn *fontname*	Uses the given font
-font *fontname*	Uses the given font
-geometry *geom*	Uses given size and location
-ls	Turns shell into login shell
-sb	Turns on scrollbar

Copying and Pasting between xterm Windows

One of the best benefits of **xterm** over the console terminal is that you can copy and paste text between **xterm** windows. This is very handy if you edit documents. You can view one document in one **xterm** window and edit another in a different **xterm** window, copying and pasting between the two.

Xterm is highly configurable, but in the default configuration, you select text by holding down the left mouse button and dragging over the text you want to select. Double-clicking over a word selects just that word. Triple-clicking anywhere in a line selects the entire line.

To paste, press the middle mouse button. The text will be inserted, just as if you typed it.

Xterm just presents a shell window. Inside the **xterm** window, you run text-based shell programs, few of which know anything about the mouse and selecting text. Therefore, you have to ensure that the program you run within the **xterm** window is ready for the pasted text. In the **elvis** text editor, for example, you should enter input mode by typing **i** in command mode.

Elvis does not support middle-mouse button pastes, which is very annoying. To paste in **elvis**, you must hold down the **Shift** key while you press the middle mouse button.

Our fix is to use a different **vi** clone that comes with Linux, called **vim**. **Vim** fully supports mouse pasting in **xterm** windows without the hassle of **elvis**.

Other Shell Window Programs

In addition to the ubiquitous **xterm**, Linux ships with a few other shell programs, including **color_xterm**, **rxvt**, and **shelltool**.

If you want a shell with color, use **color_xterm**. This program acts just like **xterm**, but it presents a lot more color. For example, when you make a directory listing with **ls**, **color_xterm** presents directories in one color and ordinary files in another.

The **rxvt** program is very similar to **xterm**. Many claim that **rxvt** uses a smaller memory footprint than **xterm**, but we find its quirks aren't worth the difference (particularly with Linux shared libraries, which reduce **xterm**'s memory footprint to a reasonable level).

If you use Open Look applications on a Sun system at work, you will find yourself right at home with **shelltool**, found in **/usr/openwin/bin**.

You must have loaded the Open Look applications when you installed Linux to have this program. We recommend you install these programs, which also include the **olwm** and **olvwm** window managers.

All in all, we tend to only use **xterm** instead of other shell window programs, because **xterm** remains constant on all the UNIX systems we use, at home and at work.

Starting X Automatically at Boot-Up and Creating an X Login Screen

Up to now, we've been running **startx** to begin an X session. You still need to login at the console and start X yourself (or use the automatic method we describe later). In addition to this method, there's a way to set up an X login screen, using XDM. *XDM* stands for the X Display Manager; it is a means to control an X session. As such, XDM is generally much nicer to the user, as it automatically starts the X server and presents a graphical login window, like the one shown in Figure 3.7.

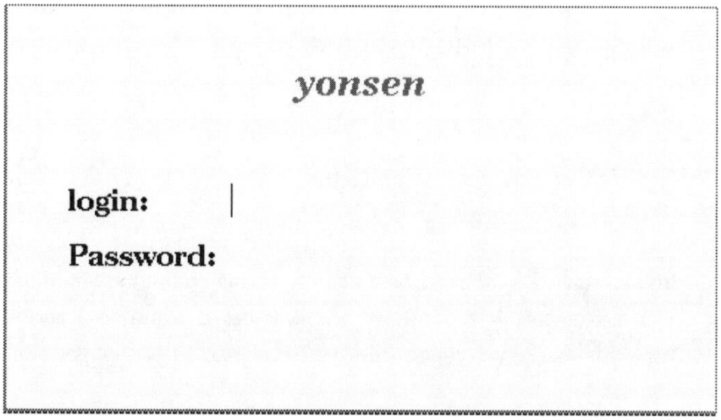

Figure 3.7 A graphical login window.

The X Display Manager is run from a program called **xdm**. While **xdm** takes a little getting used to, we like it better than the **startx/xinit** that we've been running so far. This is because **start**x (which runs **xinit**) requires you to login to a text screen and then start up X (via **startx**). **Xdm** allows you to log directly into an X session.

Xdm also allows one program to control your workstation's console and a number of X terminals. If you're interested in this, look in Appendix A for books that cover **xdm**.

To set up **xdm**, you need to edit at least one system file, a key file used when booting Linux; this is a serious endeavor. *Always* back up any system file before you edit it.

UNIX Run-Levels

Xdm is usually set to trigger what is called a *run-level*. With a few exceptions, run-levels in UNIX is an arbitrary concept that mostly follows ancient UNIX traditions. The run-level *S* implies a single-user stand-alone system.

In Linux, run-level 1 and higher are multiuser. This means that more than one user is allowed to login. On many systems, run-level 3 starts networking. This is also the default Linux run-level. Linux has special run-levels for power-fail (which shuts the system down) and the Vulcan death-grip (**Ctrl-Alt-Backspace**).

You can get some ideas about run-levels by looking in the **/etc/inittab** file. In **/etc/inittab**, one of the first entries will be something like the following:

```
# Default runlevel.
id:3:initdefault:
```

 In Slackware 2.3 (and the first edition of this book), the Linux default run-level was 5. The default X run-level was 6. It has changed to 3 and 4, respectively. Now, run-level 6 will reboot the system, a great surprise if you want it to run X.

This states that the default system run-level is 3. When Linux boots up, it will boot into run-level 3. Later in the **/etc/inittab** file, you'll find something like:

```
x1:4:wait:/etc/rc.d/rc.4
```

This states that on entry to run-level 4, **/etc/rc.d/rc.4** should be run. This file, then, starts up the X Display Manager, which presents an X login screen.

On our system, **/etc/rc.d/rc.4** starts the following program:

```
# Tell the viewers what's going to happen...
echo "Starting up the X Window System V.11 R.6..."

# Call the "xdm" program.
exec /usr/X11R6/bin/xdm -nodaemon
```

This is what starts up **xdm**. To get **xdm** up and running, all you should really have to do is edit the **/etc/inittab** as **root** and change the following line:

```
id:3:initdefault:
```

to

```
id:4:initdefault:
```

That's it. Everything else comes preconfigured. You may want to change the configuration, but you have a good start.

After making these changes, when you next boot Linux, you'll boot into run-level 4 rather than run-level 3. The process of going into run-level 4 will start **xdm**, because of what's in the **/etc/rc.d/rc.4** file.

Before doing this, though, make a copy of **/etc/inittab**. You also should test **xdm** before setting the system to boot into it, because you always want to be able to boot Linux. (Making a mistake in **/etc/inittab** can result in a Linux that won't boot.) To test **xdm**, you can type in the following command as root, to change to run-level 4 now:

```
# init 4
```

This will jump you to run-level 4. Be patient; this command takes a while.

Be sure that X is not running when you do this. You should be logged in as root at the console.

If you set up your **.login** or **.profile** file to automatically call **startx** when you login (see "Starting X Automatically on Login" later), you must disable this first. These two methods for starting X conflict. Quit X and then comment out those lines you added to the **.login** or **.profile** file, for example:

```
if ( `tty` == '/dev/tty1' ) then
#    Commented out.
#    startx
endif
```

After a while, you should see a graphical login screen. It is best to test **xdm** using init 4 first, to see if everything is set up correctly. Try to login and see what happens. If it works, you're in business and you can confidently modify the **/etc/inittab** file.

The **xdm** configuration files are in **/usr/lib/X11/xdm**. If you want to change the background color for the login screen, look in **Xsetup_0** in that directory. You probably won't have to edit much in **/usr/lib/X11/xdm**, especially for a stand-alone Linux system without X terminals on the network. (If your needs are more demanding, you'll need to look into a book on X, such as *The UNIX System Administrator's Guide to X*; see Appendix A for more on this.)

User Accounts Under Xdm

While you probably won't have to edit any of the **xdm** system files in **/usr/lib/X11/xdm**, it's likely you'll have to edit files in your home directory. By default, **xdm** runs a file named **.xsession** from your home directory, instead of the **.xinitrc** that is run by **startx** (and **xinit**).

To create the **.xsession** file, you can start by copying your **.xinitrc** file to **.xsession** in your home directory. (Remember to put in the leading period on the filename in your home directory.) Then modify this file like you changed the **.xinitrc** file.

Here's a copy of our **.xsession** file:

```
#!/bin/sh
userresources=$HOME/.Xresources
usermodmap=$HOME/.Xmodmap
sysresources=/usr/X11R6/lib/X11/xinit/.Xresources
sysmodmap=/usr/X11R6/lib/X11/xinit/.Xmodmap


# merge in defaults and keymaps

if [ -f $sysresources ]; then
    xrdb -merge $sysresources
fi


if [ -f $sysmodmap ]; then
    xmodmap $sysmodmap
fi


if [ -f $userresources ]; then
    xrdb -merge $userresources
fi


if [ -f $usermodmap ]; then
    xmodmap $usermodmap
fi
```

```
# start some nice programs
xsetroot -solid SteelBlue

xterm -geom 80x32+264+0 -ls &
xterm -geom 80x32+0+250 -ls &
oclock -geom -7-7 &
exec fvwm
```

If you don't want to start up X at boot time, you may want to start X every time you login.

Starting X Automatically on Login

If you don't set up **xdm**, you'll need to type in **startx** after you login to get X and all these applications in your **.xinitrc** file started. If you don't like to enter **startx** every time you login, and you're sure that you want to run X every time you login, you can put the **startx** command in your **.login** or **.profile** file (depending on the shell you use, **csh** or **ksh**). If you do, be sure that you're running from the console only. Otherwise, the **.login** or **.profile** file will error out if they get run from elsewhere (such as when you login over a serial line or from another virtual terminal).

The way to check for this is to check the result of the **tty** program. The **tty** program returns the current device file used for your terminal. When run from an **xterm** shell window, **tty** will print out something like **/dev/ttyp1** (for the first pseudo-terminal device). But, when run from the console (from the first virtual terminal), **tty** will print out **/dev/tty1**. When run from the second virtual terminal, **tty** prints out **/dev/tty2** so we can check for **/dev/tty1**.

To do this, we can enter **tty** at the console (before starting X):

```
$ tty
/dev/tty1
```

Use the value **tty** returns for *you*, not necessarily the value *we* received.

Armed with this information, you can edit your **.login** file (presuming you use the C shell, **csh**, as your shell) to add the following lines:

```
if ( `tty` == '/dev/tty1' ) then
    startx
endif
```

This will start up X when you login at the console. You can also set up your account to log you out when you quit X. Most of the time, we begin X at login and quit X when we want to logout. If this fits your pattern, you can change the **.login** file to contain the following:

```
if ( `tty` == '/dev/tty1' ) then
    startx
    logout
endif
```

The X Font Server

The X font server is a special program that can scale fonts. This ability dramatically increases the already-prolific set of X fonts available on your system (use the **xlsfonts** command to list these fonts). To get the font server up and running, you must:

- Configure the font server and tell it where to get fonts.
- Configure the font server to start up before X does.
- Configure the X server to communicate with the font server.

To configure the font server, we need to tell it where to find the scalable fonts. Luckily, Linux comes with a workable preconfigured file, **/usr/X11R6/lib/X11/fs/config**.

To start the font server, use the **xfs** (short for *X font server*) command. Enter the following command as root:

```
# xfs -port 7000 &
```

This uses the default configuration file, **/usr/X11R6/lib/X11/fs/config,** and runs on TCP/IP port 7000 (an arbitrary port to which the X font server defaults).

Once started, we can verify that the font server is running by using the **fsinfo** command:

```
gilbert:/$ fsinfo -server hostname:port
```

You need to fill in the hostname and port number. For example, with a hostname of *eric* and the default port number of *7000*, the command would be:

```
gilbert:/$ fsinfo -server eric:7000
```

You should see output like the following:

```
name of server: eric:7000
version number: 2
vendor string:  X Consortium
vendor release number:  6000
maximum request size:   16384 longwords (65536 bytes)
number of catalogues:   1
         all
Number of alternate servers: 0
number of extensions:   0
```

Once you verify that the font server is running, you can set up XFree86 to communicate with the font server. This is necessary so that X applications can take advantage of the font server's fonts.

To get the X server ready to accept the font server, you need to adjust its font path, or **fp**. Enter the following commands:

```
gilbert:/$ xset +fp tcp/eric:7000
gilbert:/$ xset fp rehash
```

In your case, you need to replace *eric* with your system's hostname. The first command tells the X server to use a TCP/IP port as a sort of font directory; the *tcp/hostname:port* syntax is the standard way to do this. The second command tells the X server to query again for all the available fonts.

If you're running **xdm** (see "Starting X at Boot-Up" earlier), you should stop that, verify that things work manually, and then set up **xdm** again. Problems with the font server may cause X to quit. If X quits, this may prevent an X-based login, leaving you in an unhappy situation.

Setting a Screen Background Image

In X, you can display a bitmap image, a solid color, or a graphics file as your screen background, depending on the program you use to accomplish this task.

The **xsetroot** program sets the screen background color. It can also set the screen background to a monochrome bitmap. Our **.xinitrc** file sets the background color to SteelBlue. Other good screen background colors include bisque3 and MediumTurquoise. You can see the whole list of X color names in the text file **/usr/lib/X11/rgb.txt**. This file contains a number of entries, including:

```
255 239 213 PapayaWhip
255 235 205 BlanchedAlmond
 50 205  50 LimeGreen
```

The **xsetroot** program can also be used to set the screen background to a monochrome bitmap, stored in an X bitmap file. The syntax for setting the screen background to a bitmap is:

```
gilbert:/$ xsetroot -bitmap filename -fg fore -bg back
```

where *filename* is the name of the file containing the bitmap and the *fore* and *back* are optional parameters that set the image's foreground and background color, respectively. Use the color names from the **rgb.txt** file explained earlier.

For example, if you have an X bitmap file named **prisoner.xb**, you can set it to be tiled over the screen background with the following command:

```
gilbert:/$ xsetroot -bitmap prisoner.xb
```

You'll see a screen like that shown in Figure 3.8.

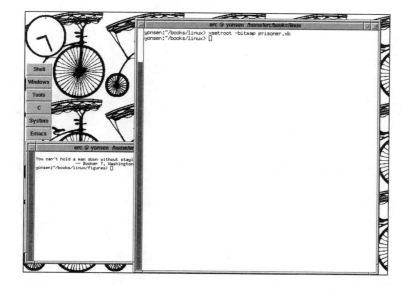

Figure 3.8 Using a bitmap as the screen background.

Because the image looks good in black and white, we skip the *-fg* and *-bg* options to **xsetroot** (and leave the famous penny-farthing bicycle alone).

If, instead of an X bitmap file, you have a GIF, TIFF, or JPEG image, you can use **xv** to display the image. **Xv** is a very neat image and file manager that sports the ability to convert images from one format to another and a way cool Visual Schnauzer. Normally, you display images in **xv**'s window, but it can also display images on the screen background, also called the *root window*.

For **xv**, use the following syntax to display an image on the root window:

```
gilbert:/$ xv -quit -root -max filename
```

where *filename* is the name of the file you want to display. When you run this command on an image file, you'll see a result like the one in Figure 3.9.

Figure 3.9 Using **xv** to set an image file for the screen background.

With complicated color images, you can soon fill up your colormap from the screen background image. This may lead to color flashing as X programs run out of colors in the default colormap and therefore create their own colormaps.

The Fvwm Window Manager

The window manager is one of the most important applications you'll run, as it sits around every application window on the screen and can influence how the windows work. The de facto window manager for Linux is **fvwm**.

This window manager provides a great deal of control over the way you interact with X, especially because **fvwm** supports a host of configuration options. While you can run any window manager you want, **fvwm** seems to be the most popular in the Linux world. It's not documented in many places or X books, so we'll show you how to set up **fvwm** for your Linux system.

You can run only one window manager at a time.

Configuring Fvwm

Most window managers under X support a configuration file. Usually, this file is located in a dot file in your home directory. Most window managers also follow a naming convention for their configuration file. For the **mwm** window manager, the file is named **.mwmrc**. For **twm**, it's **.twmrc**. For **fvwm**, it's **.fvwmrc**.

At startup, **fvwm** will look for your customizations in a file named **.fvwmrc** in your home directory. If you have no **.fvwmrc** file (which is likely when you start out), **fvwm** will look for a system file named **/usr/lib/X11/fvwm/system.fvwmrc**. If that file, too, is missing, **fvwm** will exit.

Because **fvwm** is a very complex window manager, you should copy the **system.fvwmrc** file or one of the example files to your home directory and name it **.fvwmrc**. By starting from a working example, you'll find it a lot easier than creating a **.fvwmrc** file from scratch.

Once you find the **fvwm** system directory, you'll see a number of sample configurations in the **sample_configs** directory. It's easiest to configure **fvwm** from a working model, so you can either copy **system.fvwmrc** or one of the files in the **sample_configs** directory.

Once you have copied a working configuration file into your home directory, the next step is to start customizing. The **.fvwmrc** file is very long, so we'll provide an overview of the areas you're most likely to customize and then provide an example **.fvwmrc** file—a very long example—that you can use. Just browsing this example should give you plenty of ideas. In addition to our example, you may want to look at the **fvwm** example files mentioned earlier and look at **fvwm**'s online-manual page.

In the **.fvwmrc** file, the order of items is very important. It's best to start with a working example and then search for the items we mention. Change the item's value, but leave the item itself in the same relative position in the **.fvwmrc** file.

Configuring Fonts and Colors

The foremost area you'll likely customize in the **.fvwmrc** file is fonts and colors.

Each window manager, including **fvwm**, allows only one application at a time to get keyboard input. This window, usually called the *active window* or the *keyboard focus window*, is usually highlighted by the window manager. In the **.fvwmrc** file, the *HiForeColor* sets the text foreground color for the active window's title. The *HiBackColor* sets the active titlebar color. The *StdForeColor* and *StdBackColor* work similarly for nonactive windows.

We use the following colors (copied from the default **.fvwmrc** file):

```
StdForeColor        Black
StdBackColor        #60a0c0


# this is used for the selected window
HiForeColor         Black
HiBackColor         #c06077
```

Window managers usually support two policies for selecting which window is made active: *click-to-focus* and *focus-follows-mouse*. Few people agree on which is better (Microsoft has decided click-to-focus is better, though). Choose the mode you want.

If you want focus-follows-mouse, ensure that the following line is commented out:

```
#ClickToFocus
```

If you want click-to-focus, then uncomment (remove the # character) the same line:

```
ClickToFocus
```

For fonts, you can control a number of the fonts used by **fvwm**:

```
Font       -adobe-helvetica-medium-r-*-*-14-*-*-*-*-*-*-*
#Font      -*-times-medium-i-*-*-*-140-*-*-*-*-*-*
```

```
WindowFont  -adobe-helvetica-bold-r-*-*-12-*-*-*-*-*-*-*
#IconFont   -adobe-helvetica-medium-r-*-*-11-*-*-*-*-*-*-*
IconFont    fixed
```

The asterisks (*) in the font names are wildcards. We only specify the minimum amount of data necessary to get Helvetica fonts at 10 and 12 point. A few fonts are commented out. You can uncomment these lines (and comment out the corresponding line) to try these other fonts, or type in your own font names.

By default, **fvwm** asks you to place each new window that appears on the screen. This can be a real pain, so we usually ask **fvwm** to place windows for us—you can always move them later—by setting the oddly named RandomPlacement option. Uncomment the following line to get this effect:

```
RandomPlacement
```

You also need to comment out the following line:

```
#NoPPosition
```

By default, **fvwm** places no border around dialog windows (called *transient windows* in X terminology). To make **fvwm** act more like the Motif window manager, uncomment the following line:

```
# If you want decorated transient windows,
# uncomment this:
# Ensure that a titlebar appears on dialogs.
DecorateTransients
```

Testing Your Fvwm Configuration

Now that we've made a change to our **.fvwmrc** file, it's time to test our new configuration. To do this, you need to restart **fvwm**. You can either quit X and restart everything or call up **Fvwm**'s root window menu, where you'll find a **Restart fvwm** choice. (It may be on a submenu.) You can access **fvwm**'s root menu by holding down the left mouse button over the screen background.

Turning off the Virtual Desktop

Both XFree86 and **fvwm** provide the ability to use *virtual screen space*, screen space beyond the confines of your monitor's resolution. XFree86 calls this a *virtual screen*, and **fvwm** calls this a *virtual desktop*.

These two methods tend to conflict, and frankly, we don't have much use for either kind of virtual screen space, as we don't run that many X applications at once and we can iconify windows to get them out of the way. Furthermore, it's easy to accidentally warp to one of **fvwm**'s virtual desktop spaces, which tends to get annoying.

Because of all this, we turn off **fvwm**'s virtual desktop in our **.fvwmrc** file with the following:

```
DeskTopSize 1x1
```

You specify the desktop value in units of the screen size; *1x1* means no virtual desktop.

Placing Icons

Fvwm's defaults result in bizarrely placed icons, with hidden icons strewn throughout the screen. We want to change this. To do so, use the *IconBox* command in the **.fvwmrc** file. We like our icons to go across the top of the screen, but we start from an offset of about 130 pixels to leave room for the round **oclock** window we place in the upper-left corner of the screen. (See our **.xinitrc** file, listed earlier.)

The *IconBox* specifies a rectangular area where you want the icons to appear. Here's our area:

```
IconBox 130 5 600 15
```

Configuring the Good Stuff

Fvwm also supports something called *modules*, add-ons that you can configure and run. The most popular add-on is called *GoodStuff*; it places a window on your screen from which you can launch applications or menus, sort of like a toolbar or the Windows 95 command area at the bottom of the screen.

Then you can turn on GoodStuff by uncommenting the GoodStuff lines in the *InitFunction* and *RestartFunctions* sections:

```
Function "InitFunction"
#Module "I" FvwmBanner
#Exec    "I" xpmroot /usr/include/X11/pixmaps/fvwm.xpm &
Module "I" GoodStuff
#Module "I" FvwmPager 0 3
#Exec    "I" exec xterm -geometry 80x64+0+0 &
#Wait    "I" xterm
#Desk    "I" 0 2
#Exec    "I" exec xmh -font fixed -geometry 507x750+0+0 &
#Wait    "I" xmh
#Desk    "I" 0 0
EndFunction


Function "RestartFunction"
#Exec    "I" xsetroot -solid "#266294"
Module "I" GoodStuff
#Module "I" FvwmPager 0 3
EndFunction
```

Either way works. The *InitFunction* section allows you to specify a set of X applications to launch at **fvwm** startup. Because this overlaps with the **.xinitrc** file, we typically skip starting any applications in the *InitFunction* section.

Toward a Motif-Like Look and Feel

One of **fvwm**'s claims to fame is that it is a free window manager that looks a lot like the Motif window manager, **mwm,** used on just about every commercial version of UNIX. Unfortunately, while **fvwm** looks like Motif, it doesn't act as much like **mwm** as you'd expect. The similar look of **fvwm** can fool you.

Take heart, though, as there are a few things you can do to make
fvwm act more like **mwm**. Take a look at our **.fvwmrc** file, later, and
you'll see a lot of **mwm**-like behavior.

Putting It All Together

To put all this together, the following is our **.fvwmrc** file. You can use
this as a base for your modifications. We don't expect you to type this
in. Instead, we provide it as a source of ideas and information for
configuring **fvwm** to your liking. The only lines we changed—and there
are only a few—are marked in italic type.

```
########################################
# set up the colors
#
# OK some people like bright clear colors on
# their window decorations.
# These people, I guess would mostly be from nice
# sunny/good weather places
# line California.
#
# StdForeColor       Black
# StdBackColor       LightSkyBlue
# HiForeColor        yellow
# HiBackColor        PeachPuff1
# PagerBackColor     BlanchedAlmond

# Me, I'm from Upstate New York and live
# in New Hampshire, so I prefer
# these dark muddy colors...

# this is used for nonselected windows,
# menus, and the panner
StdForeColor       Black
StdBackColor       #60a0c0
```

```
# this is used for the selected window
HiForeColor        Black
HiBackColor        #c06077


PagerBackColor     #5c54c0
PagerForeColor     orchid


StickyForeColor    Black
StickyBackColor    #60c0a0


# Menu colors
MenuForeColor          Black
MenuBackColor          grey
MenuStippleColor       SlateGrey


#####################################
# Now the fonts - one for menus, another
# for window titles, another for icons
Font        -adobe-helvetica-medium-r-*-*-14-*-*-*-*-*-*-*
#Font       -*-times-medium-i-*-*-*-140-*-*-*-*-*-*
WindowFont -adobe-helvetica-bold-r-*-*-12-*-*-*-*-*-*-*
#IconFont   -adobe-helvetica-medium-r-*-*-11-*-*-*-*-*-*-*
IconFont    fixed


#####################################
# Set up the major operating modes
#
#######      FOCUS STUFF      ########
# Set windows to autoraise after 750
# milliseconds if you like it.
# Autoraise can sometimes obscure pop-up
# windows. Performance is now
# similar to olvwm's auto-raise feature.
#AutoRaise 750


# Normally, we'll be in focus-followsmouse
```

```
# mode, but uncomment this
# for mwm-style click-to-focus
#ClickToFocus


#######     ICON STUFF    #########
# Auto Place Icons is a nice feature....
# This creates two icon boxes, one on the
# left side, then one on the
# bottom. Leaves room in the upper left
# for my clock and xbiff,
# room on the bottom for the Pager.
#IconBox -150 90 -5 -140
#IconBox 5 -140 -140 -5
#IconBox -70 1 -1 -140
IconBox 130 5 600 15


# If you uncomment this, and make sure
# that the WindowList is bound to
# something, it works pretty much
# like an icon manager.
#SuppressIcons


# StubbornIcons makes icons de-iconify into
# their original position on the
# desktop, instead of on the current page.
#StubbornIcons


# With AutoPlacement, icons will normally
# place themselves underneath active
# windows. This option changes that.
StubbornIconPlacement


# If you want ALL you icons to follow you around
# the desktop (Sticky), try this
#StickyIcons
```

```
######      MWM EMULATION     #######
#
# My feeling is that everyone should use
# MWMDecorHints and MWMFunctionHints,
# since some applications depend on having
# the window manager respect them.

# MWMFunction hints parses the function
# information in the MOTIF_WM_HINTS
# property, and prohibits use of these
# functions on the window. Appropriate
# portions of the window decorations are removed.
MWMFunctionHints

# MWM is kinda picky about what can be done
# to transients, and it was keeping
# me from iconifying some windows that I
# like to iconify, so here's an
# over-ride that will allow me to do the
# operation, even tough the menu
# item is shaded out.
MWMHintOverride

# MWMDecor hints parses the decoration
# information in the MOTIF_WM_HINTS
# property, and removes these decoratons
# from the window. This does not affect
# the functions that can be performed via the menus.
MWMDecorHints

# These are affect minor aspects for the
# look-and-feel.
# Sub-menus placement mwm-style?
MWMMenus
# mwm-style border reliefs (less deep
```

```
# than default fvwm) ?
# MWMBorders
# Maximize button does mwm-inversion thingy
# MWMButtons

###      MISCELLANEOUS STUFF      ####
# If you don't like the default 150 msec click delay
# for the complex functions
# change this and uncomment it.
#ClickTime 150

# OpaqueMove has a number (N) attached
# to it (default 5).
# if the window occupies less than
# N% of the screen,
# then opaque move is used. 0 <= N <= 100
OpaqueMove 100

# flip by whole pages on the edge of the screen.
#EdgeScroll 100 100

# A modest delay before flipping pages seems
# to be nice...
# I thresh in a 50 pixel Move-resistance too,
# just so people
# can try it out.
#EdgeResistance 250 50

# I like to use a large virtual screen and move
# from page to page with the
# pager.
#EdgeResistance 10000 0

####      WINDOW PLACEMENT      ######
# RandomPlacement prevents user interaction
# while placing windows:
```

```
# Make windows appear without requiring user
# interaction to place them.
RandomPlacement


# SmartPlacement makes new windows pop-up
# in blank regions of screen
# if possible, or falls back to random
# or interactive placement.
#SmartPlacement


# With SmartPlacement, windows will normally
# place themselves over icons.
# Uncomment this to change that.
#StubbornPlacement


# NoPPosition instructs fvwm to ignore
# the PPosition field in window
# geometry hints. Emacs annoyingly sets
# PPosition to (0,0)!
#NoPPosition


#########        DECORATIONS      ######
# If you want decorated transient windows,
# uncomment this:
# Ensure that a title-bar appears on dialogs.
DecorateTransients


####################################
# Set up the virtual desktop and pager


# Set the desk top size in units of
# physical screen size.
# No virtual desktop.
DeskTopSize 1x1


# and the reduction scale used
```

```
# for the panner/pager
# No virtual desktop.
#DeskTopScale 36


# Use the Fvwm Pager
# No virtual desktop.
#Pager 5 5


######################################
# Module path and paths to the icons
#
# ModulePath is a colon-separated list, just
# like regular unix PATH
ModulePath /usr/lib/X11/fvwm
PixmapPath /usr/include/X11/pixmaps/
IconPath   /usr/include/X11/bitmaps/


######################################
# Set the decoration styles and window options
# Order is important!!!!
# If compatible styles are set for a
# single window in multiple Style
# commands, then the styles are ORed
# together. If conflicting styles
# are set, the last one specified is used.


# These commands should command before any
# menus or functions are defined,
# and before the internal pager is started.


# change the default width.
Style "*" BorderWidth 5, HandleWidth 5, Color Black/#60a0c0,Icon
unknown1.xpm


Style "Fvwm*"     NoTitle, Sticky, WindowListSkip
Style "Fvwm Pager" StaysOnTop
```

```
Style "FvwmBanner" StaysOnTop
Style "GoodStuff"  NoTitle, NoHandles, Sticky,
WindowListSkip,BorderWidth 0
Style "*lock"      NoTitle, NoHandles, Sticky, WindowListSkip
Style "xbiff"      NoTitle,           Sticky, WindowListSkip
Style "Maker"      StartsOnDesk 1
Style "matlab"     StartsOnDesk 3
Style "signal"     StartsOnDesk 3
Style "rxvt"       Icon  term.xpm
Style "xterm"      Icon xterm.xpm, Color black/grey
Style "Appointment" Icon datebook.xpm
Style "xcalc"      Icon xcalc.xpm
Style "xbiff"      Icon mail1.xpm
Style "xmh"        Icon mail1.xpm, StartsOnDesk 2
Style "xman"       Icon xman.xpm
Style "xvgr"       Icon graphs.xpm
Style "matlab"     Icon math4.xpm
Style "xmag"       Icon mag_glass.xpm
Style "xgraph"     Icon graphs.xpm
Style "GoodStuff"  Icon toolbox.xpm


####################################

# Stuff to do at start-up

Function "InitFunction"
#Module "I" FvwmBanner
#Exec   "I" xpmroot /usr/include/X11/pixmaps/fvwm.xpm &
#Module "I" GoodStuff
#Module "I" FvwmPager 0 3
#Exec   "I" exec xterm -geometry 80x64+0+0 &
#Wait   "I" xterm
#Desk   "I" 0 2
#Exec   "I" exec xmh -font fixed -geometry 507x750+0+0 &
#Wait   "I" xmh
#Desk   "I" 0 0
```

```
EndFunction

Function "RestartFunction"
#Exec    "I" xsetroot -solid "#266294"
#Module "I" GoodStuff
#Module "I" FvwmPager 0 3
EndFunction

# Now define some handy complex functions.

# This one moves and then raises the
# window if you drag the mouse,
# only raises the window if you click,
# or does a RaiseLower if you double
# click
Function "Move-or-Raise"
    Move       "Motion"
    Raise      "Motion"
    Raise      "Click"
    RaiseLower "DoubleClick"
EndFunction

# This one maximizes vertically if you click
# (leaving room for the GoodStuff bar at the
# bottom) or does a full maximization
# if you double-click, or a true full vertical
# maximization if you just hold the mouse button down.
Function "maximize_func"
    Maximize    "Motion" 0 100
    Maximize    "Click" 0 80
    Maximize    "DoubleClick" 100 100
EndFunction

# This one moves and then lowers the window
# if you drag the mouse, only lowers the window
# if you click,  or does a RaiseLower if you double
# click
```

```
Function "Move-or-Lower"
    Move        "Motion"
    Lower       "Motion"
    Lower       "Click"
    RaiseLower  "DoubleClick"
EndFunction

# This one moves or (de)iconifies:
Function "Move-or-Iconify"
    Move        "Motion"
    Iconify     "DoubleClick"
EndFunction

# This one resizes and then raises the window
# if you drag the mouse,
# only raises the window if you click,
# or does a RaiseLower if you double
# click
Function "Resize-or-Raise"
    Resize      "Motion"
    Raise       "Motion"
    Raise       "Click"
    RaiseLower  "DoubleClick"
EndFunction

# This is provided as a hint only.
# Move to a known page on the desktop,
# then start an application in a
# known location. Could also switch to a
# known desktop, I guess
#Function "abs_coord"
#GoToPage "Immediate"   1,1
#Exec    "Immediate" exec xcalc -geometry +100+100&
#EndFunction

####################################
```

```
#now define the menus - defer bindings until later

Popup "Shells"
Title   "Shells"
  Exec    "Xterm (7x14 font)"      exec /usr/bin/X11/xterm -sb -sl
500 -j -ls -fn 7x14 &
  Exec    "Color Rxvt (VT100 emulator)" exec /usr/bin/X11/rxvt -
font 7x14 -ls &
  Exec    "Color Xterm (7x14 font)"      exec
/usr/bin/X11/color_xterm -sb -sl 500 -j -ls -fn 7x14 &
  Exec    "Large Xterm (10x20 font)"      exec /usr/bin/X11/xterm
-sb -sl 500 -j -ls -fn 10x20 &
  Exec    "Large Rxvt (10x20 font)"       exec /usr/bin/X11/rxvt -
font 10x20 -ls &
  Exec    "Large Color Xterm (10x20 font)"       exec
/usr/bin/X11/color_xterm -sb -sl 500 -j -ls -fn 10x20 &
EndPopup

Popup "Screensaver"
  Title    "Screensaver"
  Exec    "Bat"      exec xlock -nolock -nice 0 -mode bat &
  Exec    "Blank"    exec xlock -nolock -nice 0 -mode blank &
  Exec    "Blot"     exec xlock -nolock -nice 0 -mode blot &
  Exec    "Bob"      exec xlock -nolock -nice 0 -mode bob &
  Exec    "Bounce"   exec xlock -nolock -nice 0 -mode bounce &
  Exec    "Flame"    exec xlock -nolock -nice 0 -mode flame &
  Exec    "Galaxy"   exec xlock -nolock -nice 0 -mode galaxy &
  Exec    "Grav"     exec xlock -nolock -nice 0 -mode grav &
  Exec    "Helix"    exec xlock -nolock -nice 0 -mode helix &
  Exec    "Hop"      exec xlock -nolock -nice 0 -mode hop   &
  Exec    "Hyper"    exec xlock -nolock -nice 0 -mode hyper &
  Exec    "Kaleid"   exec xlock -nolock -nice 0 -mode kaleid &
  Exec    "Life"     exec xlock -nolock -nice 0 -mode life  &
  Exec    "Life3d"   exec xlock -nolock -nice 0 -mode life3d   &
  Exec    "Maze"     exec xlock -nolock -nice 0 -mode maze &
  Exec    "Pyro"     exec xlock -nolock -nice 0 -mode pyro &
  Exec    "Qix"      exec xlock -nolock -nice 0 -mode qix &
```

```
    Exec    "Random"    exec xlock -nolock -nice 0 -mode random &
    Exec    "Rect"      exec xlock -nolock -nice 0 -mode rect &
    Exec    "Rock"      exec xlock -nolock -nice 0 -mode rock &
    Exec    "Rotor"     exec xlock -nolock -nice 0 -mode rotor &
    Exec    "Sphere"    exec xlock -nolock -nice 0 -mode sphere &
    Exec    "Spline"    exec xlock -nolock -nice 0 -mode spline &
    Exec    "Swarm"     exec xlock -nolock -nice 0 -mode swarm &
    Exec    "Wator"     exec xlock -nolock -nice 0 -mode wator &
    Exec    "Worm"      exec xlock -nolock -nice 0 -mode worm &
    Exec    "World"     exec xlock -nolock -nice 0 -mode world &
EndPopup

Popup "Screenlock"
    Title   "Lock Screen"
    Exec    "Bat"       exec xlock -nice 0 -mode bat &
    Exec    "Blank"     exec xlock -nice 0 -mode blank &
    Exec    "Blot"      exec xlock -nice 0 -mode blot &
    Exec    "Bob"       exec xlock -nice 0 -mode bob &
    Exec    "Bounce"    exec xlock -nice 0 -mode bounce &
    Exec    "Flame"     exec xlock -nice 0 -mode flame &
    Exec    "Galaxy"    exec xlock -nice 0 -mode galaxy &
    Exec    "Grav"      exec xlock -nice 0 -mode grav &
    Exec    "Helix"     exec xlock -nice 0 -mode helix &
    Exec    "Hop"       exec xlock -nice 0 -mode hop   &
    Exec    "Hyper"     exec xlock -nice 0 -mode hyper &
    Exec    "Kaleid"    exec xlock -nice 0 -mode kaleid &
    Exec    "Life"      exec xlock -nice 0 -mode life   &
    Exec    "Life3d"    exec xlock -nice 0 -mode life3d   &
    Exec    "Maze"      exec xlock -nice 0 -mode maze &
    Exec    "Pyro"      exec xlock -nice 0 -mode pyro &
    Exec    "Qix"       exec xlock -nice 0 -mode qix &
    Exec    "Random"    exec xlock -nice 0 -mode random &
    Exec    "Rect"      exec xlock -nice 0 -mode rect &
    Exec    "Rock"      exec xlock -nice 0 -mode rock &
    Exec    "Rotor"     exec xlock -nice 0 -mode rotor &
    Exec    "Sphere"    exec xlock -nice 0 -mode sphere &
```

```
   Exec    "Spline"    exec xlock -nice 0 -mode spline &
   Exec    "Swarm"     exec xlock -nice 0 -mode swarm &
   Exec    "Wator"     exec xlock -nice 0 -mode wator &
   Exec    "Worm"      exec xlock -nice 0 -mode worm &
   Exec    "World"     exec xlock -nice 0 -mode world &
EndPopup

Popup "Games"
   Title   "Games"
   Exec    "Maze"      exec maze &
   Exec    "Spider"    exec spider &
   Exec    "Workman"   exec workman &
   Exec    "Xboard"    exec xboard &
   Exec    "Xcuckoo"   exec xcuckoo &
   Exec    "Xeyes"     exec xeyes &
   Exec    "Xhextris"  exec xhextris &
   Exec    "Xlander"   exec xlander &
   Exec    "Xlogo"     exec xlogo &
   Exec    "Xmahjongg" exec xmahjongg &
   Exec    "Xroach"    exec xroach &
   Exec    "Xtetris"   exec xtetris &
   Exec    "Xvier"     exec xvier &
EndPopup

Popup "Applications"
   Title   "Applications"
   Exec    "Ghostview"    exec ghostview &
   Exec    "GNU Emacs"    exec emacs &
   Exec    "Lucid Emacs"  exec lemacs &
   Exec    "Seyon"        exec seyon -modem /dev/modem &
   Exec    "XV"           exec xv &
   Exec    "X3270"        exec x3270 &
   Exec    "Xedit"        exec xedit &
   Exec    "Xfig"         exec xfig &
   Exec    "Xfilemanager" exec xfilemanager &
   Exec    "Xfm"          exec xfm &
```

```
    Exec     "Xfractint"        exec rxvt -font 7x14 -e xfractint
map=chroma &
    Exec     "Xgrab"            exec xgrab &
    Exec     "Xpaint"           exec xpaint &
    Exec     "Xspread"          exec xspread &
    Exec     "Xxgdb"            exec xxgdb &
EndPopup


# This menu is invoked as a sub-menu
# - it allows you to quit,
# restart, or switch to another WM.
Popup "Quit-Verify"
    Title    "Really Quit Fvwm?"
    Quit     "Yes, Really Quit"
    Restart "Restart Fvwm"    fvwm
    Restart "Start twm"       twm
    Restart "Start tvtwm"     tvtwm
    Restart "Start mwm"       mwm
    Restart "Start olvwm"     /usr/openwin/bin/olvwm
    Restart "Start olwm"      /usr/openwin/bin/olwm
    Nop ""
    Nop "No, Don't Quit"
EndPopup


# Provides a list of modules to fire off
Popup "Module-Popup"
    Title   "Modules"
    Module  "GoodStuff" GoodStuff
    Module  "Clean-Up"  FvwmClean
    Module  "Identify"  FvwmIdent
    Module  "SaveDesktop"   FvwmSave
    Module  "Debug"     FvwmDebug
    Module  "Pager"         FvwmPager 0 3
    Module  "FvwmWinList"   FvwmWinList
EndPopup


# This menu will fire up some very common utilities
```

```
Popup "Utilities"
    Title  "Utilities"
        Exec   "Top"             exec rxvt  -font 7x14 -T Top -n Top -e
top &
        Exec   "Calculator"   exec xcalc &
        Exec   "Xman"         exec xman &
        Exec   "Xmag"         exec xmag &
        Exec   "Oclock"       exec oclock &
        Nop    ""
        Popup  "Applications"  Applications
        Nop    ""
        Popup  "Shells"        Shells
        Nop    ""
        Popup  "Games"         Games
        Nop    ""
        Popup  "Screensaver"   Screensaver
        Nop    ""
        Popup  "Lock Screen"   Screenlock
    Nop ""
    Popup   "Modules"   Module-Popup
    Nop ""
    Popup   "Exit Fvwm" Quit-Verify
        Nop       ""
        Refresh "Refresh Screen"
EndPopup


# This defines the most common window operations
# Modified to be more like Motif window manager.
Popup "Window Ops"
    Title      "Window Ops"
    Function   "Move    (Alt-F7)"      Move-or-Raise
    Function   "Resize  (Alt-F8)"   Resize-or-Raise
    Raise      "Restore  (Alt-F5)"
    Lower      "Lower (Alt-F3)"
    Iconify    "Minimize (Alt-F9)"
    Function   "Maximize (Alt-F10)"      maximize_func
    Nop        ""
```

```
    Destroy      "Destroy"
    Delete       "Delete"
    Nop        " "
    Refresh      "Refresh Screen"
EndPopup


# A trimmeddown version of "Window Ops",
# good for binding to decorations
Popup "Window Ops2"
    Function     "Move (Alt-F7)"     Move-or-Raise
    Function     "Resize"     Resize-or-Raise
    Raise        "Raise"
    Lower        "Lower"
    Iconify      "Iconify"
    Stick        "(Un)Stick"
    Nop          " "
    Destroy      "Destroy"
    Delete       "Delete"
    Nop          " "
    Module       "ScrollBar"     FvwmScroll 2 2
EndPopup


#####################################
# One more complex function - couldn't be
# defined earlier because it used
# pop-up menus.
#
# This creates a Motif-ish sticky menu for
# the titlebar window-ops
# pop-up
# Menu acts like normal twm menu if you
# just hold the button down,
# but if you click instead, the menu
# stays up, Motif style
# Was Window Ops2
Function "window_ops_func"
```

```
      PopUp    "Click"     Window Ops
      PopUp    "Motion"    Window Ops
# Motif would add
Delete   "DoubleClick"
EndFunction


#####################################
# This defines the mouse bindings

# First, for the mouse in the root window
# Button 1 gives the Utilities menu
# Button 2 gives the Window Ops menu
# Button 3 gives the WindowList (like TwmWindows)
# I use the AnyModifier (A) option for the
# modifier field, so you can hold down
# any shift-control-whatever combination you want!

#      Button    Context Modifi  Function
Mouse 1    R        A         PopUp "Utilities"
Mouse 2    R        A         PopUp "Window Ops"
Mouse 3        R        A         WindowList
#Mouse 3        R        A         Module "winlist" FvwmWinList transient

# Now the title bar buttons
# Any button in the left titlebar button gives the window ops menu
# Any button in the right titlebar button iconifies the window
# Any button in the rightmost titlebar button maximizes
# Note the use of "Mouse 0" for AnyButton.

#      Button    Context Modifi  Function
Mouse 0    1        A         Function "window_ops_func"
Mouse 0    2        A         Function "maximize_func"
Mouse 0    4        A         Iconify

# Now the rest of the frame
# Here I invoke my complex functions for
# Move-or-lower, Move-or-raise,
```

```
# and Resize-or-Raise.
# Button 1 in the corner pieces, with any
# modifiers, gives resize or raise
# Allow resizing from window border, like mwm.
Mouse 1     FS  A    Function "Resize-or-Raise"
# Button 1 in the title, sides, or icon,
# w/ any modifiers, gives move or raise
Mouse 1     T  A    Function "Move-or-Raise"

# Button 1 in an icon gives move for a
# drag, de-iconify for a double-click,
# nothing for a single click
# Button 2 in an icon, w/ any modifiers,
# gives de-iconify

Mouse 1     I   A    Function "Move-or-Iconify"
Mouse 2     I   A    Iconify

# Button 2 in the corners, sides, or titlebar
# gives the window ops menu
Mouse 2     FST A    Function "window_ops_func"
# Button 3 anywhere in the decoration
# (except the title bar buttons)
# does a raise-lower
Mouse 3     TSIF   A    RaiseLower

# Button 3 in the window, with the Modifier-1
# key (usually Alt or diamond)
# gives Raise-Lower. Used to use control
# here, but that interferes with xterm
Mouse 3        W     M      RaiseLower

######################################
# Now some keyboard shortcuts.

# Arrow Keys
# press arrow + control anywhere,
```

```
# and scroll by 1 page
Key Left     A   C   Scroll -100 0
Key Right    A   C   Scroll +100 +0
Key Up       A   C   Scroll +0   -100
Key Down     A   C   Scroll +0   +100

# press arrow + meta key,
# and scroll by 1/10 of a page
Key Left     A   M   Scroll -10 +0
Key Right    A   M   Scroll +10 +0
Key Up       A   M   Scroll +0   -10
Key Down     A   M   Scroll +0   +10

# press shift arrow + control anywhere,
# and move the pointer by 1% of a page
Key Left     A   SC  CursorMove -1 0
Key Right    A   SC  CursorMove +1 +0
Key Up       A   SC  CursorMove +0   -1
Key Down     A   SC  CursorMove +0   +1

# press shift arrow + meta key and
# move the pointer by 1/10 of a page
Key Left     A   SM  CursorMove -10 +0
Key Right    A   SM  CursorMove +10 +0
Key Up       A   SM  CursorMove +0   -10
Key Down     A   SM  CursorMove +0   +10

# Keyboard accelerators
#Key F1      A   M   Popup "Utilities"
#Key F1      A   M   Popup "Utilities"
#Key F2      A   M   Popup "Window Ops"
#Key F3      A   M   Module "WindowList" FvwmWinList
#Key F4      A   M   Iconify
#Key F5      A   M   Move
#Key F6      A   M   Resize
#Key F7      A   M   CirculateUp
```

```
#Key F8     A    M    CirculateDown
#
Key F1         WFST    M      Raise
Key F2         WFST    M      Delete
Key F3         WFST    M      Lower
Key F4         WFST    M      Destroy
Key F5         WFST    M      Raise
Key F6         A       M      WindowList
Key F7         WFST    M      Move
Key F8         WFST    M      Resize
Key F9         WFST    M      Iconify
Key F10        WFST    M      Maximize


#Page Up/Dapge Down keys are used to
# scroll by one desktop page
# in any context, press page up/down + control
# in root context, just pressing page up/down is OK
#
# I prefer the non-wrapping scroll. These
# are for example purposes only
#Key Next    A       C       Scroll 100000 0
#Key Next    R       N       Scroll 100000 0
#Key Prior   A       C       Scroll -100000 0
#Key Prior   R       N       Scroll -100000 0


#####################################
#####################################
#Definitions used by the modules


######### GoodStuff button-bar ######
# Colors
*GoodStuffFore Black
*GoodStuffBack #908090

# Font
*GoodStuffFont -adobe-helvetica-bold-r-*-*-10-*-*-*-*-*-*-*
```

```
# Geometry - really likes to pick its own size, but giving a position
is OK
*GoodStuffGeometry -1-90


# Layout: specify rows or columns, not both
*GoodStuffColumns 1


# Define the buttons to use....
*GoodStuff Kill     rbomb.xpm    Destroy


# xterm or rxvts on remote machines can be done like this
# Output redirection is csh style, not sh style
# You will want to substitute your own hosts here!


#*GoodStuff Dopey   rterm.xpm    Exec "dopey" rsh dopey "exec xterm
-T dopey -display $HOSTDISPLAY </dev/null >&/dev/null & "&
#*GoodStuff Grumpy  rterm.xpm    Exec "grumpy" rsh grumpy "exec
xterm -T grumpy -display $HOSTDISPLAY </dev/null >&/dev/null & "&
#*GoodStuff Snoopy  rterm.xpm    Exec "snoopy" rsh snoopy "exec
xterm -T snoopy -display $HOSTDISPLAY </dev/null >&/dev/null & "&
#*GoodStuff Xcalc    rcalc.xpm    Exec "Calculator" xcalc &
#*GoodStuff mail     mail2.xpm     Exec "xmh" xmh &


#*GoodStuff Paging  clamp.xpm    TogglePage
#*GoodStuff xclock  clock.xpm    Swallow "xclock" xclock -bg
\#908090 -geometry -1500-1500 -padding 0 &


########## No Clutter ###############
# I only wrote NoClutter as a simple test
# case, but maybe some big sites like
# universities really have usage problems
# (too many open windows)....
# Time delays are in seconds.
*FvwmNoClutter 3600 Iconify 1
*FvwmNoClutter 86400 Delete
*FvwmNoCLutter 172800 Destroy


########## Window-Identifier ########
```

```
# Just choose colors and a fonts
*FvwmIdentBack MidnightBlue
*FvwmIdentFore Yellow
*FvwmIdentFont -adobe-helvetica-medium-r-*-*-12-*-*-*-*-*-*-*


############## Pager ################
*FvwmPagerBack #908090
*FvwmPagerFore #484048
*FvwmPagerFont -adobe-helvetica-bold-r-*-*-10-*-*-*-*-*-*-*
*FvwmPagerHilight #cab3ca
*FvwmPagerGeometry -1-1
*FvwmPagerLabel 0 Misc
*FvwmPagerLabel 1 FrameMaker
*FvwmPagerLabel 2 Mail
*FvwmPagerLabel 3 Matlab
*FvwmPagerSmallFont 5x8


##############FvwmWinList############
*FvwmWinListBack #908090
*FvwmWinListFore Black
*FvwmWinListFont -adobe-helvetica-bold-r-*-*-10-*-*-*-*-*-*-*
*FvwmWinListAction Click1 Iconify -1,Focus
*FvwmWinListAction Click2 Iconify
*FvwmWinListAction Click3 Module "FvwmIdent" FvwmIdent
*FvwmWinListUseSkipList
*FvwmWinListGeometry +0-1
```

Exiting X from Fvwm

To exit from **fvwm** and usually quit X (if **fvwm** is the last X application in your **.xinitrc** or **.xsession** file), you usually call up the **fvwm** root menu and quit. The default choices are Exit Fvwm, which invokes a submenu to confirm, and Yes, Really Quit.

Summary

The X Window System is a graphical interface used by Linux, and it comes in the form of XFree86, a version of X optimized for the PC architecture.

This chapter deals with one of the most tedious, nonintuitive, and uninspiring aspects of Linux installation and configuration—messing around with XFree86. You learned about all the mundane details that go into a typical XFree86 configuration process, including mucking around with various files and settings.

X runs through a series of configuration files after it's launched. Some of these files control what applications begin when X begins, while other files add functionality in the form of the X Display Manager.

Once you have X up and running, you can run some of the many neat X-based programs that ship with the Slackware distribution. One of the handiest is **xterm**, an admittedly blah program that gives you a UNIX-like terminal (and, by extension, access to the UNIX command line). We find that most Linux users use **xterm**, making it one of the most popular X Window applications. In this chapter we discuss **xterm**, how to configure it, and how to use it.

The **fvwm** window manager is advertised as being Motif-like, and it is—on the surface. After you use it for a while, you'll learn that it doesn't respond to the same commands as the Motif window manager (**mwm**), and all in all it works differently than does **mwm**.

In the next chapter we'll cover additional Linux tools, both character-based and X-based.

Section II

Using Linux

Now that you have Linux installed and configured on your PC, it's time for the fun part—actually using it.

Chapter 4 covers basic Linux tools that you'll probably use every day in some fashion. The coverage here focuses on tools that are unique to Linux, whether they be features not found in other UNIX implementations or features found in the UNIX world that have been slightly changed for use under Linux. A good example of this is the **elvis** text editor, which is a clone of the ubiquitous **vi** editor.

Chapter 5 covers additional Linux tools that you probably won't use every day, but that will still come in handy. This would include the **emacs** text editor and the Mtools, which are specific to Linux and allow Linux to interoperate mare easily with the PC architecture.

Chapter 6 introduces basic system administration and the tools you'll need to use Linux on a long-term basis, whether you're working on a standalone system or a network. These include utilities for hard-disk usage, managing users, and scheduling tasks.

Basic Linux Tools

This chapter covers:

- Linux tools
- The Linux filesystem
- File types
- File permissions
- Basic Linux commands
- Wildcards
- Other ways of viewing files
- Linux and passwords
- Linux shells
- Using the **elvis** text editor

Linux Tools

Because it's a UNIX workalike, you'd expect Linux to toe the line when it comes to UNIX design philosophy and user tools. Design philosophy? Yes. As an operating system, UNIX can be seen as a collection of tools, some more important than others. Because UNIX (and Linux, for that matter) originally evolved through the contributions of a widespread computing community, UNIX tools tend to spring up in response to specific situations: When a problem needed to be solved, either a new command was added or new options were added to old commands.

This tool-based approach is what gives UNIX much of its perceived complexity. Compared to Microsoft Windows and the Macintosh operating system, the use of UNIX tools like **vi** and **ls** may seem to be fairly archaic and nonintuitive. For the outsider, they are.

But once you spend some time with UNIX and its command structure, you'll see that there's a great deal of logic underlying the UNIX operating system—and by extension, the Linux operating system. Once you've mastered a few Linux commands, you can move on to more complex command lines and more complex computing chores. We'll begin this chapter with a discussion of basic UNIX/Linux commands and concepts. In the next chapter, we'll discuss more advanced Linux tools. The tools in this chapter can be run from a command line or under the X Window System in an **xterm** window.

If you're a computing neophyte, you may want to check out a basic UNIX text (such as *teach yourself . . . UNIX, Third Edition*—MIS:Press) for a more detailed explanation of UNIX directories, files, commands, command lines, pipes, and standard input/output. See Appendix A for details.

The Linux Filesystem

Linux organizes your information in *files*. Files can contain text, programming information, shell scripts, or virtually any other kind of information.

We're not going to spend a lot of time on this basic concept here or on the different types of files under the UNIX operating system; if you're not sure what a file is, you should check out one of the basic UNIX texts listed in Appendix A. However, there are some things you should know about how Linux treats files:

- **Linux has no practical limit on the length of filenames.** While there are some internal limits on filename size (namely, 256 characters), you're probably not going to run into these limits. If you're frustrated by DOS's eight-dot-three filename limitation, you'll be pleased with this aspect of Linux. However, if you're using Linux on a network with other forms of UNIX, you'll probably want to limit your filenames to a 14-character limit, because this is the general limit in the UNIX world.

- **Linux has few limitations on what characters can be used in filenames.** Generally speaking, you shouldn't use the following characters in filenames:

  ! @ # $ % ^ & ( ) [ ] { } ' " ? | ; < > ` + - \ / . ..

  These characters have a tendency to conflict with the shell. In addition, you can't use spaces in the middle of a filename.

- **With Linux, case always counts, and that includes filenames.** Under Linux, **report**, **Report**, and **REPORT** are three different files.

A file can be looked at in a few different ways when it comes to the name. When we refer to files throughout this chapter, we're mainly speaking about the filename itself (like **test**) and not the *absolute pathname*. Under Linux, an absolute filename is the name of the file as measured from the root directory. Therefore, a file that's stored in a subdirectory (which you'll learn about later in this chapter) named **/home/kevinr** would have an absolute pathname of **/home/kevinr/test**. When we refer to **test** without a reference to the subdirectory containing it, we're referring to its *relative pathname*. There's a lot more rigmarole to do with relative pathnames, but you'll probably not deal with it all that often.

One difference from MS-DOS that you'll notice: With Linux, there's no such thing as drive names. There's a single filesystem, and any differences in physical media are pretty much abstracted away. This is why the CD-ROM drive actually appears as part of the filesystem as **/cdrom**. Similarly, the floppy drive is represented by a device driver, not a physical drive letter. (There are ways that Linux deals with floppy drives; some of them will be covered in Chapter 5.)

File Types

Under Linux, a file can be one of several types:

- Ordinary files
- Directories
- Links
- Special device files

We're not going to spend a lot of time discussing each of these file types; you should be able to see the difference between them in the short explanations here. If you want more information about UNIX file types, check out one of the UNIX texts listed in Appendix A.

Ordinary Files

Ordinary files win the Linux prize for truth in advertising; they tend to be rather ordinary. Generally speaking, you'll spend most of your time working with ordinary files of some sort:

- *Text files* are made up of ASCII text. For example, when you create a file in **emacs**, you're creating a text file. In addition, if you create source-code files for use in programming, you're creating text files.

- *Data files* may contain special characters not contained in the ASCII set. For example, the **xv** graphics editor creates and edits files in various graphics formats. Because these files contain non-ASCII characters, they are data files. The same would go for files created by a database manager or a spreadsheet manager.

- *Command text files*, also known as *shell scripts*, contain ASCII characters but are marked differently from other Linux files.

- *Executable files* are binary program files that are created when source-code files are compiled.

Directories

Directories are, well, directories. Under Linux, a directory is also a file that contains information about the directory. (Talk about the ultimate in self-referential logic…) You'll learn more about directories soon, but the important thing to know is that directories can have the same sort of limitations—i.e., permissions—as can files.

Links

A *link* is a reference to another file within the filesystem. This allows a file to be in two (or more) places at the same time—in its original file location and at the reference elsewhere in the filesystem. You'll learn more about links later in this chapter.

Special Device Files

In a sense, you've already covered this type of file in Chapter 2, when you learned how Linux refers to various portions of the PC architecture, such as **/dev/hda** for the hard drive. These references are called *device files*, and they are used by Linux to represent physical portions of the PC. Under Linux—and under UNIX, for that matter—everything is a file, whether it a collection of data, a device file representing a physical piece of hardware (such as a printer, disk drive, etc.), or the kernel of the operating system itself. Similarly, even if you've installed Linux on a PC with multiple hard drives, you'll never see a difference in the way Linux treats the separate drives; there will be only one large filesystem.

How Linux Organizes Files and Directories

Most important Linux commands deal with the management of files and directories. Therefore, it's important that we take a moment and explain exactly how Linux treats these files and directories.

Like DOS, Windows, the Macintosh OS, and other versions of UNIX, Linux stores files in a hierarchical fashion; files are stored in directories, and directories (or subdirectories) are stored in other directories. The only directory that's not a subdirectory of another directory is the *root* directory. This directory doesn't have a name (like **bin**, as seen in Table 4.1). Instead, the root directory is indicated by a slash (/). This is the opposite of MS-DOS, which uses the backslash (\) to indicate the root directory. The directory above the current directory in the hierarchy is called the *parent* directory. The Linux installation process creates quite a few directories, including the main subdirectories of the root directory. It's handy to know what's contained in these directories; they'll be the first place to look for specific files. Table 4.1 lists the main directories found in the root directory.

Table 4.1 The Main Subdirectories of the Root Directory

Directory	Contents
bin	Binary files
boot	Information needed to boot the system
cdrom	CD-ROM drive, if Linux supports your CD-ROM drive
dev	Device drivers
etc	Miscellaneous files, mostly used in system administration
home	The home directory for users
lib	Programming libraries
tmp	Temporary storage of temporary files
usr	Commands
var	System definitions

NOTE Case counts in Linux across the board, as you'll learn time and time again. (This is different from DOS, where case doesn't matter.) If you tell Linux to look for a directory named **BIN**, the system won't find this directory. However, if you tell Linux to look for **bin**, the system will find it.

The same goes for Linux commands—when we tell you to use the **cd** command, we mean **cd**, not **Cd**, **CD**, or **cD**. Again, this is different from DOS.

Depending on how you installed Linux, you may also have a directory called **dos**, **dosc**, or something similar, which contains the MS-DOS partition on your hard drive.

Your Home Directory

When you set up a user account in Chapter 2, you also created a *home* directory for the user (in this case, you). You can think of your home directory as a base for operations. When you login the system, you're automatically placed in this directory, and default files for important applications (such as **emacs**) have been automatically been copied to this directory. Generally, it's a good idea to name the directory the same as the login name of the user; in Chapter 2, for example, the home directory was named **kevinr**. The absolute filename of this home directory is **/home/kevinr**.

You should keep all your files in your home directory. In fact, the default Linux installation gives you no choice other than to store your files in this directory, as file permissions don't allow you to write to any other directories. (The root user, on the other hand, can do anything to any directory.) You can create subdirectories, however, to better help you organize the many files that you'll inevitably create as a result of your Linux usage.

You can *always* use the tilde character (~) as a shortcut for the home directory, as you'll see in the following commands.

Moving Between Directories with Cd

At any given time, you can be placed in only one directory, which is your *current* or *working* directory. If you visualize the directory scheme as a hierarchy, you can also visualize moving between various parts of that hierarchy. The Linux command that allows you to move between directories is **cd**. You can use to the **cd** command to point to a specific directory:

```
gilbert:/$ cd /usr
gilbert:/usr$
```

The Bourne Again SHell, or **bash**, is set up by default on Linux systems. **Bash** is designed to show the name of the machine on a prompt (in this instance, *gilbert*), as well as the current directory. (A colon is used to separate the machine name and the current directory.) As you can see in the previous example, the first line shows that the current directory is /, or the root directory. In the second line—after running the **cd** command—the current directory is **/usr**.

We're getting ahead of ourselves here a bit, diving into UNIX commands without every really describing them. For now, suffice it to say that a *command* is a direct instruction to the Linux system.

The **cd** command can be used in many different ways. You can use it to make the root directory your current directory:

```
gilbert:/usr$ cd /
gilbert:/$
```

You can also use it to move up a single directory in the hierarchy. In the next example, your current directory is **/usr/doc** and you want to make the **/usr** directory your current directory. To do this, you'll need to know that Linux always represents the current directory with a period (.) and the parent directory with two periods (..). The following command line, then, would move your current directory to the parent directory:

```
gilbert:/usr/doc$ cd ..
gilbert:/usr$
```

The explanation probably made this example seem more complex than it is.

You can also use **cd** to make a subdirectory your current directory. The trick here is knowing that you'll want to move to a directory relative to your current directory. Knowing that **doc** is a subdirectory of the current directory **/usr**, you would move to the **doc** directory with the following command line:

```
gilbert:/usr$ cd doc
gilbert:/usr/doc$
```

However, if you used the following command line, you'd experience failure:

```
gilbert:/usr$ cd /doc
bash: /doc: No such file or directory
```

You're generating this error message because **doc** and **/doc** would be two different directories—**doc** exists as a subdirectory of the current directory, while **/doc** would need to be a subdirectory of the root directory (hence the leading slash). Beginners are sometimes confused by this point.

Another command line that would generate a failure is:

```
gilbert:~$ cd..
bash: cd..: not found
```

Without the space between the **cd** command and the notation for the higher-level command, the shell doesn't understand your request.

You can also move to your home directory at any time, no matter what the current directory is, with the following command:

```
gilbert:/usr$ cd ~
gilbert:~$
```

The tilde (~) symbol can be used at any time and in other commands as shorthand for your home directory. In addition, using **cd** without a new directory specification will automatically lead you to your home directory:

```
gilbert:/usr$ cd
gilbert:~$
```

There's really only one restriction to the **cd** command: You must have execute permission for the directory you're switching to.

If you decide to go with another Linux shell that *doesn't* list the current directory (see "Linux Shells," later in this chapter) at the beginning of the prompt, you'll need to use the **pwd** (short for *print working directory*) command to print the name of the current working directory:

```
gilbert:/usr$ pwd
/usr
```

File Permissions and Linux

When you first use your Linux system and are not logged in as the root user, you might be in for some rude surprises when you try to write to a directory that's not your own home directory. Essentially, Linux will tell you that you cannot write to the directory.

Because UNIX is a creature centered around security, Linux allows *permissions* to be designated for files and directories. If you lack the proper permissions, you can't change files or directories. The root user, of course, has the proper permissions to access every file in the Linux filesystem (which means that you shouldn't expect absolute security if you're working on a larger system). Under Linux, there are three different levels of permissions: *owner*, *group*, and *world*.

Permissions are an extremely frustrating part of Linux if you're a new user. While there are permissions under DOS, they are not frequently used.

To find what permissions are applied to files, use the following command line:

```
gilbert:/$ ls -l
-rwxrwxrwx  1 kevinr  group1     512 Apr  3 19:12 test
-rwxrwxrwx  1 kevinr  group1     512 Apr  3 19:27 test.bk
drwxrwxrwx  1 kevinr  group1    2146 Apr  1 04:41 memos
-rwx------  1 kevinr  group1     854 Apr  2 19:12 data
```

There's actually a rhyme and reason to the mess of numbers and letters presented here, but it's best explained going right to left in columns (and focusing on the first line of the listings):

- The eighth column (**test**) lists the filename.
- The seventh column (**19:12**) lists the time the file was created.
- The sixth column (**Apr 3**) lists the date the file was created.
- The fifth column (**512**) lists the size of the file in bytes.

- The fourth column (**group1**) lists the group the file belongs to. (We'll explain this later.)

- The third column (**kevinr**) lists the owner of the file.

- The second column (**1**) shows the number of links to the file.

- The first column (**-rwxrwxrwx**) lists the permissions associated with the file and the type of the file.

The leading hyphen (**-**) tells us that the file is an ordinary file, which was covered earlier in this section. When you do an **ls -l**, you'll see various file-type listings, shown in Table 4.2.

Table 4.2 File Types Listed with the ls -l Command Line

Listing	File Type
-	Ordinary file.
d	Directory.
l	Link.

There are other file types listed with this command, but you won't usually see them with Linux.

Permission Lines

The remainder of the first column, covering specific permissions, commands most of our attention in this discussion. Basically, the permissions are broken down into three groups. Remember that permissions are applied to the owner of the file (in this case, **kevinr**), the group of the file (in this case, **group1**), and the world at large. Applying this trinity to a permission line of **rwxrwxrwx**, we can see that the owner has the ability to read the file (indicated by *r*), write the file (indicated by *w*), and execute the file (indicated by *x*). Moving on, the group has the ability to read the file (indicated by *r*), write the file (indicated by *w*), and execute the file (indicated by *x*). Finally, the world has the ability to read the file (indicated by *r*), write the file (indicated by *w*), and execute the file (indicated by *x*). In other words, this file is free game for anyone with access to your Linux filesystem.

Things are a little different with the following listing:

```
-rwx------  1 kevinr  group1    854 Apr  2 19:12 data
```

When there are no letters indicating a permission—as in the case with the hyphen—the permissions are restricted. With this file, the owner has the ability to read the file (indicated by *r*), write the file (indicated by *w*), and execute the file (indicated by *w*). However, no one else has *any* permissions with this file.

With most of the Linux operating system, you'll see a permission like **rwxr-xr-x**, with **root** being the owner of the file. In this instance, an average user (that is, someone not logged in as **root**) has the ability to execute files (an important capability to have) and read the files but lacks the ability to write (that is, change) the file. This protection exists for many reasons, but basically it exists to prevent users from wreaking unanticipated havoc.

When you install and configure new software on your Linux system and want to install it in one of the standard file locations, you'll need to login as **root**.

Changing Permissions

The Linux command **chmod** changes file permissions. You may want to change permissions for some popular directories in order to avoid logging in as **root** to install or configure software.

Unless you have write permission for a file or directory, you can't change the permissions. Of course, this means that you need to be logged in as **root** in order to change permissions.

Permissions can be changed in *numeric* or *symbolic* form. Neither method is what could be called intuitive, so we'll spend some time explaining each of them.

The Numeric Method

The numeric method uses numbers to track permissions. Like the permissions listings earlier in this section, the numeric method divides permissions into threes, albeit in a different manner.

The numeric method forces you to add three different sets of numbers in determining who has which permissions. The actual types of permissions (owner, group, world) haven't changed—only the method of listing them.

You'll use *modes* to track permissions, as seen in Table 4.3.

Table 4.3 Modes and Their Meanings

Mode	Meaning
400	Owner has read permission.
200	Owner has write permission.
100	Owner has execute permission.
040	Group has read permission.
020	Group has write permission.
010	Group has execute permission.
004	World has read permission.
002	World has write permission.
001	World has execute permission.

You must now translate these numbers into the numeric form by adding them together. For example, using the following directory listing:

```
-rwx--x--x  1 kevinr  group1    854 Apr  2 19:12 test
```

we arrive at a numeric permission of 711:

400	Owner has read permission.
200	Owner has write permission.
100	Owner has execute permission.
010	Group has execute permission.
001	World has execute permission.
———	
711	

A file or directory that's totally open to the world would have a permission of 777; a file or directory inaccessible to anyone would have a permission of 000.

Changing the permissions entails combining the desired permissions with the **chmod** command. For example, to change the file permissions of the **test** command to make it totally accessible to all users, you'd use the following command line:

```
gilbert:/$ chmod 777 test
```

To change the permissions so that only the owner of the file has the ability to totally access the file and at the same time permission is denied to every other user, you'd use the following command line:

```
gilbert:/$ chmod 700 test
```

To change the permissions so that the owner of the file has the ability to totally access the file, but other users and the group have the ability to read and execute (but not change) the file, you'd use the following command line:

```
gilbert:/$ chmod 744 test
```

The Symbolic Method

When using the numeric method, you don't need to know the existing permissions of the file, which means that you need enter only the desired permissions. The other main method of setting permissions, called the *symbolic* method, requires that you know the existing permissions, as you're setting new permissions relative to the existing permissions.

The symbolic method eschews numerals and uses letters instead. And it's very precise in adding or subtracting permissions relative to existing permissions. For example, the following command line gives execute permissions to the world (all users):

```
gilbert:/$ chmod o+x data
```

Here, *o* refers to "others" (in **chmod** parlance, the world), *x* refers to execute permission, and the plus sign (+) adds the execute permission to others. If a minus sign (-) were used, this command line would remove execute permission from others.

The symbolic method uses some quirky language, as you've already seen with the reference to others. The owner of the file is referred to as the user, and setting permissions for the owner means using *u*:

```
gilbert:/$ chmod u+x data
```

Setting the permission for the group is a matter of using *g*:

```
gilbert:/$ chmod g+x data
```

These statements, of course, would be meaningless if the users already had the ability to execute the file.

Table 4.4 lists the various symbols used with the **chmod** command.

Table 4.4 Symbols Used with the Symbolic Method

Symbol	Meaning
u	User (owner of the file).
g	Group.
o	Other (the world).
a	Everyone (the owner, the group, and the world).
+	Adds permission.
-	Removes permission.
r	Read permission.
w	Write permission.
x	Execute permission.
t	Sets the "sticky bit" on a directory.

If you create your own shell scripts or use the Perl language, you'll need to set permissions to make your scripts usable.

Changing Ownerships and Permissions

In the act of creating a file or directory, you automatically assign permissions to the file or directory. To see what permissions are the default, use the **umask** command:

```
$ umask
744
```

This means that the owner of the file has full privileges, while your group and the world have the ability to read the file. To change this permission, you'll again use the **umask** command, listing a new permission on the command line:

```
$ umask 007
```

This may look odd, and indeed it is odd. The **umask** command changes permissions relative to a baseline of 777. The input to the **umask** command is therefore subtracted from the baseline 777, leaving you with the total of 770, meaning that the owner of the file and the group have full permissions to the file, while the rest of the world has no permissions at all.

In the same way, you're automatically the owner of a file when you create it, but there may be times when you want to transfer this ownership to another user. You can do so with the **chown** command, provided you're logged in the system as the root user. (You didn't think you could change the ownership logged in as an ordinary user, did you? If *anyone* could change the ownership of a file, security in the UNIX operating system would be nonexistent.) When using the **chown** (short for change ownership, by the way) command, you list the new owner of the command and the file in question:

```
gilbert:~$ chown pat report
```

You can also transfer ownership of an entire directory by using the *-R* option to the **chown** command:

```
gilbert:~$ chown -R pat reports_1996
```

Similarly, the **chgrp** command changes group ownership of a file, listing the new group membership and the file in question:

```
gilbert:~$ chgrp linux_book chap4
```

The Sticky Bit

In our continuing obsession with security, we present information about the sticky bit. In the past, UNIX hackers used to get around file permissions by messing with entire directories, as most system administrators would forget to set restrictive permissions for the directory itself.

The sticky bit was a response to this security problem. Linux allows you to set the sticky bit, which makes a directory impregnable to everyone but the owner of a directory and the root user. To set the sticky bit, use the **chmod** command in the following manner:

```
gilbert:/$ chmod +t directoryname
```

Once the sticky bit is set, no one (except the root user and the owner of the directory) has the ability to move or delete files in a directory, no matter what permissions are associated with a file.

Dealing with Files and Directories

We've thrown around the term *command* a great deal without ever really defining it (our copy editor is probably gnawing her red pen by this point), but we're assuming you know what a command is and how you give a command to the computer. And you also know that the combination of a command and any options is called a *command line*.

 NOTE Under Linux, commands can be run at a command line or under the X Window System in an **xterm** window (which we covered in Chapter 3). However, there are some cases when there's an X Window version of the UNIX command; for example, there's a version of **man** for the X Window System, called **xman**, that you should use instead. In this chapter, we'll also note the X Window version.

If you've used MS-DOS for any extended period, you'll instantly recognize the Linux counterparts presented here. If you've used Microsoft Windows for an extended period and have been hidden from the command line, you may be somewhat confused initially when you run through this series of Linux commands. And if you're a UNIX workstation user, you'll find that there might be slight differences between the commands/options and the version of UNIX you're used to working with. (If you're a Cray supercomputer user, you're *really* slumming.)

This section will touch only on the most basic and useful Linux commands. For a more complete listing of Linux commands, check out *Linux in Plain English*—coming out shortly—or *teach yourself . . . UNIX, Third Edition* (MIS:Press) both listed in Appendix A.

You've already learned about the **cd** and **pwd** commands, which are used to move between directories and print the working directory, respectively. There are many more Linux commands used to deal with directories and files.

Listing Files and Directories with Ls and Dir

You'll use the **ls** command, short for *list*, quite often—probably every time you use Linux, as a matter of fact. You've already used **ls** in a discussion of permissions. The following command lists the contents of the current directory or a specified directory:

```
gilbert:/$ ls
bin/        dev/       home/         mnt/       sbin/      var/
boot/       dos/       lib/          proc/      tmp/       vmlinuz
cdrom/      etc/       lost+found    root/      usr/
```

If you're a UNIX user, this is probably not the version of **ls** you're used to, especially if you try this command on your own Linux box. The **ls** version contained with Linux is actually the GNU version of **ls**. As such, it makes several improvements to the basic **ls** command found on other versions of UNIX. One improvement, which we can't show you in the confines of a black-and-white text, is the addition of color to indicate directories (which will appear on your color monitor as blue) and special types of files. (Later in this section we'll explain how to change these colors and what the colors mean.) Linux also uses slashes after the name to indicate directories.

In addition, **ls** (by default) sorts files and directories in ASCII order, in columns. That's why the first column contains the directories beginning with *b* and *c*, followed by the rest of the alphabet. If there were directories that began with any capital letter, they'd be listed first; the directory **X/** would appear before **bin/**, because under ASCII uppercase letters precede lowercase letters.

 The Bourne Again SHell, **bash**, also supports the **dir** command in a limited sense. The **dir** command does the same thing as the **ls -l** command, which will be explained later in this section. DOS users will be relieved to know that their familiar **dir** command can also be used under Linux.

You can use one of the many command-line options to the **ls** command. For example, if you use the **ls** command in your home directory, you'll discover that there are no apparent files to be found:

```
gilbert:~$ ls
gilbert:~$
```

However, if you run the command with the *-a* option, you'll see the following:

```
gilbert:~$ ls -a
./        .bash_history    .kermrc       .lessrc
../       .emacs           .less         .term/
```

The files beginning with the period (.) are called *hidden* files. Actually, they're not so hidden as to be mysterious; they're merely hidden when you use the **ls** command to search for files. The *-a* option tells the **ls** command to look for *all* files.

There are two other listings—. and ..—that may be unfamiliar if you're not a UNIX user. The single period (.) is merely another way to display the current directory, while the double period (..) is used to display the parent directory.

The *-l* (ell, not one) option to **ls** prints a long list of the directory's contents:

```
gilbert:~$ ls -l
```

The **ls** command can also be used to determine the existence of a single file in short form:

```
gilbert:~$ ls data
data
```

or in long form:

```
gilbert:~$ ls -l data
-rwx------  1 kevinr  group1     854 Apr  2 19:12 data
```

Table 4.5 summarizes the **ls** command's important options.

Table 4.5 A Summary of the Ls Command Options

Option	Result
-a	Lists all files, including hidden files.
-A	Lists all files, except for the . and .. listings.
-c	Sorts files by the time they were last changed, rather than by the default ASCII order, beginning with the oldest file.
-d	Lists only the name of a directory, not its contents.
-l	Lists files and directories in long format.
-r	Lists the contents in reverse order.
-t	Sorts files by the time they were last changed beginning with the newest file.
-x	Lists files and sorts them across the page instead of by columns.

The **ls** command isn't the only tool for viewing files and directories on a Linux system. If you've installed XFree86, there's a file manager that can be used to graphically display the contents of your Linux system (see Chapter 5 for details). And there's a command-line tool, the Midnight Commander, that works similarly to the Norton Commander (a once-popular MS-DOS application) (see Chapter 5 for details).

Changing the Ls Colors

Although we can't show you, **ls** does indeed display different types of files in different colors. While you probably don't want to change these colors, Linux gives you the ability to do so. (Indeed, Linux gives you the ability to do a great many things you'll probably never bother to do, but that's to the credit of the people who put Linux together.) The settings for these colors are stored in the file **/etc/DIR_COLORS**, and this file is used by all users. If you want to change these settings, you need to copy this file to your home directory, rename the file **.dir_colors** (making it a hidden file), and edit the listings in the file. As with many of the configuration files used with Linux, there's enough comments in the default **/etc/DIR_COLORS** to guide you through any editing session.

Wildcards

Like UNIX (and DOS, for that matter), Linux supports wildcards in command lines and shells scripts. A *wildcard* is merely shorthand for a character or a string of characters. Wildcards can come in handy if you're looking for a file and you've forgotten the specific filename (geez, I *know* the file ends in *1996*), or if you want to see a list of files that fall within specific parameters (such as ending with *.c*, useful if you plan on using Linux for software development).

There are three types of Linux wildcards: *, ?, and [...]. Each will be explained.

Technically, wildcards are the province of the shell, and in theory a discussion of wildcards should take place with a discussion of shells. For our purposes, however, we're going to discuss wildcards at this point in the Linux discussion, because what we're saying here applies to all shells.

In the previous section covering the **ls** command, we covered the command's use when it's applied to single files. However, there may be times when you want to list a set of files that share a common characteristic, such as ending with *.c*. In this instance, you can tell **ls** to look for every file that ends with *.c*, using the following command line:

```
gilbert:~$ ls *.c
aardvark.c      stuff.c      titles.c      xylophone.c
```

In this instance, **ls** is told to substitute * for any portion of a filename preceding an ending of *.c*. And, as you can see from the list of files, the command was successful. The **ls** is used to match any number of characters in a string, including zero characters:

```
gilbert:~$ ls titles*
titles     titles.c
```

In the case of *titles*, the wildcard matched zero characters.

The asterisk (*) can be used at the beginning or end of a wildcard expression. You can also use more than one asterisk in an expression:

```
gilbert:~$ ls t*.*
titles.c
```

If you wanted to list the files with the string *titles* anywhere in the filename, you could use the following command line:

```
gilbert:~$ ls *titles*
subtitles     titles     titles.c
```

The asterisk wildcard is the most expansive wildcard available. On the other end of the spectrum is the question-mark wildcard, which is used to match a single character:

```
gilbert:~$ ls title?
titles
```

In this instance, **ls** did not match **titles.c**, which contains *two* characters after the search string of *title*. **Titles**, meanwhile, contained only one character after the search string of *title*, which matched the parameters of the **ls** command.

The final wildcard is used to return specific characters, as defined by brackets (**[]**). For example, you're looking through a directory filled with memos from the last 12 months. Since you've been a good Linux user, you've been placing a number at the end of every file, signifying the month it was written. (Yes, we know you're not likely to have too many files if you've just installed Linux. Think of this advice as something you'll need in the future.) You want to track down a memo you wrote sometime in the summer, but you can't remember the name of the file, and a reading through the directory listings don't spark a memory. In this instance, you'll want to narrow down the directory listings to files ending in *6, 7*, or *8* (corresponding to June, July, and August). To do this with the **ls** command, you'd enter **6–8** in brackets:

```
gilbert:~/memos$ ls *[6-8]
golf.8        golfanne.8    golfpat.6     golfjim.6
golftod.6     golftom.7
```

This narrows down the list of files returned by **ls**. It also means you probably play too much golf.

In the preceding example, we asked **ls** to return files that ended with a range of characters, i.e., in *6, 7*, or *8*. You can also use this wildcard to return a single character:

```
gilbert:~/memos$ ls *[6]
golfpat.6     golfjim.6     golftod.6
```

If you're searching for a character (remembering, of course, that Linux distinguishes between uppercase and lowercase letters at all times) or range of characters, you can list them in the brackets:

```
gilbert:~/memos$ ls report.[Ee]rc
report.Erc     report.erc
```

Wildcards can be used with any Linux command.

Creating Directories with Mkdir

The **mkdir** command is used to create directories. If you plan on using Linux for most of your day-to-day stuff, we advise creating directories to help organize the many files Linux (and any other version of UNIX, for that matter) creates. Using **mkdir** is simple:

```
gilbert:~$ mkdir directory
```

where *directory* is the name of the directory you want to create. To create a directory named **letters** in your home directory, you'd use the following command:

```
gilbert:~$ mkdir letters
```

To see if the directory was really created, you can use the **ls** command:

```
gilbert:~$ ls
letters/     text
```

You can also use it to create a new directory elsewhere in the directory hierarchy:

```
gilbert:~$ mkdir /users/kevin/letters
gilbert:~$ ls /users/kevin
letters/
```

Mkdir can create more than one directory on a command line:

```
gilbert:~$ mkdir letters data
gilbert:~$ ls
data/          letters/     text
```

Mkdir can also create a directory and a subdirectory in a single command line:

```
gilbert:~$ mkdir -p /letters/eric
```

Other options to **mkdir** are listed in Table 4.6.

Table 4.6 Other Options to the Mkdir Command

Option	Result
m *mode*	Sets the mode for the new directory.

Using Cat

The **cat** command does so many things under the UNIX and Linux operating systems, it's a wonder you don't use it for everything. On a very basic level, **cat** can be used to view the contents of a file:

```
gilbert:~$ cat filename
```

where *filename* is the name of the file you want to view. For example, to view the contents of a file named **test**, you'd use the following command line:

```
gilbert:~$ cat test
This is our Linux test file. Big whoop.
```

Cat, by default, displays its output to the screen. However, **cat** can be told to send its output elsewhere, which brings us to another of its many uses: It can also be used to store a file under a different filename, much in the manner of the **cp** command (which will be covered later in this chapter). For example, to create another copy of the **test** file (which we'll call **memo.kr**), you'd use the following command line:

```
gilbert:~$ cat test > memo.kr
gilbert:~$ ls
memo.kr     test
```

In this example, **cat** uses the output from the **test** file as the input for the **memo.kr** file.

Cat can also be used to create simple ASCII files; we say *simple* because **cat** sends your keyboard input directly to a file, rather than giving you the chance to edit the file. (The full-screen editors **elvis** and **emacs** can be used to edit files.) To create a simple file named **memo**, you'd use the following command line:

```
gilbert:~$ cat > memo
```

Anything you type would go directly into the **memo** file one line at a time. When creating a file like this, there are a few things to remember:

- Hit the **Enter** key at the end of every line. Otherwise, part of your typing will end up in the ether.
- You can move within the line using the **Backspace** key (well, partially, anyway; **Backspace** will merely delete the preceding character). You can't move to a previous line, however.
- Type **Ctrl-D** when you're finished typing.

The **Ctrl-D** sequence can be used whenever you run a Linux command that requires keyboard input.

Finally, **cat** can be used to combine files. For example, you can add to the aforementioned **memo** file with the following command line:

```
gilbert:~$ cat >> memo
```

Whatever you type will be added to the **memo** file. The previous rules apply. In addition, you can redirect two existing files as input to a new third file:

```
gilbert:~$ cat memo1 memo2 > memo3
```

The order of the files on the command line determines the order of the data in the new file.

There are a host of options to the **cat** command; they are listed in Table 4.7.

Table 4.7 Options to the Cat Command

Option	Result
-b	Numbers all lines, except for those not containing characters.
-n	Numbers all lines.
-s	Replaces a series of blank lines with a single blank line.
-v	Prints nonprinting (i.e., control) characters.

Other Ways to View a File

Linux contains two handy tools for viewing a file: **more** and **less**. The **more** command is pretty simple; the following command line launches **more** with the file **test**:

```
gilbert:~$ more test
```

The **more** command presents one page of text at a time, with the percentage of text displayed at the bottom of the screen. Use the **Enter** key to move forward one line in the document, or press the **Spacebar** to move ahead an entire page. Unfortunately, you can't move back to the beginning of a file once it's scrolled by.

In addition, **more** gives you the ability to search for a specific text string, by typing:

```
/string
```

where *string* is the text string you want to search for.

Where Less is More Than More

The **less** command isn't part of the standard UNIX distribution, but it's a very useful addition to the Linux command set. The **less** command provides more options when viewing a file—namely, the ability to move both forward and backward through a file. Again, to use **less** to view the file named **test**, you'd use the following command line:

```
gilbert:~$ less test
```

As with **more**, you can use the /*string* option to search for text.

A big advantage to **less** is its ability to search backward through a file by pressing **b**.

An X Window version of this program, **xless**, is also included as part of Slackware.

Using Head and Tail to View Portions of a File

If a file is especially large, you may not want to load all of it and try to scroll through it, particularly if you're just interested in a quick glance at its contents. In this case, you can use the **head** command to view the beginning of the fil, or tail to view the end of the file. For both commands, the default is to display 10 lines. Therefore, to display the first 10 lines of the file **report**, you'd use the following command line:

```
gilbert:~$ head report
```

To view the last 10 lines of the file **report**, you'd use the following command line:

```
gilbert:~$ tail report
```

To change the default of 10 lines, you'd specify a new number as an argument to the command; the following, for example, displays the first 20 lines of the file **report**:

```
gilbert:~$ head -20 report
```

Viewing an Octal Dump with Od

Finally, there's the **od** command, which allows you to view an octal dump of a file:

```
$ od filename
```

where *filename* is the name of the file to be viewed.

Finding the Magic Number with File

After you've been working on your Linux system for a while, you'll accumulate many files if you do any serious work at all. If you're a careful worker, you'll be able to keep track of files by their locations and filenames. However, if you're not a careful worker, you may run into situations where you have no idea what a file contains. You don't want to view a binary file with **cat** or another command designed to view text files, because doing so will probably result in huge amounts of garbage being displayed to your screen (which may require you to try and relogin your system).

Linux features a command, **file**, that will look at a file and return specific information about the contents of the file (most of the time, anyway). The UNIX world of late has supported *magic numbers*, and in theory these numbers—found somewhere in the binary file—should match a database of magic numbers on your system. (These magic numbers can be found in the **/etc/magic** file.) To run **file** on a file named **45edfsdwe**, you'd use the following command line:

```
gilbert:~$ file 45edfsdwe
```

At the very least, **file** will tell you the file's type (executable, ordinary, etc.) and how it's compiled (such as *dynamically linked*). If you're lucky, the **file** command will also tell you if the file is related to your machine. However, if this file is merely text, you'll see the following information:

```
gilbert:~$ file 45edfsdwe
45edfsdwe                        text
```

Copying Files with Cp

The **cp** command is used to copy existing files. When you use the **cp** command, the original file is left intact. This is handy when copying files to another user's machine (provided you're networked, of course) or to another directory for backup purposes. (There are more formal ways to make system backups on your Linux system, of course, but the **cp** command works well for single files or small groups of files.) The following command line copies a file named **textfile** to the **/home/eric** directory:

```
gilbert:~$ cp textfile /home/eric
```

When this command is run, the file named **textfile** will appear in both your home directory and *eric's* home directory.

You may want to give **textfile** a new name when it's moved to the new directory. In this case, you're giving **textfile** a new name of **textfile.kr** when it's moved to the **/home/eric** directory:

```
gilbert:~$ cp textfile /home/eric/textfile.kr
```

 Linux will do exactly what you tell it to do. In some cases, this is a good thing. In other cases, this is a very bad thing—as can be the case with the **cp** and **mv** commands.

If (using the previous command-line example) there were already a file called **textfile.kr** in the **/home/eric** directory, the **cp** command would overwrite the existing file with the new file. The **cp** command, by default, doesn't check to see if there's a file already in that directory with the same name. (The same goes for the **mv** command; this will be covered in the next section, "Moving and Renaming Files with mv.")

On the other hand, both the **cp** and **mv** commands have an option (*-i*) that prevents you from overwriting existing files, as seen in this command line:

```
gilbert:~$ cp -i textfile /home/eric/textfile.kr
cp: overwrite `textfile.kr'?
```

If you type **y**, **cp** will overwrite the existing **textfile.kr**. If you type anything else, **cp** will not overwrite the file.

Options to the **cp** command are listed in Table 4.8.

Copying Directories with Cp

cp also has the power to copy entire directories (including all files and subdirectories), in the form of the *-r* option:

```
gilbert:~$ cp -r /users/data /users/eric
```

Table 4.8 Options to the cp Command

Option	Result
-d	Maintains a symbolic link as a link rather than as a copy of the original file.
-i	Prevents overwriting of existing files with the same filename.
-p	Retains the existing permissions.
-r	Copies the entire directory structure, including subdirectories.
-v	Runs in verbose mode; lists each file as it's copied.

Moving and Renaming Files with Mv

The **mv** command is used to move files from one directory to another. This command doesn't leave a copy of the original file in the original location (for that, use the **cp** command); it deletes the original copy and inserts the new copy in the new location.

The following command line would move the **textfile** file to the new home (~) location:

```
gilbert:/usr$ mv textfile ~
```

If you were to run the **ls**, you'd find that **textfile** didn't appear in /**usr**, but was now located in your home directory.

In this example, **textfile** retains its current filename, no matter where you move it. You can also use the **mv** command to rename a file. (In fact, it's one of the few ways to actually rename a file, because there's no command for doing so within Linux.) The following command changes the **textfile** filename to **aardvark**:

```
gilbert:~$ mv textfile aardvark
```

The following command line would move **textfile** to a new directory *and* give it a new filename of **aardvark**:

```
gilbert:/usr$ mv textfile ~/aardvark
```

Linux can be fairly harsh when you're moving and renaming files. For example, the **mv** command will overwrite an existing file with a renamed file and not warn you. If you ran the following command line and a file named **aardvark** already existed in your home directory, you'd be in trouble:

```
gilbert:/usr$ mv textfile ~/aardvark
```

as **mv** would overwrite the original **aardvark** file with the new **aardvark** file. To avoid this problem, use the-*i* option with the **mv** command:

```
gilbert:/usr$ mv -i textfile ~/aardvark

mv: overwrite 'aardvark'?
```

Type **y** if you want to overwrite **aardvark, n** (or any other key) if you do not. A summary of the options to **mv** are listed in Table 4.9.

Table 4.9 A Summary of the Mv Command Options

Option	Result
-f	Overwrites existing file.
-I	Checks before overwriting existing files.

Removing Files with Rm

The **rm** (short for *remove*) command removes files. Simple enough, right? To remove a file, simply list it on the command line:

```
gilbert:~$ rm aardvark
```

Aardvark will then be swiftly and painlessly removed—so swiftly that you won't have a chance to confirm your choice. However, like the other commands listed in this chapter, you can tell Linux to confirm your file deletions, in the form of the -*i* option:

```
gilbert:~$ rm -i aardvark
rm: remove 'aardvark'?
```

Type **y** if you want to remove **aardvark, n** (or any other key) if you do not. Other options to the **rm** command are listed in Table 4.10.

Table 4.10 Options to the Rm Command

Option	Result
-f	Removes the file without any input from you.
-i	Runs in interactive mode.
-v	Runs in verbose mode, which means files are listed as they are removed.

Be warned that when you remove a file under Linux, you're *really* removing the file from existence.

If you're a PC or Macintosh user, you may have gotten spoiled by utilities like The Norton Utilities, which can "unerase" files that have been erased. At this time, no such utilities exist for Linux.

Be careful when you combine the **rm** command and wildcards, because a wildcard—especially an asterisk—in the wrong spot can wreak havoc with your system. For example, let's say that you wanted to delete all the files ending with *.golf* on your system (let's say the boss is beginning to be a little suspicious about your afternoon field trips and you want to remove any incriminating evidence). So you tell Linux to remove all files ending with *golf*— or you think you are, anyway:

```
gilbert:~/memos$ rm * golf
```

Disaster ensues. Because you placed a space between the asterisk wildcard and the rest of the command line, the **rm** command uses only the asterisk as an argument, ignoring the *golf* part of the command line. Since *every* file is returned by the asterisk wildcard, you've just removed all the files in your current directory. (By the way, the chance of this happening is an excellent argument for using the *-i* option at all times and setting it up as an alias.)

Viewing Online-Manual Pages with Man

One of the handiest feature of UNIX—and by extension, of Linux—is the existence of online-manual pages, which detail the workings of specific commands. These online-manual pages (commonly referred to as *man* pages) will list the purpose of a given command, any command-line options, and perhaps other information. (For example, **man** pages created by the FSF for use with GNU commands tend to be rather verbose, going into the entire purpose of the command and listing any known bugs.) While this sort of information isn't as useful as a full online help system (for example, you can't look up a **man** page for any topics at all; **man** pages are written for specific commands), it still can help you a great deal, especially if you know a certain command can come close to doing what you want, but you need to know the precise option that yields the desired behavior.

To view an online-manual page, combine the name of the command with the **man** command:

```
gilbert:/$ man man
```

You'll then see the information shown in Figure 4.1.

```
man(1)                                                              man(1)

NAME
       man - format and display the on-line manual pages
       manpath - determine user's search path for man pages

SYNOPSIS
       man [-adfhktw] [-m  system] [-p string] [-C config_file]
       [-M path] [-P pager] [-S section_list] [section] name  ...

DESCRIPTION
       man formats  and displays the on-line manual pages.  This
       version knows about  the  MANPATH  and  PAGER  environment
       variables, so you can have your own set(s) of personal man
       pages and choose whatever program you like to display  the
       formatted pages.  If section is specified, man only looks
       in that section of the manual.  You may also  specify  the
       order to search the sections for entries and which prepro-
       cessors to run  on  the  source  files  via  command  line
       options  or  environment  variables.  If name contains a /
       then it is first tried as a filename, so that you can  do
       man ./foo.5 or even man /cd/foo/bar.1.gz.

OPTIONS
       -C  config_file
              Specify  the man.config file to use; the default is
              /usr/lib/man.config. (See man.config(5).)

line 1
```

Figure 4.1 The **man** command in action.

The **man** page for **man** is obviously a multipage document, as evidenced by the information at the bottom of the screen, because the bottom sentence isn't complete. To move up and down through the entire **man** page by entire pages, use the **PageUp** and **PageDown** keys; to move up and down the **man** page line by line, use the keyboard cursor keys (↑ and ↓). To quit the **man** command and get a command prompt, press the **q** key (short for *quit*).

There's an X Window equivalent of **man**, called **xman**, shown in Figure 4.2. You should use this command when running XFree86.

```
┌────────────────────────────────────────────────────────────┐
│ ● Manual Page                                            ⊡  │
├─────────────────┬──────────────────────────────────────────┤
│ Options │ Sections │              Xman Help                 │
├────────────────────────────────────────────────────────────┤
│                                                              │
│   XMAN is an X Window System manual browsing tool.           │
│                                                              │
│                                                              │
│   GETTING STARTED                                            │
│                                                              │
│   By default, xman starts by creating a small window that contains │
│   three "buttons" (places on which to click a pointer button). Two of │
│   these buttons, Help and Quit, are self-explanatory. The third, Manual │
│   Page, creates a new manual page browser window; you may use this │
│   button to open a new manual page any time xman is running.  │
│                                                              │
│   A new manual page starts up displaying this help information. The │
│   manual page contains three sections. In the upper left corner are two │
│   menu buttons. When the mouse is clicked on either of these buttons a │
│   menu is popped up. The contents of these menus is described below. │
│   Directly to the right of the menu buttons is an informational display. │
│   This display usually contains the name of the directory or manual page │
│   being displayed. It is also used to display warning messages and the │
│   current version of xman. The last and largest section is the │
│   information display. This section of the application contains either │
│   a list of manual pages to choose from or the text of a manual page. │
│                                                              │
└────────────────────────────────────────────────────────────┘
```

Figure 4.2 The **xman** command in action.

The **bash** shell contains its own help mechanism, which will be covered later in this chapter.

Finding Files

The **find** command included with Linux (actually the GNU **find** command) is very similar to the **find** command that ships with most other versions of UNIX—that is, the GNU version is maddeningly complex and nonintuitive to use. At its best, **find** will search your entire filesystem for a specific file. At its worse, **find** will return every file on the system, leaving you scratching your head about how to proceed with a useful search.

Still, you shouldn't run into too many problems with **find** if you remember one thing: You need to make sure all the elements of the command line are properly organized. For example, you won't find the following command line very useful:

```
gilbert:~$ find *
```

as it returns all the files in your current directory. Similarly, the following command line will list *every* file (at a dizzying speed, no less) on your Linux system:

```
gilbert:/$ find *
```

a move guaranteed to give you a headache. (Remember, Linux does exactly what you tell it to do.)

Instead, you'll need to slow down and figure out how to use the **find** command. Let's say you want to find the directory location of a file named **test.bk**. First, you need to tell **find** how to search for a file. We know the name of the file, so we begin our command line by telling **find** to search by filename. We do so with the *-name* option:

```
gilbert:/$ find * -name
```

This is a start. Now we need to tell **find** what to look for. We do this by adding the name of the file:

```
gilbert:~$ find * -name test.bk
```

If you wanted, you could use a wildcard instead of listing the specific filename. With or without a wildcard, however, the command should work.

If you're working with a large filesystem, you may want to run the **find** command in the background. This is accomplished by adding an ampersand to the command line:

```
gilbert:~$ find * -name test.bk &
```

Running this command in the background allows you to do work while the **find** command searches for the file. For more information on running commands in the background, check out the section "Background Commands and Multitasking" later in this chapter.

 When looking at other Linux texts, you'll be able to see who actually wrote the book using Linux and who wrote the book with a knowledge of UNIX and not much experience with Linux by the way the **find** command is explained. In most versions of UNIX, the **find** command requires that *-print* be added to the end of the command line and that the name of the search be in quotation marks. The GNU version of **find** requires neither.

There's a lot more to the **find** command, as it encompasses an amazing amount of complexity that's meant for large-scale systems more than for the needs of the average Linux user. If you're interested in knowing more about the **find** command, use the following command line:

```
gilbert:~$ man find
```

Linking Files

Linux allows you to create links to other files. As a matter of fact, when you installed Linux, you unwittingly set up dozens of linked files (which you'd see if you did an **ls -l** listing of many of the XFree86-related directories). If you're a single user, you probably won't have much need to link files; after all, you're not sharing data with anyone else, and you're not necessarily trying to distribute data efficiently in limited disk space.

However, if you're using Linux on a network, you may find it advantageous to create a linked file or two. For example, you're working with Pat and Eric on a large project, and you want to share a file containing important addresses. This file is updated regularly by all of you. Instead of all three of you maintaining separate files and trying to synchronize the changes regularly, the better move would be to create one main file and create links to that file. In this way, all changes can be seen by the other users, and there's less of an administrative hassle in keeping the file current. It also cuts down on the hard disk space needed, as there's only one file actually stored on the hard drive.

To link a file named **addresses** to Eric's home directory, you'd use the following command line:

```
gilbert:~$ ln addresses /home/eric
```

To link a file named **addresses** to Pat's home directory, you'd use the following command line:

```
gilbert:~$ ln addresses /home/pat
```

After this is done, Eric and Pat will see the file **addresses** in their directories. However, the actual file won't be in their directory; instead, a link to the file **addresses** in *your* home directory will be there. There's one drawback to this, however; you can't delete the original file **addresses** until the links have been deleted, as Linux treats all hard links equally. Therefore, to get rid of **addresses**, you'd need to remove (with the **rm** command) **/home/eric/addresses** and **/home/pat/addresses** before you remove the **addresses** file in your directory. If you haven't created many links, you can probably keep track of this; if you have, you may find that you haven't kept good track of the links and you may be stymied in your attempt to delete the original file.

Some UNIX purists advise setting up links whenever possible, arguing that hard-disk space should be conserved at all times. However, we're not of this mindset. Indeed, the fewer links you can create, the better it will be for all of you. System administrators need to set up links occasionally, so this practice should be mainly reserved for them. We present the mechanics of creating links, but we don't endorse the practice on a large scale.

Symbolic Links

In the preceding examples, we covered what's known as *hard links*. (After seeing what you need to go through to delete a linked file, you know why they're called *hard*.) Linux also supports *symbolic links*; unlike hard links, symbolic links don't need to be physically deleted if you want to delete the original linked file. (There are some other differences, of course, but they aren't important to this discussion.)

To set up a symbolic link, use the *-s* option to the **ln** command:

```
gilbert:~$ ln -s addresses /home/pat
```

Viewing a File with Cal

The **cal** command lists a one-month calendar:

```
gilbert:~$ cal
```

If you want to view a calendar for the entire year (in this case, 1995), enter the following command line:

```
gilbert:~$ cal 1995
```

To stop the scrolling, type **Ctrl-S**; to start it again, type **Ctrl-Q**. To stop the calendar entirely, type **Ctrl-D**.

Virtual Terminals

Linux allows you to be in more than one place at a time, with the notion of *virtual terminals*. UNIX, inherently, supports multiple users on a system at any given time. A virtual terminal allows you to login more than once on a Linux box. While this may not be something you would normally do, there may be times when it will come in handy; for example, Chapter 6 will outline a time when it's convenient to login as another user when using the X Window System in order to kill some errant processes. While doing this, you'll still be logged in the initial terminal.

To move between virtual terminals, you type **Alt-F***n*, where **F***n* is the function key associated with the terminal. (It is *not* the **Fn** key found on most laptops. On laptops, the **Fn** key is used basically as a **Shift** key for the function keys.) The initial login to a Linux system is always associated with the **F1** function key, so any additional logins will begin with the **F2** key.

When you're finished in the virtual terminal, you should logout with the following command:

```
logout
```

Linux and Passwords

When you added a user account, you set up a password for that account. Depending on your usage, the password you select may or may not be important. On the one hand, it's nice to have some security on a machine containing all your work, even if only to deter the mischievous actions of a fellow family member. On the other hand, you don't want to be messing with an obscure (and forgettable) password, especially if you won't be using Linux every day.

So the choice about your password is really yours. If you're installing Linux in a corporate environment, however, you should follow these basic rules regarding passwords:

- Your password must be longer than two characters, but generally not more than eight characters long. In addition, it must begin with a lowercase letter.

- Always use a password longer than six characters. The longer the password, the harder it is to hack.

- Don't use a password based on personal information. You may think it's clever to use your dog's name as a password, but anyone who knows you can make an informed guess about your password. Similarly, don't use your spouse's name, your lover's name (however romantic it may be), your middle name, your job title, or any other readily available information about you.

- Don't use a word that can be found in a dictionary. Hackers have been known to throw a computer-based dictionary at login prompts, waiting for one of the words to open the door.

- Make sure your password is memorable but meaningless to anyone but you. Let's say that Kirby Puckett is your favorite baseball player. You were ecstatic the last time the Twins won the World Series. Put them together and you have **puck1991** as a password.

- There's a time-honored trick in the UNIX world to combine an easily remembered password with the vagaries of system security. First, choose a word that you know you'll remember, like the aforementioned *kirby*. Then look at your keyboard. For your real password, use the keys to the upper left of the keys for our word. In this case, the password becomes **u84g6**.

- Never send your password over electronic mail, no matter how many times lovely spies named Natasha ask you for it.
- Don't scrawl your password on a Post-It note and stick it next to your terminal.

Changing Your Password with Passwd

If you do want to change your password, you'd use the **passwd** command (not to be confused with the **pwd** command, covered earlier in this chapter):

```
gilbert:~$ passwd
Changing password for kevinr
Enter old password:
Enter new password:
Re-type new password:
Password changed.
```

When you type in the old and new passwords, the characters won't be shown on the screen.

Linux Shells

A *shell* acts as the intermediary between you and the raw operating system, interpreting your commands into a form the operating system can understand. In addition, a shell adds much of the functionality we've discussed in this chapter and adds even more when (or if) you start programming your own shell scripts.

As you'll remember from Chapter 2, you set up a shell when you add a new user to your system, the default being **bash**. How much emphasis you put on the shell depends on your UNIX background and needs. On the one hand, if you're used to working with a particular shell, you should use that shell (or its equivalent) in Linux. On the other hand, if you're not experienced with any particular shell, you should stick with the default shell under Linux, **bash**.

Several shells ship with Linux:

- **bash**, or the Bourne Again SHell. This contribution from the Free Software Foundation is the default Linux shell and probably the most popular Linux shell. **Bash** is compatible with the Bourne shell (**sh**), which means it will run scripts written for the Bourne shell. In addition, **bash** adds some popular features not found in the original Bourne shell, such as the **history** command (which will be covered later in this section) and command-line editing. By and large, you'll want to stick with **bash** unless you have some reason to switch.

- **csh**, the C shell. This widely available shell is also popular, and because it's available on most UNIX platforms, you may be familiar with it. The C shell originated the notion of command history, but it doesn't offer command-line editing.

- **sh**, the original Bourne shell. It offers compatibility with **bash** and Bourne scripts from other implementations of UNIX. However, the original Bourne shell does not offer command history or command-line editing.

- **pdksh**, the Public Domain Korn shell. This is a free version of the commercial Korn shell, which in many ways combines the best aspects of the C and Bourne shells, such as command-line editing and command history. Be warned that it's not exactly like the commercial Korn shell, and if you decide to move existing Korn scripts from another UNIX box, you may find that they don't totally work on **pdksh**.

- **tcsh**, an enhanced version of the C shell that supports command-line editing. In most ways, this is the best choice for C shell users who want the equivalent on their Linux box.

- **ash**, a trimmed-down shell used when memory is extremely tight.

- **zsh**, the Z shell. Yet another Bourne-compatible shell.

To list the shell you're using, use the following command line:

```
gilbert:~$ echo $SHELL
bash
```

As noted, the **bash** shell is very popular on Linux, and unless there's a reason to switch, you'll probably want to stick with it. (It also is POSIX-compliant, if that means anything to you.) However, if you do want to switch shells, Linux includes a command to do so, **chsh**:

```
gilbert:~$ chsh
Enter password:
The current shell is: /bin/bash
You can choose one of the following:
1. /bin/sh
2. /bin/bash
3. /bin/tcsh
4. /bin/csh
5. /bin/zsh
6. /bin/ash
Enter a number between 1 and 6: 4
Shell changed.
```

Because of the overwhelming popularity of **bash**, we're going to focus on it in our discussion of the shell in this chapter.

Your Environment

If you've been around UNIX and the X Window System long enough, you know that phrases sometimes have two different meanings depending on their context.

One such word under UNIX is *environment*. On the one hand, your *environment* refers to the various tools you've configured, like your shell and your home directory. On the other hand, in a discussion of shells, *environment* means something a little different: the variables used by your system.

Variables

In Linux parlance, variables allow a user to define information with both a name and a value that may change over the course of time. This is to allow a vast number of users to do the same thing in different locations (for example, the $SHELL variable allows anyone to set their own prompt, while all the system needs to know is that there is a $SHELL variable) while giving a lot of flexibility to users.

Under Linux, there are two kinds of variables: environment variables and shell variables. The difference is simple: an *environment variable* is set by the system and is available to all users, while a *shell variable* is managed by the shell and available only when the user is logged in the system and running the shell.

For the most part, you'll use shell variables, even on a single-user Linux installation. Setting these variables is a matter of using a simple formula:

```
$ VARIABLENAME=VARIABLEVALUE
```

where *VARIABLENAME* is the name of the variable and *VARIABLEVALUE* is the value of the variable. Some popular shell variables are listed in Table 4.11.

Table 4.11 Useful Shell Variables

Variable	Meaning
HOME	Your home directory.
LOGNAME	Your login name.
PATH	Lists the directories the shell will look in when searching for a command.
PS1	Prompt.
SHELL	Your shell, of course.

Many of these variables were set when you installed Linux. (It's probably dawned on you by now that the **setup** program in Chapter 2 did a lot more work under the hood than you thought.) There are some others, such as PS1, that you might want to change.

Variables can best be explained with a simple example that you might end up running across. When you run a command, Linux doesn't automatically know where to find the file; instead, the shell looks through a series of directories that are defined by the PATH statement. (This is why you may run into an error message when you throw a program in a nonstandard directory and try to run it when this nonstandard directory is not your current directory.) To see what's defined by the PATH statement, use the following command line:

```
$ echo $PATH
/usr/bin:/usr/local/bin:usr/bin/X11:.
```

The colons separate the directories searched by the shell when in search of an executable. (As you might expect, the PATH variable lists the most common locations for commands.) The listing ends with a dot, which tells the shell to look in the current directory for the command. (Interestingly, Linux doesn't automatically assume that the current directory should be searched.)

Background Commands and Multitasking

The shell also provides the capability to run multiple commands at one time. In computer parlance, this is called *multitasking*, and it's one of the prime selling points of the Linux operating system.

Multitasking merely means that the system can do more than one thing at a time and that it can set priorities among these different tasks. While this may be something that should be easily achieved given the power of the personal computer, it's not, as Macintosh and PC users are still waiting for an operating system that's truly multitasking (as opposed to being able to run more than one task at a given time). With the emergence of the X Window System, this capability isn't as important as it once was for the end user, even though X relies heavily on commands run in the background, as you'll see in Chapter 6, but there may be times when you need to run commands in the background from the command line.

Running a command in the background is a simple matter—you just add an ampersand (**&**) to the end of the command line. In fact, earlier in this chapter, the following command line was used as an example:

```
gilbert:~$ Ffind * -name test.bk &
```

NOTE

For the most part, you don't need to run commands in the background when running X Window.

Not every command need be run in the background; performance under Linux is pretty snappy for most tasks. Some commands that might take a long time to complete, such as **TeX**, should be run in the background, especially if you're formatting a large document.

Processes

Multiple requests to the shell are called *processes*. As these requests are made, the shell numbers them. These numbers are important if you want to kill a process. To see a list of processes, use the **ps** command:

```
gilbert:/$ ps
  PID TTY STAT   TIME COMMAND
   71 v01 S      0:00 -bash
   72 v02 S      0:00 /sbin/agetty 38400 tty2 linux
   73 v03 S      0:00 /sbin/agetty 38400 tty3 linux
   74 v04 S      0:00 /sbin/agetty 38400 tty4 linux
   75 v05 S      0:00 /sbin/agetty 38400 tty5 linux
   76 v06 S      0:00 /sbin/agetty 38400 tty6 linux
   83 v01 R      0:00 ps
```

There are always at least two processes running when you use the **ps** command: the shell process (in this case, **bash**) and the **ps** process. (Unlike other versions of UNIX, Linux does not return the **init** process as part of **ps**.) However, you'll rarely see a **ps** command with only two processes. When the Linux system boots, it usually starts a series of processes, mostly related to networking and communications. A program may generate a series of processes. If you're running the X Window System, your list of processes will be considerably longer.

Standard Input and Output

The shell, technically, is responsible for the UNIX practice of standard input and output. You've stumbled across the practice several times in this chapter (a review of the **cat** command shows that), but now it's time to formally lay out the practice.

In general, Linux programs assume that input comes from the keyboard and output goes to the monitor. (That's why it's *standard*.) To deviate from this standard practice, you need to specify the difference. This is done on the command line, mostly through the use of greater-than (>) and less-than (<) symbols.

For starters, you can redirect standard input to use an existing file as input for a program rather than keyboard entry. In this case, you must point input from the file to the command in the following manner:

```
gilbert:/$ cat < data
```

Here, the file **data** is input for the **cat** command, as opposed to normal keyboard entry.

In another variation of standard input/output, you can send the output of a command to a file. This is a very useful variation, as many commands generate output that's too voluminous to read as it whizzes by on your screen. For example, you may want to redirect the output of the **ls** command to a file and look at that output with a text editor or a viewer like **less**. In this case, you'd direct output to a file:

```
gilbert:/$ ls > listings
```

In addition, you've already seen how standard input and output can be used to append information to an existing file:

```
gilbert:~$ cat >> memo
```

Table 4.12 lists the major input/output commands.

Table 4.12 Standard Shell Input/Output Commands

Symbol	Usage	Result
>	*command > filename*	Output from *command* is sent to *filename*.
<	*command < filename*	Input from *filename* is sent to *command*.
>>	*command >> filename*	Output from *command* is appended to *filename*.
|	*command1 | command2*	Run *command1* and send the output to *command2*.

There are many places where redirection comes in handy. For example, you can send output from the command directly to a printer when using standard input/output:

```
gilbert:~$ ls | lp
```

Pipes

The previous example is a *pipe*, and it's what distinguishes a pipe from standard input/output. Redirection can only work with files and commands; a file can be used as input for a command, and a file is the recipient of output from a command. With a pipe, you can join commands, sending the output from one command to another command. A pipe is rather simple:

```
gilbert:~$ command1 | command2
```

Here, the output from *command1* is piped to *command2*. (Naturally, the entire command line is called a *pipeline*.)

You can combine a number of pipes on a command line, as in the following:

```
gilbert:~$ ls *.c | grep arg | lp
```

This command line would search for all the files ending with *.c* in your current directory and send that list to the **grep** command, which searches these files for the string *arg* and sends all these matching lines to the **lp** command, which directs the printer to spit them out.

Command History

Bash supports *command history*, which tracks which commands you've run and lets you choose among them when you need to run another command. For example, you may want to reuse a command you've recently run but don't want to go through the trouble of typing it in. In this case, you could use the **history** command and scroll between a list of previous commands:

```
gilbert:~$ history
1. cal
2. ln -s addresses /home/pat
3. ln addresses /home/eric
4. history
```

With this list, you can press the **Up** and **Down Arrow** keys (↑ and ↓) to move between the previous command lines. If there's a long list of previous commands and you want to run a specific one, you can enter its number and the command will appear on the command line.

Other shells offer this capability, albeit in different forms.

Minimal Completion

Although you may not use the facility too often, the **bash** shell's ability to complete words on a command line may be convenient for you. For example, we've been working a lot with a file named **test** in this chapter. (In fact, you're probably sick of hearing about it.) We know you want to see this file again, so run the **cat** command to view it one more time. However, instead of typing out the entire name of the file, stop when you have a command line that looks like this (*without* pressing the **Enter** key):

```
gilbert:~$ cat te
```

At this point, press the **Tab** key. Magically, the rest of the word *test* will appear on the command line. This is because you've given **bash** enough information to actually complete the command line for you. **Bash** actually goes through the directory and finds the filename that logically matches the beginning of the information you've entered. This capability can also be used to complete commands.

In our case, however, there were two files that met our conditions.

Aliases

The shell is responsible for administering one of the handiest things in Linux: setting up an alias.

Basically, an *alias* is a keyboard shortcut for a longer command line. Unless you've specified a directory in your PATH, you need to specify an absolute pathname to launch a command. Because many commands—such as some of the X Window applications—are buried deep within the hierarchy, you may have to enter a very long command line to launch them.

That's where you can set up an alias for that long command line. Basically, you use the **alias** command to tell the shell to use a short string in place of the long command line. In addition, you can use aliases to turn a potentially dangerous command into a less-dangerous command (as was the case in the discussion of the **rm** command earlier in this chapter). While **bash** does support the **dir** command (the same as in MS-DOS), you could always set up aliases for your favorite DOS commands and their Linux counterparts. Let's say you're used to working with the DOS **copy** command and just can't get used to the Linux **cp** command. You could set up an alias like the following:

```
gilbert:~$ alias copy='cp'
```

If you run this command line, you can use both **copy** or **cp** to do the same thing. You don't lose the functionality of **cp**; you're merely telling **bash** to call it when you enter **copy**.

Be careful to follow the structure shown in the example. You can't insert any spaces between the two commands, and you must be sure to use single quote marks.

To turn off an alias, use the **unalias** command:

```
gilbert:~$ unalias copy
```

When you run the **alias** command from the command line, it's only good for the current session. To make it a permanent fixture, you need to add it to your **.profile** file, found in your home directory. This file is launched every time you launch Linux, and it's here that you can really customize your system. Again, this level of customization is beyond the scope of this book; see Appendix A for a list of books that can help you with UNIX system configuration.

Using Help in Bash

The **help** command summons a summary of the **bash** shell commands, of which **alias** is a part. Basically, there are commands that are part of the Linux operating system, and there are shell commands specific to a shell. Many of these shell commands can be found in most shells, but there are also many differences between shells.

These commands are handy when creating shell scripts. While we're not going to get into the finer points of shell scripts here (you're welcome to peruse Appendix A for a list of UNIX books that cover scripts), it's handy to know that there is a way to get a list of shell commands from a command line like the following:

```
gilbert:~$ help | more
```

We use a pipe to the **more** command because the output of the **help** command is so long that much of the output will scroll past you. Running the command line yields the following output:

```
GNU bash, version 1.16.6(1)
Shell commands that are defined internally. Type `help' to see this
list.
Type `help name' to find out more about the function `name'.
Use `info bash' to find out more about the shell in general.

A star (*) next to a name means that the command is disabled.
%[DIGITS | WORD] [&]          . [filename]
:                             [ arg... ]
alias [ name[=value] ... ]    bg [job_spec]
bind [-lvd] [-m keymap] [-f filena break [n]
builtin {shell-builtin [arg ...]] case WORD in [PATTERN [|PATTERN].
cd [dir]                      command [-pVv] [command [arg ...]]
continue [n]                  declare [-[frxi]] name[=value] ...
dirs [-l]                     echo [-neE] [arg ...]
enable [-n] [name ...]        eval [arg ...]
```

```
exec [ [-] file [redirection ...]] exit [n]
export [-n] [-f] [name ...] or exp fc [-e name] [-nlr] [first] [last
fg [job_spec]                      for NAME [in WORDS ... ;] do COMMA
function NAME { COMMANDS ; } or NA getopts optstring name [arg]
hash [-r] [name ...]               help [pattern ...]
history [n] [ [-awrn] [filename]]  if COMMANDS; then COMMANDS; [elif
jobs [-lnp] [jobspec ...] | jobs - kill [-s sigspec | -sigspec] [pid
let arg [arg ...]                  local name [=value] ...
logout                             popd [+n | -n]
pushd [dir | +n | -n]              pwd
read [-r] name ...]                readonly [-n] [-f] [name ...] or r
return [n]                         select NAME [in WORDS ... ;] do CD
set [—abefhknotuvxldHCP] [-o opti  shift [n]
source filename                    suspend [f]
test [expr]                        times
trap [arg] [signal_spec]           type [-all] [-type | -path] [name
typeset [-[frxi]] name[=value] ... ulimit [-Shacdmstfpnuv [limit]]
umask [-S] [mode]                  unalias [-a] [name ...]
unset [-f] [-v] [name ...]         until COMMANDS; do COMMANDS; done
variables - Some variable names an wait [n]
while COMMANDS; do COMMANDS; done { COMMANDS }
```

The Elvis/Vi Text Editor

In Linux, the chore of text editing falls on a few different editors, and these vary greatly in terms of capabilities. As you'll recall from Chapter 2, we presented some advice as to which text editors to install. We're going to follow this up by focusing on one of the text editors we advised installing: **elvis** (which installs automatically), while saving a discussion of **emacs** for Chapter 5, after you've had some experience with the X Window System. We're not going to get into a religious war about **vi** or **emacs**; we'll present explanations of both.

Using the Elvis Text Editor

The full-screen **elvis** text editor is a clone of the **vi** text editor, which appears on most (but not all) UNIX systems. (Because you're not technically using the same **vi** found on other UNIX systems, we'll use the proper terminology here and refer to **elvis**. However, whenever you see **elvis** as part of a command, you can substitute **vi** if that's what you're used to.)

Elvis is used for editing text (ASCII) files, which have a wide application in the Linux operating system—text files are used for shell scripts, input to text processors, input for electronic mail, and programming source code files. **Elvis** works from the command line, and you can invoke it without a file loaded:

```
gilbert:/$ elvis
```

or with a file loaded:

```
gilbert:/$ elvis textfile
```

Without a file, **elvis** will look something like Figure 4.3.

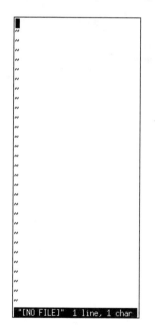

Figure 4.3 Elvis without a file loaded.

With a file loaded, **elvis** will look something like Figure 4.4.

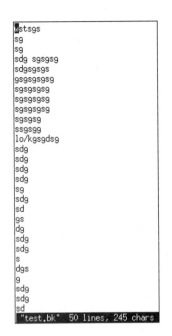

Figure 4.4 Elvis with a file loaded.

You can also invoke **elvis** using the following command lines:

```
gilbert:/$ vi
gilbert:/$ ex
gilbert:/$ view
gilbert:/$ input
```

These command-line variations can be confusing, because they all call the **elvis** editor. Basically, you can think of **vi** and **elvis** doing the same thing. If you run **view** with a file specified, you're starting **elvis** in read-only mode. (This is the equivalent of **elvis -R** run from the command line.) And if you run **input** with a file specified, you're starting **elvis** in input mode.

Input mode? Yes, **elvis** works with two modes (as does **vi**): command and input (input mode is the same as insert mode, for you **vi** users out there). The two modes are pretty straightforward: command mode is used to send a command to **elvis**, while input mode creates the text making up the file. You'll notice the difference immediately if you load **elvis** from the command line and then assume you can begin typing immediately into the file; chances are good that you'll end up generating a series of annoying beeps, as **elvis** begins in command mode and won't accept most keyboard input. The exception is if you accidentally type **i**, which puts **elvis** in input mode.

When in input mode, you can go ahead and type. When you do, you'll notice that **elvis** doesn't insert line breaks at the end of the line; the line shifts to the right, with previously input text scrolling off the page. Line breaks (in the form of an **Enter** keystroke) must be entered at the end of each line.

When you're ready to save the file, you must switch to command mode and enter the proper command. Pressing the **Esc** key will switch you to command mode; **elvis** by default won't tell you if it's in input or command mode. (If you're not sure you switched to command mode, hit the **Esc** key again. If you are in command mode, the only damage you can do is generate an annoying beep.) To enter a command in **elvis**, you must preface it with a semicolon (:). For example, the following would save a file in **elvis**:

```
:w file
```

where *file* is the name of the file to be saved. To save a file and quit **elvis**, use the following command:

```
:wq file
```

where *file* is the name of the file to be saved. (The command **ZZ**—sans leading colon—does the same thing.) To quit **elvis** without saving a file, use the following command:

```
:q!
```

Elvis and Memory

There's one important thing to remember when dealing with **elvis**: As you edit a file, you're editing a file that's been loaded into your system's RAM (or, in **elvis** parlance, a *bufffer*). You're not making a single change to the copy of the file on your hard drive. You can delete all the contents of the file loaded into RAM, or you can make a set of drastic changes, but the changes will be meaningless until you explicitly save the file to disk in the manner described in the previous section. If you're not happy with the changes, you can quit **elvis** without saving the file with the following command:

```
:q!
```

If you are happy with the changes, save the file to disk, and the previous version of the file is gone.

Creating a Text File

Elvis can be as simple or as complex as you want. On the one hand, it's really easy to create or edit a text file; all you need to know are the following steps:

- Launch **elvis** from the command line.
- Switch to insert mode by typing I.
- Type.
- When you want to save the file and exit **elvis**, press the **Esc** key (which moves you to command mode), type **:wq** *filename* (use your own filename here), followed by **Enter**. The file is saved, and your command prompt reappears.

Moving through Your Document

If you're running **elvis** from the command line (as opposed to running it under the X Window System), you'll find that your mouse won't help much. If your documents get too long, you'll need to learn about some of the nifty shortcuts that can be used to move through a document.

The easiest way to move through a document in **elvis** is to use the cursor and page-movement keys that exist on your keyboard (**PageUp**, **PageDown**). The **PageUp** and **PageDown** keys will move you up and down a single page; if there's less than a page of text to scroll to, you'll be placed at the beginning or the end of the file. Similarly, the up and down cursor keys (↑ and ↓) can be used to move the cursor through the document; if you press the up cursor (↑) key at the top of the screen, the previous line will scroll to the top.

However, there's one quirk with **elvis** (which maintain compatibility with **vi**, by the way): the left and right cursor keys (← and →) can be used only to maneuver through the current line of text. If you're at the end of the line and expect to use the right cursor key (→) to move to the following line, you'll be greeted by a beep and a cursor stuck on that last character; only the up and down cursor keys (↑ and ↓) can be used to move between lines.

For the most part, the cursor and page-movement keys should serve your scrolling needs in **elvis**. However, should you require some additional capabilities, Table 4.13 lists some other useful cursor and scrolling commands.

Table 4.13 Elvis Cursor and Scrolling Commands

Command	Result
0 (zero)	Moves the cursor to the beginning of the current line.
b	Moves the cursor to the beginning of the current word.
)	Moves the cursor to the end of the document.
$	Moves the cursor to the end of the current line.
e	Moves the cursor to the end of the current word.
w	Moves the cursor to the beginning of the next word.
nG	Moves the cursor to the beginning of line *n*.
H	Moves the cursor to the beginning of the file.
G	Moves the cursor to the beginning of the last line in the file.

Undoing the Last Command

Elvis can undo the last command (unless you've saved the file to disk, in which case all changes are set in stone); to do so, go to command mode with **Esc** and type **u** (for *undo*).

More on Elvis

This is about all you'll need to know about **elvis**. To be honest, it's not a very complex application, and given your probable text-processing needs, there's little need to spend much time mastering its every nuance. There are many other options to **elvis**, but most of them are of interest only to the hard-core user. To see what additional actions you can take with **elvis**, use the following command line:

```
gilbert:~$ man elvis
```

Before we leave the discussion of **elvis,** we'd like to point out that we managed to cover the topic without making one cheap pun about the King.

Printing Files

When you installed Linux, you were prompted about the location of the printer connected to your PC. If you're like 99 percent of the PC users out there, you have a printer connected to your parallel port. If you're installing Linux on a UNIX network, you'll use the previously installed printer or set up a printer per the UNIX printing system (which varies considerably).

In this section, we'll assume you've installed the printer on the parallel port and told Linux of this installation. (If this isn't the case, check with a standard UNIX text to see how printers are treated on UNIX networks.) To see what printers Linux thinks are connected to the network, use **lpc**:

```
gilbert:/$ lpc
lpc>
```

This command will present you with a series of options. These commands, for the most part, relate to printing a specific file on a specific printer.

NOTE This section assumes that you're printing a file directly from the command line. Some other applications—primarily Ghostscript—deal with printers on their own, which you'll learn in Chapter 5.

You can also use the standard **lpr** command to print files:

```
gilbert:/$ lpr filename
```

where *filename* is the name of the file you want to print. The command copies *filename* to a spool directory, and from there the file is actually printed. After you run the **lpr** command, you can edit the file you're printing, but the changes won't be reflected in the printed pages.

To check on the status of a print request, use the **lpq** command:

```
gilbert:/$ lpq
```

You'll be given information about the printer, the status of pending print jobs (what's being printed, what's next in line), and a job ID.

This ID is important if you want to cancel the print request; for this, you'd use the **lprm** command in conjunction with the job ID:

```
gilbert:/$ lprm 213
```

If you want to cancel *all* the print requests (in other words, your printer jammed and you want to begin the print sequence from scratch), use the following command line:

```
gilbert:/$ lprm -
```

Summary

This chapter covered the basic Linux commands and concepts, beginning with an explanation of how Linux organizes files and directories. There's nothing too obscure about these concepts, as Linux pretty much falls in line with the rest of the UNIX world. But these concepts are still worth reviewing, even if you're an experienced UNIX user.

A number of Linux commands were explained: **cd** (for moving between directories), **pwd** (which prints the current directory), **ls** (which lists the contents of the current directory or another specified directory), **mkdir** (which creates a directory), **rm** (which removes a file), **rmdir** (which removes a directory), and more.

Quite a lot of space was spent on permissions, which can trip up even the most experienced of UNIX users at times. Also covered are the commands that deal with permissions: **chmod** (which changes permissions) and **umask** (which defines how permissions are set when you create a file or directory).

How Linux deals with passwords is another important section of this chapter. When you installed Linux, you set up a password. Covered here is a further explanation of passwords, followed by coverage of the **passwd** command, which is used for changing passwords.

The many tools for viewing files were covered: **more** (used to scroll through a file), **less** (the more flexible successor to **more**), **head** (used to view the beginning of a file), **tail** (used to view the end of a file), and **od** (which displays an octal dump of a file).

The shell acts as the intermediary between you and the operating system. As such, the shell has a ton of power over your actions on the Linux operating system—it manages things like standard input and output, redirection, processes, and multitasking. The default shell under Linux is **bash** from the Free Software Foundation.

The **elvis** text editor (a clone of **vi**) is a useful text editor. The basic operations in **vi** were covered, although we advise the reader to check out the online-manual pages for this command.

To print a file with Linux, use the **lpr** command. A set of utilities— **lpc**, **lpq**, **lprm**—assist in the task of managing print requests.

This chapter covered a lot of ground, but it barely scratches the surface when it comes to useful Linux commands and concepts. In the next chapter, we'll move on to some basic Linux applications that you'll find useful for your everyday work.

Linux
Applications

This chapter covers:

- Neat Linux applications
- Using **emacs**
- Text-processing tools: **groff**, **TeX**, **texinfo**, and **sed**
- Printing with Ghostscript
- Compressing your files with **gzip**
- Archiving your files with **tar**
- Using the MTools
- System-administration tools
- X Window applications
- Emulating DOS and Windows
- Games for fun and enjoyment

A Wealth of Features

In Chapter 4 you were exposed to a lot of what Linux has to offer in your daily work. However, that chapter barely scratched the surface of Linux's many tools—particularly the tools found in the Slackware distribution.

In this chapter, we extend our discussion of Linux tools, focusing on some specific topics. However, we're not going to cover every single Linux tool, especially not those tools that can be found in most distributions of UNIX. Here, we'll discuss tools that are unique to Linux or (in the case of **gzip** and **tar**) that come in slightly different versions from the rest of the UNIX world. (You'll see what we mean when we discuss **tar** and its compression capabilities.) Because Linux contains most of the standard UNIX commands, we strongly advise you to purchase a guide to UNIX (many are listed in Appendix A) to use as a guide to the more common UNIX commands; we won't spend time here covering useful commands like **grep**, for example. They're adequately covered in other texts, and there's very little to distinguish the Linux version of these commands from the mainstream UNIX version.

With that in mind, it's time to cover the many tools that make Linux unique when compared to both other operating systems and other versions of UNIX.

Using Emacs

The **elvis/vi** text editor covered in Chapter 4 is a pure text editor; all it did was allow you to open or create a text file and edit it in a full-screen layout. (It also performs this basic capability in a very confusing manner, forcing you to distinguish between command and input modes.)

The **emacs** text editor goes a little further in its capabilities and is easier to use. Created by Richard Stallman and controlled by the Free Software Foundation, **emacs** has evolved into an essential piece of software for most UNIX users, even though **emacs** ships with relatively few commercial implementations of UNIX; its appeal is such that system administrators are willing to go the extra mile and obtain it for use on their systems.

Although we're not going to get into the religious war that separates **vi** and **emacs** editors, we do think that **emacs** is worth checking out, especially if you've not used either text editor extensively. **Emacs** offers many things not found in **vi**:

- **Emacs** allows you to edit more than one file at a time and to cut and paste between files.
- **Emacs** features online help—a rarity in the Linux/UNIX world.
- A spelling checker, based on the UNIX **spell** command, can be accessed from a pull-down menu.
- With pull-down menus and a graphical interface (though, sadly, without what-you-see-is-what-you-get capabilities), **emacs** comes closest to a true word processor in the Linux world.

Beginners will probably get a little more out of **emacs** than other Linux text-editing tools, if only because the basic commands are always available in pull down menus. In addition, **emacs** can be used for a host of other functions, including the reading of electronic mail and Usenet news, and the editing of source-code files for C, Lisp, and **TeX**.

This discussion will center around the X Window version that ships with the Slackware distribution of Linux (version 19.30.1). If you've decided to forego the joys of X, you should have installed the non-X version of **emacs** that was available during the Linux installation process. You can go back and install that version if you're not using X; however, if you installed the X Window version of **emacs**, you should remove that version from your system before installing the non-X version.

If you do use the non-X version of **emacs**, you'll be able to follow along with this section of the chapter, for the most part. We'll provide keyboard equivalents to the commands listed here.

To launch **emacs** without a file loaded, type the following command line in an **xterm** window:

```
gilbert:/# emacs
```

as seen in Figure 5.1.

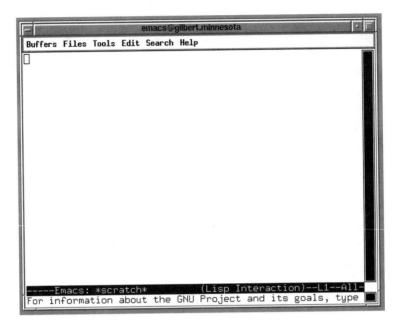

Figure 5.1 Emacs without a file loaded.

You can also load **emacs** with a file loaded, specifying the file on the command line:

```
gilbert:/# emacs filename
```

where *filename* is the name of the file. (Remember that if filename isn't found on your PATH or in the current directory, you'll need to list an absolute filename.)

If you've used any other computing system or another X Window application, you'll feel fairly comfortable in **emacs**. There are some changes in terminology that might throw you off; for example, you don't edit separate files (you edit buffers), and the mechanism for showing your position in a document is not called the cursor, but the *point*. (In this chapter, we'll use the term *cursor*.)

Emacs and Commands

With **emacs**, there is usually more than one way to perform a command, especially with the X Window version.

One method is through keyboard shortcuts. Every **emacs** function can be performed via the keyboard, usually in conjunction with the **Ctrl** and **Alt** keys. (In some **emacs** documentation, there will be references to the **Meta** key rather than the **Alt** key; this reference is more for the users of other UNIX systems that lack an **Alt** key on their keyboard. This is, of course, not the case with Linux.) Most of the time, the **Ctrl** and **Alt** keys are literally shortcuts for full commands, which you could enter if you were truly inclined.

There's one thing to note when working with keyboard sequences: When you see notation like **Ctrl-x Ctrl-f**, this means you hold down the **Ctrl** key and then press the **x** and **f** keys in sequence. (No, you don't need to release the **Ctrl** key between the **x** and **f** keys.)

The other method is through a pull-down menu. As you can see from Figure 5.2, **emacs** provides some pull-down menus (Buffers, File, Edit, and Help). Be warned that these menus don't work the same way as pull-down menus in the Microsoft Windows, Macintosh, or OS/2 environments. In these situations, a menu choice acts as a gateway to another action, either a dialog box or another menu.

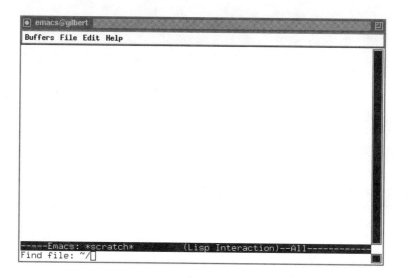

Figure 5.2 Emacs before loading a file.

Essentially, pull-down menus in the **emacs** environment act as gateways for the **emacs** command line, which can be found on the bottom of the screen. For example, go ahead and choose **Open File** from the File pull-down menu (or the keyboard equivalent of **Ctrl-x Ctrl-f**) You won't see a fancy dialog box that allows you to choose from a list of existing files. Instead, you'll see a line at the bottom of the Emacs window that lists the current directory, as shown in Figure 5.2.

Here is where you can choose your directory. After doing so, you'll see a list of files, as shown in Figure 5.3.

```
 emacs@gilbert                                              
Buffers File Operate Mark Regexp Immediate Subdir Help
 /root:
 total 143
 drwxr-x--x   5 root      root       1024 Apr 28 03:58 .
 drwxr-xr-x  18 root      root       1024 Apr 24 00:26 ..
 -rw-r--r--   1 root      root        433 Aug 11  1993 .Xdefau\
lts
 -rw-r--r--   1 root      root       2502 Apr 28 03:41 .bash_h\
istory
 -rw-r--r--   1 root      root       2938 Apr  4  1993 .emacs
 -rw-r--r--   1 root      root        164 Mar 30 02:59 .kermrc
 -rw-r--r--   1 root      root         34 Mar 30 02:59 .less
 -rw-r--r--   1 root      root        114 May  7  1993 .lessrc
 drwxr-xr-x   2 root      root       1024 Mar 30 02:39 .seyon
 drwxr-xr-x   2 root      root       1024 Mar 29 09:31 .term
 lrwxrwxrwx   1 root      root          8 Mar 29 09:31 INSTALL\
 -> /var/adm
 -rw-r--r--   1 root      root     127299 Apr 24 00:25 fig7_14\
.xwd
 lrwxrwxrwx   1 root      root         14 Mar 29 09:31 linux -\
> /usr/src/linux
 -rw-r--r--   1 root      root        117 Apr 22 11:30 man.man
--%%-Dired: ~                          (Dired by name)--Top----
Reading directory /root/...done
```

Figure 5.3 Emacs with a directory listing.

If you look at Figure 5.3 closely, you'll see that the number of pull-down menu choices has dramatically increased. Depending on the context, **emacs** will display varying sets of pull-down menus.

The list in Figure 5.3 is meant as a way to show options; the contents are read-only, and you can't scroll among them to actually select a file or directory; instead, you continue to choose **Open File** from the File menu (**Ctrl-x Ctrl-f**) and manually insert the file or directory name. In short, the **Open File** menu choice is actually a shortcut both to the **emacs** command line and to the **ls -l** command line.

After you choose a file, you'll see something like Figure 5.4. Hopefully, your file contains more than the gibberish shown in the figure.

Figure 5.4 emacs with a file loaded.

Again, you'll note that the menu bar for **emacs** has changed slightly, in reaction to the context of editing a simple text file. In Figure 5.4, **emacs** gives us the name of the file (*test*), the mode (*Fundamental*), and the amount of the file that is displayed on the screen (in this case, *22 percent*).

Notice that the status bar on the bottom of the **emacs** window has also changed. In the previous screen shots, the status bar listed *Lisp Interaction*, without the name of a file (which made sense, because we didn't have a file loaded). This leads us to a major feature of **emacs**: modes.

The Many Modes of Emacs

You've already seen **emacs** change behavior when presented with a different context: different pull-down menus for different chores. Another sign of **emacs'** flexibility is in its support of modes, which essentially changes **emacs** depending on the usage.

For example, Figures 5.1 and 5.2 showed **emacs** in Lisp Interaction mode. If you were a Lisp programmer, this mode might be important to you. However, most of you will be interested in other **emacs** modes—particularly the mode found in Figure 5.4, Fundamental mode. This is the mode used to edit ASCII files. There are other modes for **emacs** that you may end up using, however, such as the modes for editing C and **TeX** source-code files.

Creating and Editing Files

Most of what **emacs** does is pretty straightforward; as you've already learned, most actions can be done from the pull-down menu or from keyboard equivalents.

After you launch **emacs** from a command line, you're presented with a blank screen. If you're creating a new file, go ahead and start typing. **emacs** will wrap words at the end of a column, but in an unusual manner, displaying a slash (/) to indicate that a word is continued on the following line (as shown in Figure 5.5).

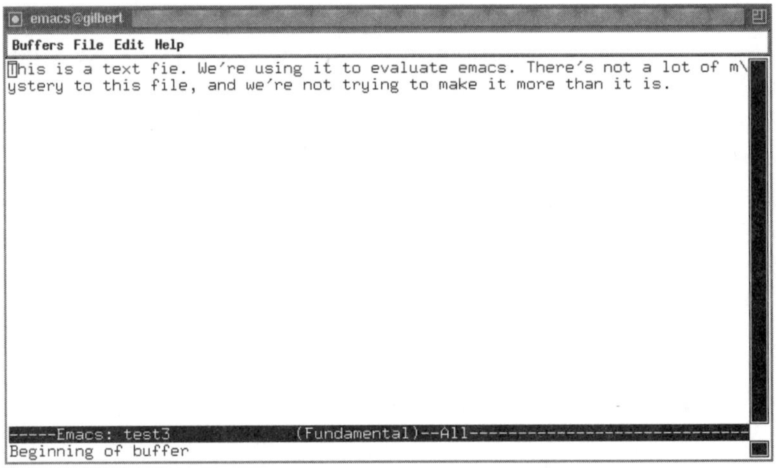

Figure 5.5 Emacs displaying text.

This version of **emacs** performs just like any other text editor when it comes to cursor commands and such; there are a few quirks to watch for, however:

- The cursor keys (↑, ↓, ←, and →) are used slightly differently than you'd think. The up arrow (↑) moves the cursor to the beginning line of the current paragraph; pressing it twice moves the cursor to the beginning of the file. The down arrow ($\downarrow$) moves the cursor to the end of the current paragraph; pressing it twice moves the cursor into the following paragraph. However, the left and right arrow keys ($\leftarrow$, and $\rightarrow$) work as you would expect them to.

- The **PageUp** and **PageDn** commands apply to the position of the document in the **emacs** buffer. If the entire document is displayed in a window, these commands won't do anything.

- The **Home** and **End** keys are used to mark text and to position the cursor at the beginning or end of a document.

- The **Backspace** and **Delete** keys should work as you'd expect. (This is one of the advantages of Linux on the PC architecture; Linux assumes that there's standard PC equipment present, and by and large that assumption will be valid. There are mechanisms for remapping keys should Linux not work as you'd expect, but these sorts of problems are minimized under Linux and XFree86.)

In addition, there are a host of keyboard commands for maneuvering through a document, as listed in Table 5.1.

Table 5.1 Emacs Cursor Commands

Command	Moves...
Ctrl-a	the cursor to the beginning of the current line.
Ctrl-b	the cursor backward one character.
Ctrl-e	the cursor to the end of the current line.
Ctrl-f	the cursor forward one character.
Ctrl-n	the cursor to the next line.
Ctrl-p	the cursor to the previous line.
Ctrl-v	the document ahead one page.
Alt-v	the document back one page.
Alt-<	the cursor to the beginning of the document.
Alt->	the cursor to the end of the document.

Buffers

In UNIX parlance, a *buffer* is a portion of memory set aside for a specific task. In **emacs**, a buffer can contain an existing file or a new file in progress. When a file is in a buffer, it exists separately from something stored on the hard disk; you can make changes to the buffer, but they won't be reflected in the version stored on disk. Only when you explicitly save the file to disk will the changes be made permanently. This sometimes trips up new computer users, who assume that whatever appears on the screen is exactly mirrored at all times on the disk.

Emacs allows you to view multiple buffers and to cut and paste between the buffers. To see which buffers are currently open, select **Buffers** from the menu bar (or type **Ctrl-x Ctrl-b**). You'll see something like Figure 5.6.

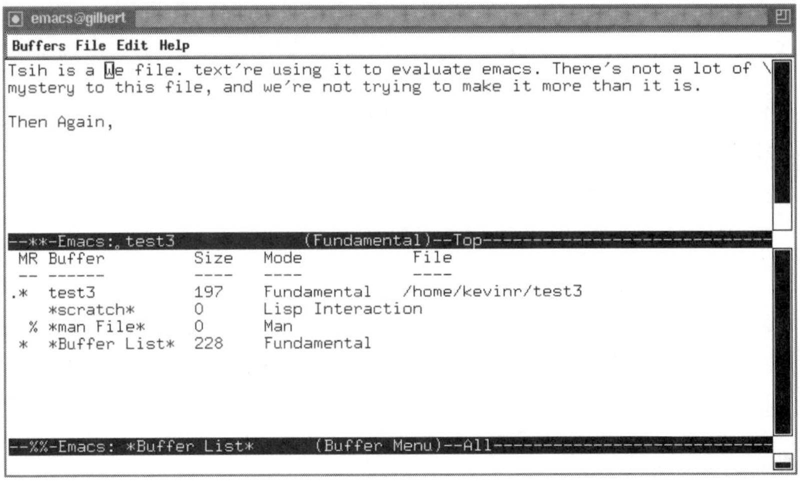

Figure 5.6 Buffers in **emacs**.

Emacs and Help

There's one additional area where **emacs** is superior to most other Linux text-editing tools: the presence of true online help. To access the online help, you can choose Help from the pull-down menu, which gives you a list of selections. Some of the help is context-sensitive and relates to what you're doing at the moment (such as the help for modes), and there are general help topics and a tutorial.

A good place to start with the online help is with the **Info** menu choice (**Ctrl-h I**), which provides a general overview of **emacs** online help (as shown in Figure 5.7). And **Ctrl-h t** provides a decent tutorial.

```
┌──────────────────────────────────────────────────────────────────────┐
│ ◉ emacs@gilbert                                                     ᴇ⅃ │
├──────────────────────────────────────────────────────────────────────┤
│ Buffers File Edit Help                                                 │
│ File: dir       Node: Top       This is the top of the INFO tree       │
│   This (the Directory node) gives a menu of major topics. Typing "d"   │
│   returns here, "q" exits, "?" lists all INFO commands, "h" gives a    │
│   primer for first-timers, "mTexinfo<Return>" visits Texinfo topic, etc.│
│   --- PLEASE ADD DOCUMENTATION TO THIS TREE. (See INFO topic first.) ---│
│ * Menu: The list of major topics begins on the next line.              │
│                                                                        │
│ Developing in C and C++:                                               │
│ =========================                                              │
│ * GCC: (gcc).            Information about the gcc Compiler             │
│ * CPP: (cpp).            The C Preprozessor                             │
│ * Make: (make).          The GNU make Utility                          │
│ * GDB: (gdb).            The GNU Debugger                               │
│                                                                        │
│ Libraries and program generators:                                      │
│ ==================================                                     │
│ * glibc: (libc).         The standard C runtime library.               │
│ * iostream: (iostream).  The GNU C++ iostream library.                 │
│ * Libg++: (libg++).      The G++ Library                               │
│ * gmp: (gmp).            GNU MP arbitrary precision arithmetic library.│
│ * Regex: (regex).        The GNU regular expression library.           │
│ * Termcap: (termcap).    The termcap library, which enables application progr\│
│ --%%-Info:  (dir)Top     (Info Narrow)--Top----------------------------│
│ menu-bar help info                                                   ■ │
└──────────────────────────────────────────────────────────────────────┘
```

Figure 5.7 The **emacs** help screen.

There will be further discussion of the **emacs** help system later in this chapter in the section entitled "Using Texinfo."

A Basic Emacs Tutorial

Many Linux users won't care about **emacs**' bell and whistles; they only care about creating and editing documents. In that spirit, we present this minitutorial that covers the creation and editing of text files under **emacs**.

You already know how to load **emacs**. If you want to create a new file, go ahead and type. If you want to load an existing file and didn't specify the file on the command line, you can open it by selecting **Open File** (**Ctrl-x Ctrl-f**) from the File menu.

To edit the file, you can use the basic movement and editing keys on the keyboard. When it's time to save your file, you can select Save Buffer (**Ctrl-x Ctrl-s**) from the File menu; if you're working with an existing file, you should select Save Buffer As (**Ctrl-x Ctrl-w**) from the File menu, but using the existing filename.

To quit **emacs**, select Exit Emacs from the File menu or type **Ctrl-x Ctrl-c**. If you haven't saved any changes to the file, **emacs** will make sure you want to quit and give you the option of saving the file at that time.

The Undo Command

Emacs also allows you to undo your most recent action; naturally enough, the **Undo** menu selection from the Edit menu does just this. (The keyboard equivalent is **Ctrl-_**.)

Editing Text

When you edit existing text, you can go one of two ways. Old-time UNIX and **emacs** users make a big deal about the scads of commands that are used to delete and edit text. We're modernists (relatively speaking), so we're into the more recent (and handier) methods of doing things.

For example, to cut and copy text, there's a host of commands for cutting existing text, saving it to a buffer, and then reinserting the buffer in either the existing file or a new file. We find it's a lot easier to use the mouse to mark a section of text and then use the menu choices in the Edit menu to make the changes (cut, copy, and paste). If you're used to this trinity of choices from the Windows, Macintosh, or OS/2 worlds, you'll feel comfortable with them under Linux:

- The Cut (**Ctrl-w**) menu choice cuts the marked text and saves it to another buffer.
- The Copy (**Alt-w**) menu choice copies the marked text to a buffer, leaving the marked text intact.
- The Paste (**Ctrl-y**) menu choice pastes the text in the buffer where the cursor is positioned.

There are two things to note here: The keyboard equivalents for these mechanisms aren't the same as the keyboard equivalents under Windows, Macintosh, or OS/2, and marked text is grayed when you select it with the mouse but not when you release the mouse. The text is still marked; you just can't tell.

Deleting text involves the same sort of mechanisms: marking text with the mouse and then using the Clear menu choice (no keyboard equivalent, interestingly enough) from the Edit menu to delete the text. (You can't use the **Backspace** or **Delete** key to delete marked text.) There are also a host of keyboard commands for deleting text (if you're a devoted touch-typist and can't bear the thought of using a mouse), as listed in Table 5.2.

Table 5.2 Delete Commands in **Emacs**

Command	Deletes...
Delete	the character to the left of the cursor.
Backspace	the character to the left of the cursor.
Ctrl-d	the character beneath the cursor.
Ctrl-k	all characters to the end of the line.
Alt-d	to the beginning of the next word.
Alt-Delete	all characters to the beginning of the previous word.

Finally, **emacs** features a slew of keyboard commands for changing existing text. Most of these selections aren't found in a menu, so you'll need to perform them from the keyboard. We list them in Table 5.3.

Table 5.3 Additional **Emacs** Editing Commands

Command	Result
Ctrl-t	Transposes the character under the cursor with the character before the cursor.
Alt-t	Transposes the word under the cursor with the word before the cursor.
Ctrl-x Ctrl-t	Transposes the current line with the next line in the document; remember that under **emacs** a line can be a paragraph if there's no carriage return at the end of a line.
Alt-l (ell)	Changes the case of a word to lowercase; if your cursor is positioned in the middle of the word, **emacs** only changes the case of the letters in the remainder of the word.
Alt-u	Changes the case of a word to uppercase; if your cursor is positioned in the middle of the word, **emacs** only changes the case of the letters in the remainder of the word.
Alt-c	Capitalizes the word, provided the cursor is at the beginning of the word.

Searching and Replacing

When it comes to searching and replacing text, **emacs** is not a very sophisticated player, but you'll probably have little need for the more extensive search-and-replace facilities found in a commercial word processor.

To search for a specific string, select Search from the Edit menu. The bottom of the window will feature the following input mechanism:

```
Search:
```

At that point you can enter the string of text to look for, moving forward through the document from the current cursor position, not from the beginning of the file.

If you choose **Ctrl-s** from the keyboard, you'll get a slightly different search mechanism, as you'll see by the bottom of the window:

```
I-search:
```

This search is *incremental*, which means that **emacs** moves through the document based on your first keystroke (if you type **t**, it will move to the first *t* it finds).

To perform a search-and-replace operation, select Query-Replace from the Edit menu. **Emacs** will prompt you for the text to search for and the text to replace it with. Armed with this, **emacs** will move to the first occurrence of the search text in the buffer, asking if you do want to replace the text (type **y** for *yes* or **n** for *no*).

Spell Checking

Emacs features a spelling checker that's really an extension of the UNIX **spell** command, **ispell**. If you select Spell from the Edit menu, you'll see a host of choices that allow you to check the spelling in the buffer, the spelling of a particular word, or the spelling using a different or foreign language dictionary. This menu also allows you to make changes to a dictionary (a good thing, especially if you're writing a book and use a lot of words that aren't in the standard dictionary).

 Linux also supports the **spell** command, if you wish to run it from the command line.

Printing in Emacs

To print a file in **emacs**, select Print Buffer from the File menu (there's no keyboard equivalent). This has the same effect as running **lpr** from the command line.

Quitting Emacs

The sequence **Ctrl-x Ctrl-c** will save the current buffer and quit **emacs**. You can also use the Exit Emacs choice on the Files menu.

There's a lot more to **emacs** than what we list here; realistically, all we can do is offer an overview of **emacs** and let you poke around the rest, figuring out which of **emacs'** many capabilities best fit your situation.

Xedit

A considerably less sophisticated editing tool is **xedit**, but it is one you might find useful nevertheless. **Xedit** is a simple text editor, where the screen is split into different areas used for editing text and creating drafts of text.

You can launch **xedit** from the **fvwm** menu or from an **xterm** window. If you specify a file on the command line, that file will be loaded into **xedit**. For an X Window application, there's not a whole lot to do with the mouse; you can basically load and save a file via buttons and select text, but other actions are accomplished via a set of **Ctrl-** and **Alt**-key combinations. These combinations are listed in Table 5.4.

Table 5.4 Important Editing Actions with Xedit

Key Combination	Action
Alt-Del	Deletes the previous word.
Alt-Backspace	Deletes the next word.
Alt-<	Moves the displayed text to the beginning of the file.
Alt->	Moves the displayed text to the end of the file.
Alt-]	Moves the displayed text ahead one paragraph.
Alt-[	Moves the displayed text backward one paragraph.

Continued...

Key Combination	Action
Alt-b	Moves the cursor to the beginning of the previous word.
Alt-d	Deletes the word after the current cursor position.
Alt-f	Moves the cursor to the beginning of the next word.
Alt-h	Deletes the word prior to the current cursor position.
Alt-i	Inserts a file.
Alt-k	Deletes the text to the end of the current paragraph.
Alt-q	Makes the current text into a paragraph, with indent and newline.
Alt-v	Moves the cursor to the beginning of the previous page.
Alt-y	Inserts the selection at the current cursor position.
Alt-z	Scrolls the displayed text one line down.
Ctrl-a	Moves the cursor to the beginning of the line.
Ctrl-b	Moves the cursor backward one character.
Ctrl-d	Deletes the character after the cursor.
Ctrl-e	Moves the cursor to the end of the line.
Ctrl-f	Moves the cursor forward one character.
Ctrl-h	Deletes the character before the cursor.
Ctrl-j	Inserts a newline character and indents the following line.
Ctrl-k	Deletes to the end of the line.
Ctrl-l	Redraws the display.
Ctrl-m	Inserts a newline character.
Ctrl-n	Moves the cursor to the next line.
Ctrl-o	Inserts a newline and moves the cursor to the previous line.
Ctrl-p	Moves the cursor to the previous line.
Ctrl-r	Performs a search-and-replace before the current cursor position.
Ctrl-s	Performs a search-and-replace after the current cursor position.
Ctrl-t	Transposes the characters on either side of the cursor.
Ctrl-v	Repositions the page to the following page.
Ctrl-w	Deletes the selected text.
Ctrl-y	Undeletes the last text deleted with **Ctrl-w**.

For more on **xedit**, check out its online **man** page, best viewed with **xman**.

Textedit

If you're coming from a Sun Microsystems environment, you may be more comfortable with the **textedit** text editor:

```
gilbert:$ textedit
```

This text editor features the familiar Open Look buttons for opening and managing files. It's a basic text editor, complete with search-and-replace capabilities and the ability to copy selections to a Clipboard.

To get more information about **textedit**, check out its online **man** page:

```
gilbert:$ xman
```

Other Text-Editing Tools

If these text editors don't fit your needs, you're welcome to try out some of the other text editors:

- **Vim** is a **vi**-compatible text editor (only the **q** command is missing). It adds to the basic **vi** command set with several shell-like features, including command-line history, filename completion, and more.

- **Jove** is *Jonathan's Own Version of Emacs,* and it works pretty much like **emacs** in the major ways, using buffers and such. If you yearn for **emacs** in text mode and you installed **emacs** to run under the X Window System, you can use **jove** and pretty much feel right at home (although there are some areas where **jove** differs significantly from **emacs**; you can read all about it in the online **man** pages).

- **Joe** is *Joe's Own Editor* (notice how these software creators name things after themselves?), and it's basically a text editor that supports some old WordStar conventions. (History lesson: WordStar is a text editor that used to be very big in the MS-DOS world; Windows pretty much wiped it out.) When you think of WordStar, you should think of **Ctrl**-key combinations used to perform basic tasks, and that's exactly what you'll find in **joe**.

- If you're a UNIX old-timer, you might feel comfortable with the **ed** text editor (which can also be summoned under the **red** command). The Slackware Linux version is very limited; you can only edit files in the current directory and you cannot execute shell commands.

Text-Processing Tools

Like the UNIX operating system as a whole, Linux offers many tools for text processing, in addition to the text-editing tools already covered in this chapter and in Chapter 4. This split requires a little background first, however.

As you've been told repeatedly throughout the course of this book, UNIX (and by extension, Linux) is built upon a set of specialized commands, as computing chores are divided between many small-scale, specific commands. To create a document, for example, you can't merely call on a word processor like WordPerfect and create a document from beginning to end, with fancy layouts and such. While **emacs** does do many of the things a good Windows or Macintosh word processor would do, it's still limited when it comes to page layouts and other things associated with advanced word processing and rudimentary desktop publishing.

That weakness is actually inherent in the UNIX operating system, which delegates small tasks to small commands. Traditionally, creating a document within UNIX has involved three sets of tools:

- Text editors, such as **vi** or **emacs**
- Text processors, such as **groff** or **TeX**
- Printing commands, such as **lpr**

In this chapter and in Chapter 4, you've learned about the major text editors in Linux. In this section, we'll run down the major text processors in Linux; then we'll discuss printing in Linux.

Groff: The Traditional Standard

Early in its history, UNIX was viewed as the perfect front end to a robust printing system. (This is how early UNIX development was justified at Bell Labs, as a matter of fact.) As a result, there are many text-processing tools in UNIX. Some of them have been superseded by commercial what-you-see-is-what-you-get text editing/processing packages in the commercial world (such as FrameMaker and WordPerfect). However, for most of your basic text-processing needs, you'll find that **groff** and its brethren fit the bill.

Roff was an original text-processing tool from the Bell Lab days of UNIX, which evolved into various other tools (like **troff** and **psroff**). **Roff** and its descendants were viewed as text-processing filters, which would take the output of a text editor (properly formatted with **roff** commands, of course) and send it to a specific printer. These formatting commands could include columns, fonts, boxes, and other layout elements.

The Slackware version of Linux features **groff**, the Free Software Foundation version of **troff**. **Groff** and its accompanying utilities allow you to format documents for a wide range of devices, including PostScript printers (using the **ps** device driver), **TeX**, X Window programs, and other line printers.

Using Groff

As mentioned, **groff** is a text processor, which means it takes input from a text editor (like **vi** or **emacs**) and prepares it for output on another device. For your part, you must input **groff** formatting commands into your text document.

Groff formatting commands begin with a backslash (\) or a period (.). **groff** takes these commands and interprets them for the output device. For example, you may want to input the text found in Figure 5.8, using **vi** or **emacs**, saving the file as **rules** in your home directory.

You can also send the **groff**-formatted document to the default printer, using the following command line:

```
gilbert:~/$ groff rules | lpr
```

```
.po 1i
.ce1
\s12\fBLinux Rules!\fR


\s10This monthly issue of \fILinux Rules!\fR features 20 more reasons
why Linus is the ultimate operating system. Some of the reasons
include:
.in 5
* Linux is way cool!
* Linux is better than DOS at \fIeverything\fR.
* Only smart people like us use Linux.
```
```
\s10Do we need to say more?
```

Figure 5.8 Input for the **groff** text processor.

You can run the **rules** file and see the result on the screen using the following command line:

```
gilbert:~/$ groff rules
```

After running the text in Figure 5.8 through **groff**, the result will look like Figure 5.9.

Linux Rules!

This monthly issue of *Linux Rules!* features 20 more reasons why Linux is the ultimate operating system. Some of the reasons include:

> * Linux is way cool!
> * Linux is better than DOS at *everything*.
> * Only smart people like us use Linux.

Do we need to say more?

Figure 5.9 The document after it was run through **groff**.

There are some things to note when using **groff**:

- **Groff** automatically fills to the right margin, even if you insert your own carriage returns in the text document. To stop this from happening, insert **.nf** at the beginning of the document; this is short for *no fill*.
- **Groff** automatically justifies the text; spaces between words are increased to allow the text to be stretched across the page. We're not fans of this spacing, Since it results in some awkward-looking lines, especially when you're working with longer words. We usually tell **groff** to stop justifying the text, which means inserting the **.ad** command at the beginning of the file.
- As you can tell from Figure 5.9, we tagged some bold and italic words with commands that begin with \f; for example, the \fB command turns on bold formatting, while the \fI command turns on italic formatting. These commands stay in effect until you explicitly turn them off with the \fR command.
- The first line of the little message is in 12-point type, as opposed to the 10-point type used in the rest of the message. The \s command, followed by a number, enters the point size. (This is valid only for devices that can handle different point sizes, of course; older line printers do not.)
- Dot commands must appear on their own line; these lines won't appear at all in the document. Backslash commands, on the other hand, can appear anywhere in the document.

Some useful **groff** commands are listed in Table 5.5.

As always, you can check out the online **man** page for a command by specifying it on the command line:

```
gilbert:~/$ man groff
```

Creating Man Pages with Groff

Programmers or system administrators on larger systems will want to check out the use of **groff** to create online-manual pages. To create them, you'd go through the same document-creation process found in the previous section: formatting pages in **elvis** or **emacs** and then running the documents through the **groff** text processor. However, to create an online-manual page, you'd need to run the page through **groff** with two options: -*Tascii* (which tells **groff** to output in ASCII text, rather than formatting for a printer; the default is PostScript) and -*man* (which tells **groff** to use the manual-page macros).

Groff is also capable of outputting for other devices and software applications. An option of -*Tdvi* produces files in the **TeX** device-independent DVI format.

Table 5.5 Useful Groff Formatting Commands

Command	Result
.ad	Turns off text justification.
.bp	Inserts a page break.
.ce n	Centers the next n lines; if no number is specified, only the following line will be centered.
.fi	Tells **groff** to fill the text lines (counters **.nf**).
.ft n	Changes the font to n (**B** for bold, and so on).
\fn	Changes the font to n (**B** for bold, and so on).
.in n	Indents the following lines by n spaces.
.ls n	Sets the line spacing on a document. For example, **.ls 2** would change the spacing to double-spaced; the default is single-spaced.
.na	Turns on text justification (counters **.ad**).
.nf	Tells **groff** not to fill the lines of text.
.pl n	Sets the number of lines on a page to n; the default is 66 lines to a page.
.po ni	Sets the left margin; 1I (one ell) would set the left margin to 1 inch—you must set this or the printing will begin at the absolute left of the page (you can use centimeters instead of inches by using c instead of i).
.ps n	Changes the point size to n.
\sn	Changes the point size to n.
.sp n	Sets the number of lines to skip by n; to skip a specific space, use ni for inches or nc for centimeters.
.ti n	Indents the first line of the following paragraphs by n spaces.
.un n	Underlines the following line; if a number (n) is specified, then n lines will be underlined. This must be used with entire lines, as you can't just underline a specific word.

Using TeX

Biblical scholar and programming whiz Donald E. Knuth developed **TeX** (pronounced *tech*) to handle the tough typesetting chores that other computer tools couldn't handle at the time, such as mathematical and foreign-language formatting. **TeX** works like **groff**: You create the source file in **elvis** or **emacs**, and then you run the file through **TeX**. Linux also features **LaTeX**, a series of useful macros for use with **TeX**, as well as scads of fonts for use with **TeX**. (Academics will find that these fonts are worth the price of Linux on their own; the fonts cover all major and most minor dialects, even descending into the world of fantasy with fonts for Klingon.)

In this book, we're not going to spend a lot of time covering **TeX**. When you installed Linux from the CD-ROMs, you were prompted about whether you wanted to install **TeX** and the accompanying fonts. If you didn't do so at the time, you can run the **setup** program again and install the **TeX** disksets. The usage of **TeX** is somewhat involved; if your work involves this sort of precise mathematical formatting, you will want to check out one of the many books covering **TeX**. On top of that list would be Knuth's own *The TeXbook*. In addition, Leslie Lamport (the creator of **LaTeX**) documented **LaTeX** in the *LaTeX User's Guide and Reference Manual*.

Using Texinfo

Hypertext meets Linux with the **texinfo** text-formatting program, courtesy of the same folks who brought us **emacs**. **Texinfo** is a relatively new attempt in the UNIX/Linux world to provide useful documentation for users of all sorts. The goal of **texinfo** is to create information files that be accessed from help systems within applications, from the command line, or printed in a traditional manual. The benefit, of course, is that documentation only needs be changed on one source file. Since this makes the creation of useful online documentation easier, we certainly applaud the effort—UNIX has a reputation for being too cryptic, and **texinfo** is a way to bring online help to the masses.

The nice thing is that the Free Software Foundation practices what it preaches, placing most of its online help in **texinfo** files. In fact, if you use **emacs**, you'll want to check out the **texinfo** files that **emacs** uses in the Help menu (you can also access these files by typing **Ctrl-h I**).

We show the top level of the info files in Figure 5.10.

```
● emacs@gilbert
Buffers File Edit Help
File: dir          Node: Top        This is the top of the INFO tree
    This (the Directory node) gives a menu of major topics. Typing "d"
    returns here, "q" exits, "?" lists all INFO commands, "h" gives a
    primer for first-timers, "mTexinfo<Return>" visits Texinfo topic, etc.
    --- PLEASE ADD DOCUMENTATION TO THIS TREE. (See INFO topic first.) ---
* Menu: The list of major topics begins on the next line.

Developing in C and C++:
========================
* GCC: (gcc).           Information about the gcc Compiler
* CPP: (cpp).           The C Preprozessor
* Make: (make).         The GNU make Utility
* GDB: (gdb).           The GNU Debugger

Libraries and program generators:
=================================
* glibc: (libc).        The standard C runtime library.
* iostream: (iostream). The GNU C++ iostream library.
* Libg++: (libg++).     The G++ Library
* gmp: (gmp).           GNU MP arbitrary precision arithmetic library.
--%%-Info:  (dir)Top      (Info Narrow)--Top-----------------------------
Composing main Info directory...done                                   ■
```

Figure 5.10 The Info mode for **emacs**.

Although you can't see the entire page from the figure, this portion of the **emacs** documentation actually acts as the documentation for all the offerings of the Free Software Foundation, most of which are found within the Slackware implementation of Linux. For example, if you scroll down the Info page, you'll actually run into the documentation for **texinfo** itself, as we show in Figure 5.11.

You don't need to access these Info files through **emacs**. You can do so by using the following command line:

```
gilbert:/$ info
```

The result is shown in Figure 5.12.

As you can see from Figure 5.12, the documentation for **texinfo** is completely online, which makes further coverage in this chapter somewhat redundant. The files listed in Figure 5.12 can tell you anything about the creation of **texinfo** pages that you'll ever want to know.

```
● emacs@gilbert                                                          ⬚
Buffers File Edit Help
File: texi.info,  Node: Top,  Next: Copying,  Prev: (dir),  Up: (dir)   ■

Texinfo
*******

   Texinfo is a documentation system that uses a single source file to
produce both on-line information and printed output.

   The first part of this master menu lists the major nodes in this Info
document, including the @-command and concept indices.  The rest of the
menu lists all the lower level nodes in the document.

   This is Edition 2.18 of the Texinfo documentation, 26 March 1993,
for Texinfo Version 2.

* Menu:

* Copying::                          Your rights.
* Overview::                         Texinfo in brief.
* Texinfo Mode::                     How to use Texinfo mode.
* Beginning a File::                 What is at the beginning of a Texinfo file?
* Ending a File::                    What is at the end of a Texinfo file?
* Structuring::                      How to create chapters, sections, subsections,
                                       appendices, and other parts.
--%%-Info:  (texi.info.gz)Top        (Info Narrow)--Top---------------------   ■
```

Figure 5.11 Online documentation for the **texinfo** system.

```
● xterm                                                                  ⬚
File: dir       Node: Top       This is the top of the INFO tree
  This (the Directory node) gives a menu of major topics. Typing "d"
  returns here, "q" exits, "?" lists all INFO commands, "h" gives a
  primer for first-timers, "mTexinfo<Return>" visits Texinfo topic, etc.
  --- PLEASE ADD DOCUMENTATION TO THIS TREE. (See INFO topic first.) ---
* Menu: The list of major topics begins on the next line.

Developing in C and C++:
========================
* GCC: (gcc).          Information about the gcc Compiler
* CPP: (cpp).          The C Preprozessor
* Make: (make).        The GNU make Utility
* GDB: (gdb).          The GNU Debugger

Libraries and program generators:
=================================
* glibc: (libc).       The standard C runtime library.
* iostream: (iostream). The GNU C++ iostream library.
* Libg++: (libg++).    The G++ Library
* gmp: (gmp).          GNU MP arbitrary precision arithmetic library.
* Regex: (regex).      The GNU regular expression library.
* Termcap: (termcap).  The termcap library, which enables application programs
                       to handle all types of character-display terminals.
* Gperf: (gperf).      Hash Gererator
* Bison: (bison).      bison, and not yacc
* Flex: (flex).        Fast lexical analyzer
* ipc: (ipc).          System V inter process communication system calls.
* M4: (m4).            GNU 'm4' macro processor

Other languages:
================
* mst: (mst).          The GNU Smalltalk programming language.
* GAWK: (gawk).        The GNU version of awk
* Emacs Lisp: (elisp). The language of emacs.
* CL: (cl).            Partial Common Lisp support for Emacs Lisp.

Using Emacs & Co.
=================
```

Figure 5.12 The **info** command in action.

Using Sed

The **sed** (streams editor) command isn't really a text editor, nor is it really a text processor. However, it can be used as a text processor—or rather, as an interactive text processor. Or you can think of **sed** as a filtering text editor; procedurally, you use the **sed** command with the following steps:

- Read in text from a file.
- Make changes in the text.
- Display new text on screen or save to a file.

These procedures are all specified in one command line. A typical **sed** command line should look something like this:

```
gilbert:~$ sed -n -e operation -f scriptfilename filename
```

where *-n* refers to a specific line or lines, *operation* refers to one of the many available **sed** operations, *scriptfilename* refers to a file that contains a longer list of **sed** operations, and *filename* refers to the file that **sed** works on.

The various command-line options are explained in greater detail in Table 5.6.

Table 5.6 Sed Command-Line Options

Command	Result
-e	Explicitly tells **sed** that what follows is an operation; if you only use one operation, you can omit the -e.
-f	Specifies a script file; if you plan on using many operations regularly, it's best to save them in a script file for future use.
-n	Specifies a specific line number or a range of line numbers to use.

Go ahead and create a text file called **test**:

```
This is a test of the Emergency Linux system. This is a test.
If this were an actual document, we probably would take it
more seriously than we do this flippant, unorganized memo.
```

Let's begin by using **sed** to display only a portion of the file **test**, like the second and third lines. Do so with:

```
$ sed -n '2,3p' test
```

On your display, you'd see the following:

```
If this were an actual document, we probably would take it
more seriously than we do this flippant, unorganized memo.
```

If we wanted to write the results of our command to a file, we could do so as follows:

```
$ sed -n '2,3p' w filename test
```

where *filename* is the name of a file.

Some things to note in our little examples:

- Because we used only one operation, we omitted the -e option.
- We listed the command within single quotes, which tells **sed** that everything contained in the quotes is part of the same operation.
- We specified certain lines for **sed** to work on. If no lines are specified, **sed** assumes that it is to work on the entire file.

Printing, of course, is not the only operation available to **sed** users. We list the major operations in Table 5.7.

Like most UNIX commands, **sed** can be used with pipes and other commands. If you want more information about **sed**, we suggest that you consult the other references cited in Appendix A. You can also get more information about **sed** from the online-manual page:

```
gilbert:~$ man sed
```

Table 5.7 Sed Operations

Operation	Result
a*string*	Adds the *string*.
c*string*	Changes specified lines to the specified *string*.
d	Deletes specified lines or strings.
I	Inserts specified string before specified lines.
l	Lists the file or specified portions thereof—useful because it displays characters normally used for formatting; for example, tabs are printed with the > character.
p	Prints to standard output—unless specified otherwise, your screen.
r *filename*	Inserts an entire file after a specific line.
s/*string1*/*string2*/	Substitutes *string1* for *string2*.
w *filename*	Writes specified lines to *filename*.

Printing with Ghostscript Under Linux

Printing in Linux isn't a very intuitive topic to grasp. (Of course, neither is printing on any PC, for that matter, thanks to a lack of standards between hardware and software.) Most standalone Linux users are going to connect their printers to their PC's parallel port, as this is the accepted way of doing things in the PC world. Of course, some PC owners will be stubborn and use a serial port for a printer, despite all the headaches this will cause.

On one level, printing with Linux is a simple matter, as long as your printer is connected to the parallel port and you don't want to do more than print simple ASCII text. (When you installed Linux, you were asked where the printer was installed; if your printer was connected to the first parallel port, the answer would have been *LPT1* in DOS parlance.) For this level, the basic Linux printing tools (**lpr, pr**) will work just fine, which is how the topic was covered in Chapter 4. The problem becomes a little more pronounced when you want to print graphics and fonts, especially those formatted with PostScript.

Additional information about printing and Linux can be gleaned from Grant Taylor and Brian McCauley's excellent **PRINTING-HOWTO**, contained on the accompanying CD-ROMs.

Using Ghostscript

Many UNIX documents are distributed in the PostScript format (even the Linux Documentation Project uses PostScript-formatted documents, although HTML docs are also available). PostScript, as we all know, is a commercial product under the watchful eye of Adobe. Because Adobe doesn't give away PostScript for free, in order to access PostScript files on the noncommercial Linux operating system, a workaround was needed. Once again the Free Software Foundation came to the rescue, with Ghostscript.

Ghostscript is actually the umbrella term for many smaller programs that allow you to view and print PostScript-formatted documents. (Remember we told you the UNIX operating system is merely a collection of tools?) Ghostview, is the X Window application program for viewing PostScript-formatted documents.) When you installed Slackware Linux (which we covered in Chapter 2), you should have installed all the files necessary to run Ghostscript, including a set of fonts. These files can be found in **/usr/lib/ghostscript** on the first CD-ROM.

Ghostscript requires the X Window System to be running, but is actually launched from a command line in an **xterm** window. As we said, Ghostscript is actually a set of programs, but the program you'll end up using the most is the interpreter, which takes a file and displays the PostScript formatting in anticipation of printing the document. To launch the interpreter, use the following command line:

```
$ gs filename(s)
```

where *filename(s)* refers to the file or files that you want rendered. If you specify multiple files, **gs** will display each file in order.

To view a PostScript file with Ghostview, just specify the file on the command line:

```
$ ghostview file.ps
```

The menu selections for Ghostview are pretty self-evident.

Basically, Ghostscript and Ghostview should work right out of the box if you have X Window and its fonts installed correctly.

Unlike a normal Linux application, which can write directly to the printer, it takes a little bit of work to print a PostScript-formatted file, especially on most PC-based printers. Unlike the UNIX and Macintosh printer worlds, PostScript isn't the *lingua franca* of the PC printer world. Printers listed in Table 5.8 are supported by Ghostscript.

Table 5.8 Printers and Fax Formats Supported by Ghostscript

Name	Printer
ap3250	Epson AP3250 printer
appledmp	Apple dot matrix printer (should also work with Imagewriter)
bj10e	Canon Bubblejet BJ10e
bj200	Canon Bubblejet BJ200
bjc600	Canon Color Bubblejet BJC-600 and BJC-4000
bjc800	Canon Color Bubblejet BJC-800
cdeskjet	HP DeskJet 500C with 1 bit/pixel color
cdjcolor	HP DeskJet 500C with 24 bit/pixel color and high-quality color (Floyd-Steinberg) dithering; also good for DeskJet 540C
cdjmono	HP DeskJet 500C printing black only; also good for DeskJet 510, 520, and 540C (black only)
cdj500	HP DeskJet 500C (same as cdjcolor)
cdj550	HP DeskJet 550C/560C
cp50	Mitsubishi CP50 color printer
declj250	alternate DEC LJ250 driver
deskjet	HP DeskJet and DeskJet Plus
dfaxhigh	DigiBoard DigiFAX software format (high resolution)
dfaxlow	DigiFAX low (normal) resolution
djet500	HP DeskJet 500
djet500c	HP DeskJet 500C alternate driver (does not work on 550C or 560C)
dnj650c	HP DesignJet 650C

Name	Printer
epson	Epson-compatible dot matrix printers (9- or 24-pin)
eps9mid	Epson-compatible 9-pin, interleaved lines (intermediate resolution)
eps9high	Epson-compatible 9-pin, interleaved lines (triple resolution)
epsonc	Epson LQ-2550 and Fujitsu 3400/2400/1200 color printers
faxg3	Group 3 fax, with EOLs but no header or EOD
faxg32d	Group 3 2-D fax, with EOLs but no header or EOD
faxg4	Group 4 fax, with EOLs but no header or EOD
ibmpro	IBM 9-pin Proprinter
imagen	Imagen ImPress printers
iwhi	Apple Imagewriter in high-resolution mode
iwlo	Apple Imagewriter in low-resolution mode
iwlq	Apple Imagewriter LQ in 320 x 216 dpi mode
jetp3852	IBM Jetprinter ink-jet color printer (Model #3852)
laserjet	HP LaserJet
la50	DEC LA50 printer
la70	DEC LA70 printer
la70t	DEC LA70 printer with low-resolution text enhancement
la75	DEC LA75 printer
la75plus	DEC LA75plus printer
lbp8	Canon LBP-8II laser printer
lips3	Canon LIPS III laser printer in English (CaPSL) mode
ln03	DEC LN03 printer
lj250	DEC LJ250 Companion color printer
ljet2p	HP LaserJet IId/IIp/III* with TIFF compression
ljet3	HP LaserJet III* with Delta Row compression
ljet3d	HP LaserJet IIID with duplex capability
ljet4	HP LaserJet 4 (defaults to 600 dpi)
lj4dith	HP LaserJet 4 with Floyd-Steinberg dithering
ljetplus	HP LaserJet Plus

Continued...

Name	Printer
lp2563	HP 2563B line printer
m8510	C.Itoh M8510 printer
necp6	NEC P6/P6+/P60 printers at 360 x 360 DPI resolution
nwp533	Sony Microsystems NWP533 laser printer (Sony only)
oce9050	OCE 9050 printer
oki182	Okidata MicroLine 182
okiibm	Okidata MicroLine IBM-compatible printers
paintjet	alternate H-P PaintJet color printer
pj	HP PaintJet XL driver
pjetxl	alternate HP PaintJet XL driver
pjxl	HP PaintJet XL color printer
pjxl300	HP PaintJet XL300 color printer; also good for PaintJet 1200C
r4081	Ricoh 4081 laser printer
sj48	StarJet 48 inkjet printer
sparc	SPARCprinter
st800	Epson Stylus 800 printer
stcolor	Epson Stylus Color
t4693d2	Tektronix 4693d color printer, 2 bits per R/G/B component
t4693d4	Tektronix 4693d color printer, 4 bits per R/G/B component
t4693d8	Tektronix 4693d color printer, 8 bits per R/G/B component
tek4696	Tektronix 4695/4696 inkjet plotter
tiffcrle	TIFF "CCITT RLE 1-dim" (= Group 3 fax with no EOLs)
tiffg3	TIFF Group 3 fax (with EOLs)
tiffg32d	TIFF Group 3 2-D fax
tiffg4	TIFF Group 4 fax
xes	Xerox XES printers (2700, 3700, 4045, etc.)

Ghostscript also supports a number of graphic file formats, as listed in Table 5.9.

Table 5.9 Graphical File Formats Supported in Ghostscript

Format	Explanation
bit	plain bits, monochrome
bitrgb	plain bits, RGB
bitcmyk	plain bits, CMYK
bmpmono	monochrome MS Windows .BMP file format
bmp16	4-bit (EGA/VGA) .BMP file format
bmp256	8-bit (256-color) .BMP file format
bmp16m	24-bit .BMP file format
cgmmono	monochrome (black-and-white) CGM (low-level output only)
cgm8	8-bit (256-color) CGM (low-level output only)
cgm24	24-bit color CGM (low-level output only)
cif	CIF file format for VLSI
mgrmono	1-bit monochrome MGR devices
mgrgray2	2-bit gray scale MGR devices
mgrgray4	4-bit gray scale MGR devices
mgrgray8	8-bit gray scale MGR devices
mgr4	4-bit (VGA) color MGR devices
mgr8	8-bit color MGR devices
pcxmono	PCX file format, monochrome (1-bit black and white)
pcxgray	PCX file format, 8-bit gray scale
pcx16	PCX file format, 4-bit planar (EGA/VGA) color
pcx256	PCX file format, 8-bit chunky color
pcx24b	PCX file format, 24-bit color (3 8-bit planes)
pbm	Portable Bitmap (plain format)
pbmraw	Portable Bitmap (raw format)
pgm	Portable Graymap (plain format)
pgmraw	Portable Graymap (raw format)
pgnm	Portable Graymap (plain format), optimizing to PBM if possible

Continued...

Format	Explanation
pgnmraw	Portable Graymap (raw format), optimizing to PBM if possible
pnm	portable pixmap (plain format) (RGB), optimizing to PGM or PBM if possible
pnmraw	portable pixmap (raw format) (RGB), optimizing to PGM or PBM if possible
ppm	portable pixmap (plain format) (RGB)
ppmraw	portable pixmap (raw format) (RGB)
psmono	PostScript (Level 1) monochrome image
sgirgb	SGI RGB pixmap format
tiff24nc	TIFF 24-bit RGB, no compression (NeXT standard format)
tifflzw	TIFF LZW (tag = 5) (monochrome)
tiffpack	TIFF PackBits (tag = 32773) (monochrome)

This information was gathered from the Ghostscript Home Page at *http://www.cs.wisc.edu/~ ghost/aladdin/index.html*. Not all of these formats are supported in the version of Ghostscript (2.6.2) that you installed as part of Slackware Linux. To see what formats are supported, use the following command line:

```
$ gs -h
```

If you want a file format that isn't supported by Slackware Linux, you'll need to recompile Ghostscript. Information about this can be found in **/usr/lib/ghostscript/docs**.

In addition, some of the formats and devices listed in Tables 5.8 and 5.9 are supported only in the commercial release (3.5.3) of Ghostscript from Aladdin. Basically, the free releases of Ghostscript from Aladdin lag a full release behind the commercial version. If you plan on using Ghostscript regularly, we suggest you upgrade to the full commercial version; see *http://www.cs.wisc.edu/~ ghost/ghostscript/index.html* for details.

Font Tools

X Window users have access to a wide variety of fonts, which you first learned about in Chapter 3. To see which fonts are available on your Linux system, use the **xlsfonts** command:

```
gilbert:$ xlsfonts
```

If you do this, you'll probably suffer from whiplash as the long list of fonts scrolls by. That's why we usually pipe the output to a file or to the **more** command, which displays the font list one page at a time:

```
gilbert:$ xlsfonts : more
-adobe-courier-bold-i-normal—0-0-0-0-m-0-iso8859-1
...
```

To see what fonts are offered by your font server (assuming you've installed one; again, this is a topic you covered in Chapter 3), use the **fslsfonts** command:

```
gilbert:$ fslsfonts
```

Again, you might want to pipe the output to a file or to the **more** command.

To get information about your specific font server, use the **fsinfo** command:

```
gilbert:$ fsinfo
```

To look at all the characters in a particular font, use the **xfd** command, as shown in Figure 5.13:

```
gilbert:# xfd -fn variable
```

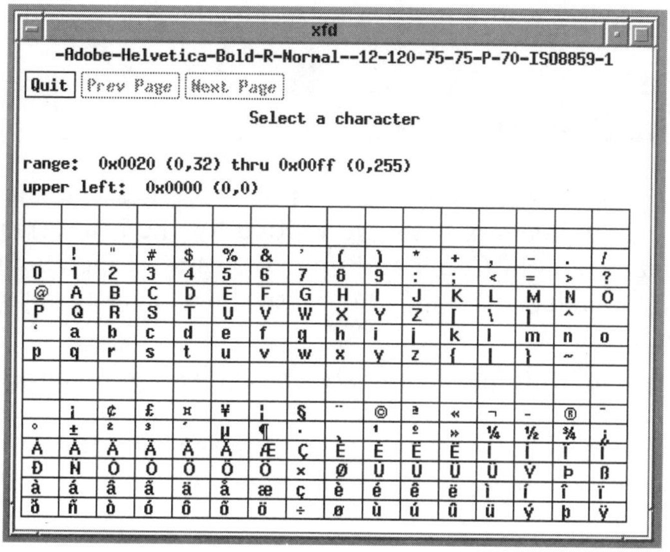

Figure 5.13 The **xfd** command in action.

You can also use the **xfontsel** command to browse through your fonts, as shown in Figure 5.14.

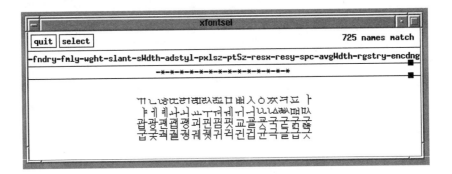

Figure 5.14 The **xfontsel** command in action.

File Managers

In Chapter 3 we introduced the idea of *file managers*—programs that present a graphical look to the Slackware Linux operating system, either when running in command-line mode or with the X Window System. In this section, we'll take a look at some of the file managers included with Slackware Linux, as well as one that we included on the second CD-ROM.

Midnight Commander

The Midnight Commander is a clone of the Norton Commander, one of the more useful pieces of software written for the MS-DOS operating system. The Midnight Command approaches the functionality of the Norton Commander, allowing you to move, rename, and copy files and directories.

Basically, the Midnight Commander divides file management into four screens: Two display file directories (so you can see where files and directories are going and where they have been), one is a shell command line (where you can directly enter shell commands), and one is a menu bar. (If the menu bar isn't present, you can summon it by moving the mouse to the top of the screen or pressing the **F9** key.)

Using the Mouse

When you installed Slackware Linux, you were asked about installing mouse support for Linux when running in a command-line mode—chiefly, the **gpm** mouse server—and at that time we recommended that you do not, because **gpm** support may conflict with the mouse functionality of the X Window System.

However, if you're not going to use the X Window System and you want to use the mouse in Midnight Commander, you should go back to the **setup** program and install the **gpm** mouse support.

If you run the Midnight Commander under X Window, you should have the functionality of the mouse.

You'll want to use Midnight Commander with a mouse; its greatest virtues lie in its ability to click on files and directories in order to perform further actions on them. You can perform all of your Slackware Linux computing tasks from within Midnight Commander; to launch an application, you can just double-click on its executable command, and if you want to associate a filename extension with an application (say, associating all files ending in *.doc* or *.txt* with **emacs**), you can do so.

Launching the Midnight Commander

You can launch the Midnight Commander with the following command line:

```
gilbert:$ mc
```

If you're using Midnight Commander under X, you should use the following command line in an **xterm** window:

```
gilbert:$ mc -x
```

There are a host of command-line options for Midnight Commander, some of which are listed in Table 5.10.

Table 5.10 Command-Line Options for Midnight Commander

Option	Result
-b	Switches display from color to black and white.
-c	Switches display from black and white to color.
-C *arg*	Changes the color to *arg*.
-d	Disables mouse support.
-f	Midnight Commander can be built with a specified set of search paths; this option displays them.
-V	Displays the current version number.
-x	Tells Midnight Commander that it is running in an **xterm** window, allowing support of screen modes and mouse escape sequences.

Midnight Commander is also complex when it comes to features (in other words, there are a lot of them, and they're not always apparent), so it's best to review the online documentation for Midnight Commander before you spend a lot of time trying to figure it out. You can get a full description of Midnight Commander by perusing its **man** page:

```
gilbert:$ man mc
```

or

```
gilbert:$ xman
```

Xfm

An X Window equivalent to Midnight Commander is **xfm**, which presents a graphical look at your applications and files.

Before you actually use **xfm**, you need to configure it by running a short script file called **xfm.install**:

```
gilbert:$ xfm.install
```

This copies configuration files to your home directory.

You can launch it from an **xterm** window:

```
gilbert:$ xfm
```

Xfm opens with two windows: one showing the contents of the current directory and one that lists configured applications. Ordinary files are represented by paper pages (like in the Macintosh operating system), links are represented by pages containing a chain, applications are represented by a page showing a little window, the parent directory is represented by a file folder with two arrows pointing up, and other directories are represented by plain file folders.

There are three pull-down menus in the main **xfm** window: File, Folder, and View. The File menu covers basic file actions (such as creating a new file; deleting, linking, and moving files; and selecting a set of files in order to perform actions on a group), the Folder menu does the same for directories, and the View menu governs how files are represented (like whether or not to display the extended file information, hidden files, and so on). You can drag and drop icons representing files.

Using the Application Manager

After you configure **xfm**, a set of applications appears in your Applications window. This doesn't mean that you actually have all these applications available on your Slackware Linux system; it means that an icon is available in case you want to install these applications. (For example, Slackware Linux doesn't ship with Mosaic, but there's an icon available.)

To change what's displayed in the Applications window, you'll need to edit the **.xfm** file (note the leading period, which means that the file is hidden) located in your **$HOME** directory:

```
gilbert:~$ xedit .xfm
```

Many of the applications, however, are included with Slackware Linux, such as **xterm**, **emacs**, **textedit**, **mail**, **calculator**, **manual** (a shortcut to the **xman** command), In addition, the **Toolbox** icon presents a new window that displays shortcuts to the **exec**, **xxgdb**, **make**, **gzip**, **tar -cfv**, tar -cfvz, zip, uuencode, grep, find, and xfmtype commands. The Graphics icon presents a new window that displays shortcuts to various graphics utilities (which will be covered later in this chapter).

Command-Line Options

There are only three command-line options to xfm:

- **-appmgr**, which launches only the application manager and not the file manager.
- **-filemgr**, which launches only the file manager and not the application manager.
- **-version**, which displays the version number of xfm.

To get more information about xfm, you can read its online man page:

```
gilbert:$ xman
```

Tkdesk

While xfm is a perfectly fine file manager, we've included another really good file manager, tkdesk, on the second CD-ROM. Tkdesk is one of the best written, most useful Linux applications around. It manages your files with an interface that looks a lot like that of the Windows Explorer, as shown in Figure 5.15.

You can configure tkdesk from within the application itself—a major advance for UNIX applications. You can use tkdesk to launch applications with its handy task bar. You can also associate file types with programs, so you simply have to double-clock on a .GIF file, for example, to launch xv, an image-viewing program.

Figure 5.15 Managing your files with **tkdesk**.

Compressing and Archiving Your Files

When you start poking around the Internet and see that most of the files end with cryptic suffixes like **.gz** and **.tar**, you know you've wandered past your background in older versions of UNIX—and past the PC and Macintosh worlds, for that matter.

These suffixes are important, however, if you plan on grabbing software from an FTP site and installing it on your Linux system. In addition, you may find the tools responsible for these suffixes to be very useful as you archive files or prepare them for transmission to other systems, either directly or via the Internet.

Essentially, a suffix of **.gz** means that a file has been compressed using the GNU **gzip** utility, and as you poke around the Linux software world, you'll see that it's very common. **gzip** is not the only UNIX/Linux utility for compressing files; the traditional **compress** command is also supported, while this release of Slackware Linux now features the **zip** and **unzip** commands, which maintain conformity with the famous **PKZip** compression format from PKWare. All of these commands do essentially the same thing: They take an ASCII or binary file (or a defined set of files) and shrink them into a smaller file. This file can then be sent via the Internet or electronic mail faster. Most UNIX systems come with both **compress** and **pack** (and their counterparts, **uncompress** and **unpack**).

Because **gzip** and **zip** come with your Linux system, they are probably the commands you'll want to concentrate on. **Gunzip** (the counterpart to **gzip**) can be used on files compressed with **compress** and **pack**, which means that it will work with the vast majority of compressed files in the UNIX world. **Zip** will work with files zipped up with software in the MS-DOS, Macintosh, and Windows worlds; as this format is prevalent on the Internet, you'll want to become familiar with it if you begin to surf the Internet on a regular basis. In a sense, you don't need to know what command the file was compressed with—in other words, you don't need to worry about an extension of **.z** versus **.Z** versus **.gz**—**gzip** will work on them all. Similarly, you can use **zip** if you see a file ending with **.zip**. If you're working with compressed files for distribution to the rest of the world, you'll want to be careful about using **gzip**; after all, not all UNIX users have **gzip**, although most Internet users seem to (judging by the number of **gzip**-compressed files on various FTP sites).

We're not going to get into recommendations about which compression utility to use. There are versions of **gzip** for other operating systems, such as MS-DOS, although they tend not to be widely distributed. Similarly, because **PKZip** is available at no charge for every major operating system, it's become the format of choice in the MS-DOS and Windows worlds. (The major compression utility in the Macintosh world, StuffIt, isn't available for other operating systems.) As more Internet information is archived in **.zip** files, it's become perhaps the major compression format overall in the computer world. Because you have both commands available, it's up to you to choose the right format for your circumstances.

Extended documentation on **gzip** can be found in the GNU **texinfo** documentation discussed earlier in this chapter, while you can get more information about **zip** from its online **man** entry:

```
gilbert:$ man zip
```

or

```
gilbert:$ xman
```

In the following two sections, we'll cover both **gzip** and **zip**.

Using Gzip

The **gzip** command works in the following steps:

- Compress the specified file.
- Save the compressed file to disk, adding a *.gz* to the old filename; compressing a file named **test** will yield a new filename of **test.gz**.
- Delete the original file.

For example, you may begin with a directory that contains the following files:

```
#test#       fig7_10.xwd     fig7_12.xwd     test.bk
#test3#      fig7_11.xwd     test            test3
```

Let's say you want to compress the file named **test**. You'd do so with the following command line:

```
gilbert:/home/kevinr# gzip test
```

A listing of the current directory would yield the following result:

```
#test#        fig7_10.xwd    fig7_12.xwd    test.gz
#test3#       fig7_11.xwd    test.bk        test3
```

The file **test** has been replaced by **test.gz**. If you're used to working in the PC or Macintosh world, you may be used to working with **PKZip** from PKWare. However, **gzip** and **PKZip** don't work exactly the same. For starters, **gzip** won't compress multiple files into a single archive via wildcards in the way **PKZip** does. If you run the following command line:

```
gilbert:/home/kevinr# gzip te*
```

A listing of the current directory would yield the following result:

```
#test#        fig7_10.xwd    fig7_12.xwd    test.gz
#test3#       fig7_11.xwd    test.bk.gz     test3.gz
```

The original files beginning with *te* have replaced by individual files beginning with *te* and ending with *.gz*.

To see to what extent a file has been compressed, use the *-l* (*ell*) option to **gzip** on a compressed file:

```
gilbert:/home/kevinr# gzip -l test.gz
compressed  uncompr.  ratio  uncompressed_name
      122   245       59.5%  test
```

The 59.5 percent is actually a tad low for a file compressed with **gzip**; however, because we started with a relatively small file, the compression factor isn't as extensive as it would be with a larger file. However, some large files that are already compressed (namely, graphics files in the JPEG and GIF formats) can't be compressed to a great extent by **gzip**.

Using Gunzip

The **gunzip** command can be used to uncompress any compressed file, whether the compression was performed with the **gzip**, **compress**, or **pack** command. It's simple to use—just combine it with the name of the compressed file:

```
gilbert:/home/kevinr# gunzip test.gz
```

When you uncompress a file, the compressed file is automatically deleted from the system. If you're uncompressing a file and you're not quite sure about its contents, you may want to copy the file into another directory, leaving the original compressed file intact.

Using Zip

The **zip** command compresses a set of files into a single, compact archive. It can be uncompressed and scanned by versions of **zip** in the MS-DOS, Windows, Windows 95, Windows NT, Macintosh, OS/2, and VMS worlds. There are some limits to this compatibility; the Linux **zip** creates zipped files that can be read only by newer versions of **pkzip**— 2.04g or newer. (Note that **zip** was not created by Phil Katz or PKWare, so don't expect any support from them.)

To zip a set of files (in this case, all the commands in the existing directory), use a command line like the following:

```
gilbert:$ zip *
```

This is already different from **gzip**, which is used only to compress a single file; you can specify a range of filenames using wildcards with **zip**. As **zip** zips the files, the progress will be reported to the screen. When you compress these files, the original files are unchanged (as opposed to **gzip**, where the originals are deleted after being included in the archive).

There are a host of command-line options to **zip**. To translate the UNIX end-of-line character (linefeed) into the combination carriage-return/linefeed that MS-DOS prefers (useful when you're exchanging text or source-code files with MS-DOS/Windows users; *don't* use this option when sending binaries!), use the *-l* (*ell*) option, as in the following example:

```
gilbert:$ zip -l *.c
```

Similarly, when you're passing files to MS-DOS/Windows users, you must take into account the fact that MS-DOS can't handle long filenames or handle files that contain two periods. The *-k* option tries to make the UNIX filenames conform to MS-DOS conventions:

```
gilbert:$ zip -k file.zip *.c
```

You can add files to an existing **zip** file with the *-g* option:

```
gilbert:$ zip -g file.zip *.c
```

Occasionally a zipped file will be damaged in transit, the result of a byte or two being dropped. **zip** is smart enough to detect the damage and to give you the means to repair the damage. After **zip** tells you that an archive is damaged, use the *-F* option to fix it:

```
gilbert:$ zip -F damaged.zip
```

If you want to run **zip** in "quiet" mode—that is, without returning any output to the screen as files are individually compressed (useful if you use **zip** in a pipe or a shell script)—use the *-q* option:

```
gilbert:$ zip -q zipfile.zip *.c
```

You can get more information about **zip** from the online **man** pages:

```
gilbert:$ man zip
```

or

```
gilbert:$ xman
```

Be warned, however, that the **man** pages are not 100 percent accurate. Don't be surprised if some of the listed options (such as *-e* and *-ee*, used for encryption) don't work with your version of **zip**.

Related Zip Commands

To unzip a zipped archive, use the **unzip** command:

```
gilbert:$ unzip zipfile.zip
```

To unzip a file as part of a pipe, use **funzip**:

```
gilbert:$ funzip zipfile.zip: command
```

To search through an archive using the **egrep** command, use **zipgrep**:

```
gilbert:$ zipgrep zipfile.zip
```

Other related commands include **zipcloak, zipinfo, zipnote,** and **zipsplit.**

Using Tar

As noted, the **gzip** command doesn't work with a set of files; it works only on a single specified file. If you want to compress a set of files, you'll first need to create an archive of files and then compress the archive. The UNIX/Linux **tar** (tape archive) command does just this.

Tar doesn't actually compress any files in the archive. It merely combines the files and retains the directory structure in one large archive.

Again, if you're wandering around the Internet and various FTP sites, you'll probably run into files that end with **.tar.gz**; this means that a set of files has been archived with **tar** and then compressed with **gzip**. And if you decide to do system backups—which we strongly advise you to do—the **tar** command is the first step in creating that archive.

The **tar** command is somewhat involved; it's not difficult to use, but its options tend to be obscure. However, a few examples of **tar** in action should clear things up for you.

Let's say you want to back up all the files in an important directory—**/home/patrick**—to make sure your work isn't lost to the world. Before you use **tar**, make sure your current directory is **/home/patrick** and then use the following command line to back up the contents of the directory:

```
gilbert:~/patrick tar cvf archive.tar .
```

This command line will create an archived file named **archive.tar** in the current directory, through the use of the following functions and options:

- *c*, which creates the archive file.
- *v*, which tells **tar** to be verbose (that is, to report on the files being archived) as it archives the contents of the directory.
- *f*, which specifies that **archive.tar** is the filename of the archive.

It doesn't matter much what order the functions and options are in; older versions of **tar** required that a function immediately follow the command in the command line, but the version of **tar** that ships with Linux lacks this requirement. However, it's usually a good idea to put *f* as your final option, because this is where you specify a filename.

Tar also leaves the existing files in the directory intact (unlike **gzip**, which removes the original file). **Tar** doesn't require a hyphen (-) before functions and options. However, you can use one if you please; it won't cause any effect to the command line.

The command line ends with a period (.), which tells **tar** to use all the contents of the current directory as input for the archive file. (**tar** will also archive hidden files.) You can also use **tar** with wildcards (using **c*** instead of . at the end of the command line would archive all files in the current directory beginning with *c*). In addition, you can specify a directory to be archived, giving either a pathname (**home/patrick**) or a pathname relative to the current directory (for instance, you can specify **patrick** if the current directory is /**home**). However, you cannot use absolute filenames to create an archive; **tar** will remove the leading slash (/) from the pathname to make sure that important files aren't overwritten when the file is unarchived. (You'll see why later in this section.) When you specify a directory to be archived, **tar** will also archive any subdirectories and maintain the directory structure. In fact, it's considered good practice to create a subdirectory specifically for the archived material; in that way, users won't have problems when unarchiving your materials on their systems.

After you run **tar**, you end up with another Linux file subject to the same rules that all Linux files must follow. You could copy this file to a floppy disk or to another directory in the Linux file system, you could save it to a tape drive or recordable CD-ROM drive, or you could compress it using **gzip** (as explained earlier in this chapter). Because all UNIX users have access to the **tar** command, you can pass the file along to other users and know that they can unarchive your archive. In addition, there are versions of **tar** for the MS-DOS and Macintosh operating systems, so your archive can be used by most computer users.

Functions and Options

When we used **tar** in the previous section, we specified *cvf* on the command line. This bears further explanation.

Tar requires the use of functions and options on the command line. If you enter a command line lacking a function, **tar** will report an error. In our sample command line, we used c as the obligatory function, following it up with the optional *v* and *f* options.

Important **tar** functions and options are listed in Tables 5.11 and 5.12. We present them in case you need some of the more obscure functions; for the most part, the only functions you'll use are c, x, and t.

Table 5.11 Important Functions in Tar

Function	Result
A	Appends files to an existing archive.
c	Creates a new archive.
d	Compares existing files in the filesystem to the files in the archive, making sure that no existing files are overwritten.
r	Appends specified files to the end of an existing archive.
t	Lists of the contents of an existing archive.
u	Updates files in the filesystem if the archive contains newer versions.
x	Extracts files and directories from the archive.

Table 5.12 Important Options in Tar

Function	Result
f *filename*	Specifies a *filename* for the archive.
k	Keeps existing files.
M	Creates a multivolume archive.
v	Works in verbose mode, which means that **tar** lists the files being archives or unarchived; we always use this option to make sure **tar** is really archiving the files we want archived.
z	Zips a file (using **gzip**) while also creating the archive (this option will be explained later in this chapter).

These are the major functions and options for **tar**, but there are many others that apply to other situations. For a full list of the functions and options for the GNU version of **tar**, use the following command line:

```
gilbert:~$ man tar
```

or use the **info** command to view the **texinfo** explanation of **tar**.

Unarchiving an Archive

You'll also use **tar** to unarchive a **tar** file, using a command line that looks like the following:

```
gilbert:~$ tar xvf archive.tar
```

This will unarchive the files and create any subdirectories found in the archive. However, these subdirectories will be created as subdirectories of the current working directory. In the preceding command line, if there's a directory named **stuff**, it will be created as a subdirectory of the user's home directory. When files are archived, **tar** automatically strips the leading slash (/), which denotes an absolute pathname. If you've been a good UNIX citizen, you've created an archive based on a new subdirectory, so all the files that are unarchived will be in their own subdirectory.

To see what files are in an archive, use the *t* function with **tar**:

```
gilbert:~$ tar tvf archive.tar
drwxr-xr-x kevinr/users        0 Apr 23 00:57 1995 home/kevinr/
-rw-r-r- kevinr/users        164 Mar 30 02:59 1995 home/kevinr/.kermrc
-rw-r-r- kevinr/users         34 Jun  6 15:16 1993 home/kevinr/.less
-rw-r-r- kevinr/users        114 Nov 23 19:22 1993 home/kevinr/.lessrc
drwxr-xr-x kevinr/users        0 Mar 29 09:31 1995 home/kevinr/.term
-rwxr-xr-x kevinr/users     2730 Mar 30 02:59 1995 home/kevinr/.term/termrc
-rw-r-r- kevinr/users       3016 May 13 16:39 1994 home/kevinr/.emacs
-rw-r-r- kevinr/users        471 Apr 20 03:12 1995 home/kevinr/.bash_history
-rw-r-r- root/root           197 Apr 21 00:04 1995 home/kevinr/test3
-rw-r-r- root/root           247 Apr 20 03:33 1995 home/kevinr/#test#
-rw-r-r- root/root           197 Apr 21 00:18 1995 home/kevinr/#test3#
-rw-r-r- root/root        268399 Apr 22 11:48 1995 home/kevinr/fig7_10.xwd
-rw-r-r- kevinr/users        122 Apr  6 10:13 1995 home/kevinr/test.gz
-rw-r-r- root/root        325889 Apr 22 12:03 1995 home/kevinr/fig7_11.xwd
-rw-r-r- root/root        252107 Apr 22 12:01 1995 home/kevinr/fig7_12.xwd
-rw-r-r- kevinr/users        245 Apr  8 09:22 1995 home/kevinr/test.bk
```

The *t* function merely tells **tar** to display the contents of the archive; there's no extraction of files. Armed with this knowledge, however, we could go ahead and unarchive a specific file or files. For example, to unarchive the file **test.bk**, you'd use the following command line:

```
gilbert:~$ tar xvf archive.tar home/kevinr/test.bk
```

Using the Z Option

As we've mentioned repeatedly here, you'll probably use the **tar** command in conjunction with the **gzip** command, creating an archived and compressed file. Because Linux works with tools from the Free Software Foundation, you can expect some integration of similar tools (as you've seen with **emacs** and **texinfo**). This integration is extended with an option unique to the GNU versions of **tar** and **gzip**: the *z* option. This handy function allows you to both archive and compress a file or set of files by using the *z* options with **tar**. For example, you could use the following command line to both archive and compress a set of files:

```
gilbert:~$ tar cvzf archive.tar.gz .
```

You must specify the **.tar** and **.gz** extensions when creating an archive using the *z* option, as opposed to the separate use of **gzip** where a **.gz** extension is added automatically.

To both unarchive and uncompress a file, you'd use the following command line:

```
gilbert:~$ tar xvzf archive.tar.gz
```

Making System Backups

In our discussion of **tar** and **gzip**, we didn't really get into making backups of your systems. If you've been exposed at all to computing (by now you should be), you should know to back up your system regularly. Computing systems fail, though not as often as they did in the past, and you should always make it a point to back up critical data.

Of course, what constitutes *critical data* depends on your viewpoint. Some users feel comfortable backing up their entire system, particularly if they've made many configuration changes to their Linux installation. (This would include recompiling the kernel.) Others may feel comfortable backing up only selected system files, knowing that Linux is on a CD-ROM and can be easily reinstalled.

Backups really fall in two categories: system files and data files. The system files, of course, are the configuration files that you've adapted for your own particular usage; these would include any hidden configuration files as well as the configuration files used for the X Window System. On the other hand, data files are your actual work; if you've been programming an application, for example, you'll want to save those data files in a backup frequently. And you'll probably want to save the files—both hidden and public—in your home directory and in the home directories of your users if you're a system administrator.

Our larger point is that there's no rule to fit all the circumstances surrounding a backup. If you're a system administrator and you need to save a large number of files, you should be using **tar**, **gzip**, and a tape drive to archive files. If you're just looking at saving a few smaller files or a single directory, you can use **tar** and **gzip** to create a smaller file that can be copied directly to a floppy disk.

Using a Floppy for Backups

Linux allows you to directly write to a floppy disk. You don't need to mount the disk drive or create a Linux filesystem before writing to it. Even if the diskette is formatted with MS-DOS, Linux will write over the existing contents of the file. (In other words, if you've got important files on a diskette and don't want them to be wiped out by Linux, don't use a device driver to access the floppy. Later in this chapter we'll discuss Linux commands for accessing the MS-DOS-formatted floppy.)

Linux assumes that the first disk drive on a PC is **/dev/fd0**. You can use the **tar** command to send its output to this drive instead of to a file:

```
gilbert:~$ tar cvf /dev/fd0 .
```

If the contents of the archived files are too large to fit on one floppy, you'll need to create a multivolume archive; you can do so with the M (remembering that case counts in Linux; using m instead of M will yield a different result!) option to **tar**, as in the following command line:

```
gilbert:~$ tar cvMf /dev/fd0 .
```

In this instance, you'll want to keep careful track of your floppies; if they get out of order or you accidentally lose a diskette, you run the risk of ruining the entire archive.

Of course, if you use the -z option to **tar**, you may be able to fit an entire archive on a single floppy.

Using a Tape Drive for Backups

You can write to a tape drive for a backup directly with the **tar** command. However, which device you write to depends on your system setup.

If you're using a tape drive that runs from the floppy controller (as is the case with most QIC-type drives, for example), you'll need to specify **/dev/rft0** as your device:

```
gilbert:~$ tar cvf /dev/rft0 .
```

This creates an archive on the tape drive.

There's a little more to creating this tape archive than might appear. For example, if you're using a QIC-type tape drive, there's no way to format these tapes under Linux; you'll need to use the DOS utilities to format a tape (see, there was a reason to keep that DOS partition!) or buy preformatted tapes.

In addition, there's the sticky issue of exactly how much data you can throw on a tape. Most newer QIC-type drives rewind automatically every use. However, Linux can't deal with this rewinding, and there's no way to create a marker on the tape to place multiple backups on the same tape. How wasteful this seems depends on who is paying for the tape; quite honestly, you can get by with just two tapes, performing weekly backups revolving the two tapes and reformatting between.

Another option is to use a nonrewinding tape device driver, which can be specified as **/dev/nrft0** (or another number in the sequence, depending on your system setup). Your command line would look something like this:

```
gilbert:~$ tar cvf /dev/nrft0 .
```

In this manner you could create several archives.

When using **/dev/nrft0** you'll have to rewind the tape on your own and then look for separate archives. To rewind the tape after you're finished creating archives, use the **mt** command:

```
gilbert:~$ mt /dev/nrft0 rewind
```

The **mt** command is a wonderful thing. If you've worked with tape drives at all, you know that they can run into problems when they're only partially used; they become "loose" and can jam. The **mt** command allows you to forward a tape to the end and then rewind, in a command line like the following:

```
gilbert:~$ mt /dev/nrft0 retension
```

Finally, the **mt** command allows you to specify files on a tape drive, in case you don't want to use **tar** to unarchive all of them. This gets you into some tricky ground, however, because Linux still can't recognize the file makers on a tape drive, and your efforts are in effect tricking Linux into accessing the correct files. Let's say you've rewound the tape but you want to grab the second file on the tape. In this case, you must tell Linux to look for the next file on the tape—or in **mt** parlance, the first file past the current file. You'd use the following command line:

```
gilbert:~$ mt /dev/nrft0 fsf 1
```

The same thing could be used to move the tape placement to the third or fourth files on the tape, using the following command lines (respectively):

```
gilbert:~$ mt /dev/nrft0 fsf 2
```

and

```
gilbert:~$ mt /dev/nrft0 fsf 3
```

In addition, there's another twist to **mt**. You can't move between sequential files on a tape drive and then try to grab more than one file; with **mt**, you must move to the first file in question and then move to the next file in question. If you want to grab the fifth and sixth files in a tape, you must first move to the fifth file, use **tar** to unarchive it, and then move to the sixth file separately, keeping in mind that **mt** moves in relation to the current file. Therefore, you'd use a sequence like the following:

```
gilbert:~$ mt /dev/nrft0 fsf 4
```

remembering that you're moving in relation to the first file on the tape; after you use **tar**, you'd use the following command line:

```
gilbert:~$ mt /dev/nrft0 fsf 1
```

remembering that the sixth file is the first file after the fifth file.

You can also back up to a tape drive, such as a QIC or DAT tape drive, connected to a SCSI board. In this case, you'll use a command line like the following:

```
gilbert:~$ mt /dev/rst0 .
```

if you want to use a rewinding device and the SCSI device is numbered 0, or use:

```
gilbert:~$ mt /dev/nrst0 .
```

for a rewinding device and the SCSI device is numbered 0.

The **mt** command also allows you to access tapes made by different devices. For the most part, you shouldn't have problems reading a DAT tape created on another system. However, you can run into problems if the other UNIX system used a different block size when creating the tape. In this case, your attempts to read the file will result in error messages. To avoid these, you'll need to use **mt** to specify a new block size, as in the following command line:

```
gilbert:~$ mt setblk blocksize
```

There are a host of additional options to the **mt** command; as always, you're encouraged to peruse the online-manual page:

```
gilbert:~$ man mt
```

or

```
gilbert:~$ xman
```

Commands Specific to the PC Architecture: MTools

The **mt** command is but one of many Linux commands that are expressly designed for the many quirks of the PC architecture—specifically on DOS-formatted floppy disks. The MTools commands are designed to take these quirks into account when performing many routine tasks.

In short, the need for the *m*-series of commands exists because DOS files and UNIX files are structured a little differently, which is something you'll need to watch for, especially if you're using floppy drives. In fact, you can wipe out a good DOS floppy disk by using a UNIX command to copy a file to it. (We learned this the hard way.)

Therefore, you'll want to check out the *m*-series of commands, used specifically to deal with the quirks of the DOS and Linux architectures and the differences between them.

Using Mdir to View the Contents of a DOS Directory

This straightforward command is used to list the contents of a DOS directory:

```
gilbert:~$ mdir
```

The default for **mdir** and the rest of the MTools, is **A:** (in other words, your first floppy drive). Because a DOS partition can be mounted from Linux, the *m*-series of commands won't accept **C:** as an input.

Using Mcd to Change Directories

The **mcd** command changes directories on the floppy drive (the default is the root directory on **A:**). Without an argument, it displays the current device and working directory:

```
gilbert:~$ mcd
A:/
```

Using Mcopy to Copy Files

As noted, the UNIX **cp** command can be destructive to an MS-DOS file structure on a floppy. To copy a file from within Linux to a DOS floppy, you'll want to use the **mcopy** command:

```
gilbert:~$ mcopy -t textfile a:textfile
```

As you probably noticed, the **mcopy** command uses the DOS convention of naming floppy drives (as opposed to the UNIX **dev** designations).

Here **mcopy** was used to copy a file named **textfile** (presumably containing text) to the **A:** floppy drive. The *-t* option was used because UNIX and DOS have different ways of dealing with linefeeds, and this option is specifically for text-file translation.

There are only a few other command-line options to **mcopy**. In a show of mercy on the part of its designers, **mcopy** will warn you if you're overwriting an existing file. In order to ignore this mercy, you'd need to run **mcopy** with the *-n* option:

```
gilbert:~$ mcopy -n textfile a:textfile
```

If you want to be told about each file movement as it happens, use the verbose mode, as launched by the *-v* option:

```
gilbert:~$ mcopy -v textfile a:textfile
```

Also, remember that you must always conform to the DOS eight-dot-three naming convention when working with DOS files.

The **mread** and **mwrite** commands do the same thing.

Using Mren to Rename DOS Files

The **mren** command renames DOS files:

```
gilbert:~$ mren oldfile.nam newfile.nam
```

Remember that you must always conform to the DOS eight-dot-three naming convention when working with DOS files.

Using Mdel to Delete DOS Files

The **mdel** command, predictably enough, is used to delete files from a DOS directory. For example, to delete **textfile** from the **A:** floppy drive, you'd use the following command line:

```
gilbert:~$ mdel a:textfile
```

Using Mtype to View a DOS File

If you want to view the contents of a DOS file on a floppy, use the **mtype** command to display the file:

```
gilbert:~$ mtype filename
```

If you're viewing an ASCII file, use the *-t* option:

```
gilbert:~$ mtype -t filename
```

Using Mmd to Create a DOS Directory

You can create a DOS directory with the **mmd** command:

```
gilbert:~$ mmd newdirec.tor
```

Remember that you must always conform to the DOS eight-dot-three naming convention when working with DOS directories.

Using Mrd to Remove a DOS Directory

If you're not happy with the directory you created with **mmd**, you can delete it with the **mrd** command:

```
gilbert:~$ mrd newdirec.tor
```

Using Mread to Copy a DOS File to Linux

The **mread** command transfers a DOS file to a Linux file, making appropriate conversions if necessary. This command actually works on two different levels: It can be used to transfer a single file to a UNIX file, or it can be used to transfer a set of DOS files to a Linux directory. In the first usage, you'll need to specify both the DOS and UNIX filenames:

```
gilbert:~$ mread dosfile unixfile
```

To copy a set of files to a specific UNIX directory, specify the DOS files (yes, you can use wildcards) and then the UNIX directory:

```
gilbert:~$ mread *.* /home/kevinr
```

If a file of the same name already exists in the destination directory, **mread** will warn you before overwriting the file.

There are a few useful options to **mread**:

- *-t*, which converts a DOS text file to a UNIX text file, stripping DOS carriage returns from the destination file.
- *-m*, which preserves the time stamps on the original DOS files.
- *-n*, which removes the overwriting-prevention mechanisms.

The **mcopy** command will also copy files between DOS and Linux.

Using Mwrite to Write a UNIX File to DOS

The **mwrite** command writes a UNIX file to a DOS-formatted diskette:

```
gilbert:~$ mwrite unixfile dosfile
```

If a file of the same name already exists in the destination diskette, **mwrite** will warn you before overwriting the file.

There are a few useful options to **mwrite**:

- *-t*, which converts a UNIX text file to a DOS text file, adding DOS carriage returns to the destination file.
- *-m*, which preserves the time stamps on the original Linux files.
- *-n*, which removes the overwriting-prevention mechanisms.

The **mcopy** command will also copy files between DOS and Linux.

Using Mformat to Format a Diskette

The **mformat** command adds the basics of a DOS file system (FAT, boot sector, and a root directory) to a UNIX-formatted diskette. To format a diskette in drive **A:**, you'd use the following:

```
gilbert:~$ mformat a:
```

Mformat also supports a number of options:

- *-t*, which sets the number of tracks (not sectors).
- *-h*, which sets the number of heads.
- *-s*, which sets the sectors per track.
- *-l*, which sets the volume label.

The **mformat** command will work only with a diskette that's already been formatted for UNIX. Its usefulness is actually more limited than may appear at first glance.

Using Mlabel to Designate a Volume Label

The **mlabel** command displays a current DOS volume label and then asks for a new label; if you don't enter anything at the prompt, **mlabel** merely removes the existing volume label without adding a new one. The only option to **mlabel**, *-v*, runs the command in verbose mode (always a good thing if you're working with an unfamiliar command).

Using Mattrib to Change the DOS File Attributes

If you're exchanging files with a DOS machine, you may (however, the chance is pretty remote) run into conflicts with the file's attributes (which are akin to the Linux file permissions). A DOS file can have be read-only (*r*), archived (*a*), system (*s*), or hidden (*h*). You can use **mattrib** to change these permissions; **+** to add the attribute (highly unlikely) or **-** to remove the attribute (more likely, although you probably won't be messing much with DOS file attributes). For example, to change a file from hidden to unhidden, you'd use the following command line:

```
gilbert:~$ mattrib -h filename
```

To remove the read-only designation from a file, use a command line like the following:

```
gilbert:~$ mattrib -r filename
```

To make the file a regular file and not a system file, you'd use a command line like the following:

```
gilbert:~$ mattrib -s filename
```

To make the file a file that can be archived (how DOS allows files to be archived is a rather twisted and sordid tale; let's just leave it at that), you'd use a command line like the following:

```
gilbert:~$ mattrib -a filename
```

To add the attributes in the preceding examples, you'd substitute **+** for **-**.

These commands assume that you're working with drive **A:**. If you're working with a file on your hard drive, you can designate an absolute filename on the command line (using the DOS practice of a backslash between directories), but be sure and enclose the absolute filename in quotation marks or your Linux shell will choke on the filename.

Graphics Tools

Much of the purpose of the X Window System is to bring graphical computing tools to a text-based operating system, UNIX (or, in this case, Linux). Hence the presence of many X-only tools designed to create and edit graphics of all sorts. We'll review some of them here.

Bitmap

This simple program is used for creating *bitmaps*, small rectangular drawings that can be inserted directly into C programming code and can be used for icons, cursor shapes, tile and stipple patterns, and more. It's shown in Figure 5.16.

When you launch the **bitmap** command, you're presented with a grid representing the image. You can use the accompanying settings to create shapes (like curves). If you're using **bitmap** to create cursors, you can designate a point as a *hot spot*, which determines where the cursor is pointing. Bitmaps can be inverted or folded.

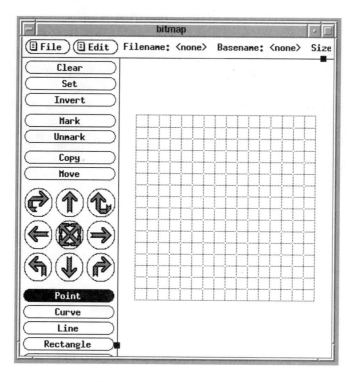

Figure 5.16 The **bitmap** program.

Additional utilities (**bmtoa** and **atobm**) can be used to convert the final bitmap file to and from ASCII strings.

Xfig

Xfig is a handy program for creating small drawings that use circles, squares, polygons, other shapes, and text (such as flowcharts). You can start with a blank screen or an existing file. Your work can be saved in LaTeX, PostScript, PIC, or PiCTeX formats.

Xfractint

This program is used to generate *fractals*, multicolored shapes that evolve from a set of parameters that you provide. These parameters may include a number of colors and the size of a window, as well as the pattern used as the basis for the fractal. (Many patterns are included with **xfractint**.)

This is a rather odd program in that it takes input from the **xterm** window while displaying the output in a separate X window. When you run **xfractint** for the first time, you may be focused on the new X window and not on the old **xterm**; however, when you see that the new window stays black and the **xterm** demands input, you'll figure it out.

To run **xfractint**, use the following command line:

```
gilbert:$ xfractint
```

There are several command-line options, which you can review in the online **man** pages:

```
gilbert:$ xman
```

Xpaint

This simple paint program can be used to create and modify graphics files; if you've ever used MacPaint for the Macintosh, you'll quickly get the hang of **xpaint**. (Some of the cursors used in MacPaint can also be found in **xpaint**, as a matter of fact.) Supported file formats include

Portable Bitmap (PPM), X bitmap (XBM), TIFF, GIF, PostScript, XPM, and more. **Xpaint** is shown in Figure 5.17.

When you launch **xpaint**, you're presented with a window containing painting tools, such as a solid brush, a paint can, editing tools, and text input. You must either create a new "canvas" or open an existing file, which will then open a new window. Basically, the use of **xpaint** comes down to working in these two windows (at least two windows, anyway; you're welcome to open several "canvases").

Further information can be gleamed from the online **man** page.

Figure 5.17 xpaint

Xv

This is an excellent graphics-editing package from John Bradley. Basically, this package can be used to display GIF, JPEG, TIFF, Portable Bitmap (PBM, PGM, PPM), X bitmap, BMP, PCX, Iris RGB, XPM, XWD, and PostScript files. It's shown in Figure 5.18.

Basically, you can use **xv** to view and manipulate these graphics files. For example, you can perform the following actions on a supported graphics file:

- When you change the size of the window, you change the size of the image. If you change the proportions of the window, you change the proportions of the image. These changes will be saved to file if you want.
- Graphics can be rotated in 90-degree increments.
- A picture can be flipped vertically or horizontally.
- Cropping pictures is a matter of defining one portion of the graphic and discarding the rest.

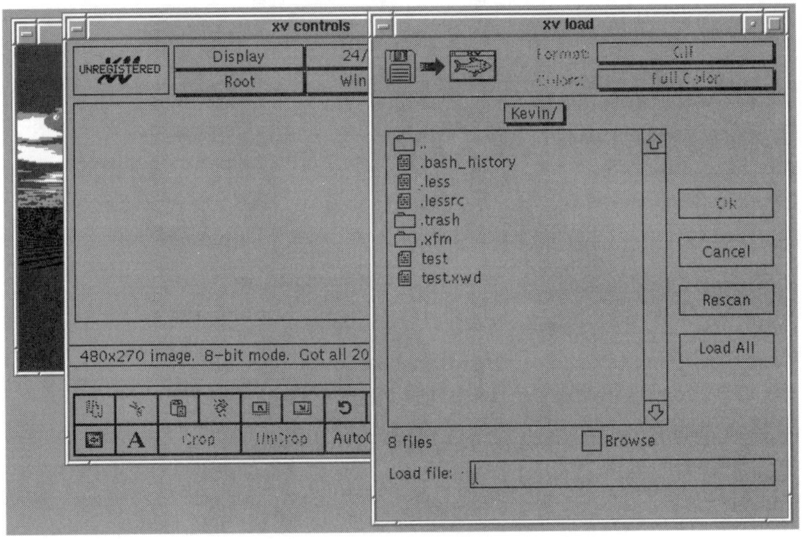

Figure 5.18 Xv when loading a file.

- A portion of a graphic can be magnified and then saved in that resolution.
- You can change the RGB values of a graphic or produce a stippled version using black and white.
- File conversions can be performed, as graphics imported in any format can be saved to any other format supported by **xv**.

The version of **xv** that ships with Slackware Linux is unregistered shareware. If you use **xv** we strongly encourage you to register it with Bradley. You can find further information about **xv** in **usr/doc/xv/xv.blurb**, while the entire documentation formatted in PostScript (which you must first unzip using **gunzip**) can be found at **usr/doc/xv/xvdocs.ps.gz**.

The JPEG Utilities

There are a series of commands that allow the manipulation and conversion of JPEG files. This is perhaps a more important capability than you might think; JPEG is becoming (along with GIF) one of the prevalent graphics file formats of the World Wide Web. If you're planning on doing any Web work (surfing or publishing), you'll want to know about these JPEG tools.

Cjpeg

This simple command compresses a graphics file (in the GIF, Portable Bitmap [PBM], BMP, GIF, Targa, and RLE formats) and converts it to the JPEG format, popular in the World Wide Web world. To convert the file **image.gif** to a JPEG file, you'd use the following command line:

```
gilbert:$ cjpeg -gif image.gif > image.jpg
```

Djpeg

This simple command decompresses a JPEG file and converts it to a file format that can more easily be handled by Slackware Linux (Portable Bitmap [PBM], BMP, GIF, Targa, or RLE). You select the file format on the command line. For example, to convert the file **image.jpg** to a GIF format, you'd use the following command line:

```
gilbert:$ djpeg -gif image.jpg > image.gif
```

Rdjpgcom and Wrjpgcom

The **rdjpgcom** command prints out any "comment blocks" found in a JPEG file. These comments are used to annotate images, both for the person viewing the image and for the person managing a set of images. To view the comments in the file **image.jpg**, you'd use the following command line:

```
gilbert:$ rdjpgcom image.jpg
```

Conversely, the **wrjpgcom** command is used to add a comment block to a JPEG file. You can add the comment directly from the command line, but you must specify a new filename and the original filename (this command will not overwrite an existing file):

```
gilbert:$ wrjpgcom -comment "This is a comment" old.jpg > new.jpg
```

or add an existing file (in our example, **add.txt**) to the comment block:

```
gilbert:$ wrjpgcom -cfile comment.txt < old.jpg > new.jpg
```

Miscellaneous Tools

There are many more command-line and X Window tools that ship as part of Slackware Linux. Here are some you'll find useful.

Clocks

If you want to *constantly* know what time it is, you can run the **oclock** or **xclock** commands, which place a clock on your screen, displaying the current time (as shown in Figure 5.19).

Figure 5.19 Oclock (left) and **xclock** (right).

In Figure 5.19, we're showing the clocks with no command-line options. However, you can customize **oclock** on the command line; some of the options are listed in Tables 5.13 and 5.14.

Table 5.13 Some Oclock Command-Line Options

Option	Changes...
-bd *color*	the border color to the specified *color*.
-bg *color*	the background color to the specified *color*.
-fg *color*	the foreground color to the specified *color*.
-hour *color*	the foreground color to the specified *color*.
-jewel *color*	the jewel color to the specified *color*.
-minute *color*	the minute-hand color to the specified *color*.
-transparent	the appearance so that only the hands, border, and jewel of the clock are showing.

Table 5.14 Some xclock Command-Line Options

Option	Changes...
-analog	the display from digital to analog.
-chime	the sound setting so the clock will ring twice on the hour and once on the half-hour.
-digital or **-d**	the display to digital.
-hands *color*	the color of the hands to *color*.

Xdpyinfo and Xev

The **xdpyinfo** command displays information about the X Window System:

```
gilbert:# xdpyinfo
name of display:    :0.0
version number:     11.0
```

```
version string:    The XFree86 Project, Inc
vendor release number:    3120
maximum request size:  4194300 bytes
motion buffer size: 0
bitmap unit, bit order, padding:   8, MSBFirst, 32
image byte order:  LSBFirst
number of supported pixmap formats:    2
supported pixmap formats:
    depth 1, bits_per_pixel 1, scanline_pad 32
    depth 4, bits_per_pixel 8, scanline_pad 32
keycode range:    minimum 8, maximum 134
focus:  window 0xc000d, revert to Parent
number of extensions:    10
    BIG-REQUESTS
    MIS-SCREEN-SAVER
    MIT-SHM
    MIT-SUNDRY-NONSTANDARD
    Multi-Buffering
    SHAPE
    SYNC
    XC-MISC
    XFree86-VidModeExtension
    XTEST
default screen number:    0
number of screens:    1

  ...
```

Admittedly, most of this information isn't going to mean anything to you unless you're already conversant with the X Window System. If you do know X, however, you can get a lot of useful information about your system via **xdpyinfo**. Because our goal here isn't to teach you about the intricacies of X, we recommend that you peruse one of the X Window texts recommended in Appendix A.

Similar to **xdpyinfo** on the usefulness scale is **xev**, which opens a window and returns information about the events the window generates. Again, if you know nothing about X, this information will be rather useless—but if you do know about X and (specifically) events, this information can be useful.

Xlock

The **xlock** command locks your system until a correct password is entered. For those who are into security, this gives you a tool to keep others from accessing your system when you step away. Be careful, however, that you don't accidentally invoke **xlock** and forget your password.

Xmag

The **xmag** command (as summoned from an **xterm** window or an **fvwm** menu) is used to magnify a portion of the screen, as shown in Figure 5.20.

Figure 5.20 Magnifying a portion of the screen with **xmag**.

Xman

We've spent much time referring to **xman** throughout the course of this book and have assumed that you know how to use it. Basically, **xman** is very simple. When you launch **xman** from an **xterm** window or from an **fvwm** menu, you'll be presented with a small window. It's from here you can summon a dialog box used to load an online **man** page, call for help, or quit the application. When this window is active, you can also use **Ctrl-S** to summon another dialog box used to actually load the page. This dialog box has a text-entry field in which you enter the command name and two buttons used to choose whether you want to search for the exact **man** page (**Manual Page**) or for something *like* the string you entered (**Apropos**).

After you decide which **man** page to load, a new window appears with the rendered **man** page.

Sc and Xspread

The **sc** command (designed to be run in command-line mode) launches a full-screen spreadsheet program. There's actually a lot of complexity to **sc**, which you'll learn about if you peruse the online **man** page:

```
gilbert:$ man sc
```

The **xspread** spreadsheet is based on the **sc** spreadsheet. Basically, it's the mechanism for using **sc** in an X window.

Emulators

You've got to hand it to the idealistic nature of the Linux community: It envisions a more perfect world, where no matter what operating system your software is written for, you should be able to use that software under Linux in some manner.

That's why we have a whole set of Linux software packages that allow you to run software written for Windows, DOS, CP/M, and Macintosh software. While on one level it seems rather silly to be launching a tool to run Windows applications under Linux when one could just run Windows anyway, it helps to know that these projects were launched in the days when hard disks were expensive and most people just didn't want to bother having two or more operating systems on a single computer. Now, when anything smaller than a 1.2-gigabyte hard disk on a PC is really an insult, these concerns are lessened.

We've included the tools for running Windows and DOS programs on the second CD-ROM, but these versions may be outdated by the time you read this chapter. Most of this software can be found at *sunsite.unc.edu*, in the **/pub/Linux/system/Emulators** directory. Table 5.15 lists an index of the software from this directory, current as of the writing of this book. In addition, there's a subdirectory named **dosemu**, which contains DOS emulators. The contents of this directory are listed in Table 5.16.

Table 5.15 A Directory Listing of /pub/Linux/system/Emulators

File	Explanation
68k-simulator.tar.gz	MC-68000 simulator for the X Window System
alec64-1.11-bin.tar.gz	Commodore 64 emulator
apple2.tar.Z	Apple IIe emulator for X and Linux
apple2_videx.tar.Z	Another part of the Apple emulator
bsvc-1.0.4.tar.z	Microprocessor simulator (Motorola 68000, Hector 1600)
cpm-0.2.tar.gz	Z80 and CP/M emulator
executorElf199p.tar.gz	Executor Macintosh emulator (demo) (ELF version)
executor-linuxaout-199p.tar.gz	Executor Macintosh emulator (demo) (a.out version)
vice-0.10.0.tar.gz	Commodore C64/C128/PET/VIC20 emulators
x48-0.4.0.tar.gz	HP48 calculator software emulator
xzx-0.5.4.tar.gz	X-based ZX Spectrum emulator

Table 5.16 A Directory Listing of /pub/Linux/system/Emulators/dosemu

File	Explanation
Win3.1_Dosemu.HOWTO.gz	Information on getting **dosemu** to run Windows
dosemu-HOWTO-52.3.ps	**dosemu-HOWTO** for version 0.53.3 (in PostScript format)
dosemu-HOWTO-52.3.txt	**dosemu-HOWTO** for version 0.53.3 (in ASCII format)
dosemu0.60.4.tgz	Source code for **dosemu** 0.60.4
garrot02.tar.gz	Returns **dosemu** idle time to system
xdos0.4a.tgz	DOS emulator designed for X, to be run in an **xterm** window

Emulating DOS under Linux

If you're hot to run DOS programs under Linux, you'll want to check out **dosemu** or **xdos** (they're the same software, essentially, with one difference: **xdos** will run in an X Window window with mouse support; **dosemu** does not). **Dosemu** is found on the second CD-ROM in the **contrib** directory (**dosemu0.60.4.tgz**).

Strictly speaking, neither **dosemu** nor **xdos** is a DOS emulator even though they're referred to as such in the documentation (the *emu* in **dosemu** refers to *emulator*). **Dosemu** runs a virtual DOS machine on the Intel-based PC architecture (much in the same manner that OS/2 handles DOS sessions). You'll need to compile **dosemu** for use on your own machine; the HOWTO file details the exact procedure.

Emulating Microsoft Windows under Linux

If there's one area where Microsoft Windows is superior to Linux, it's in the vast amount of software that runs under Windows. That's why a team of volunteers is working on WINE, the Windows Emulator (or, by some other accounts, Wine Is Not an Emulator; both are correct, apparently). WINE allows you to run Microsoft Windows binaries under Linux.

For more information on WINE, you can set your WWW browser to *http://www.asgardpro.com/wine*, or you can grab it directly via FTP from these sites:

ftp://tsx-11.mit.edu/pub/linux/ALPHA/Wine/development/
ftp://sunsite.unc.edu/pub/Linux/ALPHA/wine/
ftp://ftp.infomagic.com/pub/mirrors/linux/wine/development/
ftp://aris.com/pub/linux/ALPHA/Wine/development/

In addition, the WINE Home Page lists a set of FTP sites in Europe.

Be warned, however, that WINE is still considered a development project more for experienced developers than casual users, which means you use it at your own risk. We have, however, included the most recent version (at the time this book went to production, anyway) on the second CD-ROM.

Windows 95 Window Manager

In addition to WINE, if you really like the Windows 95 interface, you can run a variant of the **fvwm** window manager, called **fvwm95**. While you configure **fvwm95** almost exactly the same as **fvwm** (see Chapter 3 on configuring **fvwm**), what you see is something very close to the Windows 95 window manager, as shown in Figure 5.21.

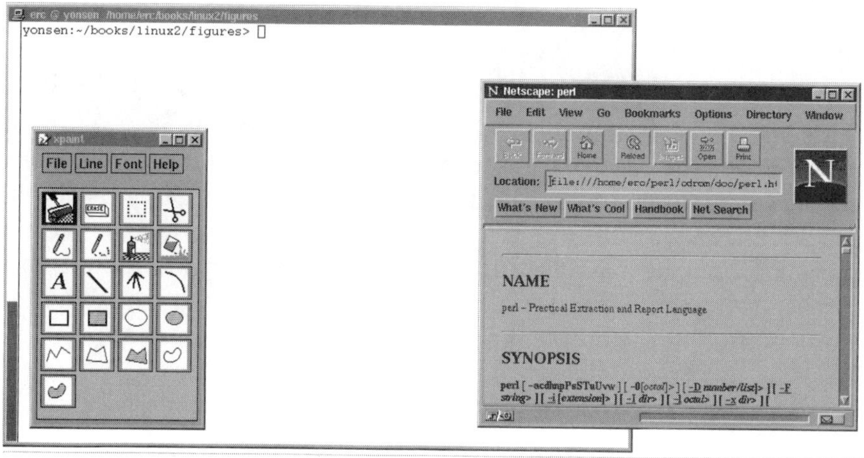

Figure 5.21 Linux screens look a lot like Windows 95 with **fvwm95**.

It's important to note that you're still running the X Window System and still running Linux, although the look **fvwm95** provides can really fool you. You'll find **fvwm95** on the second CD-ROM.

Some Math Tools

Linux and UNIX have wide usage in the academic world, where math tools are important. Most of us won't need elaborate math tools; here are a few rudimentary tools that you'll probably use.

The Bc Command

Even though the proliferation of ubiquitous and inexpensive calculators has made this command somewhat obsolete, the **bc** command—especially in the Free Software Foundation version included with Linux—can still be used as a very functional calculator. Use it as follows:

```
gilbert:~$ bc
1+1
2
quit
```

The preceding example was performed on a 486-based PC, not a Pentium.

This simple equation shows how to use **bc**: Type it as a command line, hit **Enter** (or **Return**), enter your equation, hit **Enter** (or **Return**), read the calculation, and type **quit** when you're done. Obviously, other more advanced features are available, such as square roots, converting numbers from one base to another, determining prime factors, and control statements for writing programs. Consult your system documentation or the online **man** page for further information.

Dc

The **dc** calculator uses reverse-polish calculation and provides the ability to define and call macros.

Calculator

Calculator (as summoned from an **xterm** window or a **fvwm** menu) presents a scientific-style calculator with some advanced functionality. It's shown in Figure 5.22.

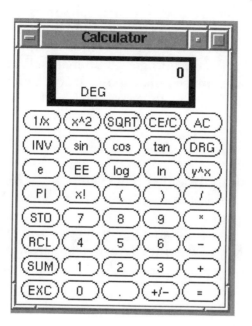

Figure 5.22 The **Calculator** command.

Games

All work and no play makes you a mighty boring Linux user. When you get tired of coding applications or creating documents with Linux, there are plenty of diversions included with the Linux operating system. Games come in terminal or X Window implementations.

Terminal Games

These games do not require X Window and run either in text mode or with proprietary graphics. These games are stored in the **/usr/games** directory unless noted otherwise. If you need more information about any of these games, you can check out their accompanying **man** pages.

Abuse

Abuse (**abuse**) is an arcade game from Crack Dot Com that pits you against a horde of angry aliens; your goal is to kill as many as you possibly can. In many ways, **abuse** is structured like DOOM—you get a limited version as part of the Slackware Linux distribution, and you can register for an additional fee to get additional bells and whistles. The most recent version of **abuse** can be found at *http://www.crack.com*, while additional information about **abuse** can be found at **/usr/games/abuse-1.05**. An X Window version, **xabuse**, is also available.

Arithmetic

If you've successfully installed Slackware Linux, you can probably handle the simple math problems posed by **arithmetic**. You're presented with a series of equations; to end the test, press **Ctrl-C**. If you're really competitive, however, you'll note that you're judged at the end by both the number of correct answers and how fast you answered the questions.

Atc

If you lack enough stress in your life, you can try your hand at **atc**, the Air Traffic Controller game. You need to get planes in and out of your busy airport.

Backgammon

It will only take you a minute to get acclimated to **backgammon** if you've ever played the game. If you're unfamiliar with backgammon, you may want to run the **teachgammon** command (discussed later in this section).

Bcd

This fast-paced program converts input as punch cards, paper tape, or Morse code.

Boggle

In this game (**bog**), you try to create words from a set of 12 letters. The rules are somewhat arcane; it seems to accepts some words and not others.

Caesar

This odd utility, in the words from the **man** page, "attempts to decrypt caesar cyphers using English letter frequency statistics," whatever that means. Then again, it may be someone's idea of a good joke. Try it for yourself.

Canfield

This is a Solitaire-type game. Definitely read the directions before trying to play it.

Cribbage

This text-only cribbage game (**cribbage**) can be played in long form or short form. Be warned that it's not the most reliable Cribbage game in the computer world; more than once it tried to award us lower points than we deserved. (Let's just say we spent too many hours in college playing cribbage and have a more-than-passing familiarity with the game.) Still, you'll probably find yourself wasting some time with it if you have any interest in Cribbage.

DOOM

There's little we can add to a discussion of this highly popular game, where your goal is to kill as many sentient bad guys as possible. If you've installed Linux properly, you should have no problem roaming the halls in search of targets. You even get a working WAD file that allows you to have some sound effects if you have a sound board up and running. DOOM actually comes in two versions: **sdoom** for terminal mode and **xdoom** for X Window.

Factor

This small program factors integers. That's entertainment!

Fish

This is a computer version of the venerable Go Fish that most of us played at one time or another in our childhood development. If you didn't, here's your chance.

Fortune

This command churns out a pithy quote every time it is run. When you installed Linux, you had the option of calling **fortune** every time a user logs in a Linux system.

Hangman

This is another child's game brought to the Linux world.

Hunt

This low-tech hunting game doesn't quite have the flash of DOOM or Abuse, but it's fun if you're on a network; the purpose here is to wipe out fellow network users.

Lizards

This wonderfully low-res arcade game was developed in the spirit of Eugene Jarvis: some cheesy graphics, a maze where things fall, and stolid protagonists that move up and down and left and right. It's definitely worth a try.

Mille

If you remember Mille Bournes (which isn't even around anymore, to the best of our knowledge), then you'll love this card game. If not, don't bother.

Monop

This test-based version of the venerable Monopoly board game is pretty decent, if you're really into Monopoly. It's not much fun playing by yourself, though; all you can do is go into debt and buy everything you land on.

Morse

In case the **bcd** command was too fast-paced for you, the **morse** command translates your keyboard input into Morse code. Use **Ctrl-C** to end the excitement.

Number

This command translates numerals (*12*) into words (*twelve*).

Paranoia

This text-based game gives you a set of binary choices in an attempt to solve a mystery. You're guaranteed to die at some point in this game—kinda like real life, when you stop to think about it—but otherwise you wander through a series of situations and make the appropriate decisions.

Pom

The current phase of the moon is displayed by entering **pom**. As the **man** page states, this command is "useful for selecting software completion target dates and predicting managerial behavior."

Ppt

The **ppt** command takes your input and creates the on-screen equivalent of punched paper tape. Takes us back to our high-school computing days, playing Oregon Trail on a timeshare mainframe maintained by MECC.

Primes

The **primes** command prints out a list of prime numbers, beginning with the number you enter.

Rain

The **rain** command randomly generates a pattern on your screen, giving the appearance of rainfall.

Robots

The **robots** command launches a two-dimensional board game where your goal is to kill the evil robots, but in an unusual fashion—you lack weapons, and your only tool to kill the evil robots is to make them run into one another. When things get hairy, you can teleport to another location on the grid.

Sail

The **sail** command launches a two-dimensional board game where your goal is to take command of a Man of War and fight other network users outfitted similarly. You can choose from many historical sea battles or opt to play a scenario from *Star Trek*. This game is older than the PC itself; it was first written for use on a DEC PDP 11/70 minicomputer in the fall of 1980. (By the way, the **man** pages for **sail** are probably more interesting than the game itself.)

Sasteroids

The **sasteroids** command launches a clone of the Atari Asteroids game we all grew up with. This version incorporates color and shades, rather than the endearing outlines used in the original.

Snake

The **snake** command begins a game where your goal is to snarf up dollar signs ($) while avoiding a series of *s*'s (representing the snake).

Teachgammon

This command teaches you how to play backgammon.

Tetris

This addictive game requires you to juggle geometric forms in an attempt to create uninterrupted rows before the pile gets too high. There is an X Window version (**xtetris**) available that's easier to play.

Trek

This command launches a *Star Trek* game (although, for legal reasons, the term *Star Trek* is never used). Your purpose is to patrol a quadrant and pursue the bad guys. This game is pre–*TNG*, however; the purpose is to kill as many Klingons as possible.

Tetris

This addictive game requires you to juggle geometric forms in an attempt to create uninterrupted rows before the pile gets too high. There is an X Window version (**xtetris**) available that's easier to play, while this version is written for terminals connected to a Linux box.

Wargames

The **war games** command is an interesting twist on the shoot-'em-up games found elsewhere in the Linux system.

Worm

The **worm** command causes you to become a two-dimensional worm, and your goal is to eat letters to see how long you can become.

Worms

As opposed to **worm**, the **worms** command creates what is purported to be worms on your screen, which dance as if in the throes of Blakean ecstasy.

Wump

The **wump** command launches a text-based game where your goal is to hunt the Wumpus through a series of 20 rooms located in a cave. You must watch out for bats and pits.

X Window Games

In addition to the **xdoom**, **xtetris**, and **xabuse** games mentioned in the previous section, there are a host of X-specific games that ship with this version of Slackware Linux. You can find most of them in **/usr/X11R6/bin**. Some of them can be launched directly from the Games menu found on **fvwm**. Most of them have **man** pages, which are best viewed from **xman**.

> For some reason, games called **xcuckoo** and **xhextris** are installed in the default **fvwm** Games menu. These games do not ship with Slackware Linux.

Ico

This command opens a window and causes a geometric shape to bounce around the screen. This command is used mostly by sales geeks to show how fast their X-based computers will run, as if the elemental task of bouncing a wire object is any indication of the processing power of a machine.

Workman

This application plays musical CDs from the CD-ROM drive. The **man** page (best viewed with **xman**) is in error, however, when it states that **workman** works only with SunCD drives; we've found that it works with any CD-ROM supported through Linux. However, be warned that there are a few rules—undocumented ones, at that—when dealing with **workman**:

- You need to have permission to use the CD-ROM. (Remember when we told you that Linux treats everything as a file, even the devices?) Most users do not have the proper permissions to use **workman**. You'll need to run the **chmod** command as **root** to change the permissions.
- After **workman** is launched, you cannot open the CD-ROM drive.

You can also run **workman** in text-only mode (i.e., without X Window running) by entering the following command line:

```
gilbert:$ workbone
```

Xboard

The **xboard** command summons a chess board that runs GNU Chess, which is considered to be a rather polished implementation of chess (in other words, really good chess players can be challenged by it). The game is timed, and there are a host of options.

Xlander

Do you ever get the feeling that many of the participants in Linux development spent far too much time in video arcades in the 1970s and early 1980s? You will after playing **xlander**, which is an X Window version of the old Lunar Lander arcade game. Your task is to successfully land on the moon, avoiding a crash.

Xlogo

This command opens a window displaying an official X logo. This is used mostly by sales geeks to show that X is indeed running on the machine they are hawking.

Xmaze

This maze (actually launched by the **maze** command) is used mostly by sales geeks to show how fast their X-based computers will run, as if the elemental task of finishing a maze is any indication of the processing power of a machine.

Xeyes

Not truly a game, **xeyes** is the X Window version of the standard programming exercise that never fails to entertain—a pair of eyes that follow the cursor.

Xmahjongg

This is a pretty decent X Window version of the ancient board game.

Xroach

After launching **xroach**, a single roach scurries around your screen before hiding underneath a window. If you iconify the window after a while, you'll see that the roach has multiplied into several roaches, all of which scurry around your screen before finding refuge under yet another window or icon. Big-city residents who spent time in roach-infested apartments will feel right at home.

If you begin this game from an **xterm** window with the *-squish* option, you can kill the little suckers with your mouse.

Xspider

Spider is a double-deck Solitaire game that tends to be complicated.

Xvier

The goal of this board game is to get four stones in a row, either diagonally or in a column. The trick with **xvier** is that you must begin at the bottom of the board and work your way up.

Summary

This chapter began with a list of neat Linux applications and then went into an extended discussion of the **emacs** text editor. Part of the GNU Project, **emacs** is a full-featured text editor that runs both in character mode and under the X Window System. While **emacs** may take some getting used to for some users, it's both easy to use and powerful at the same time—a combination you don't find every day in the Linux software world.

Linux contains a number of text processors, which take the output from a text editor and turn it into something a printer can understand. Primary among these tools are **groff**, the GNU version of **troff**; **TeX**, the high-end text-processing tool from Donald Knuth; and **texinfo**, the formatting tool from the Free Software Foundation. In addition, **sed** was covered as a text processor, although it contains elements of both text editors and text processors.

Printing straight text is one thing, but printing graphics and text under Linux is quite another. Luckily, there are tools for editing and printing PostScript-formatted document, in the form of Ghostscript.

Linux contains a number of tools for compressing and archiving files, including **gzip**, **zip**, and **gunzip**, as well as the UNIX **tar** command (as implemented by the FSF, of course). These tools can be handy when grabbing software from the Internet, as well as when you want to create system backups to protect against disaster.

Linux also features a number of tools specific to the PC architecture. These commands, called the MTools, allow Linux to access DOS-style parts of the PC, such as the floppy drive that contained a DOS-formatted floppy, as well as perform some basic DOS functions, such as creating and deleting directories. These commands, by and large, are for use with the floppy drive.

The chapter also included a discussion of various emulators: **dosemu** and **xdos**, which emulate the MS-DOS operating system, and WINE, which runs Microsoft Windows applications.

The Slackware distribution of Linux also features more than a few games, including the popular DOOM and the golden oldie Tetris (in both character-mode and X Window versions).

Basic Linux System Administration

This chapter covers:

- System-administration tools
- Using the **passwd** file
- Deleting users
- Managing groups
- Creating bootdisks
- Using **cron** and **crontab**
- Scheduling commands
- Adding new swap space
- Mounting filesystems
- Creating a message of the day

System-Administration Tools

If you're working on a stand alone Linux system, you're wearing two hats: the hat of a user and the hat of a system administrator. Of course, when you installed Linux in Chapter 2 and set up a user account, you were fulfilling the role of a system administrator. Congratulations!

In fact, setting up and maintaining accounts is one of the more important tasks you have as a system administrator. If you plan on letting other people (i.e., the family or a co-worker) use your Linux system, you should set up user accounts for them, complete with passwords, groups, and home directories. This isn't necessarily a difficult task, but it's one you should know a little about as you continue your Linux education.

There's nothing unique about Linux system administration as opposed to UNIX system administration. All the actions detailed in this chapter are also true of the UNIX world, and if you have any experience at all with UNIX system administration, you can easily make your way through Linux.

System administration is a world unto itself. The brief introduction here barely scratches the surface of UNIX system administration. We've found that the best way to learn UNIX system administration is to just dive right in and do it. Normally, you can't do much damage to a Linux system unless you start recompiling kernels or messing with boot records and such. The actions described in this chapter won't lead to any irreversible problems.

Using the Passwd File

Linux stores information about users in the **/etc/passwd** file (not to be confused with the **passwd** command, of course). As a matter of fact, Linux stores a lot of system-configuration information in this file, as is evidenced by the following excerpt:

```
halt:x:7:0:halt:/sbin:/sbin/halt
operator:x:11:0:operator:/root:/bin/bash
root:x:0:0::/root:/bin/bash
shutdown:x:6:0:shutdown:/sbin:/sbin/shutdown
```

```
sync:x:5:0:sync:/sbin:/bin/sync
bin:x:1:1:bin:/bin:
ftp:x:404:1::/home/ftp:/bin/bash
daemon:x:2:2:daemon: sbin:
adm:x:3:4:adm:/var/adm:
lp:x:4:7:lp:/var/spool/lpd:
mail:x:8:12:mail:/var/spool/mail:
postmaster:x:14:12:postmaster:/var/spool/mail:/bin/bash
news:x:9:13:news:/usr/lib/news:
uucp:x:10:14:uucp:/var/spool/uucppublic:
man:x:13:15:man:/usr/man:
games:x:12:100:games:/usr/games:
nobody:x:65534:100:nobody:/dev/null:
kevinr:x:1000:100:Kevin Reichard,,,:/home/kevinr:/bin/bash
```

Most of these commands specify the paths associated with specific commands, such as the path for **man** pages. If you want to change these defaults (for example, if you're using **uucp** to connect to other systems and other systems are connecting to yours, this would be the place to change the **uucp** default path), here's the place to do it.

Our real concern, however, is with the final line of the file, concerning the configuration for user *kevinr*:

```
kevinr:x:1000:100:Kevin Reichard,,,:/home/kevinr:/bin/bash
```

We'll break this line down as an example of how Linux deals with user entries:

- *kevinr* refers to the user name.
- *X* is the placeholder for the encrypted password. The actual encrypted text is kept in a separate file called **/etc/shadow/**. To help keep the system secure, **/etc/shadow** can only be read by the root user. If this field contains an asterisk (*) instead of an *x*, this means the account is disabled (something you'll learn about later in this chapter).
- *1000* is the user ID, a numeral the system uses to track the account. Instead of dealing with *kevinr* when working with file

permissions and such, the system deals with *1000* or the equivalent user ID.

- *100* is the group ID (you'll learn about groups later in this chapter).
- *Kevin Reichard* is the full name of the user; this entry can contain additional information about the user.
- */home/kevinr* refers to the user's home directory.
- */bin/bash* refers to the user's default shell.

Not every field needs to be used, but there needs to be spaces left for them (:).

As you can see from the previous example, the root user has a slightly different line from a normal user; in this case, zeros are used in the user ID and group ID fields.

This file is where you'd check for the current user configuration, not to add new users. You can make changes to this file that will be reflected in the system as a whole; for example, you can give the user a new ID by merely changing the appropriate number in the user ID field. However, there are ramifications to doing this; because the system tracks file ownership and group membership by user ID and not by user name, this change will mean that all the files that the user used to own would be in ownership limbo; you'd need to manually change the ownership of the files with the **chown** command. Unless you absolutely must change the user ID for a user, you're best off avoiding this maneuver.

The **adduser** command, which you first encountered in Chapter 2, can be used to add users. This command can be run by the root or superuser at any time:

```
gilbert:/# adduser
```

Deleting Accounts

The flip side of adding accounts is, of course, deleting accounts. If you're working on a smaller system, you don't need to worry too much about deleting accounts, unless you have a situation where a disgruntled employee may have the opportunity to wreak havoc on your system.

Deleting an account is a multifaceted affair, however, as you must delete every reference to the user in the Linux system. This means removing the user's entry from **/etc/passwd**, removing the user's home directory (the **rm -r** command line will do so, although you should really make sure there's nothing valuable in the directory), transferring ownership of the removed user's files, deleting references to the user from any group files (which you'll learn about in the next section), ending any **cron** or **at** jobs begun by the user (both are explained later in this chapter), and making sure that the mail subsystem doesn't continue to acknowledge the user's existence. You'll also want to delete the user's mail file, which is kept in **/usr/spool/mail**, with the filename being the user's name. Most of this work can be done automatically with the **userdel** command. For example, to remove the *kevinr* account:

```
userdel -r kevinr
```

You may also want to disable an account rather than delete it outright. In this case, you'd merely throw an asterisk (*) in the second field of the **/etc/passwd** file. The following would temporarily disable *kevinr*'s account:

```
kevinr:*:1000:100:Kevin Reichard:/home/kevinr:/bin/bash
```

Managing Groups

In the UNIX world, groups have a long history as a mechanism for dividing access to certain files. Anyone who's worked with a network of any sort realizes that giving only some members access to a set of files enhances security and makes organizational chores go easier.

Linux supports groups; each file is owned by both a user and a group. By using the *ls -l* (that's *ell*, not *one*) command line, you can get the full permissions line for a file:

```
gilbert:~$ ls -l
-rwxrw-r--   1 kevinr users    87619 Apr 23 23:39 addresses.dat
```

This tells us that the file **addresses.dat** is owned by both the individual user *kevinr* and the group *users*; that *kevinr* can read, write, and execute the file; and that the *users* group can read and write the file. All other users can only read the file.

Here are the contents of a typical **/etc/group** file:

```
root::0:root
bin::1:root,bin,daemon
daemon::2:root,bin,daemon
sys::3:root,bin,adm
adm::4:root,adm,daemon
tty::5:
disk::6:root,adm
lp::7:lp
mem::8:
kmem::9:
wheel::10:root
floppy::11:root
mail::12:mail
news::13:news
uucp::14:uucp
man::15:man
users::100:kevinr,pat,erc
execs::101:kevinr,pat
nogroup::-1:
```

As you can see, most of the listings in a **/etc/group** file have very little to do with a user group and more to do with applications and other ownership issues. You can tell which lines have to do with user groups, as they are numbered above 100 (this is a Linux convention). In the preceding example, these two lines are reserved for user groups:

```
users::100:kevinr,pat,erc
execs::101:kevinr,pat
```

This is actually an incomplete listing, as evidenced by the double colon, which means that a field has been left out. Normally the lines in the **/etc/group** file are listed in the following format:

```
groupname:password:groupID:users
```

This field is blank because most systems don't bother setting up passwords for groups. Whether or not this is a huge security breach is debatable; to be honest, setting up a password for a group is a pain. Most of you won't need to deal with it, and those who do may want to consider investing in a more advanced UNIX system-administration tome.

Logging in as Su

When you want to work as the root user (for the purposes of adding and deleting users, for example), you don't need to logoff the system and then login again as root; instead, you can login as the superuser:

```
gilbert:~$ su
gilbert:/home/kevinr#
```

Note that the previous home directory was listed as ~, but it is changed to **/home/kevinr** after logging in as superuser.

There's another important reason to login as **su** (in addition to having others on your Linux system login as superuser, in instances where there are multiple administrators on the network): When someone is logged in as **root**, the system only notes that **root** logged on the system. However, when someone uses **su** to login for root privileges, there's a record of the login in the file **/var/adm/messages**:

```
Apr 27 22:06:30 gilbert su: kevinr on /dev/tty1
```

To quit using the system as superuser, use **exit** or **bye**:

```
gilbert:/home/kevinr# exit
exit
gilbert:~$
```

More on the Messages File

The **/var/adm/messages** file can be a very useful tool if you're trying to track down problems with your Linux system, as it logs all system activity, including the system configuration when booting Linux. The following section shows the messages logged to **/var/adm/messages** when Linux is booted:

```
Kernel logging (proc) started.
Console: colour EGA+ 80x25, 1 virtual console (max 63)
Serial driver version 4.00 with no serial options enabled
tty00 at 0x03f8 (irq = 4) is a 16450
tty01 at 0x02f8 (irq = 3) is a 16450
lp_init: lp0 exists, using polling driver
ftape: allocated 3 buffers aligned at: 00230000
SBPCD version 2.6 Eberhard Moenkeberg <emoenke@gwdg.de>
SBPCD: Looking for a SoundBlaster/Matsushita CD-ROM drive
SBPCD:
SBPCD: = = = = = = = = = = W A R N I N G = = = = = = = = = = =
SBPCD: Auto-Probing can cause a hang (f.e. touching an ethernet
card).
SBPCD: If that happens, you have to reboot and use the
SBPCD: LILO (kernel) command-line feature like:
SBPCD:
SBPCD:    LILO boot: linux sbpcd=0x230,SoundBlaster
SBPCD: or like:
SBPCD:    LILO boot: linux sbpcd=0x300,LaserMate
SBPCD: or like:
SBPCD:    LILO boot: linux sbpcd=0x330,SPEA
SBPCD:
SBPCD: with your REAL address.
SBPCD: = = = = = = = = = = END of WARNING = = = = = = = = = = =
SBPCD:
SBPCD: Trying to detect a SoundBlaster CD-ROM drive at 0x230.
SBPCD: - Drive 0: CR-563-x (0.80)
SBPCD: 1 SoundBlaster CD-ROM drive(s) at 0x0230.
SBPCD: init done.
```

```
Calibrating delay loop.. ok - 25.04 BogoMips

scsi : 0 hosts.

Memory: 14652k/16384k available (976k kernel code, 384k reserved, 372k data)

This processor honours the WP bit even when in supervisor mode. Good.

Floppy drive(s): fd0 is 1.44M

FDC 0 is a 8272A

Swansea University Computer Society NET3.017

Swansea University Computer Society TCP/IP for NET3.017

IP Protocols: ICMP, UDP, TCP

PPP: version 0.2.7 (4 channels) NEW_TTY_DRIVERS OPTIMIZE_FLAGS

TCP compression code copyright 1989 Regents of the University of
California

PPP line discipline registered.

SLIP: version 0.7.5-NET3.014-NEWTTY (4 channels)

CSLIP: code copyright 1989 Regents of the University of California

eth0: 3c505 not found

eth0: D-Link DE-600 pocket adapter: not at I/O 0x378.

D-Link DE-620 pocket adapter not identified in the printer port

Checking 386/387 coupling... Ok, fpu using exception 16 error reporting.

Checking 'hlt' instruction... Ok.

Linux version 1.1.59 (root@fuzzy) (gcc version 2.5.8) #5 Sat Oct
ÊÊ29 15:50:31 CDT 1994

Partition check:

   hda: WDC AC2340H, 325MB w/128KB Cache, CHS=1010/12/55,
   MaxMult=16

   hda: hda1 hda2

VFS: Mounted root (ext2 filesystem) readonly.

Max size:332509   Log zone size:2048

First datazone:152   Root inode number 155648

ISO9660 Extensions: RRIP_1991A

gilbert login: ROOT LOGIN ON tty1
```

Most of this code is pretty self-evident, but we'll take a few minutes to explain what a few of the lines mean, in order of appearance. The first line of the code, obviously, shows that the system started logging actions. The next line:

```
Console: colour EGA+ 80x25, 1 virtual console (max 63)
```

tells what resolution Linux is running in. This resolution applies only to Linux running in text mode, not when running the X Window System. The lines:

```
tty00 at 0x03f8 (irq = 4) is a 16450
tty01 at 0x02f8 (irq = 3) is a 16450
```

both refer to the serial devices on the PC and their corresponding IRQs. As you'll recall from Chapter 2, *tty00* is the equivalent of COM1 (in other words, the first serial port). This also tells us that the serial port features a 16450 UART chip, which you'll find useful for high-speed communications.

The next set of lines beginning with *SBPCD* refer to configuration factors when using a SoundBlaster Pro sound card/CD-ROM drive, as the system automatically polls the device to make sure it's functional. The line:

```
Memory: 14652k/16384k available (976k kernel code, 384k reserved,
372k data)
```

refers to the amount of RAM the system has. In this case, as 16MB of RAM are indeed installed on the PC, this means that Linux can see all of it. The line:

```
Floppy drive(s): fd0 is 1.44M
```

refers to the floppy drive, which Linux does recognize as a high-density 3.5-inch drive on *fd0*. The line:

```
eth0: 3c505 not found
```

refers to an unsuccessful search for an Ethernet card—no surprise, as this particular machine is lacking such a device. However, the following lines:

```
Swansea University Computer Society NET3.017
Swansea University Computer Society TCP/IP for NET3.017
IP Protocols: ICMP, UDP, TCP
PPP: version 0.2.7 (4 channels) NEW_TTY_DRIVERS OPTIMIZE_FLAGS
```

```
    TCP compression code copyright 1989 Regents of the University of
California
    PPP line discipline registered.
    SLIP: version 0.7.5-NET3.014-NEWTTY (4 channels)
    CSLIP: code copyright 1989 Regents of the University of California
```

show that this machine supports the SLIP and PPP remote-login protocols, which means that this machine could login to an Internet host. The line:

```
    ISO9660 Extensions: RRIP_1991A
```

tells us that the CD-ROM drive supports the ISO-9660 extensions. Finally, the line:

```
    gilbert login: ROOT LOGIN ON tty1
```

tells us that a root user logged in the system.

Error Messages

The previous section relied on a small section of the **/var/adm/messages** file; if you take a look, you'll see a very large file if you've been using Linux for any amount of time. For example, you'll see who logged on and off the system, even if the login was unsuccessful, as in the following line:

```
    Mar 31 14:48:51 gilbert login: 1 LOGIN FAILURE ON tty1, root]
```

To see just the messages relevant to the most recent boot, you can use the **dmesg** command. This produces a bit of output, so you'll probably want to pipe your output to **less**:

```
    dmesg | less
```

Boot Options

In Chapter 2, we guided you through a Linux installation and emphasized the use of **loadlin** as a way of launching Linux. If you bought the first edition of this book, you know that this is a change in the way we recommend you launch Linux, but we don't mean to imply that **loadlin** is the only way to launch Linux. In this section, we'll discuss some of the alternatives, beginning with the creation of a bootdisk and ending with a look at LILO.

Creating a Bootdisk

When you installed Linux from the accompanying CD-ROM, you were asked if you wanted to create a boot floppy. You might have refused to do so, thinking to yourself, "I don't need a stinkin' boot floppy!"

Then you might have had a small problem booting your Linux system. You might have made a small error when compiling a kernel, for example, which could lead to all sort of panic messages when Linux fails to load. And that's when you smack yourself on the head and curse yourself for not creating a boot floppy.

Basically, a boot floppy contains the **root** partition, allowing you to boot the Linux kernel. PCs are designed to boot from sector 0, cylinder 0 of the boot drive, and most PCs are configured to first look to the **A:** drive for the boot information. If the information isn't found there—and most of the time it isn't—then the PC is configured to look to sector 0, cylinder 0 of the hard drive. (Check your PC's BIOS configuration to see if this is valid. For example, the advanced setup in the popular AMD BIOS series has an option to change the boot drive.)

When a Linux system is booted from a floppy, all it means is that the kernel or LILO is configured to be found in the beginning of the boot floppy, thus ensuring that Linux will be loaded. This information is stored in a file named **vmlinuz**; it's a compressed file that's expanded and run when you boot your system. It's the same file that exists on your hard disk; the only difference is the media, not the contents of the kernel. When you boot from floppy, you're loading the kernel, which then looks to the hard drive for the rest of the operating system files. This can also be useful if you're testing a new kernel.

Some people like to boot their system from their floppy; this leaves the boot sector on a hard drive safe for another operating system. There's nothing wrong with booting from floppy for Linux and leaving the boot information on the hard drive for DOS or Windows.

The Slackware **setup** program contains the tools needed to create a new boot floppy. The Slackware **makebootdisk** command is useful for creating a new bootdisk without having to go through the reconfiguration menus in the **setup** program. To use it, just supply the name of the kernel file to use:

```
makebootdisk zImage
```

Makebootdisk will then put up a simple menu that allows you to produce one or more Linux bootdisks. These may be LILO bootdisks (these contain a small root partition and allow more boot options) or simple bootdisks (just a kernel file written directly to floppy).

You can also create a new floppy from scratch. There are many ways to go about it, and the **BOOTDISK-HOWTO** from Graham Chapman (*grahamc@zeta.org.au*) contained on the first accompanying CD-ROM is actually an excellent overview of the many options.

Here, however, we'll present a down-and-dirty way of creating a bootdisk. With Linux loaded and you logged in as the root user (superuser), you can merely use the **rdev** command to specify a kernel file and its root device. The following command will tell **vmlinuz** to set the root device to drive **A:**

```
gilbert:/home/kevinr# rdev vmlinuz /dev/fd0
```

 It's a good idea to make a copy of **vmlinuz** before doing anything to it.

You can tell **rdev** to use any device, including hard drives and SCSI drives.

After that, copy **vmlinuz** to the floppy:

```
gilbert:/home/kevinr# cp vmlinuz /dev/fd0
```

If you're more comfortable with the **dd** command, you can use it in the place of **cp**. However, be warned that you have to use a few parameters (*if, of*) with it. To accomplish the same action with **dd** that we just performed with **cp**, you'd use the following command line:

```
gilbert:/home/kevinr# dd if=vmlinuz of=/dev/fd0
```

If you're not sure what the kernel is using for a root device, type **rdev** on a command line by itself:

```
gilbert:/home/kevinr# rdev
```

To learn more about the **rdev** command, summon its online help:

```
gilbert:/home/kevinr# rdev -h
```

These steps will give you a basic and functional boot floppy. There are many other things you can do to a boot floppy—you can include a filesystem and a set of basic UNIX commands or you can include a set of utilities that will allow you to restore a system backup from tape or other storage device. Again, the **BOOTDISK-HOWTO** provides an excellent overview of the subject and can point you to the many directions you can take with a boot floppy.

Recovery Packages

There are several recovery packages in the Linux world that will create diskettes specially designed for those occasions where you need to boot from a floppy. We've included them all on the second accompanying CD-ROM. Following is a list of the packages.

Bootkit

Bootkit (from Scott Burkett) uses menus to create rescue disks, both for the purpose of booting a system and for saving the contents of a corrupted system. You can also grab it from *sunsite.unc.edu*; the file is **/pub/Linux/system/Recovery/Bootkit-vvv.tar.gz**.

CatRescue

CatRescue (from Oleg Kibirev) creates rescue disks and provides some handy information on recovering from a system failure. You can also grab it via FTP from *gd.cs.csufresno.edu/pub/sun4bin/src/CatRescue100.tgz*.

Rescue Shell Scripts

Rescue Shell Scripts (from Thomas Heiling) features shell scripts for creating boot and boot/root diskettes. You can also grab it via FTP from *sunsite.unc.edu:/pub/Linux/system/Recovery/rescue.tgz*.

What to Do If You Forget Your Password

We've all done it, particularly when working on systems where we don't login every day. Mere users can forget their passwords, and system administrators have the tools to change their passwords and set up new accounts.

On the other hand, as a system administrator, you're supposed to be infallible. If you forget your password, there's no higher entity to bail you out. Forgetting your password is another good reason for creating a boot floppy. In these cases, you can boot the system from floppy, mount the **/root** partition (if necessary), remove the existing password from the **/etc/shadow** file (although the password is encrypted, the entire entry can be deleted), and then reboot from hard disk, where you can create a new password.

This small section should serve as a cautionary note to anyone who assumes that their Linux system is secure—it's not. If you can boot a system from a floppy, you have access to the entire filesystem.

Using LILO

In the first edition of this book, we advised you to install Linux using LILO, the Linux Loader. In this edition, we do not. The reason for the change is quite simple: We've found that using **loadlin** is a much better alternative for new users. LILO can be a tad churlish and unforgiving— if you make an error when setting up LILO, you've pretty much munged up the boot record of your PC. (Yet *another* reason to create a boot floppy!) And given these days of multiple operating systems coexisting on PCs, we find that many users want to have the option to go to Linux from their other operating systems, and under these circumstances **loadlin** works best.

However, some will want to go with LILO as their boot tool. We always give people—especially experienced users—an option.

What is LILO?

Basically, *LILO* is a program that controls your boot drive's Master Boot Record, or MBR. When you turn on your computer, the BIOS checks your MBR for instructions on how to proceed.

When you install LILO, you're telling the MBR to actually invoke the LILO program upon boot. LILO can be programmed to wait for a certain time before actually loading Linux, and it can be used to boot other operating systems, such as DOS and OS/2.

LILO's actually a pretty simple beast, and the configuration process here makes it even simpler. LILO works with a configuration file that's generated automatically through this **setup** program. You can run this program whenever you want, actually; you could use **loadlin** and then adapt LILO after you get to a certain point in your Linux education. Your first move will be to start the process by running the **setup** program, then mark any operating systems you want to appear in this configuration file. Because you want Linux to be able to boot, you'll want to begin by specifying Linux. After that, you can designate another operating system (MS-DOS or OS/2) as a possible boot option. You'll want to specify Linux first, however, so that it appears first in the configuration file. When you're finished running through these queries, you'll end up with a file that looks like this:

```
# LILO configuration file
# generated by 'liloconfig'
#
# Start LILO global section
boot = /dev/hda
#compact         # faster, but won't work on all systems.
delay = 50
```

```
vga = normal      # force sane state
ramdisk = 0       # paranoia setting
# End LILO global section
# Linux bootable partition config begins
image = /vmlinuz
  root = /dev/hda2
  label = Linux
  read-only # Non-UMSDOS filesystems should be mounted read-only for checking
# Linux bootable partition config ends
# DOS bootable partition config begins
other = /dev/hda1
  label = DOS
  table = /dev/hda
# DOS bootable partition config ends
```

This file is stored as **/etc/lilo.conf**.

You'll also be asked about how long to wait before loading Linux. LILO is pretty handy in that it lets you specify a period of time (5 seconds or 30 seconds) between when LILO loads and when the first operating system is loaded. (In the **/etc/lilo.conf** file, this appears as the numeral *50* if you chose **5** seconds, and *300* if you chose **30** seconds.) This gives you time to specify another operating system to boot, should you want to boot DOS or OS/2 instead of Linux. This is done by pressing the left **Shift** key after LILO loads, which then gives you the prompt:

```
boot:
```

If you specify DOS, then DOS will boot from the DOS partition (provided, of course, that you've marked this partition as a boot partition). Pressing the **Tab** key gives you a list of options.

If you're using OS/2's Boot Manager, you may want to use that for the primary boot loader and use LILO to boot Linux.

Removing LILO

There are several ways to remove LILO. The version of LILO on the CD-ROM allows you to remove it from the boot sector with the following command line:

```
gilbert:~$ lilo -u
```

A better way may be to use the following command when running DOS:

```
C:> FDISK /MBR
```

This tells DOS to install DOS, not LILO, as the controller of the MBR.

Scheduling Events

Linux features a number of system-administration tools that allow you to schedule events at specific times; for example, you may want to schedule a system backup in the middle of the night. These tools are covered in the next few sections.

The Nice Command

Sometimes you'll run a command and not care too much when it's completed, such as when you issue a command right before you leave for lunch. When time is not of the essence—especially on large, multiuser systems that may not contain quite enough hardware firepower to support so many users—you may want to use the nice command in conjunction with other commands, so named because you're being nice to the system. Use it at the beginning of the command line:

```
gilbert:~$ nice command filename
```

For example, if you're performing an extremely complicated sort with many files, you may want to launch the sort using **nice** before that typical two-hour lunch.

The At Command

Of course, some lunches can expand to three or even four hours, depending on the libations involved. If you're not sure you'll be back in the office in time to run an important command, you can use the **at** command.

Seriously, you're more likely to use the **at** command to relieve pressure on the system by running system-intensive commands in the middle of the night, to send mail messages involving long-distance charges when rates are lowest, or to back up a large hard disk at some regular interval.

Using **at** is simple, as you first specify a time for execution, followed by the command line. To set up a specific command, type the following:

```
gilbert:~$ at 11am
```

At is very flexible about defining the time when the command is to be run; you can use a time, as in our example, or you can use a more precise number based on military time.

After you hit the **Enter** (or **Return**) key, you'll be placed on the next line, without a prompt. As you recall, this is the Linux method of asking for additional input. (Usually, anyway; there are exceptions.) This is where you provide the command that at is to execute; end each command by hitting the **Enter** (or **Return**) key. When you're finished, type **Ctrl-D**.

The system's response is a single line of information that confirms when the command (designated by the system with a job-ID of many digits) will be run. This job-ID is very valuable information. Should you need to see a list of pending job-IDs, use **at** with the -*l* option:

```
gilbert:~$ at -1
```

If you want to cancel a pending command scheduled with **at**, use **at** with the -*r* (remove) option:

```
gilbert:~$ at -r job-ID
```

For procedures you need to perform again and again, **cron**, covered later in this chapter, is likely to be a better tool than **at**.

The Batch Command

The **batch** command combines many commands into one command line, which is then run in the background without any prompting on your part. Use **batch** as follows:

```
gilbert:~$ batch
```

End the command by hitting the **Enter** (or **Return**) key. As with **at**, you'll be placed on a new line, as batch waits for additional input. Go ahead and type in the commands, ending each by hitting the **Enter** (or **Return**) key. When you're finishing entering commands, type **Ctrl-D**.

You'll then be presented with a command prompt, so go ahead with your other work as your batch commands are quietly executed by the system. If your commands require some sort of confirmation message or output delivered to you, the message will be conveyed as a mail message; you won't find messages popping up on your screen while you're in the middle of some other action.

Elsewhere in this book, we have discussed running programs in the background using the ampersand. There are some fundamental differences between background tasks and **batch**:

- Commands issued to **batch** are accorded even less priority than commands run in the background.
- With **batch**, commands will continue to execute even if you logoff the system; background tasks are killed if you logoff the system.
- Background tasks will interrupt you should your background command specify some kind of output or confirmation. **Batch** does not; as we noted, confirmation or output is sent as a mail message.

The Cron Command

System administrators have all the fun—or used to, anyway, as evidenced by the **cron** command. **cron** started life as a tool for system administration, allowing the system administrator to schedule regular tasks unattended.

Why use **cron**? As we said earlier, it allows you to schedule regular tasks unattended. You may want to back up your data to tape drive weekly, or even daily. You may want to send yourself a mail message to remind you of important noncomputer chores. Or you may want to send electronic mail to other UNIX systems late at night when the long-distance rates are lower.

In some ways, the **at** command accomplishes the same as the **cron** command. So why use **cron**? Because you can set it up to perform regular tasks. With **at**, you can only set up a single task to be performed at one specific time. Because **at** is much easier to use, we recommend using it in one-time situations, and use **cron** in repetitive situations.

There are two parts to **cron**: The **crontab** file and the actual **cron** command. We'll cover each.

Creating a Crontab File

As we said earlier, the **crontab** file contains the tasks that are to be performed regularly. You have your own personal **crontab** file, stored in the **/usr/lib/crontab** directory. Such a file is not created automatically when you install Linux; it's up to you to create the file—though not directly. The **crontab** file installation and the structure of the actual file can be confusing.

You can use **vi** or **emacs** to create a **crontab** file. However, you can't save the file directly in the **/usr/lib/crontab** directory; instead, you must save it under a different name and use the **cron** command to install it. We'll guide you through a typical file creation and installation.

There are six fields to a **crontab** file, each separated by a space. The first five fields specify exactly when the command is to be run; the sixth field is the command itself.

Let's say that we wanted to run a command every morning at 8:30 a.m. The structure of the **crontab** line looks something like this:

```
30 8 * * * command
```

The exact values associated with the five fields are listed in Table 7.1.

Table 7.1 Fields in a Crontab Line

Field	Meaning
1	Minutes after the hour
2	Hour, in 24-hour format
3	Day of the month
4	Month
5	Day of the week

Some things to note when creating a **crontab** file:

- Asterisks (*) are used to specify when commands are to be run in every instance of the value of the field. An asterisk in the third field means to run the command every day of every month, an asterisk in the fourth field means to run the command every month, an asterisk in the fifth field means to run the command every day of every week.

- Days of the week are referenced somewhat strangely. The week begins with a *0* for Sunday and ends with a *6* for Saturday. (Computer people, especially on UNIX, are famous for starting to count with *0* rather than the more common *1* used by others.)

- Times are specified in military (24-hour) time. Thus 10 p.m. is specified as *22*.

- Ranges can be specified, instead of specific days and times. For example, you can perform the command only on the 15th and 30th days of the month by using *15,30* in the third field. (Just make sure you adjust it in February.) Or you can specify that a command be run only in the fall months by using *10-12* in the fourth field. These two methods can be combined: running a command in spring and fall means using *4-6,10-12* in the fourth field.

After creating our crontab file (which must be saved under a filename of anything but **crontab**; we'll call it **ourfile**), we can then install it, using the **crontab** command:

```
gilbert:~$ crontab ourfile
```

Cron then takes **ourfile**, copies it, and saves the copy under our username in the **/usr/lib/crontab** directory, with a filename of **/usr/lib/crontab/ourname**. If we want to make changes to our **cron** configuration, we must edit our original file (which still exists—remember, **cron** only makes a copy) and then reinstall it using **crontab**. If we want to totally remove the file, we must use the **crontab** command with the *-r* option:

```
$ crontab -r
```

To prevent mischief or some unintended damage, we are allowed access to only our own **crontab** file.

Some Crontab Examples

The **crontab -l** command lists the **crontab** entry for your username. For example:

```
gilbert:~$ crontab -l


15 3 * * * /bin/sh /u/erc/my_backup
```

In this example, every night at 3:15 a.m., **cron** will invoke the Bourne shell, **sh**, and execute a shell script called **my_backup** that is stored in the **/u/erc** directory. Presumably, this script will back up certain directories to tape. The reason it's performed at 3:15 is because at this time the machine is mostly idle.

If you only wanted to back up on Mondays, you'd use the following **crontab** entry:

```
15 3 * * 1 /bin/sh /u/erc/my_backup
```

Again, we've left the time to execute the script at the arbitrary time of 3:15 a.m.

If you wanted to only perform backups on the first and fifteenth of each month, you could use the following **crontab** entry:

```
15 3 1,15 * * /bin/sh /u/erc/my_backup
```

This ends our discussion of scheduling tasks under Linux.

More on Multitasking

We discussed running commands in the background briefly in Chapter 4. This is where we extend that discussion.

Multitasking is a fancy computer-speak way of saying the operating system can do more than one thing at a time. While this may seem like a simple matter, it's really not; personal-computer users have been screaming for a multitasking operating system for (seemingly) years (though, ironically, they for the most part ignore OS/2, which handles multitasking in much the same manner as Linux).

Linux documentation doesn't often use the term multitasking (even though the rest of the computer world uses it); instead, Linux is said to be *multiprocessing*—the same thing described differently. When you run a Linux command, like **ls** or **cat**, you're running a process. When you boot the Linux operating system, you are actually launching a series of processes without consciously doing so. (If you use a graphical user interface like the X Window System, you're launching many, many processes.) On a large multiuser system, there may be literally thousands of processes running at a given time.

These processes compete with each other for computing resources. Running programs in the background, as described earlier, is a way for the Linux user to allocate resources efficiently. Such allocation is necessary to keep the system from bogging down, especially a large multiuser system with less-than-adequate resources. If there are more processes running than can fit in your system's random-access memory (RAM), then Linux uses a hard disk as extended RAM in an action called *swapping to disk*. (You've already leaned about a swap partition in Chapter 2; later in this chapter we'll discuss how to set up a swapfile after Linux has already been installed.) However, hard disks are much slower than RAM, so swapping to disk is not the most desirable of solutions; but on the PC, it may be the only solution you have.

As we said, it's important for the Linux system and user to efficiently allocate resources. Linux does this (as it does almost everything else) in hierarchical fashion: Processes beget other processes (much as directories contain subdirectories), with one process at the top of the pyramid. When a process launches another process, it uses a system call entitled a *fork*, which creates the new process.

When you boot a Linux system, the first process (process 1) launches a program called **init**, which then launches other processes. **Init** is the mother of all Linux processes—or, as referred to in Linuxdom, **init** is a *parent* to other resources, which in turn can act as parents to additional resources, called *child processes*. **Init** is, ultimately, the ancestor of all processes running on the system.

When we described the shell and its importance in running programs for you, we were referring to the shell acting as the parent and managing child processes. Unless you tell it otherwise (by issuing the **kill** command), the shell waits while you run a child and returns with a prompt after the child process is finished, or *dies*. (Telling it otherwise is accomplished through several means, background being the most common.) If a child process dies but this fact is not acknowledged by the parent, the child process becomes a *zombie*. What macabre imagery!

It's up to the operating system to keep track of these parents and children, making sure that processes don't collide. This means scheduling processes to within a fraction of a second, ensuring that all processes have access to precious CPU time. It's also up to the operating system, through the **init** program, to manage child processes that have been abandoned by their parents. These abandoned processes are called *orphans*. (Family values obviously play an important role in the Linux operating system, as they do in the Republican Party.)

Although we have mockingly referred to the high level of abstraction associated with the UNIX operating system, using names like parent, orphan, zombie, and child to describe the various stages of processes is a very useful thing; it helps both users and programmers visualize very intangible actions.

To see what processes are running on your system, use the **ps** command:

```
gilbert:~# ps
PID TTY STAT  TIME COMMAND
 49 v02 S     0:00 /sbin/getty tty2 38400 console
 50 v03 S     0:00 /sbin/getty tty3 38400 console
 51 v04 S     0:00 /sbin/getty tty4 38400 console
 52 v05 S     0:00 /sbin/getty tty5 38400 console
 53 v06 S     0:00 /sbin/getty tty6 38400 console
```

```
 73 v01 S     0:01 bash
 57 v01 S     0:00 sh /usr/X11/bin/startx
258 v01 S     0:00 xinit /usr/X11R6/lib/X11/xinit/xinitrc -
260 v01 S     0:00 twm
262 v01 S     0:00 /usr/bin/X11/oclock -geom 100x100+0+6
263 v01 S     0:00 /usr/bin/X11/xterm -ls -geom 80x24+3+372
264 v01 S     0:00 /usr/bin/X11/xterm -ls -geom 80x48+264+13
265 pp1 S     0:01 -bash
266 pp0 S     0:00 -bash
293 pp1 R     0:00 ps
 48 v01 S     0:00 -bash
```

Because we used the command on a single-user Linux machine running X Window, our list of running processes is not very long (relatively speaking, of course). If you're working on a large, multiuser system and ask for all the processes running, your list may be pages long. The fourth field, which covers the time the processes have run, may be of interest if there are some inordinately large numbers present. Most Linux commands, even very complex ones, don't take much time to complete.

We're using the **ps** command in its simplest form. Should you need more information than provided in the manner discussed here, use the **ps** command in the long form:

```
gilbert:~# ps -l
```

or in the family form:

```
gilbert:~# ps -f
```

which provides a lot of neat information, including which processes are children of other processes:

```
gilbert:~# ps -f
PID TTY STAT   TIME COMMAND
 49 v02 S     0:00 /sbin/getty tty2 38400 console
 50 v03 S     0:00 /sbin/getty tty3 38400 console
 51 v04 S     0:00 /sbin/getty tty4 38400 console
```

```
 52 v05 S      0:00 /sbin/getty tty5 38400 console
 53 v06 S      0:00 /sbin/getty tty6 38400 console
 48 v01 S      0:00 -bash
 73 v01 S      0:01  \_ bash
257 v01 S      0:00      \_ sh /usr/X11/bin/startx
258 v01 S      0:00          \_ xinit usr/X11R6/lib/X11/xinit/xinitrc -
260 v01 S      0:00              \_ twm
262 v01 S      0:00                  \_ /usr/bin/X11/oclock -geom 100x100+0+6
263 v01 S      0:00                  \_ /usr/bin/X11/xterm -ls -geom
80x24+3+37
266 pp0 S      0:00                  |   \_ -bash
264 v01 S      0:01                  \_ /usr/bin/X11/xterm -ls -geom
80x48+264+
265 pp1 S      0:02                      \_ -bash
303 pp1 R      0:00                          \_ ps -f
```

If you need to view all the processes running on the entire system (kids, don't try this at home, unless you really want a lot of information, most of it of questionable value), use:

```
gilbert:~# ps -a
```

To get a fuller view of the whole system, you can use:

```
gilbert:~# ps -au
```

Depending on the size and number of users on your system, you may regret using this option.

For our purposes, the most important column is the first one, which lists the IDs of running processes. When the kernel launches a new process, it assigns an ID number to the process. (As we saw earlier, **init** is numbered process 1.)

This number is important because it allows you to manipulate the process via the ID number. For example, there are times when you may want to kill a process because it's using too many precious system resources or not performing in the manner you anticipated. If the process is running in the foreground, you can press the **Delete** or **Break** keys (depending on your keyboard) to stop the process. (If **Delete** or **Break** doesn't work, try **Ctrl-C** or **Ctrl-D**.) If a process is running in the background or has been launched by another user at another terminal, however, you must kill the process via the **kill** command:

```
gilbert:~# kill PID
```

using the PID returned by the **ps** or other commands. This sends a signal to the process, telling it to cease and desist. Most processes don't know what to do when they receive a signal, so they commit suicide. Not all processes respond to the straight **kill** command; for example, shells ignore a **kill** command with no options. To kill a shell or other particularly stubborn processes, use **kill** with the *-9* option:

```
gilbert:~# kill -9 PID
```

This sends an unconditional kill signal to the process. If you have many processes to kill, you can wipe them all out with:

```
gilbert:~# kill 0
```

This kills all the processes in a current process group, which oversees all processes created by a common ancestor, usually the login shell.

More on the Foreground and Background

As the Linux operating system keeps track of these many processes, it must set priorities; after all, computing resources are typically finite (yes, we'd all love to have the power of a Cray for our tasks, but we make do with our underpowered multiuser systems), and some tasks are simply more important than other tasks when it comes to your attention. If a job doesn't require input from you, go ahead and run it in the background. This means that the process will run out of sight (and out of mind, too often), popping up only when the command is completed. While the command runs in the background, you're free to work on other tasks with other commands.

As you learned earlier in this book, running a process in the background is a matter of adding an ampersand (**&**) to the end of the command line:

```
$ command options &
```

For example, you should run CPU-intensive commands, such as **sort**, in the background. There's no reason for you to interact with the **sort** command as it goes through large files; your role in the process is to issue the command and then stay out of the way. The **sort** command requires no input from you, and it doesn't write to the screen as it performs the sort. The same goes for programmers who need to compile programs; their damage is done when creating the source code, not when compiling said code.

The temptation, of course, is to assume that all commands can be run in the background, but this isn't true. As a matter of fact, there's a rather limited number of commands that you should run in the background. For example, any command that relies on continued input from you, such as text editors and anything to do with electronic mail, shouldn't be run in the background.

Swap Space and Performance

When you installed Linux, you were prompted about the installation of swap space, which extends your system's random-access memory (RAM) to a physical hard disk. The notion of a swap space should be familiar to you if you've worked at all with UNIX on any sort of hardware platform, especially as you notice your hard drive thrashing when you switch between memory-intensive applications.

Linux uses paging to swap portions of memory (in this case, a page of 4096 bytes) between your RAM and the hard disk. When you consider how memory-intensive any PC-based version of UNIX is (compounded by the memory requirements of the X Window System), it's amazing Linux achieves the performance that it does. Of course, there are a few tricks used along the way: If the page from RAM derives from a read-only file, then that page is actually tossed aside and reread from hard disk when needed again. Similarly, Linux can share pages between applications; when you load two separate instances of an application at the same time, each instance of the application is actually reading from the same page of memory.

When you installed Linux, you had the option of installing a separate partition for swap space. Before getting into that, we'll go into Linux's memory-management tools and then let you decide if you really need to install more swap space.

I'm Free!

The Linux **free** command lists the amount of free RAM in your system and how much RAM is being used:

```
gilbert:~$ free
                total      used      free    shared  buffers  cached
Mem             63252      8124     55128      6484      980    3852
-/+ buffers:               3292     59960
Swap:               0         0         0
```

This output is new in Linux 1.3 and 2.0.

The **free** command lists the total amount of RAM in blocks; a *block* is equivalent to 1024 bytes, which makes the total available memory on this machine 14.99 megabytes (no, we didn't use a Pentium-based PC for this computation!). Where's the rest of the memory, because there's actually 16 megabytes installed? The **free** command literally lists the free memory; the rest is under control of the kernel and can't be accessed at any time.

Because there's not a lot happening on this machine (the **free** command was run immediately after the machine was booted), it's no surprise that only 3 megabytes or so of RAM are actually being used, while more than 11 megabytes are free. In addition, 2 megabytes are shared between processes. Contrast this to Figure 6.1, run after XFree86 is running.

```
xterm
gilbert:~$ free
               total      used      free    shared   buffers
Mem:          14648      8296      6352      5960      3112
-/+ buffers:              5184      9464
Swap:             0         0         0
gilbert:~$ █
```

Figure 6.1 Running the **free** command under X.

The numbers change quite a bit after loading X Window—all of a sudden there's only a little more than 6 megabytes free, with more than 8 megabytes in use, and more than 6 megabytes shared between processes.

The numbers in the *buffers* column refers to memory set aside by the system to use for common disk operations; instead of going to disk for every little task, Linux sets aside a portion of discretionary memory for these tasks (meaning that if RAM gets low, this memory will be freed for other purposes).

In this example, no swap space was set up when Linux was installed; hence the zeros.

Deciding Whether to Use Swap Space

If you've got 16 megabytes of RAM in your PC, as was in the case in the previous example, you probably won't need swap space, unless you're performing some computational-intensive task, such as programming. In these cases, you'll probably want to set up some swap space. However, if you didn't set up a separate swap partition when installing Linux, you're out of luck unless you want to use **fdisk** to repartition your hard drive and then reinstall Linux.

If the owner of the machine used as an example in the previous section wanted to install some swap space and not reinstall Linux, the only option would be to set up a swap file. Installing a swapfile is actually very similar to the routine for setting up a swap partition in Chapter 2, though it can be a tad involved.

It's best to perform this task logged in as **root**; otherwise, you'll probably run into file-permission problems.

Your first step is to actually set aside the space for your swap file on your hard disk, which means you'll use the **dd** command. Before you use it, however, you'll need to figure out how much hard-disk space you want to set aside for a swap file and what you want to name it (no, it's a little less involved than naming a child; you're best off just calling it **swap** and leaving it at that). For example, the following command would set up a 10MB swap space:

```
gilbert:~# dd if=/dev/zero of=/swap bs=1024 count=10240
```

The **dd** command writes data from a special device file called **/dev/zero** (don't worry; you don't need to know anything about this file past its existence in this circumstance) into a new file called **/swap**. We set the block size as 1,024, and we set aside a total of 10,240 bytes, which ends up being 10 megabytes of RAM. We chose 10 megabytes because it's a nice round number.

You've created a swapfile, but you need to format it now. Do so with the **mkswap** command (a command you should recall from the Linux installation information). In this case, you can format the **/swap** file to a size of 10,240 bytes:

```
gilbert:~# mkswap -c /swap 10240
```

To make sure that the new swap file and the rest of the file system are set up correctly, use the **sync** command:

```
gilbert:~# sync
```

You're not through yet! You still need to tell Linux that it has a swap file available. In this case, you'll use the **swapon** command, specifying the name of the swap file:

```
gilbert:~# swapon /swap
```

After doing all this, we can see from running the **free** command again (as shown in Figure 6.2) that there is indeed swap space available.

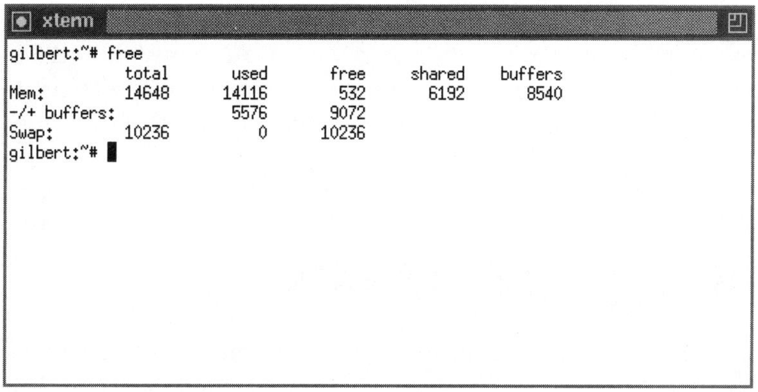

Figure 6.2 Running **free** after installing swap space.

After you've installed the swap space and you want the space to be permanently loaded on your Linux every time you boot, you'll need to add a line to the **/etc/fstab** file. This is the file that maintains the mounting of filesystems when Linux boots. It's a somewhat confusing process, but essentially the **/etc/rc.d/rc.S** file contains the following line:

```
swapon -a
```

that searches the **/etc/fstab** file for any swap spaces. If none are present, then installation continues as normal. If there is a swapfile or partition noted in **/etc/fstab**, then it is automatically mounted as Linux loads. Therefore, to make sure this swapfile loads every time Linux boots, you'll need to add to **/etc/fstab** a line like the following:

```
device          directory      type      options

/swap           none           swap      sw
```

To disable the swap partition, use the **swapoff** command:

```
gilbert:~# swapoff /swap
```

Don't delete the swap file before using the **swapoff** command.

If you're not going to be using the swap file again, you can go ahead and remove it from your system, using the **rm** command. You'll also need to edit the aforementioned **/etc/fstab** file and remove the swap file line from the file; if Linux searches for a swap file and doesn't find one, it will generate a few errors and you run the danger of risking memory integrity.

Mounting Filesystems

In UNIX parlance, to *mount* a filesystem is to tell the system that there's a device available for use. This may be a hard drive, a CD-ROM drive, or something else. When you launch Linux, the system itself mounts all the devices on your PC, and these devices are stored in your **/etc/fstab** file. (This should look somewhat familiar if you've been reading this chapter from beginning to end; accessing this file is part of installing new swap space.) A Linux startup script—usually in the **/etc/rc.d** directory—takes the information from your **/etc/fstab** file to mount the various components of your PC.

In theory, you won't need to mount anything through your Linux system if everything installed correctly. You may need to mount a new hard drive or a new CD-ROM if you make changes in your system, or you may want to mount a tape drive only when you actually need it.

However, mounting a device is rather simple. Basically, you can use the **mount** command to mount a device, specifying both the device to be mounted and the location in the filesystem where you want the device to be located. (The location must already exist, so you need to create it before using the **mount** command.) Rendered abstractly, the **mount** command looks like this:

```
gilbert:~# mount device mountlocation
```

where *device* is the name of the device and *mountlocation* is the location of the device on the filesystem. As you'll recall from Chapter 2, Linux uses a series of device names to specify devices, such as **/dev/cd0** for the first CD-ROM drive on a system, **/dev/cd1** for the second CD-ROM drive on a system, and so on. The *mountlocation* is merely the place in the filesystem where you want to be able to access the files on the device; a good place to locate a mountlocation is in the **usr** directory, and you must combine this with a name of a directory. Therefore, to mount a SCSI CD-ROM drive with a location of **/usr/cdrom**, you'd use the following command line:

```
gilbert:~# mount /dev/scd0 /usr/cdrom -rt iso9660
```

The **mount** command no longer autoprobes reliably for the filesystem type, so you'll need to specify it on the command line.

To unmount a mounted filesystem, use the **umount** command:

```
gilbert:~# umount /dev/scd0
```

Sending a Message of the Day

System administrators who have worked on other UNIX systems may be used to sending out a message of the day to all the users of the system. The same capability exists in Linux.

When a user logs in the system, the contents of the file **/etc/motd** are automatically displayed on their screen. Therefore, for you to send out a message of the day, you need to create a **/etc/motd** file. This can be done with a text editor like **vi** or **emacs**, saving a text file with a filename of **/etc/motd**.

One of the system setup scripts (**/etc/rc.d/rc.s**) creates new **/etc/motd** and **/etc/issue** messages based on the name of the running kernel. If you wish to use your own message files, you'll need to comment out the lines in this script that make the new **/etc/motd** and **/etc/issue** files, or your custom versions will be overwritten upon reboot.

Summary

This chapter covered the basic system-administration tasks you're going to run into when using Linux. This involves mundane tasks like adding and deleting users, managing groups, creating boot floppies, scheduling commands, and more. However, there's a lot more to UNIX system administration than we presented here, and if you're planning on tackling the issue, we recommend that you purchase a good UNIX system-administration book and apply the general UNIX guidelines to Linux.

The next chapter begins our coverage of extending Linux to the outside world, with a discussion of Linux serial-telecommunications tools.

Section III

Linux Communications and Networking

No operating system is an island, which is why Linux contains so many tools for dealing with the outside world.

Chapter 7 covers serial telecommunications tools such as **seyon** and **minicom**, which allow you to dial into online services and bulletin-board systems.

Chapter 8 covers Linux TCP/IP. As any good UNIX does, Linux has TCP/IP networking built in. Chapter 8 contains an overview of TCP/IP networking.

Chapter 9 covers the Internet in all its glory. Linux owes a lot to the Internet, and you'll find that a connection to the Internet is one of the most valuable things you can have as a Linux user.

Linux and Telecommunications

This chapter covers:

- Serial communications and Linux
- Using **seyon**
- The many options to **seyon**
- Using **minicom** and **xminicom**
- Options to **minicom**
- Using **rzsz**
- Getting more information about the **rzsz** commands

Expanding Your Reach via Modem

Even if you're using Linux as a standalone system, you're not limited to your little neck of the woods. Linux and its many accompanying tools allow you to connect via modem to other parts of the world, whether it be bulletin-board systems (BBSes), online services, or the Internet. Thanks to its reliance on good UNIX software, Linux also contains several tools for connecting to character-based systems like CompuServe or local bulletin-board systems.

In this chapter we will cover the many tools Linux features for serial communications, beginning with a very functional telecommunications program, **seyon**, followed by discussions of the **minicom**, **xminicom**, and **term** packages, and ending with a discussion of older UNIX telecommunications tools like **rzsz**. All the tools covered here are included in the Slackware Linux distribution.

Seyon: Telecommunications from Linux

The **seyon** telecommunications program, developed by Muhammed M. Saggaf (as immortalized in Figure 7.1), is a surprisingly functional terminal-emulation package for the X Window environment.

Seyon supports many features that can be found in popular telecommunications packages like Procomm, including a dialing directory, support for several protocols (including Zmodem), various emulation modes (including DEC VT102, Tektronix 4014, and ANSI), and translation modes (for communicating with PC-based services).

To use **seyon**, you need to have a modem and a connection to a telephone line. When you installed Linux, you were prompted about the location of the modem on your PC—in other words, the COM port connected to your modem (if your PC was typical, this would have been COM1 or COM2). This information was then translated into a device file called **/dev/modem**, which is used by input for **seyon**.

Therefore, to launch **seyon**, use the following command line:

```
gilbert:~$ seyon -modems /dev/modem
```

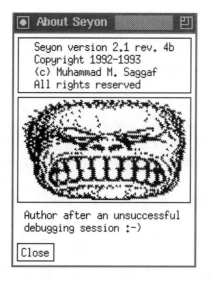

Figure 7.1 The About **Seyon** dialog box.

If you're smart, you'll set up an alias for this rather cumbersome command line. If you merely launch **seyon** with no options, you'll get an error message. After you load **seyon**, you'll see two windows, like what's shown in Figure 7.2.

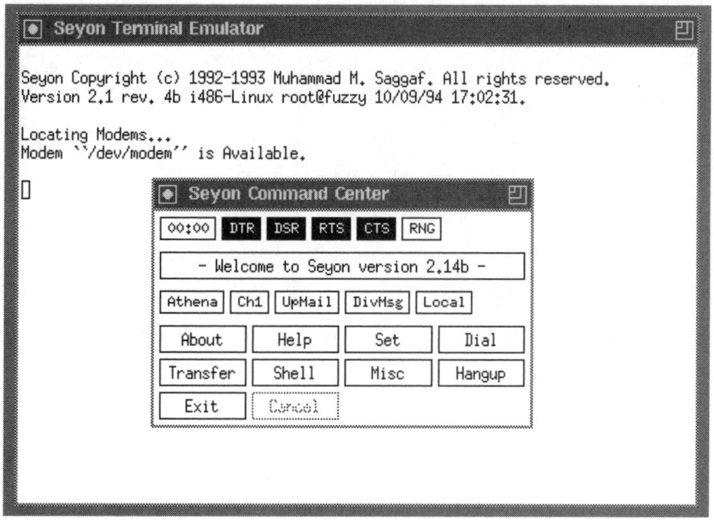

Figure 7.2 Seyon at startup.

The Command Center is where you'll spend most of your time in **seyon**. The top row of status buttons returns information from the modem (DTR, DSR, RTS, and CTS are standard telecommunications indicators, while RNG tells us that a call is going through and the number indicates the time of the call; very handy information if you're paying an online service by the minute).

The next large box is a status indicator, telling us whether **seyon** is active, awaiting a call, or making a call. If **seyon** is inactive for any period of time, various messages—most of which are on the cutesy side—will be displayed.

The next row of buttons doesn't do much as the buttons have no actions associated with them. However, the remaining buttons are what catch our interest, as they form the guts of functionality of **seyon**:

> **About** displays the humorous dialog box shown in Figure 7.1.
>
> **Help** displays the online-manual page for **seyon**. **Seyon** is capable of some pretty advanced maneuvers not covered here.
>
> **Set** opens a dialog box (shown in Figure 7.3) that contains various system settings:

- **Strip 8th** strips the eighth bit—useful for connecting to non-UNIX systems.
- **BS->DEL** functionally turns the **Backspace** key into a **Delete** key. The **Backspace** key is not universally supported in the UNIX world, and if you're communicating a lot with other UNIX hosts, you'll want to turn this feature on.
- **Meta->Esc** translates the **Meta** key into the PC **Esc** key. You'll want to leave this setting alone.
- **XON/XOFF** refers to the software flow-control setting. The default is to have this setting disabled. However, some remote hosts require XON/XOFF control; hence the need for this setting.
- **CTS/RTS** is another flow-control setting. Again, the default is disabled, but some remote hosts require it to be enabled.
- **AutoZmodem** tells **seyon** to automatically enable a Zmodem file transfer when prompted by the remote host. This is a matter of convenience.
- **IdleGuard** sends a string to the remote host if the session has

been idle. The goal is to keep the session from being terminated due to inaction, as most remotes have auto-logoff capabilities.

- The **Baud** dialog box (actually a misnomer; you're setting the bits per second, not the baud rate) sets the session speed. Unfortunately, the fastest session is 38400 bps. Generally speaking, you'll want to set the session speed higher than the actual session. When using a 14400-bps modem, you'll want to set the session speed to 19200 bps.

- **Bits** refers to, well, bits. Generally, this setting should be 7 or 8.

- **Parity** can be none, even, or odd.

- **Stop bits** can be 1 or 2.

- **Common** is a shortcut to set the bits/parity/stop bits separately; most remote hosts require a setting of 8-N-1 or 7-E-1.

- **NewLine** allows you to set an outgoing UNIX newline to be translated to a newline, a carriage return, or a newline/carriage-return combination. Most PC-based online services prefer the new line/carriage-return combination.

- **Port** sets the modem port. Of course, if you couldn't specify this when starting **seyon**, you couldn't get to this point anyway.

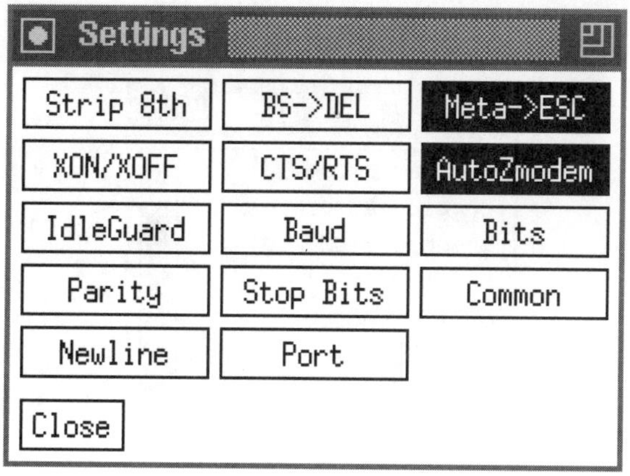

Figure 7.3 The Set dialog box.

The **Dial** button brings up a list of telephone numbers. When you first use **seyon**, you'll be presented with a long list that contains one telephone number. This is the example Seyon dialing directory, which you'll want to adapt for your own usage. This is not a difficult task (select **Edit** from the Dialing Directory dialog box), and you can use the many examples found in the example file. An edited Dialing Directory dialog box is shown in Figure 7.4.

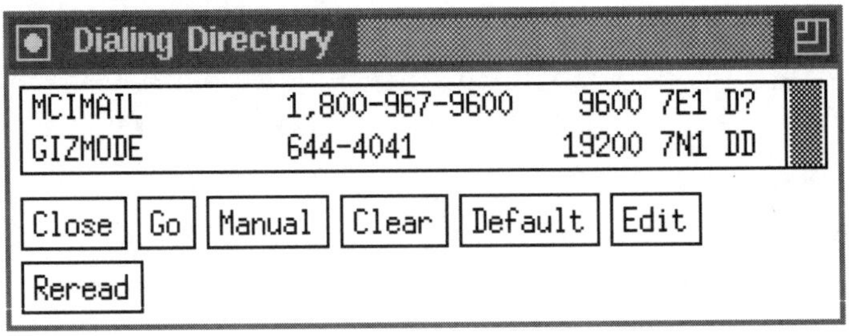

Figure 7.4 The Dialing Directory dialog box.

This dialog box also allows you to manually enter a phone number, using the current **seyon** system settings.

The Transfer dialog box (shown in Figure 7.5) allows you to send and receive files. These are actually external protocols, although the various Zmodem iterations are part of the default **seyon** installation. The Help files describe how to install other protocols within **seyon**.

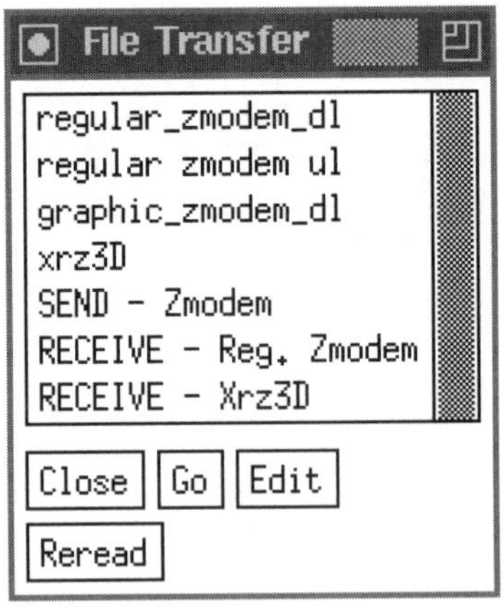

Figure 7.5 The File Transfer dialog box.

The Shell dialog box allows you to run a **shell** command from within **seyon**.

The Miscellaneous dialog box contains a set of various capabilities, including text capture, a text editor, and a file viewer. It's shown in Figure 7.6.

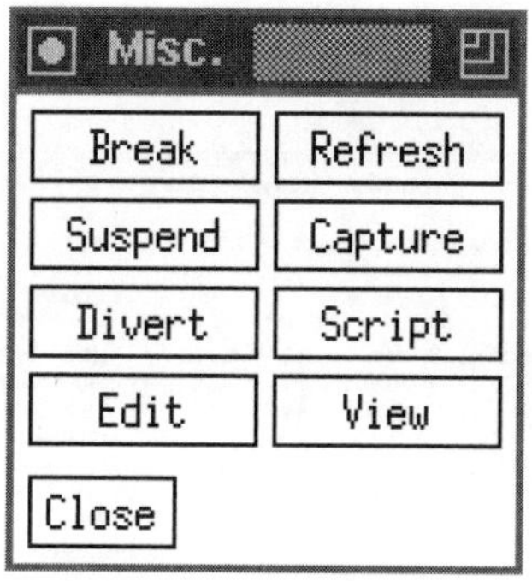

Figure 7.6 The Miscellaneous dialog box.

The **Hangup** button hangs up the current connection. The **Exit** button exits **seyon**. Finally, the **Cancel** button cancels the current operation.

This overview of Seyon should give you a pretty good idea of its capabilities. But there's a lot more to Seyon; for example, it features a slew of command-line options—too many to cover here. However, if you're serious about using Seyon regularly, you should check out its scripting mechanisms, which are akin to a formal programming language (featuring if/then statements and the like). Again, by summoning the Help files from the Command Center, you'll get a complete overview of the **seyon** scripting mechanisms.

Using Minicom and Xminicom

Seyon is an X Window-based application. However, you may not want to do everything from within X, so you might want a character-based telecommunications package. This exists in the form of **minicom**, written by Miquel van Smoorenburg. (You can also use **xminicom**, which places an X Window front end on the basic **minicom** package. Both actually work the same. Here, we'll cover **minicom**, but you can use the same commands when running **xminicom**.)

Minicom is a full-screen telecommunications package. It works similarly to other PC-based telecommunications packages, offering a menu (accessible by pressing **Ctrl-a z**) as shown in Figure 7.7. Every command is accessible with the **Ctrl-a** combination, by the way.

```
+=======================================================+
I                 Minicom Command Summary                I
I                                                        I
I          Commands can be called by CTRL-A <key>        I
I                                                        I
I            Main Functions          Other Functions     I
I                                                        I
I Dialing directory..D  run script (Go)....G I Clear Screen.......C I
I Send files.........S  Receive files......R I cOnfigure Minicom..O I
I comm Parameters....P  Add linefeed.......A I Jump to a shell....J I
I Capture on/off.....L  Hangup.............H I eXit and reset.....X I
I send break.........F  initialize Modem...M I Quit with no reset.Q I
I Terminal emulation.T  run Kermit.........K I Cursor key mode....I I
I lineWrap on/off....W  local Echo on/off..E I Help screen........Z I
I                                            I scroll Back........B I
I                                                        I
I        Select function or press Enter for none.█       I
I                                                        I
I          Written by Miquel van Smoorenburg 1991-1994   I
+=======================================================+
```

```
CTRL-A Z for help I 38400 8N1 I NOR I Minicom 1.60 1994 I VT100 I OFFLINE
```

Figure 7.7 The Minicom command summary.

To get working quickly in **minicom**, you can press **d** from this command summary. At this point you can manually enter a telephone number or press **Enter** for your dialing directory. From this menu you can also add new phone numbers, edit existing numbers, or delete unwanted entries.

To change communications parameters, type **Ctrl-a p**, which brings you to a dialog box with comm parameters, as shown in Figure 7.8.

```
+========[Comm Parameters]========+
I                                 I
I Current: 38400 8N1              I
I                                 I
I  Speed        Parity      Data  I
I                                 I
I A: 300        I: None     N: 5  I
I B: 1200       J: Even     O: 6  I
I C: 2400       K: Odd      P: 7  I
I D: 4800                   Q: 8  I
I E: 9600                         I
I F: 19200                        I
I G: 38400      L: 8-N-1          I
I H: Current    M: 7-E-1          I
I                                 I
I Choice, or <Enter> to exit? █   I
+=================================+
```

```
CTRL-A Z for help I 38400 8N1 I NOR I Minicom 1.60 1994 I VT100 I OFFLINE
```

Figure 7.8 Setting comm parameters in Minicom.

Because **minicom** is a character-based Linux program, it relies heavily on keyboard combinations. Most of these combinations are accessible from the menu shown in Figure 7.7. However, because you might not want to go to this screen for every little action, we list the key combinations in Table 7.1.

Table 7.1 Key Combinations in Minicom

Key	Result
a	Adds a linefeed to each line.
b	Scrolls back through the terminal window into the buffer.
c	Clears the screen.
d	Displays the dialing directory.
e	Turns echo on and off; useful if you're seeing two characters where you should only see one or if you're not seeing any characters when you should see some.
f	Sends a break to the remote host.
g	Runs a script.
h	Hangs up the modem.
i	Sets the cursor-key mode.
j	Jump to the shell while leaving Minicom in memory.
k	Starts a kermit session.
l	Turns capture on, saving the current session to file (**minicom.cap** is the default, although you can enter a new filename).
m	Initializes the modem.
o	Configures **minicom** (a task for when you're logged in as **root**, by the way).
p	Sets comm parameters, such as bps rate, stop bits, and parity.
q	Quits **minicom** without resetting the modem.
r	Receives a file from the remote host; the supported protocols are Zmodem, Ymodem, Xmodem, and kermit.
s	Sends a file; the supported protocols are Zmodem, Ymodem, Xmodem, and kermit..
t	Changes the terminal emulation among VT100, Minix, and ANSI.
w	Turns the line-wrap on and off.
x	Exits **minicom** and resets the modem.
z	Summons the command-summary screen.

One nice feature of Minicom is its scripting capability. While the script itself can be a shell script (the documentation explains how to implement this), Minicom allows you to set up a password with the script, preventing unauthorized usage of the script within Minicom. Having said this, there are some other acknowledged security issues with Minicom, mostly relating to its running in superuser mode. If security is an issue in your Linux system, you may want to rethink Minicom.

The online-manual page for **minicom** is quite extensive and can probably answer any questions you have.

Using Rzsz

If you're a PC user and have dabbled in telecommunications, you've probably worked with software packages that did everything: managed the dialup and login process, oversaw the file transfers, and essentially centralized all manner of serial communications. However, Linux—being the good UNIX workalike that it is—features different tools for accomplishing the same thing. Dipping into the UNIX software chest, we can come up with a few commands that allow serial communications without needing any fancy programs—or even an interface, for that matter.

The UNIX **cu** command is used to call another computer system. If you're working on a stand-alone system, you'll probably want to use Minicom or Seyon instead, but if you're working on a network that has UUCP already configured, you can use the **cu** command (which is a UUCP command) for making the initial connection.

Once you're connected to a remote system, you can use the **rzsz** set of commands to upload and download documents. Essentially, these commands implement the Zmodem, Ymodem, and Xmodem protocols from the command line, assuming that a valid connection has been made. In addition, the remote host must support the protocol you want to use. As the Zmodem protocol is already popular among most online services and bulletin-board systems, it's useful to have.

There are actually six commands in the **rzsz** distribution. As they differ slightly from other **rzsz** distributions (the **man** pages and online help messages don't match), we'll list them here and then further explain each of them:

- **rz** or **lrz** receives files via Zmodem from a remote host.
- **rb** or **lrb** receives files via Ymodem from a remote host.
- **rx** or **lrx** receives files via Xmodem from a remote host.
- **sz** or **lsz** sends files via Zmodem to a remote host.
- **sb** or **lsb** sends files via Ymodem from a remote host.
- **sx** or **lsx** sends files via Xmodem from a remote host.

To get the skinny on each of these commands, use the *-h* option to the command (additionally, this Linux distribution features online-manual pages for the **rz** and **sz** commands, shown in Figure 7.9). For example, **sb -h** on the command line gives you the following:

```
gilbert:~# sb -h
Send file(s) with ZMODEM/YMODEM/XMODEM Protocol
        (Y) = Option applies to YMODEM only
        (X) = Option applies to XMODEM only
Usage:  lsz [-2+abdefkLlNnquvwYy] [-] file ...
        lsz [-2Ceqv] -c COMMAND
        lsb [-2adfkquv] [-] file ...
        lsz [-2akquv] [-] file
```

and much more....

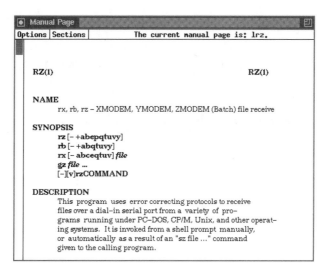

Figure 7.9 Online-manual page for rz/lrz.

How you actually use these commands will partially depend on the remote host, of course; some hosts, especially UNIX-based ones, require that you first start **rz** on the remote host and then run **sz** locally if you want to upload a file. Other hosts, particularly PC-based ones, have their own methods for handling a file upload.

Other Linux Telecommunications Tools

If none of these serial telecommunications tools strikes your fancy, you can peruse wider offerings on the Internet for more appropriate tools. Always popular, yet difficult to use and set up, is C-Kermit (available from the official *kermit.columbia.edu* FTP site, in the **/kermit/c-kermit** directory. Be warned that you'll need to use a **makefile** to create a version for Linux.

Another option is the **pcomm** telecommunications package. This package is essentially a Linux workalike to the popular DOS/Windows Procomm, featuring a dialing directory, interactive usage, and more. We've included it on the second CD-ROM, or you can grab it from the *ftp.cecer.army.mil* FTP site, in the **pcomm** directory.

Summary

This chapter covered serial communications under the Linux operating system, focusing on packages like **seyon**, **minicom**, **xminicom**, and the **rzsz** utilities.

The next chapter covers networking and Linux.

Linux Networking

This chapter covers:

- TCP/IP
- System administration and networking
- The **fwhois** command

Networking and Linux

One of the great appeals of the Linux operating system is its built-in networking connectivity. Instead of trying to make an operating system like DOS, Microsoft Windows, or MacOS deal with a network, you can work with Linux, where the network exists at the core of the operating system.

This is accomplished through TCP/IP (Transmission Control Protocol/Internet Protocol), which has become the *lingua franca* for networking in the UNIX world. Because UNIX-based systems were instrumental in forming the Internet and its predecessors, TCP/IP became the dominant protocol for communication on the Internet. TCP/IP is the major tool for networking UNIX-based computer systems, as most UNIX implementations contain support for TCP/IP. Other operating systems, such as DOS and OS/2, can also connect to TCP/IP networks, although this requires special add-on software.

Linux comes with full support for TCP/IP (provided you installed it when you installed Linux; if not, you'll need to look at reinstalling Linux or recompiling your kernel). This support comes in the form of the NET-3 set of protocols and programs. On your end, connecting to a UNIX network via TCP/IP is merely a matter of making sure your PC is correctly hooked up to the network via Ethernet card and cabling.

 Much of what's involved with Linux networking is best performed at the sysadm level. If you're a system administrator, you should follow your own configuration routines at the network level; after all, Linux installs and configures pretty much like any other PC UNIX on the network level. If you're not a system administrator, we suggest you check out Olaf Kirch's *Linux Network Administrator's Guide*, which can be found on the accompanying CD-ROM or in print at your local bookstore.

In Chapter 1 we covered supported Ethernet cards. If you need more information about setting up your Ethernet card, check out the **ETHERNET-HOWTO** on the accompanying program CD-ROM, in the **docs** directory.

Linux also allows you to make a TCP/IP connection via telephone line, using the SLIP or PPP protocol. If you want to connect to the Internet via a dialup connection, you'll need to use these tools. (We cover this in more depth in Chapter 9.)

Before you try using any of these tools, you should have some background in TCP/IP. We advise checking out Olaf Kirch's *Linux Network Administrator's Guide*, which has been printed by various sources (including the Linux Documentation Project and SSC).

In addition, the CD-ROM contains a very useful, detailed guide to TCP/IP networking and NET-3 in the form of **NET-2-HOWTO**, in the **docs** directory.

These guides should form the basis of your networking expertise. However, we'll provide a short overview of TCP/IP networking here.

TCP/IP Basics

Under a TCP/IP network, every computer on the network is assigned an IP address, including your computer. If your Linux workstation is permanently connected to a TCP/IP network, this address will remain constant. (If you're using a dialup connection to the Internet through a service provider, your IP address will be dynamically assigned when you login the service.) This address comes in four fields, such as *255.255.0.0*. This breaks down to:

subdomain.subdomain.domain.domain

You will find detailed information on IP addresses, how they're structured, and how you can acquire them on the second accompanying CD-ROM. We're not going to spend a lot of time on the intricacies of IP addresses; it's an involved subject beyond the reach of this book.

From your end, IP addresses are important for connecting to another computer on the network. (By this, we mean the *entire network*, which can include the rest of the world if you're connected to the Internet.) However, in many situations you don't need to know the specific IP address to make a connection, as you probably discovered when you see lists of Internet addresses (such as those found in Appendix A) without any IP addresses listed. Why's that? Because early in the Internet's development the decision was made to allow a Domain Name Server (DNS) to handle these dirty details. Your TCP/IP network (or your service provider) has a named DNS somewhere on the network. When you enter an Internet address like **ftp.x.org** or a mail address like

reichard@mr.net, a lookup is performed on the DNS, which then makes sure that the mail or request is routed to the proper machine. If you've installed TCP/IP on your system, you'll be running a daemon named **named** that handles the connections to the DNS.

The **fwhois** command connects to the DNS and returns information about a specific user or a domain name:

```
gilbert:~$ fwhois mr.net
Minnesota Regional Network (MR-DOM)
      511 11th Avenue South, Box 212
      Minneapolis, MN 55415


      Domain Name: MR.NET


      ....


      Record last updated on 16-Nov-93


      Domain servers in listed order:


      NS.MR.NET              137.192.240.5
      RS0.INTERNIC.NET        198.41.0.5
      RIVERSIDE.MR.NET       137.192.2.5
      SPRUCE.CIC.NET         35.42.1.100

gilbert:~$ fwhois dfazio@mr.net
Fazio, Dennis (DF202)          dfazio@mr.net
Minnesota Regional Network (MR-DOM)
      511 11th Avenue South, Box 212
      Minneapolis, MN 55415


      Record last updated on 16-Dec-91
```

The **fwhois** command also lists users on your Linux system, even if you're not connected to the Internet.

Setting up TCP/IP Information

The files that control TCP/IP configuration are stored in the **/etc** directory. When you first set up Linux and are asked about machine names and domain names, this information is sent to the **/etc/hosts** file. While you don't need to mess with this file if you're connected to the Internet (it does many of the same things that a Domain Name Server does), it's a good thing to place the names of essential servers in this file. And if you're not connected to the Internet but you are maintaining a small network, this is the place to store the IP addresses for the workstations on your system. (Again, this could be done via a DNS on your local system, but it's a lot easier to use the **/etc/hosts** file.)

Another file to check is the **/etc/networks** file, used to configured different networks in the TCP/IP subsystem. This file is summoned when the system launches, and its functions are handled by DNS servers if you're working on the Internet. Again, if you're not connected to the Internet but you want to have subnetworks and such (you really don't; we're speaking hypothetically here if you're working on a small network), you'd use this file instead of a DNS.

 If you have an ethernet card, you can configure it using the "netconfig" command. You might also need to edit /etc/rc.d/rc.modules to load support for your card.

You'll also want to run the **ifconfig** command, which essentially tells the kernel about your Ethernet card and the IP addresses if you've not done so already. To see the current state of your system, use the command with no options:

```
gilbert:/$ ifconfig
lo    Link encap:Local Loopback
      inet addr:127.0.0.1  Bcast:127.255.255.255  Mask:255.0.0.0
      UP BROADCAST LOOPBACK RUNNING  MTU:2000  Metric:1
```

```
RX packets:0 errors:0 dropped:0 overrun:0
TX packets:40 errors:0 dropped:0 overruns:0
```

In this case, we're actually using Linux without a network card or a connection to a network—but Linux thinks it's on a network using a tool called *loopback*. Loopback allows applications and daemons that need to communicate via TCP/IP to connect to local resources.

Summary

Linux networking is an involved subject and one beyond the goals of this book. You'll want to check out some of the reference works in Appendix A for more information.

Linux and the Internet

This chapter covers:

- Linux and the Internet
- SLIP and PPP
- Electronic mail
- The World Wide Web
- Web browsers
- The UUCP commands
- Using FTP
- The **telnet** command
- Using the Usenet

Getting on the Worldwide Network

The Internet has been the recipient of a ton of hype recently, and with good reason: it's one of the most exciting developments in the computer world in quite some time. As both a computer user and a Linux user, you'll greatly benefit from the many possibilities offered by the many offerings of the Internet.

As a matter of fact, you've probably noticed the many references to the Internet throughout the course of this book. It seems as though anyone who wants to do any advanced work with Linux needs a link to the Internet. (As did the authors of this book, who spent much of their time planning this book and coordinating material through electronic mail and the Internet.) Usenet newsgroups—which we cover in Appendix A—as well as great Web sites can certainly enhance your understanding and usage of the Linux operating system.

How you connect to the Internet depends on your specific circumstances, however. If you're using Linux in a corporation that's already connected to the Internet, you can merely piggyback from that connection. If you're working on a stand alone Linux workstation, you can set up your own Internet connection with the aid of an Internet service provider.

Both of these possibilities exist because of Linux's built-in networking capabilities—namely, TCP/IP, which you learned about in Chapter 8. Basically, this support for TCP/IP allows a Linux user to use another computer on the network. In Chapter 8, the computers on the network were in the same physical location as your computer. On the Internet, the computers on the network can be just about anywhere. (In other words, the Internet is basically the world's largest TCP/IP network.)

The concept behind TCP/IP networking is actually pretty simple. Each machine on the network has an individual TCP/IP address, and every other machine on the network can access this machine (if only to be denied access, of course; there are some security measures involved if need be). The extent of the network depends on your needs; some companies purposely restrict their TCP/IP networks to a very confined set of machines; other allow full access to the global Internet.

In this chapter, we'll discuss getting on the Internet using the tools built into Linux.

Finding a Window to the Internet

If you aren't connected to the Internet via a direct network connection, you'll need to make arrangements to do so. There are two ways to do this.

One method involves piggybacking off of a machine that is directly connected to the Internet. In this manner, you can essentially use the specifics of the connected machine. Connectivity tools that fall under this category include **SLiRP**, which is run in a remote UNIX shell account and makes it act like a SLIP/CSLIP account. We compiled it on an Ultrix machine and connected to it with DIP. It works great! The source for it is on the CD-ROM in /**contrib**.

The **term** program, which was covered in the first edition of this book, is no longer supported under newer versions of Linux.

Linux's SLIP and PPP Tools

If you don't have a permanent TCP/IP connection to the Internet through work or a friend, you can use Linux's SLIP and PPP tools to connect to the Internet via an Internet service provider of some sort. SLIP (Serial Line Internet Protocol) and PPP (Point-to-Point Protocol) allow you to connect to another TCP/IP machine.

To connect to the Internet via SLIP and PPP, your implementation of Linux must first support both protocols. If you installed directly from the CD-ROM, your Linux kernel will indeed support SLIP and PPP; if you look at the screen closely when you boot Linux, you'll notice that SLIP and PPP will be listed. However, if for some reason you decided to compile your own kernel, then you should have had the foresight to compile in SLIP and PPP support. (You were asked if you wanted support for these protocols as part of the **make** process.) If not, then you'll need to go back and compile a new kernel, paying special attention to the Network section of the **makefile**.

After doing that, you'll set up an account with a service provider (like Netcom, PSI, GNN, Microsoft Network, or Minnesota Regional Network), which gives you Internet access using a standard modem.

When you connect via a service provider, you'll be assigned an IP address right on the spot; the process yields a *dynamically assigned* IP address, which is then used by your Linux system to connect to the Internet.

When you set up an account, you should get a list of information from the service provider. Out of this information, you'll need to know the following:

- The access telephone number—if you don't have this number, you can't dial up the service provider.

- The IP numbers of the Domain Name Servers. These are the servers your system looks to when you want to connect to another machine on the Internet. Without these servers, your Linux system would be lost in cyberspace.

- Your username and password.

- The mechanism for logging on the system. This is a little more daunting than it looks, because it seems that every service provider handles dialup connections a little differently. As an example: our service provider uses a standard UNIX-style login procedure, where the entry of a username and a password is followed by a standard UNIX prompt:

```
Welcome to the Twin Cities MRNet dialIP Service.
User Access Verification
Username:
Password:
slip-server> ppp
```

After entering **ppp** at the command prompt, the server initiates the PPP protocol with your machine. This is not standard in the ISP world; most initiate the process immediately after you enter your password.

Basically, SLIP and PPP do the same thing. However, SLIP (the older of the two protocols) is decreasing in popularity, because PPP (quite honestly) is easier to configure and use. Linux contains the **dip** command, which handles SLIP connections to a service provider.

The **dip** command stands for *dialup IP* connections, that is, a TCP/IP connection between your Linux system and some other system. The connection is made over a serial line (and presumably a phone line and modem) instead of the traditional Ethernet or other TCP/IP connection. On top of the serial line connection, **dip** implements one of a number of serial-line Internet protocols, including SLIP, CSLIP (Compressed SLIP), and PPP.

Thus, without a direct hard-wired network link, you can establish an IP (network) link over a phone line. This is very useful for connecting to an Internet service provider. The way this works is that all data going between the two computers is sent over the serial line. At each end, the data is converted into network packets and sent to the appropriate programs. To most programs on either end, there is no real difference between this type of link and a direct network connection, except that serial-line links are typically much slower than direct network connections.

You can use **dip** for both incoming and outgoing dialup links.

When you dial out with **dip**, you can configure a chat script to set up a link to your remote system. The chat script contains things like which serial port to use, the system (host) to connect to, what speed to set the modem, the protocol (e.g., PPP, SLIP, etc.), and so on.

You can also use **dip** to manage incoming connections. Users then login normally over a serial link, but the "shell" launched on login is not **bash** or **csh**, but **diplogin**.

In this case, you can set up a program called **diplogin** as the "shell" to execute for a particular user in the **/etc/passwd** file. (Normally, **diplogin** is a link to **dip** with the -*i* option to set **dip** into input mode. Upon login, **dip** looks up the user's name in the **/etc/diphosts** file. Each entry in this file is a lot like the system password file, **/etc/passwd**. For each user, you can have an extra external dial-in password to add an extra level of security—a useful thing in the wild atmosphere of the Internet.

Upon successful login, **dip** sets up a network connection between the dial-in line and your Linux system, using the protocol specified in the **/etc/diphosts** file for the given user who logged in. Normally, this is CLSIP, SLIP, or PPP.

Dip also supports dynamic IP address allocation. See the online documentation for more on this.

NOTE

Because dialup Internet connections are so individualistic (we've dealt collectively with both static and dynamically allocated addresses), we're going to leave it up to you to configure **dip**. You'll want to read carefully through the online-manual pages for **dip**, as they contain plenty of examples. They also contain example scripts, which you can adapt to automatically log you on a remote connection.

To help make the first connection, it's very handy to run **dip** in test mode. To run it, use the following command line:

```
gilbert:/$ dip -t

dip>
```

The *-t* option tells **dip** to accept interactive commands. You can use these interactive commands to find out more information about what steps work and what steps don't while you're debugging a **dip** connection.

Unfortunately, there is no really easy way to set up **dip**. You can find out more about **dip** and its configuration options by looking in the **/usr/doc/dip** directory.

Linux's PPP Tools

We recommend that you use the PPP protocol instead of SLIP for many reasons, some technical and some not; basically, it's easier to set up PPP connections when you're using dynamically assigned IP addresses.

Not that it's that simple to set up a PPP connection. The trouble with the Linux world is that it lacks a simple tool like Trumpet Winsock to automate dialup connections to the Internet, which is why you need to slog through descriptions like the one here.

In addition to the **dip** program, Linux supports a suite of PPP-only applications. The **dip** program supports the PPP protocol, along with SLIP and CLSIP. The PPP suite of applications only supports PPP. Of these PPP-only tools, the **pppd** command acts as the PPP daemon and sits in the background awaiting PPP connections.

The **ppp-on** command brings up a connection. The **ppp-off** command brings it down. As with **dip**, there's a lot of configuration to do. This is one area of Linux that could really use some improvement. You can find out more about Linux's PPP tools by looking in the **/usr/doc/ppp** directory.

Confusing as it sounds, the **dip** program supports the PPP protocol, but not the separate PPP suite of commands. Nor do the PPP commands support **dip**. That is, you can't really mix and match **dip** with **ppp-on**, **ppp-off**, and **pppd**.

In addition to the **slip** and **ppp** suites, you can run **diald**, short for *Dial Daemon*. **Diald** maintains a pseudo-networking connection for your phone line, even if the phone line is not actively connected to the Internet. This capability allows you to only tie up your phone line when needed, because **diald** automatically reconnects when needed and hangs up when a connection is no longer necessary.

Diald is on the second CD-ROM.

Setting up a PPP Connection

Here are the steps you'll want to follow to establish a PPP connection to an Internet Service Provider, or ISP. In these situations, you're calling the same phone number and are dynamically allocated an IP address each time you login the ISP's computer.

First, you'll need to make sure that your local permissions are set up correctly. When logged in as **root**, you should edit your **/etc/hosts.deny** file to add the following line:

```
ALL: ALL
```

This prevents others from logging on your system via the Internet when you're connected to your ISP. However, you do want to allow yourself access to your own machine (we assume you do, anyway), so edit your **/etc/hosts.allow** file to add the following line:

```
ALL: 127.0.0.1
```

If you haven't done so already, you should give your own machine a name (we told how to change this in Chapter 2). This information is found in **/etc/HOSTNAME**.

Next, you'll need to tell your Linux system where to find data on the Internet. This involves adding the name of your service provider and a DNS server to the **/etc/resolv.conf** file, in the following format:

```
search mr.net
nameserver xxx.xxx.xxx.xxx
```

In this example, we told Linux to look for things like news and mail at *mr.net*. In the place of *xxx.xxx.xxx.xxx* you'll provide a DNS address as provided by your ISP.

You'll also want to take a look at **/etc/hosts**. It should contain two lines, looking something like this:

```
127.0.0.1 localhost
0.0.0.0   gilbert
```

If *127.0.0.1* is used for your machine name, change it. This should not be used when a connection to the Internet is made, because it may conflict with some Internet services.

Finally, you'll want to give Linux the username and password provided to you by your ISP in the **/etc/ppp/pap-secrets** file. This line will look something like this:

```
reichard * password
```

where *password* is the password.

One more step before you make a connection: You'll need to create a **/etc/ppp/chatscript** to include information about your ISP, particularly a phone number. The following script works with most modems:

```
TIMEOUT 5
'' ATZ
OK ATDTxxx-xxxx
ABORT 'NO CARRIER'
ABORT BUSY
ABORT 'NO DIALTONE'
ABORT WAITING
TIMEOUT 45
CONNECT "We are connected!"
TIMEOUT 5
"name:" reichard@mr.net
"word:" password
in> ppp
```

where *xxx-xxxx* is the phone number of your ISP. The final three lines are tailored to our ISP, which presents two prompts (*username:* and *password:*) as well as a command line for launching **ppp** on the host computer. You'll want to change this for your specific ISP.

Once connected, you should be able to use any of the Internet tools presented here.

Internet Tools

After you work out your connections to the Internet, you can take advantage of the network tools available under Linux.

We'll begin with a discussion of Internet mail, then we'll discuss other Internet goodies.

Using Electronic Mail

The ability to send electronic messages to individuals, groups of people, or everyone in the company is not one of the flashiest features of the Linux operating system, but it is certainly one of the most used. Other networking systems, particularly from the MS-DOS world (like Novell NetWare) lack basic electronic-mail (or e-mail) capabilities, while other operating systems featuring built-in electronic mail lack the other extensive capabilities featured in Linux.

The mail program has been an important part of UNIX almost since the very beginning. As UNIX evolved, so has mail—to an extent. The actual electronic-mail mechanisms are similar to the original mail mechanisms; changes mainly concern how a user interacts with a mail program. The procedures described here may not appear exactly the same on your system, as there are many mail programs, both UNIX- and X Window-based, that vary in how they present information to the user.

Linux gives you a few options for reading and sending mail, starting with the **mailx** command and ending with programs like **elm** and **pine**, which ship on the accompanying CD-ROMs.

Receiving Mail

Linux informs you of incoming mail when you login the system. You'll see a message like:

```
You have mail.
```

Unless you read your mail at this point, this message will reappear periodically, as the shell is automatically set up to remind you of unread mail.

To view this mail, type:

```
gilbert:/$ mail
```

You'll see something like what's shown in Figure 9.1.

The shell responds with a list of your mail messages, listed in the order they were received by your system, newest mail first. The first field lists the sender of the message, the second through fifth fields denote the time and date the message was received, the sixth field records the number of lines in the message and the size of the message (in bytes), and the final field indicates the subject of the message.

Press **Enter** to read the first message on the list. If it's a long message, the entire message will scroll by. If you want to stop scrolling the message, type **Ctrl-S**; to start it again, type **Ctrl-Q**.

```
gilbert:/# mail
Mail version 5.5 6/1/90.  Type ? for help.
"/var/spool/mail/root": 4 messages 4 unread
>U  1 root                 Thu Sep 15 02:23 132/4321  "Register with the Lin"
 U  2 volkerdi@mhd1.moorhe  Thu Sep 15 02:53  66/2758  "Welcome to Linux!"
 U  3 root                 Thu Sep 15 02:23 132/4321  "Register with the Lin"
 U  4 volkerdi@mhd1.moorhe  Thu Sep 15 02:53  66/2758  "Welcome to Linux!"
& []
```

Figure 9.1 Incoming mail.

There are two types of messages waiting for us: messages from *root* and messages from *volkerdi@mhd1.moorhead*. If you're connected to the Internet and have your own network with other users, your electronic mail can come from two sources: your own system and other systems. Mail from other systems, sent on the Internet or the Usenet, has its own unique addressing scheme (more on that in the next section). Mail from your own system uses the same login names as described in Chapter 1; these names are contained in the **/etc/passwd** file.

The newer addressing scheme, and one that is growing in popularity (mainly because of the growing popularity of the Internet), is called *domain addressing*. Structured as the exact opposite of a bang path, a domain address couples the name of the user with an address. This scheme grew out of the need for international standardization of electronic-mail addresses and provides a hierarchical structure to addressing. Essentially, the world is split into country domains, which are divided into educational domains (indicated by the suffix *.edu* in the address) and commercial domains (indicated by the suffix *.com* in the address). There are hundreds and hundreds of commercial and educational domains, and the number is growing every day.

Reading a domain address is quite simple. In the address of:

reichard@mr.net

reichard refers to the user, while *mr.net* refers to the domain. The user and domain names are separated by the at *(c)* symbol. As a user, you don't need to know the specific path a message must take, nor do you need to know the name of a gateway. With a domain address, sending a message is simple:

```
gilbert:/$ mail reichard@mr.net
```

The idea of the Internet is fairly amorphous and abstract. The Internet is technically a collection of many networks that somehow manage to talk to each other. As a user, all you need to know is a recipient's electronic-mail address; the system administrator handles the basic details of linking a system to the Internet.

If you're on the Internet, you can also receive electronic-mail from afar. To find your machine address, type **uname -n** at the prompt:

```
gilbert:/$ uname -n
gilbert
```

where *gilbert* is the name of your UNIX system, also called the *hostname*. To list all the systems you can directly communicate with, type **uname**:

```
gilbert:/$ uname
othersystem1
othersystem2
othersystem3
```

where *othersystem* refers to the other systems.

The **uname** command doesn't support this option on all systems. If this is the case, you can look in the file **/etc/hosts** covered earlier in this chapter, to get a good idea of what other systems your computer networks with.

In a large regional or nationwide network, the list of other systems can be quite large. If you want to find a specific system and you don't want to wade through a huge list of names, use **uname** in conjunction with **grep**:

```
$ uname | grep othersystem121
othersystem121
```

If the name of the other system is returned, you can send electronic mail to someone with an account on that system. In addition, you can send messages to people on the Internet if you are connected to the Internet, provided you know the exact address of the recipient.

Let's look at the first message from *root*, shown in Figure 9.2.

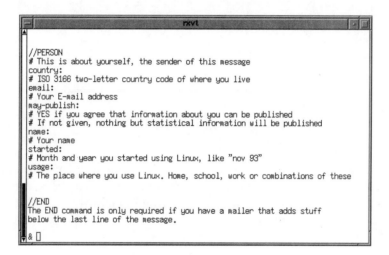

Figure 9.2 An incoming electronic-mail message.

At the beginning of an e-mail message is a *header*. With the Internet, mail may go between one or more systems on its way to you. You can't count on a direct link between systems, and because of these uncontrollable paths it may take some time for a message to reach the recipient; delivery times of 15 hours to 24 hours are not uncommon, but neither are delivery times of 10 seconds.

Creating Mail

It's very easy to create mail. (Too easy, some would say, as they survey mailboxes full of irrelevant mail messages.) To create a short message at the keyboard, simple combine **mail** with the name of the recipient, followed by a period on its own line. The resulting mail is shown in Figure 9.3.

```
& q
Saved 1 message in mbox
Held 1 message in /var/spool/mail/root
gilbert:/var/X11R6/lib# mail root
Subject: This is great!
This is great!
.
EOT
gilbert:/var/X11R6/lib# mail
Mail version 5.5 6/1/90.  Type ? for help.
"/var/spool/mail/root": 2 messages 1 new 2 unread
 U  1 root              Thu Sep 15 02:23 132/4321  "Register with the Lin"
>N  2 root@gilbert.kevinne  Fri May  5 01:44  11/381  "This is great!"
& 2
Message 2:
From root@gilbert.kevinnet Fri May  5 01:44:58 1995
Date: Fri, 5 May 1995 01:44:57 -0500
From: root <root@gilbert.kevinnet>
To: root@gilbert.kevinnet
Subject: This is great!

This is great!

&
```

Figure 9.3 Incoming mail.

As always, end input from the keyboard by typing **Ctrl-D**. Some e-mail programs also accept a single period on its own line to terminate the message, instead of **Ctrl-D**. The procedure would be the same if you were sending a message to a user on a remote machine:

```
gilbert:/$ mail reichard@mr.net
```

You can send the same message to multiple users with the *-t* option:

```
gilbert:/$ mail -t johnsone@camax.com reichard@mr.net
This, too, is a test.
.
```

The resulting message will contain multiple To: fields in the header.

Sending an existing file as the text of an electronic-mail message is almost as simple. After creating an ASCII file using **vi** or **emacs**, save the file and then redirect it as input on the command line:

```
gilbert:/$ mail johnsone@camax.com < note
```

What Do I Do with My Messages?

After you read a message, the shell presents you with a different prompt:

```
&
```

asking for a response related to the mail program. There are many actions you can take at this point; the handiest options are listed in Table 9.1.

Table 9.1 A Selection of Mail Commands

Command	Result
Return	Prints next message.
-	Prints previous message.
d	Deletes current message.
d*N*	Deletes message *N*.
dp	Deletes current message and goes to the next message.
dq	Deletes current message and quit.
u *N*	Undeletes message *N*.
s *filename*	Saves message to *filename*; if *filename* is not specified, message is saved to **$HOME/mbox**.
w *filename*	Saves message without header information to *filename*; if *filename* is not specified, message is saved to **$HOME/mbox**.
?	Lists mail commands.

Saving Messages

As we saw in Table 9.1, saving a message is simply a matter of typing:

```
? s filename
```

If you don't get many messages, it's no big deal to save them all to the same file. But if you get a lot of messages on many topics, it's a good idea to introduce some organization to your mail habits.

Let's say you're working on a project with user *erc*, and you want to keep all of his mail messages in the same file. You do so with the *s* option at the **?** prompt:

```
? s erc
```

where **erc** is the name of the file containing his mail messages. When you do this the first time, the shell creates a file named **erc**. Subsequent uses will append mail messages to the existing **erc** file.

To read this file, use **mail** with the *-f* option:

```
gilbert:/$ mail -f erc
```

Don't make the mistake of assuming your electronic mail messages are private. Because mail messages normally appear in unencrypted text files, anyone with superuser privileges, such as your system administrator, can read your mail.

Few businesses have policies regarding the privacy of electronic mail communications. When in doubt, assume that your boss can read your mail.

Other Mail Packages

As you can tell, mail sports an exceedingly primitive interface. Over the years, a crop of new mail programs have appeared, some commercial software and some free, each of which aims at making life easier for the user. Some of the free ones are included with Linux.

Xmh is an X Window front end to **mh**, as shown in Figure 9.4.

Pine is another popular electronic-mail program, shown in Figure 9.5.

Finally, there's **elm**, which is one of our favorites. Elm stands for electronic mail and it works by providing an easy-to-use interface over the standard mail program.

The basic **elm** screen looks like that shown in Figure 9.6.

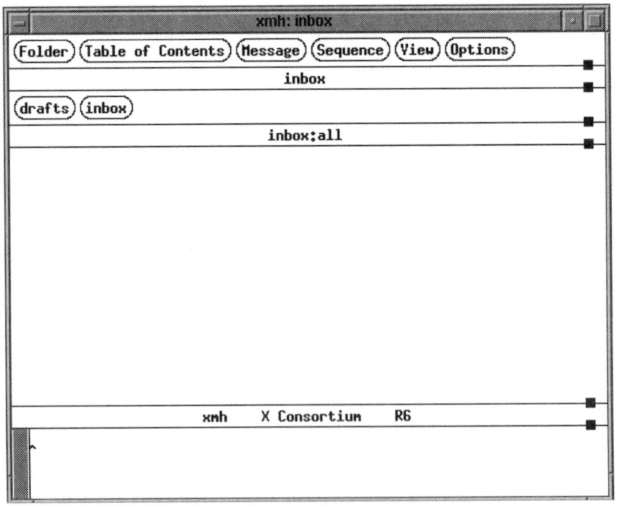

Figure 9.4 Xmh in action.

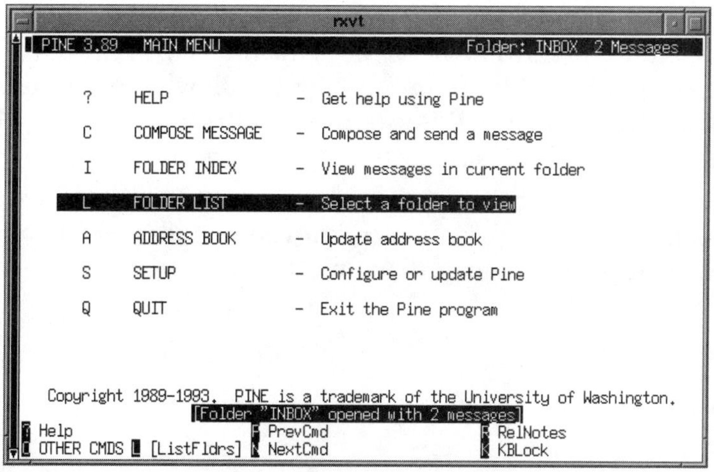

Figure 9.5 Pine in action.

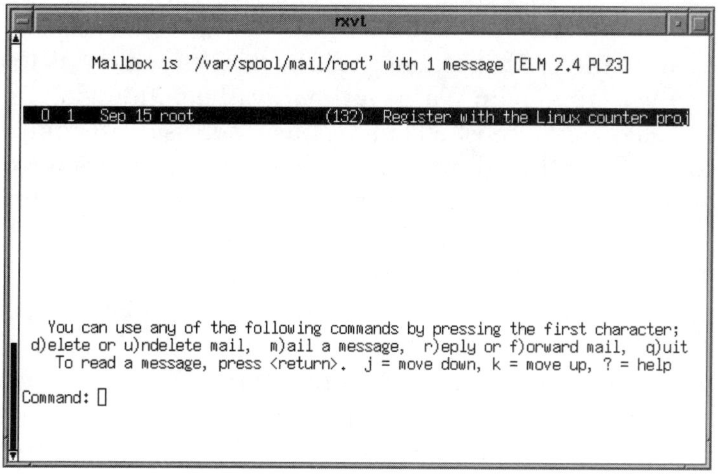

Figure 9.6 The **elm** mail program.

You can use the arrow keys on your keyboard to select a message. Pressing **Return** reads the message. Elm is so simple, fast and easy that we think you'll soon be a convert. The online help, available by typing a question mark (**?**), should get you going in no time. (Like many users, we're often too busy to read the manual. In fact, we've never read the **elm** manual—the program is that easy.)

If you've been observant, you've noticed that all the programs shown in this section work from the same mail file. This is no accident; to prevent multiple mail files from popping up all over your Linux system (as well as the entire UNIX system, if you're networked), the mail packages work from the same incoming-mail file.

Linux also supports a series of commands that allow MIME attachments to mail messages, which is a very popular way to attach files to mail messages in a manner that almost any other Internet e-mail user can understand.

Using a Web Browser

Electronic mail, of course, is a rather unglamorous function of the Internet. Most of the hoopla surrounding the Internet concerns Web pages, accessed via Web browsers. To understand these terms, a little background is in order.

By the end of the 1980s, most of the infrastructure that was to become the Internet was already in place—primarily, the nationwide linkage of computers that could almost instantaneously access other computers on the network. Before that, things like mail and newsgroups were passed along from computer to computer (mostly overnight, when phone rates were lower). When the Internet finally took shape, it became possible to access any other internetworked computer directly.

Armed with these capabilities, CERN researchers, lead by Tim Berners-Lee (now head of the WWW Consortium at MIT), developed an information-exchange structure called the *World Wide Web*, which would take advantage of these instantaneous links. A computer on the Internet has a distinct address, and a piece of software (called a *Web browser*) would use that address for instant connectivity. Pages on that internetworked machine are formatted in the HyperText Markup Language, or HTML (itself a subset of the complex Standard Generalized Markup Language, or SGML). This formatting would specify things like headlines, body text, and hypertext links to other Web resources.

It's up to the local Web browser to actually render this Web page on the local computer. For example, the Web browser will contain a tag for a headline; the Web browser uses a local font to create this headline. The same goes for body copy and hypertext links.

Popular Web Browsers

Mosaic from NCSA was the first popular Web browser, and for many users it still epitomizes the power of the Internet. Of late, however, Netscape Navigator has garnered a lot of attention as being the cutting-edge Web browser.

We're not going to play favorites here; you need to go out and grab whichever Web browser you want. We'll use Netscape Navigator in our examples, but there's nothing that wouldn't apply equally to NCSA Mosaic. In fact, there's a whole list of freeware Web browsers that have been compiled for use under Linux; you can grab them via FTP (which we'll describe later in this chapter); we've included the noncommercial ones on the second CD-ROM. They include:

- Mosaic (which has been compiled for Linux in several different versions; you'll want to check them out before committing to the download time, which can be considerable); you can grab the latest version at *ftp://ftp.NCSA.uiuc.edu/Web/Mosaic/Unix/binaries/*

- Netscape Navigator (check out *http://home.netscape.com* for more information)

- Lynx (a freeware text-only browser)

- Arena, a freeware Web browser from the WWW Consortium at MIT

- tkWWW (a freeware Web browser written in Tcl/Tk)

- SurfIt! (another freeware Web browser written in Tcl/Tk)

- Chimera (a freeware browser)

By and large, the World Wide Web is a graphical beast; most of these Web browsers (the big exception is Lynx) run under the X Window System.

Page Limits

At its core, the World Wide Web is actually an ingeniously simple thing. A Web browser, such as Mosaic or Netscape, sends a request over the network to a Web server; the request can be in one of five formats (as listed in Table 9.2 later in this chapter). The server then honors the request by sending a text file formatted in the HyperText Markup Language (HTML), which inserts *tags* in the text. The text file is then rendered by the local Web browser, which matches the tags to resources on the local machine—for example, a tag for *TITLE* would be rendered in a font and point size set up through the Web browser.

The HTML language also allows graphics and hypertext links to be embedded in the document. Most graphics files are in the GIF and XBM file formats. The hyperlinks are noted with their own tags and are usually set in a different color within the rendered document. For example, under a heading titled *Other Resources*, there may be a line colored blue that says *Sun Microsystems Home Page*. To the Web browser, however, there's an embedded Web address (in this case, *www.sun.com*). Double-clicking on *Sun Microsystems Home Page* initiates a request to the Web server *www.sun.com*. You don't need to know the *www.sun.com* address; you only need to know how to use a mouse.

You can start Netscape with the following command in an **xterm** window:

```
gilbert:/$ netscape &
```

When Netscape launches, it connects directly to a Netscape Communications home page (*home.netscape.com*). (By the way, this is a good way to test if Netscape is configured properly; if you or your system administrator has misinstalled Netscape, it will report that a connection to *home.netscape.com* has failed.)

Chances are pretty good that you won't want to spend much time wandering around the Netscape Home Page. The beauty of the World Wide Web is that it allows you to jump from Web site to Web site, either those linked to your current page or a page totally unrelated.

A page on the World Wide Web is formatted in the HyperText Markup Language. If you were to view the document in text mode—which is possible with many Web browsers, including Netscape—you'd see that the text is scattered with "tags," like *<H2>*. There's no mentions of point sizes, colors, or the like. The beginning of an HTML file looks like this:

```
<TITLE>Netscape Handbook: Graphical Elements</TITLE>
<A NAME="RTFToC0">
<B>
<FONT SIZE=+3>G</FONT><FONT SIZE=+2>raphical elements</FONT>
</B></A>
<ol>
```

```
<A HREF="../online-manual.html">Netscape Handbook: Table of
Contents</A>
<li><a href="graphics.html#RTFToC1">Netscape window</a>
<li><a href="graphics.html#RTFToC2">Point and click navigation</a>
<li><a href="graphics.html#RTFToC4">Content area and text fields</a>
<li><a href="graphics.html#RTFToC9">Security information</a>
<li><a href="graphics.html#RTFToC5">Window controls</a>
<li><a href="graphics.html#RTFToC3">Toolbar buttons</a>
<li><a href="graphics.html#RTFToC6">Directory buttons</a>
<li><a href="graphics.html#RTFToC7">Newsgroup list buttons</a>
<li><a href="graphics.html#RTFToC8">Newsgroup article buttons</a>
</ol>
<HR ALIGN="right"WIDTH=85%>
<A NAME="RTFToC1">
<FONT SIZE=+3>N</FONT><FONT SIZE=+1>etscape window</FONT>
</A>
<P>
```

This section on graphical elements describes what you see in the Netscape window. Most of the tools and text fields that help you to navigate the Internet are visible, though you have the option of hiding some tools in order to give more space on the screen to the content area.<p>

On the page describing point and click navigation, you'll find a description of each type of graphical element: colors/underlining, status indicator, progress bar, toolbar buttons, content/text fields, window controls, and menus. Subsequent pages go into more detail on how toolbar buttons, text/content fields, and window controls work. An entire section of pages is devoted to menu items, including those that let you set important options and preferences effecting the look, performance, and functionality of the Netscape window.<p>

You can open multiple Netscape windows to view multiple pages of information. The title bar of the window shows the title of currently loaded page. <P>

```
<HR ALIGN="right"WIDTH=85%>
<A NAME="RTFToC2">
<FONT SIZE=+3>P</FONT><FONT SIZE=+1>oint and click navigation</FONT>
</A>
<P>
```

The work of rendering the home page is done at the local level, matching local resources to the specifications of the Web page. You'll notice that there are a few different point sizes and typefaces on the home page. The Web document makes a reference to <TITLE>; the Web page then matches a local font and point size to the text.

A graphic is also rendered locally. When the document downloads, the graphic is sent separately, in the GIF format, which makes for quicker file transfers. (Even so, some GIF documents can be very large and take a long time to download, even at a high-speed network link.)

URL Formats

You tell a Web browser where to look by entering a Uniform Resource Locator, or URL. The WWW community has standardized on a number of URL formats, as listed in Table 9.2.

Table 9.2 URL Formats and Their Meanings, from the WWW FAQ

Format	Represents
file://ftp.microsoft.com	File at an ftp site
ftp://wuarchive.wustl.edu/mirrors	FTP site
http://info.cern.ch:80/default.html	WWW site
news:alt.hypertext	Usenet newsgroup
telnet://dra.com	Telnet connection to Internet-connected server

This means that you can connect to many Internet resources via a Web browser. Most Web browsers have a menu selection or dialog box that allows you to enter a URL.

Communications with the UUCP Commands

In many respects, the Internet is the "new wave" of UNIX communications. However, there are many UNIX and Linux users who might want to take advantage of other communications methods.

One older method is UUCP. Originally, UNIX-to-UNIX Copy Program (UUCP) was written to communicate between systems via ordinary telephone lines. The UUCP program allows you to copy files from one system to another. Today, these connections can take place between those same telephone lines via modem (at all speeds, from 2400 bits per second to 19.2 kbps), direct wiring, a local-area network, or a wide-area network connected via dedicated phone lines. Although the connection mechanisms have changed, the basic UUCP system has not; it remains mechanism-independent, which makes your life much simpler. As a user, you don't need to know the specifics of the connection mechanism; all you need to know is how to access the utilities that make communication possible.

Dealing with UUCP and the networking utilities on a configuration level is an advanced topic best left to system administrators and those with iron stomachs, suitable for dealing with the complex task of networking Linux machines.

There's no one great *überprogram* that oversees Linux connections to the outside world. Much like everything else in the Linux and UNIX worlds, the communications utilities are quite small and serve limited purposes by themselves; only when strung together do they actually make up a powerful communications system.

Why connect to the outside world? Some companies directly link far-flung offices via dedicated phone line to ensure instantaneous communication among employees. Others connect via modem over phone lines to the UUCP Network, a series of UNIX computers that pass along electronic mail and files all around the world.

In a rather confusing situation, UUCP refers both to a specific command (**uucp**) and a series of related commands (most of which begin with *uu*). In this chapter, *uucp* will refer to the specific **uucp** command, while *UUCP* will refer to the general command set.

To make things even more confusing, there's more than one implementation of the UUCP utilities on the market. In this chapter, we'll be covering the HoneyDanBer UUCP, named for its three creators (Peter Honeyman, Dan A. Nowitz, and Brian E. Redman). This implementation is supported in the version of Linux on the accompanying program CD-ROM.

A UUCP Primer

At its core, the UUCP commands allow machines to communicate directly via network links or telephone connections. They are limited in scope and are geared toward the rudimentary purposes of sending along files, electronic mail, and (sometimes) Usenet news.

In this chapter, we'll focus on the few commands you're likely to use. (If you want information about all of the UUCP commands, check Appendix A for a list of further reading material.) We'll also avoid configuration issues, which are best left to a system administrator.

Before you use **uucp**, you need to know what machines are connected to yours. The **uuname** command does just this:

```
gilbert:/$ uuname
geisha
spike
```

Why is this information important? Because you'll need to specify machine names with the **uucp** command.

Using UUCP

The **uucp** command is used to copy files from one machine to another. At first glance, in this age of Internet and the Information Superhighway, you may think that this is incredibly retro technology. And, conceptually, it is.

Realistically, however, the **uucp** command has its widest application in the corporate world, where interconnected computers are very common. In these situations, the corporate systems may not be tied to the outside world but only connected to other corporate systems. In these cases, the **uucp** command is a handy way of transferring a file from your system to the corporate headquarters in Sioux City, Iowa.

The best way to understand the **uucp** command isn't to think of it as a strange and unfamiliar networking command—just think of it as an extended version of the common **cp** command, which you used earlier in this book. Instead of downloading and uploading files from a local directory, you're using **uucp** to download and upload files from another machine.

There's an added advantage to the **uucp** command: All in all, it's a rather secure method of transferring files, when everything is set up correctly. (There's the issue of security popping up again.) The **uucp** command and the UUCP utilities can enact very specific guidelines on where files can be uploaded to or downloaded from.

Let's look at a typical **uucp** command line:

```
$ uucp chap9.txt spike!/usr/spool/uucppublic/chap9.txt
```

While this may seem to be a long command line, a closer look will show that it's actually rather simple.

The **uucp** portion of the command line, obviously, refers to the **uucp** command. This is followed by the name of the file to be copied (**chap9.txt**).

The next portion is potentially the most confusing portion for novice users, as it represents the destination of the file by name of the machine and the directory. In this case, *spike* refers to the name of the machine; the **uucp** command knows this because the name of the machine ends with an exclamation mark (!).

If the exclamation mark looks familiar, it should; remember, the Usenet method of electronic-mail addressing with bang paths makes heavy use of exclamation marks.

The exclamation mark is immediately followed by the destination directory. The **usr/spool/uucppublic** directory is a common destination for UUCP sites.

Please be aware that none of the machine names in this chapter are real. Don't use these specific examples on your own system.

Generically, the **uucp** command would look like this:

```
gilbert:/$ uucp sourcefile destinationfile
```

The **uucp** command can also be used to grab files from another machine, as long as you have the proper permissions (again, a configuration issue that we'll duck). In this case, you'll alter the **uucp** command line used earlier in this chapter. The principle is the same: use the **uucp** command to list the source file and then its destination. In this case, the remote file is the source file and a local directory is the destination:

```
gilbert:/$ uucp spike!/usr/spool/uucppublic/chap9.txt\
/usr/spool/uucppublic
```

When using the **uucp** command to download a file, all you need to do is specify the destination directory; the command assumes that the filename will remain the same and that the destination directory exists on your local machine.

Potential Problems with the Uucp Command

As many frustrated users can attest to, the **uucp** command and the greater UUCP command set are not foolproof. Perhaps the greatest frustration is that the **uucp** command isn't interactive, and there's no way to monitor the status of a file transfer. You can tell **uucp** to send you a receipt via electronic mail when the file transfer is completed:

```
gilbert:/$ uucp -m chap9.txt spike!/usr/spool/uucppublic/chap9.txt
```

However, if you don't receive the electronic mail confirmation, you can assume that the transfer has failed. Finding out why, however, isn't an easy task.

It is made somewhat easier, however, by the presence of a **logfile** that **uucp** maintains as part of the transfer process. To get at this file, use the **uulog** command:

```
$ uulog
```

This will provide a lot of output—probably too much for your troubleshooting purposes. It's probably better if you combine the **uulog** with the name of a machine:

```
$ uulog -sspike
```

Yes, *-sspike* is correct. In an oddity, the *-s* option to **uulog** must be immediately followed by the name of the machine (in this case, *spike*).

You'll then need to read through the arcane information from uulog and try to make some sense of it. Successful file transfers will end with *REMOTE REQUESTED* or *OK*.

What Can Go Wrong?

When a **uucp** connection fails, there are can be many potential culprits. The **uulog** command can be handy to discover that a connection was denied by the remote system (something like *ACCESS DENIED* will appear in the **logfile**). In this case, the login name or the password required by the remote machine may have been changed; this is a task for the system administrator to tackle.

If this isn't the case and *ACCESS DENIED* still appears in the **logfile**, it could be a simple case of a mistyped command line. If you type the wrong filename or directory, the connection will succeed, but the transfer will fail. Again, by a careful read of the **logfile**, you can determine this.

Your transfer may also be the victim of your own impatience. Not all **uucp** requests are instantaneous; many system administrators choose to queue requests and make the transfers after hour, when longdistance rates are cheaper.

Free Software and FTP

Linux also features **ftp**, a command that allows you to link directly to another computer using the network TCP/IP. Essentially, if you have a TCP/IP connection to the Internet, you can use **ftp** to connect to any public site on the Net. In this section, we'll guide you through an FTP session.

Using FTP

The **ftp** command can be used to connect to any other computer on your network running **ftp**. If your system is connected to the Internet, you can use **ftp** to access files from other Internet computers worldwide. The machines with which you network may or may not be running the UNIX or Linux operating systems; this operating-system independence is what makes FTP so widely used.

FTP is interactive software, which means it asks for information at specific times. Start it with the following:

```
gilbert:/$ ftp
ftp>
```

You'll be presented with the **ftp** prompt, where you enter special **ftp** commands. To get a list of available commands, type a question mark (**?**) or **help** at the prompt:

```
ftp> ?
or
ftp> help
```

A list of the most common FTP commands is contained in Table 9.3.

Table 9.3 Common FTP Commands

Command	Result
ascii	Use ASCII as the file-transfer type.
bell	Ring the bell when file transfer is complete.
binary	Use binary as the file-transfer type.
bye or **quit**	Terminate **ftp** session.
cd	Change directory on the remote machine.
close	End **ftp** connection to remote computer but keep local **ftp** program running.
delete *filename*	Delete *filename* on remote computer.
get *filename*	Get *filename* from the remote machine.
get *filename1 filename2*	Get *filename1* from the remote machine and save it locally as *filename2*.
help	List available commands.
mput *filename*	Copy the local *filename* to the remote machine.
pwd	List the current directory on the remote machine.

It's simple to download files from a remote machine with **ftp**. Let's say we want to grab some files from the machine named **mn.kevin.com**. (No, this isn't a real machine.) Assuming that this is a machine on the Internet that supports anonymous FTP—and our fictional machine does, of course—you would merely specify its name on the command line:

```
gilbert:/$ ftp mn.kevin.com
```

If the connection goes through, you'll receive a verification message, along with a login prompt. Because this is anonymous FTP, use *anonymous* as a login name:

```
Name: anonymous
```

You'll then be asked for a password. Some systems require you to supply your electronic-mail address, while others require *guest*. Use either. You'll then be presented with an **ftp** prompt.

The remote system has been set up to give you limited access, which means that your maneuverability is very limited and the files you want are usually close at hand. If you need to change to another directory, do so with the UNIX **cd** command.

Before embarking on the great file quest, you should know something about the files you're downloading. If they are straight C files in uncompressed, ASCII form, you can download them using the default file-transfer settings. Most larger files, especially binary files, are stored in compressed form so they take less time to transfer.

These compressed files end with *.Z*, *.z*, *.tgz*, *.zip*, or *.gz*. so they are instantly recognizable. To download compressed files, you must change to binary mode, because you're downloading binary files. Do so with:

```
ftp> binary
```

Once you are placed in the correct directory containing the file to be downloaded, start the download process with the **get** command:

```
ftp> get filename
```

As you download the file, there will be a prompt on the system, and you won't be able to enter any keystrokes.

After the file has been transferred successfully, you'll be given a message similar to the following:

```
Transfer complete
```

You may also be told the size of the file and the transfer time.

Because you're through with your file needs, close the connection with the **bye** command:

```
ftp> bye
```

What do I Do with the File?

If you download an ASCII file, you can view it using any editor, including **vi** or **emacs**. If it's a sourcecode file, you can compile it for use on your own system; we explain the process in Chapter 10. If you've downloaded a compressed binary file, you will have to uncompress it (and perhaps unarchive it) at the command line using **uncompress**, **unpack**, **tar**, or **gzip**—things you learned about in Chapter 4.

Other Networking Commands

In addition to **ftp**, which is used to transfer—copy—files from system to system, there are a number of other common networking commands. These commands work to help the connection among your computer and others on the same link. Generally, if you work at a site with multiple UNIX computers, these computers will be networked together, usually using the Ethernet network protocol. Your systems may also be networked with the worldwide Internet, which as you already know is a collection of connected networks. (Say that three times fast.)

Using the Rlogin Command

The **rlogin** command allows you to remotely login to another computer on your network (remember that if you're on the Internet, you're on a worldwide network). You must, of course, have a valid user account on any machine to which you want to login. To use **rlogin**, you need the name of the machine to login to. To login a machine named *nicollet*, you'd use a command line like the following:

```
gilbert:/$ rlogin nicollet
Password:
```

At the *Password* prompt, you may need to enter your password on machine *nicollet*, which may or may not be different from the password you use on your local machine. Once logged in, you're computing on the remote machine and can run any standard UNIX command. You also logout the same way you normally logout:

```
gilbert:/$ logout
Connection closed.
$
```

Note that after you logout from a remote machine, you're back to the command prompt at your local machine. This tends to get confusing, so be careful.

The basic form of **rlogin** is:

```
rlogin hostname
```

where *hostname* is the name of the machine to login.

Using the Telnet Command

The **telnet** command works much the same as **rlogin** does, allowing you to connect directly to a remote machine. Because the **telnet** command is considered part of the toolkit used by the Internet surfer, it's actually gained in popularity over the years.

Telnet allows you either to run a command directly on a remote machine while displaying the results on your own or to run a specific command on a remote machine (many sites that allow Telnet put restrictions on what users can run, due to security concerns). With telnet, you only need to know the address of the machine you're connecting to, such as *sunsite.unc.edu*, as illustrated by the following:

```
gilbert:/$ telnet
telnet> open sunsite.unc.edu
Trying 198.86.40.81
Connected
*************** Welcome to SunSITE.unc.edu ***************
SunSITE offers several public services via login. These include:

NO MORE PUBLIC gopher login!
Use lynx the simple WWW client to access gopher and Web areas
For a simple WAIS client (over 500 databases),   login as swais
For WAIS search of political databases,           login as politics
For WAIS search of LINUX databases,               login as linux

For a FTP session, ftp to sunsite.unc.edu. Then login as anonymous

For more information about SunSITE, send mail to info@sunsite.unc.edu

UNIX (R) System V Release 4.0 (calypso-2.oit.unc.edu)

login: swais
```

In this case, *sunsite.unc.edu* offers a variety of services to the general computing public, here centering around WAIS databases. Other Telnet sites may not offer such a wide variety of services; a site like *archie.rutgers.edu* offers only **archie** searches.

Unfortunately, Linux does not offer **archie** yet, so you'll need to use a public **archie** server to perform a search.

Sunsite.unc.edu is a public Internet site. If you're using telnet within your corporation, the rules will be slightly different. Here, *sunsite.unc.edu* offers public access; you don't need an account on *sunsite.unc.edu*, nor do you need a password. However, *sunsite.unc.edu* does put restrictions on what can be done by a visitor; for example, you can't use the standard Linux command set and your options are limited to the login selections. For a private system, you'll need an account on the remote system before you can login, and you may be subject to the same sorts of restrictions.

The Usenet and Newsgroups

The Internet's roots can be traced to the Usenet, a worldwide messaging system. The Usenet, while technically comprising a portion of the Internet, is best known for electronic-mail and newsgroup distribution.

Thousands of computers are linked—worldwide—in the loose network we call the *Usenet*, a public network of linked UNIX and non-UNIX machines, dedicated to sending information to companies, schools, universities, the government, research laboratories, and individuals. Some of these links occur over phone lines and use the uucp command to send messages back and forth, but most links nowadays go over the Internet, using the NNTP, or Network News Transfer Protocol, to send messages between machines. No matter how the messages get passed around, you can read them the same way.

The Usenet performs a variety of services, but perhaps the most popular service involves newsgroups. A *newsgroup* is a discussion of various topics, ranging from computing to sociology to boomerangs to Barney the Dinosaur. In fact, there are thousands of Usenet newsgroups. Some are trivial and a waste of bandwidth, others are of interest to only a small set of users, and others would interest a host of users. (Take a gander at *alt.sex.bestiality.barney*, and you'll see the validity of this point.)

These newsgroups are divided into classes, to better allow users to figure out what to read in the plethora of information arriving daily. Table 9.4 covers the major newsgroup classifications.

Table 9.4 The Major Usenet Newsgroup Classifications

Name	Subject
alt	alternative hierarchy, not subject to other rules
biz	business-related groups
comp	computing
misc	miscellaneous subjects
news	news about the Usenet
rec	recreational activities
sci	science
soc	social issues
talk	talk

Not only is this computer-dweeb heaven, but the Usenet provides valuable information on everything from vegetarian recipes to buying a house. There are Usenet newsgroups for just about every topic you can imagine—and then some, from *rec.sport.football.college* to *soc.culture.bulgaria*. (*Alt.buddha.short.fat.guy* was definitely a surprise the first time we saw it.) In addition, there are regional newsgroups; those of us in Minnesota have access to a wide range of newsgroups that begin with *mn*, such as *mn.forsale*.

While the Usenet can be a powerful information source, you'll also find a lot of inaccurate information, as nearly anyone can get on the Usenet. So take what you read with a grain of salt. Generally, the more technical the group, the more accurate the information you'll get. The group *comp.compilers* (information on writing compilers for computer languages) certainly contains more unbiased information than *comp.sys.next.advocacy* (advocates—an unbiased group if there ever was one—of NeXT workstations).

However, there are many Usenet newsgroups that you'll find useful. Being technical types ourselves, we regularly peruse the newsgroups relating to UNIX, the X Window System, and related topics (electronic-mail packages like Elm and Pine, software like **emacs**). Appendix A lists Linux-related newsgroups.

These classifications are broken down into specific newsgroups. The syntax of a newsgroup name is simple: the name of the classification followed by a descriptive suffix. For example, the name of the newsgroup devoted to questions concerning the UNIX operating system is *comp.unix.questions*. Note the use of periods to separate the elements. A list of some popular newsgroups is listed in Table 9.5.

Table 9.5 A Sampling of Frequently Accessed Usenet Newsgroups

Newsgroup	Topic
comp.databases	Database-management issues
comp.lang.c	C-language issues
comp.text	Text-processing issues
comp.unix.questions	Questions about the UNIX operating system
misc.jobs.offered	Job openings
sci.space.shuttle	Space exploration issues associated with the NASA space shuttle

A list of Linux-specific newsgroups is contained in Appendix A.

Newsgroups can be open or moderated. *Open newsgroups* mean that anyone can post to them, while *moderated newsgroups* have someone to review the postings before they're passed out to the general public. As you might surmise, moderated newsgroups tend to be more reliable and useful.

The Usenet newsgroups are aggressively egalitarian. News can be posted by just about anyone. Using it as a source of information requires some skepticism on your part. On the one hand, it's a great place to find very technical, specialized information—the more technical and specialized the better. Many leading figures in the computing industry regularly post information in the newsgroups. And because there's nothing new under the sun, chances are that the problem that plagues you has already been solved by someone else in the Linux world.

On the other hand, every opinion is not created equally, and a lot of ill-founded opinions can be found in most newsgroups. Veterans refer to the signal-to-noise ratio; newsgroups with a lot of ill-founded opinions and bickering are said to be filled with noise. As with any other source of information, treat what you see on the Usenet newsgroups with a healthy dose of skepticism.

Reading and Writing the News

Although all the news items are text files and could in theory could be read with **vi** or **emacs**, there are so many of them in so many separate files that it's not really feasible to read each file. A full Usenet newsfeed, that is, all the incoming message files from all the worldwide newsgroups, adds more than 50 megabytes of files to your disk each day. (Remember when we said earlier that UNIX files seem to propagate proportionally? Well, there's your example.) This is how a type of software, called *newsreaders*, evolved. Newsreaders help you sort out, with varying degrees of usefulness, what to read from the hundreds of new files that appear daily. The basic idea is to read those messages you're interested in and skip the rest. There's simply no way to read every incoming message, even if you spend all day in front of your computer.

We are not going to cover the many newsreaders in depth; Linux features several, and you're encouraged to check them all out. What you use will partially depend on how you get your news delivered. If you're on a corporate network, you'll access the news from a local server. If you're connected to the Internet via ISP, then you'll use the NNTP protocol to grab your news from the ISP news server. When you ran **setup** back in Chapter 2, you were asked about this; if you installed the wrong kind of newsreader, you can always go back to **setup** and install one more to your liking. Linux newsreaders include:

- **trn**, a reader with expanded search capabilities (shown in Figure 9.7)

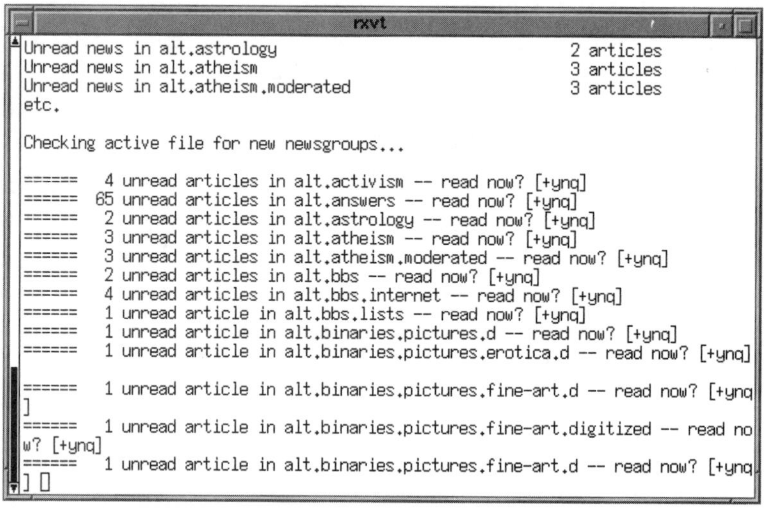

Figure 9.7 The **trn** newsreader.

- **inn**, a basic reader
- **tin**, a threaded reader that arranges messages by topic (as shown in Figure 9.8)

```
                     Group Selection (853)                        h=help
 u   1    -  Logic
 u   2    -  alt
 u   3    -  alt.activism                           Activities for activi
 u   4    -  alt.answers                            Repository for period
 u   5    -  alt.astrology                          Twinkle, twinkle, lit
 u   6    -  alt.atheism                            Discussions of atheis
 u   7    -  alt.atheism.moderated                  Atheism and related t
 u   8    -  alt.bbs                                Computer BBS systems
 u   9    -  alt.bbs.internet                       BBS systems accessibl
 u  10    -  alt.bbs.lists                          Postings of regional
 u  11    -  alt.bbs.unixbbs                        Discussion of the BBS
 u  12    -  alt.binaries
 u  13    -  alt.binaries.pictures
 u  14    -  alt.binaries.pictures.d                Discussion of posting
 u  15    -  alt.binaries.pictures.erotica          For the posting of AL
 u  16    -  alt.binaries.pictures.erotica.d        Discussion about erot

       <n>=set current to n, TAB=next unread, /=search pattern, c)atchup,
     g)oto, j=line down, k=line up, h)elp, m)ove, q)uit, r=toggle all/unread,
       s)ubscribe, S)ub pattern, u)nsubscribe, U)nsub pattern, y)ank in/out
```

Figure 9.8 The **tin** newsreader.

Slurping the News

As the Internet grows in popularity, more and more of the Usenet news gets transmitted over the Internet rather than the older **uucp** phone-line method.

Over the Internet, the Usenet news jumps from one machine to another through the NNTP. If you use NNTP to get your news, you can view the news with a Web browser such as Netscape Navigator.

In addition, a freeware program called Slurp can acquire news for you via NNTP. This is very useful for downloading select Usenet newsgroups to your Linux system. You can then read the messages offline with a newsreading program such as **xrn**, **nn**, or **trn**. We've included Slurp on the second CD-ROM.

How do I Find a File for Download?

If you're on the Usenet, you'll be surrounded by information regarding free software and how to get it. The trick is knowing where to look for it.

Some universities and corporations maintain archive sites that support anonymous FTP. These locations are referred to regularly in the newsgroup *comp.answers*.

In addition, many computer-related newsgroups will contain news items labeled *FAQ*, or *Frequently Asked Questions*. One of the frequently asked questions will (undoubtedly) concern the existence of archival sites.

And, finally, you can post a plaintive plea in a newsgroup, asking for information about a particular program. You may receive some rude comments from people who tire of answering questions from innocent beginners, but undoubtedly some kind person will answer your request with useful information.

Summary

This chapter covered Linux's many tools for connecting to other computer systems and to the Internet using TCP/IP features. These include TCP/IP connections to an existing network and dialup access using Linux's SLIP and PPP tools.

Once connected, Linux offers many commands for networking Internet access and usage, including **ftp** (which lets you transfer software from remote sites), **rlogin**, and **telnet**. You can also peruse Usenet newsgroups thanks to several newsreaders. In addition, Linux offers several mail options, including the **mail** command and the **xmh**, **pine**, and **elm** newsreaders. We've included several freeware Web browsers on the second CD-ROM.

The Usenet is a series of newsgroups. Linux features several newsreading programs.

In the next (and final) chapter, we cover programming and Linux.

Section IV

Linux Programming

The books ends with Chapter 10, an overview of Linux programming. In it you'll find explanations of Linux's programming tools (including the GNU C compiler) and its X Window programming tools.

Programming in Linux

This chapter covers:

- The GNU C compiler
- C programming
- The **cc** command
- Using **make**
- Programming under the X Window System
- Using LessTif to mimic Motif
- Using shared libraries
- Using **imake**
- Using Tcl/Tk
- A short introduction to using Perl
- Using **gawk**, the GNU Project version of **awk**

Programming under Linux

This chapter is not going to turn you into an instant Linux and X Window programmer. We will, however, show you how to program in the Linux environment. We'll cover a lot of the odd things that you're supposed to know when programming on Linux, including where the X libraries are and some interesting tidbits about how Linux uses shared libraries.

For the programmer, Linux offers all the freeware utilities and compilers you'd expect for software that relies heavily on offerings from the Free Software Foundation. Starting with the GNU C compiler, you can develop C, C++, Fortran (via **g77**), and Objective-C programs on your Linux system. In addition to these mainstream languages, Linux supports Tcl, Perl, and a host of other programming languages and second utilities. In addition, we've thrown freeware called LessTif on the second accompanying CD-ROM, for those of you who want Motif compatibility but don't want to pay for commercial software.

Your main worry is whether you've installed the proper disksets for your compiler and associated tools. (If you haven't heard of one before, a *compiler* is a tool that converts a program in text form into an executable Linux command.) Being programmers ourselves, we always recommend this; if you haven't, you can always go back and use the **setup** program to reinstall the proper disk sets.

If you're not a programmer, chances are that you'll be lost in much of this chapter. Even so, you'll find some interesting Linux utilities mentioned here. In addition, many free Linux programs come in source code-form only; you'll need to learn to compile them, so it's important to know about the process of compiling and linking C programs.

The Linux C Compiler: GNU CC

The main C and C++ compiler on Linux is the GNU **gcc**. It is an all-encompassing program and can compile a number of programming languages: C, C++, Fortran, and Objective-C. **Gcc**, or **cc**, which is linked to **gcc**, compiles C and C++ programs just like you'd expect. The command-line parameters are all standard **cc** parameters in addition to the traditional **gcc** parameters. If you're used to programming on UNIX, you'll find Linux works as you'd expect.

For those new to C programming, we'll provide a short introduction. If you're *really* new at this, you'll likely want to get a C programming book to help you out. Appendix A lists a few.

C Programming

C programs—and in fact, most programs in general—usually start in plain old text files. (Linux makes extensive use of simple text files, as you've seen throughout this book.) These text files are created with text editors like **vi** or **emacs**. Once created, C programs must be compiled with a C compiler, **cc** or **gcc** (which are one and the same on Linux). This C compiler converts the text file, which the programmer wrote, into object, or machine, code for the Intel platform. Then, object modules (files of object code) are linked together to make an executable program, a brand new Linux command. Once the process is successfully completed, you can execute this program like any other command you type at the command line. Being able to create your own command is a neat thing.

In addition to creating C or C++ programs, you can use shell scripts or write code in a number of interpreted languages including Perl and Tcl, which we cover later in this chapter. From the plethora of Linux program-creation tools, you need to choose the appropriate tool for any given task.

The first step is identifying what types of files you're dealing with. Table 10.1 lists the most common Linux file types and their common file extensions.

Most C programs are stored in one or more files that end with *.c*, for example, as **neatstuff.c** and **myprog.c**. When you compile a C file, the C compiler, **cc**, creates an object file, usually ending with *.o*. The linker (called *linkage editor* in Linux parlance), **ld**, then links the *.o* files to make an executable program. The default name for this program is **a.out**, although no one really uses **a.out** for their program names. Instead, programs have names like **ls**, **cp**, or **mv**. All of this is controlled by the **cc** command.

Table 10.1 Program File Types

File Suffix	Meaning
.a	Library
.c	C program
.C	C++ file (note the uppercase C)
.cc	C++ file
.cpp	C++ file
.cxx	C++ file
.c++	C++ file
.f	Fortran program
.for	Fortran program
.h	C or C++ include file
.hxx	C++ include file
.o	Object module (compiled from a .c file)
.pl	Perl script
.pm	Perl module script
.s	Assembly code
.sa	Shared library stubs linked with your program
.so.*n*	Run-time shared library, version number is *n*
.tcl	Tcl script
.tk	Tcl script

The Cc Command

The **cc** command executes the C compiler, which can compile and link C programs into executable commands. To test your Linux C compiler, we'll use the following short program:

```
/*
 * Example C program for Chapter 10,
 * Linux Configuration and Installation.
 */
```

```
#include <stdio.h>

int main(int argc, char** argv)

{
    /* This is a comment. */
    printf("Linux is my favorite O.S.\n");

    return 0;
}

/* chap10.c */
```

Enter the preceding code into a text file named **chap10.c**, using your favorite Linux text editor.

It's a good idea to always name C program files with a *.c* extension. This isn't required, but following conventions like this makes Linux easier to use.

After you type in this short program, you can do the following simple steps to create a working executable program from this C file.

The program you typed in was simply a text file. There's nothing in it to make it an executable command. To do so, we need to compile and link the program. Both steps are accomplished by the following **cc** command:

```
$ cc -o chap10 chap10.c
```

This command runs the C compiler, **cc**. The *-o* option tells **cc** to build a program named **chap10** (the default name without the *-o* option is the awkward **a.out**). The *chap10.c* part of the command tells **cc** to compile the file named **chap10.c**. The **cc** command both compiled and linked the program.

You should now have an executable program named **chap10**. You can execute this program by typing **chap10** at the command line. When you do, you'll see the following output:

```
$ chap10
Linux is my favorite O.S.
```

Now you're a real C programmer, ready for a lucrative new career.

Compiling the Long Way

When we used the **cc** command, **cc** first compiled the program into an object module. Then **cc** linked the object module to create an executable program, the file named **chap10**. This is very important if you need to compile more than one file into your program. Most C programs require a number of **.c** files, all of which must be compiled and linked to form one program. One of the main reasons for separating C programs into multiple files is sanity: reading a 1MB program in one file is ludicrous. And yes, C programs get to this size, and even much bigger than 1 megabyte. Some C programs we've worked on include more than a million lines of C code. You need to know how to compile multiple *.c* files into one executable command because the vast majority of Linux freeware comes in this fashion.

To use the long method of compiling and linking, we split the tasks into two steps. First, you compile all the *.c* files you require. Then you link the resulting *.o* files (we'll get into this later) into your executable program. Because we have a very small C program typed in already (you did type it in, didn't you?), we'll start with that.

Compile **chap10.c** into an object module, an *.o* file, with the following command:

```
$ cc -c chap10.c
```

If you are successful, you should see a file named **chap10.o** in your directory. The *.o* file is called the *object file* (or *object module*); it contains unlinked machine code.

The next step is to link the object files (there's usually more than one) into an executable file. To do this, we again use the *-o* option to **cc**, but this time we pass a *.o* file at the end of the command line, rather than the *.c* file we used earlier:

```
$ cc -o chap10 chap10.o
```

This command links the file **chap10.o** into the executable program **chap10**. You can place more than one object filename on the command line, as in the following example:

```
$ cc -o chap10 chap10_a.o chap10_b.o chap10_c.o
```

Normally you'll want to pick more descriptive filenames than the ones we've used.

Working with Cc

In normal operation, the **cc** command executes a number of other commands under the hood. One such command is **cpp**. The **cpp** command is the C preprocessor. This reads a C program file, a *.c* file, and expands any # directives. In the short program you typed in earlier, the #*include* directive means to include the file **stdio.h**. That is, **cpp** reads in **stdio.h** and inserts the contents right at the #*include* directive. Most C programs use one or more include files.

These include files are normally stored in **/usr/include**. If you use the angle brackets, (<) and (>), around an include filename, like **<stdio.h>**, this means that **cpp** looks for a file named **stdio.h** in the standard places, of which **/usr/include** is the default (the *-I* command-line parameter can add more directories to the include file search path; see Table 10.2 later). You can also use quotation marks (") around the filename.

All C programs are built around the section labeled main(). The main() section (called a *function* in C parlance) is executed when the program starts. Our main() function simply calls the printf() function, which prints the text between the quotation marks to your screen. As you can tell, this is not a sophisticated program.

The *n* character passed to printf() in our program means that a newline character is printed. This starts a new line. If you're used to a DOS machine, you'll note that UNIX uses a newline character where DOS uses a carriage return and then a new line. The backslash, \\, is used as a special character in C programs. Usually, a backslash is combined with another character to make a nonprintable character, such as **n** for a new line, **t** for a tab, or **a** for a bell.

Using the Cc Command

The **cc** command uses a number of command-line parameters to tell it what to do and to allow you to fine-tune the process of building executable programs from C language text files. Table 10.2 lists commonly used **cc** command-line parameters.

Table 10.2 Cc Command-Line Parameters

Parameter	Meaning
-I*directory*	Searches the given directory and **/usr/include** for include files
-c *filename.c*	Compiles the file *filename.c* and builds the object module *filename.o*; this does not create an executable command
-o *progname*	Names the executable program *progname*; the default name is **a.out**
-g	Compiles with debugging information
-O	Optimizes the program for best performance
-l*Library*	Link in the named *library*

Most UNIX compilers don't allow you to mix the *g* (include debugging information) and *O* (optimize) options, but the GNU C compiler used by Linux allows this.

There are many **cc** command-line options; use **man cc** to see them.

Linking with Libraries

For C programs, a *library* is a collection of commonly used routines that you can reuse in your programs. Most C programs require more than just the standard C library. If you look in **/usr/lib**, you'll see most of the libraries supported by Linux. Table 10.3 lists the major locations for Linux libraries.

Table 10.3 Locations for Linux Libraries

Directory	Libraries
/usr/lib	Main system libraries
/usr/openwin/lib	Open Look libraries like the Xview library
/usr/X11R6/lib	Most X Window libraries

To link with a given library, you use the *-l* command-line option to **cc**. To link with the X11 library, use *-lX11*; this is shorthand notion for linking in the library named **libX11.a** (or it's shared-library equivalent, **libX11.so**).

ELF Files

This version of Linux uses a new object module format called ELF, short for Executable and Linking Format. Programs compiled with ELF differ from those compiled in the older **a.out** format. ELF provides better support for shared libraries, the primary reason for this migration. Shared libraries save on memory usage when you run more than one program at a time, especially more than one X Window program.

Normally, you won't have to pay attention to ELF or **a.out** issues, except for one thing: the **a.out** libraries are not compatible with the ELF libraries. This is especially true for shared libraries.

Thus, you need to be careful about any Linux binary programs you acquire. If you compile everything from source code, then you're OK, as Linux will use the libraries you have on your system.

But if you pick up applications in precompiled binary format, for example, Netscape Navigator or NCSA Mosaic, you have to ensure that you have the proper shared libraries as expected by the application, or the program simply won't run.

When you install Linux (or any time later if you run the **setup** program), you can install both the **a.out** and the ELF libraries. If you have the disk space, you should load both. If you need to choose one or the other, go with ELF, as everything in the Linux world is migrating to ELF.

To see what systems your linker, **ld**, is configured for, try the following command:

```
ld -V
```

You should see output like the following:

```
ld version cygnus-2.6 (with BFD 2.6.0.14)
  Supported emulations:
   elf_i386
   i386linux
   i386coff
   m68kelf
   m68klinux
   sun4
   elf32_sparc
```

The *sparc, sun4,* and *m68k* (Motorola **68000**) are for cross-compiling. Chances
are you won't use these options.

By default, **gcc** will compile to ELF format. To verify, use the **file**
command on any executable file, such as the **chap10** file we created
earlier:

```
file chap10
```

You should see output like the following:

```
chap10: ELF 32-bit LSB executable i386 (386 and up) Version 1
```

This indicates that the default object file format on Linux is now ELF, as
expected.

The term **a.out**, unfortunately, means different things in different contexts. If
you compile a C program with **gcc**, the default output filename remains **a.out**.
Even so, this **a.out** file will appear in ELF object file format, not the older object
file format, called **a.out** format. This is yet another confusing part of Linux.

If for some reason you need to force **gcc** to compile in **a.out** format, you
can use the following command in place of **gcc**:

```
gcc -b i486-linuxaout -c foo.c -o foo
```

This command requires the **a.out** libraries. If you did not load them, this
command will fail.

Linux Shared Libraries

Linux supports a great concept called *shared libraries*. Because so many
Linux programs link in very large libraries, particularly X Window
libraries, the program size tends to grow. When you run these

programs, they take up more memory (real and virtual). To help alleviate this problem, Linux supports shared libraries, similar to Windows DLLs, or Dynamic Link Libraries. The whole purpose is that many programs can reference a single copy of the library loaded into memory. For X Window programs, this saves a lot of RAM.

The problem with Linux shared libraries is that they are very tightly linked to their version numbers. If you upgrade your version of Linux, many old applications may still demand the old versions of the shared libraries, and you may no longer have these old versions on your system. If you have a lot of Linux programs that came only in binary format (Netscape Navigator is a common program in this category), you either need to load the old shared libraries or wait until all the programs you use get upgraded. If you have the source code for the program, you can simply recompile and relink, and everything should be OK.

Programming with X

Linux comes with a number of X Window libraries, ready both for you to program with and for you to use when compiling freeware X Window applications. Unfortunately, Linux does not come with the Motif libraries, which are necessary to compile a number of neat programs, including the Mosaic Internet browser. (You can purchase the Motif libraries from a number of third parties, though; see Appendix A for details. Or, you can try a freeware version of the Motif API, called LessTif, which is described later.)

When compiling X programs, you normally don't have to do anything special to link, other than adding the X libraries to your **cc** command line. The X Window include files should be in the proper place, **/usr/include/X11** (actually a symbolic link to **/usr/X11R6/include/X11**, but good enough for the compiler).

To compile and link an X program, you can use the following command line:

```
cc -o foo foo.c -lXaw -lXt -lXext -lX11 -lSM -lICE
```

The *-l* option tells **cc** (really **ld**, as called by **cc**) to link in the named library. These libraries provide commonly used functions. The ones listed earlier provide X Window functions for the program. Thus, the -*lXaw* option tells **ld** to link in the Xaw library. By convention, this library file will be named **libXaw.a** for a static library and **libXaw.so** for a shared library.

 For more information on X and Motif programming, see URL *http://ourworld. compuserve.com/homepages/efjohnson/motif.htm* on the World Wide Web.

Using LessTif

Everyone wants to use the Motif libraries until they find out that they're an added-cost feature for Linux. Unfortunately, the Motif library is commercial software, which means you have to pay extra to get either the Motif library source code or a set of binaries for your platforms. Add to this hassle the frustrating nature of the complex Motif license for software developers, where it's almost impossible to tell if you can actually distribute your applications, and you're ready to scream.

However, we've run across a great programming effort called LessTif, which is gaining more Motif functionality each day. While it's not in completed form, we thought you might want to take a look at it, so we included it in the second CD-ROM' s **programming/lesstif** directory.

LessTif is a workalike clone of the Motif libraries. That is, it is a set of programming libraries that look and act like the Motif libraries (Xm and Mrm). Under the hood, the code is entirely different. From a programmer's perspective, though, LessTif has the same API as the Motif libraries and supports a number of Motif widgets, supporting more Motif widgets with each release. It uses public header files with the same name as their Motif counterparts.

For your programs, LessTif should allow your Motif programs to be recompiled under LessTif with no source code changes—at least in theory. We've had to make a few changes to get around the fact that LessTif is incomplete as we write this. Luckily, because LessTif is undergoing what looks like constant development, the problems we face today should gradually go away.

Distributed under the GNU license, you can use LessTif in free applications. You'll probably want to check the GNU licenses before using LessTif for commercial software.

Installing LessTif

LessTif comes in source code format. All you need to do is run **xmkmf** and then **make** in the standard way to build X programs:

```
xmkmf
make
```

If you run into any problems, there's a file named **INSTALL** with the distribution.

Problems with LessTif

The developers of LessTif clearly let you know that LessTif is not a complete Motif clone by any means. This is only natural at this early stage in LessTif's development. Even so, there's quite a few things present in LessTif that will appeal to Motif programmers.

LessTif, as incomplete free software, is not without its problems, as you'd expect. But each version gets better and better.

Editres Support

Editres is an X application and protocol that allows programs compiled with the X Toolkit (Xt) Intrinsics library to export information on widget attributes to an outside program, namely, **editres** itself.

With **editres**, for example, you can change the font, colors, and text displayed with any widget, presuming an application supports the **editres** protocol. To do this, an application must set up an event-handling function and pass the special **editres** library call, *_XEditResCheckMessages*, as the handler. For example, the following code sets this up for a Motif application:

```
#include <X11/Xmu/Editres.h>

Widget      toplevel;
void        _XEditResCheckMessages();

/* ... */

XtAddEventHandler(toplevel,
  (EventMask) 0,
  True,
  _XEditResCheckMessages,
  NULL);
```

With this set up, your Motif application will properly respond to the **editres** protocol.

The reason we mention this is that LessTif calls *XtAddEventHandler* automatically from the *Vendor* shell widget. Thus, all LessTif programs will support **editres**. But there's a slight problem with this. *_XEditResCheckMessages* resides in the X miscellaneous utilities library (**libXmu.a**) and you must be sure to link this in.

To link with LessTif, you need to link in at least the following libraries, as shown in the following command:

```
cc -o foo foo.c -lXm -lXmu -lXt -lX11
```

We mention this because you're probably not linking in the Xmu library now. It's nice that LessTif supports **editres** from the start, but you need to remember to link in the Xmu library.

All in all, for free software, it's hard to complain about LessTif. LessTif isn't ready for prime-time usage yet, but it has made great strides in recent months. You'll probably want to track its progress and conduct some tests before using it. Better yet, you may want to volunteer to help the effort.

Finding out More about LessTif

You can look up the LessTif home page on the World Wide Web by accessing *http://www.hungry.com/products/lesstif/*. You can also use FTP to acquire the latest version of LessTif, at machine *ftp.hungry.com* in the **pub/hungry/lesstif** directory.

XForms

XForms is a C library designed to dramatically simplify the creation of X programs. The basic task in XForms is creating *forms*, XForms terminology for panels, windows, or dialogs. A form is really a top-level window containing a number of widgets. By simplifying the options and coming up with a good set of default values, XForms reduces much of the complexity in creating X applications. You do pay a price in reduced flexibility, but for many application needs, XForms will be the right fit.

One of the areas of reduced freedom and complexity is widget layout. All widgets are placed in an exact position, be it in pixels, millimeters, or points (1/72 of an inch). Other widget sets, like Motif, provide an extensive set of widgets that control the layout of other widgets. Of course, widget layout is one of Motif's most troublesome aspects for developers new to the library. XForms, on the other hand, eliminates most of these options and confusion by placing widgets directly.

XForms allows you to populate your forms with widgets such as buttons, sliders, and text-entry fields. Some of the more innovative widgets include dials, clocks, and X-Y data plots. The X-Y data plots will appeal to those in the academic community who want to display data graphically.

Should the XForms base widget set be too confining for your needs, you can create "free" objects, something like the Motif drawing area widget, where your application gets a blank canvas to draw in and callbacks to handle all events. This allows a way to extend the base widget set. XForms includes an extensive API for adding new widgets.

The look and feel of XForms applications varies. You can create a variety of push-button styles, including beveled push-buttons and rounded-corner buttons, so your interface can look like Motif, Open Look, or just about anything else.

A lot of the look seems to come from older Silicon Graphics applications. Many of the widgets support neat border styles, but the menus look strange. It took us a long time to get used to the menus in

XForms; they don't interact the same as menus in most toolkits, and they take some getting used to.

On the plus side, XForms supports a number of text styles and fonts, which is great for those who don't know much about the long X font names. With smart use of the font styles, your XForms programs will look much better than most Motif programs, with much less coding.

Coding is one area where XForms excels. You can generally create a working application in a very short amount of time, with very little code.

We've included XForms in a binary version on the second CD-ROM. XForms is a copyrighted product that is freely available for *noncommercial use only*. For commercial use, you need to contact the XForms authors at *xforms@world.std.com*. We cannot stress enough the importance of following this guideline.

To acquire XForms via the Internet (there may be an updated version by the time you read this), you can FTP to one of the following sites: *bloch.phys.uwm.edu* in the **pub/xforms** directory, *ftp.cs.ruu.nl* in the **pub/XFORMS** directory, and *imageek.york.cuny.edu* in the **xforms** directory. On the Web, see *http://bragg.phys.uwm.edu/xforms*.

Programmer's Tools

In addition to the basic compiler, Linux comes with many utility programs and tools to make programming easier. The first and foremost tool is a program called **make**.

Building Programs with Make

Most C programs require more than one .c file of source code. When one of these files changes, at least one (and maybe more) of the files must get recompiled to have the executable program reflect the changes. Tending to be lazy, programmers don't want to recompile all the files if just one changed. Furthermore, these lazy programmers don't want to have to keep track of all the files that changed. This is where the tool called **make** comes in.

Make is a command that helps build or "make" UNIX programs from the C language source code files. **make** uses a set of rules, stored in a file called **Makefile**, to tell it the most efficient way to rebuild a program. You keep a **Makefile** in each directory where you develop C programs.

The **Makefile** contains a set of rules, using a rigid syntax, that describe how to build the program. Most of the rules declare which parts of the program depend on other parts. Using these dependency rules, **make** determines what has changed (based on the file modified date) and what other things depend on the file or files that changed. Then **make** executes the commands in the **Makefile** to build each thing that needs to be rebuilt.

The basic **Makefile** syntax is deceptively simple. (Linux includes the GNU **make** program, which accepts a number of rule shortcuts. For this chapter, we'll just cover the basics. Use the **man make** command to find out more about **make**.)

You start out with a so-called target. The target is something you want to build, such as our program **chap10** from the earlier example.

To create a target in the **Makefile**, begin with a new line and name the target—what you want to build—then place a colon (:) and a tab, and then list the files the target depends on. Starting on the next line, begin with a tab, then place the UNIX command used to build the target. You can have multiple commands, each of which should go on its own line, and every command line must start with a tab.

In the abstract, the **Makefile** rules look like the following:

```
what_to_build:   what_it_depends_on
command1_to_build_it
command2_to_build_it
command3_to_build_it

...

lastcommand_to_build_it
```

In the abstract, this looks confusing. Here's a more concrete example, using the **chap10** program we provided earlier.

The target we want to build is the **chap10** program. The **chap10** program (the target) depends on the object module **chap10.o**. Once we have the object module **chap10.o**, then the command line to create the **chap10** program is:

```
chap10:     chap10.o
cc -o chap10 chap10.o
```

This **make** rule states that if **chap10.o** has a more recent date, then execute the **cc** command to build the **chap10** program from the object module **chap10.o**.

This is just part of the task; we still have to compile **chap10.c** to create the object module **chap10.o**. That is, the file **chap10.o**, is said to depend on the file **chap10.c**. You build **chap10.o** from **chap10.c**. To do this, we use another **make** rule.

This time, the object module **chap10.o** depends on the text file **chap10.c**. The command to build the object module is:

```
chap10.o:     chap10.c
cc -c chap10.c
```

With this **make** rule, if you edit **chap10.c**, you'll make the file **chap10.c** have a more recent date/time than the object module **chap10.o**. This causes **make** to trigger the **cc** command to compile **chap10.c** into **chap10.o**.

You've discovered the secret to **make**'s rules. Everything depends on the date/time of the files, a very simple—but clever—idea. The idea is that if the text of the program *.c* file is modified, you better rebuild the program with **cc**. Because most users are impatient, if the *.c* file hasn't been changed, there's simply no reason (at least in our example) to rebuild the program with **cc**.

A Make Example

To try **make**, enter the following text into a file named **Makefile**:

```
#
# Test Makefile
#
```

```
# The program chap10 depends on chap10.o.
chap10:     chap10.o
    cc -o chap10 chap10.o


# The object module chap10.o depends on chap10.c.
chap10.o:     chap10.c
    cc -c chap10.c
```

This **Makefile** should be in the same directory as your sample C program file, **chap10.c**. To use **make**, we need to tell it what to make, that is, what target we want to build. In our case, we want **make** to build the program **chap10**. The following command will build this program:

```
$ make chap10
        cc -c chap10.c
        cc -o chap10 chap10.o
```

We should now have the **chap10** program ready to run. If we try **make** again, it—being very lazy—tells us there's no new work to do:

```
$ make chap10
chap10 is up to date.
```

Why? Because the **chap10** program was built, and nothing has changed. Now, edit the **chap10.c** file again or use the **touch** command to bump up the date/time associated with the file:

```
$ touch chap10.c
```

When you call **make** again, it knows it now needs to rebuild the **chap10** program, because presumably the **chap10.c** file has changed since the last time **chap10.c** was compiled with **cc**. Because **touch** only updates the date/time associated with the file and doesn't change the internals of the file in any way, we've just fooled **make**. **make** doesn't bother checking if a file is different; it merely checks the time the file was last written to, blindly assuming that no one would ever write to a file without modifying its contents. Normally, though, you don't want to fool **make**; use its simple rules to make your life easier.

Make supports a number of useful command-line parameters, as shown in Table 10.4.

Table 10.4 Make Command-Line Parameters

Parameter	Meaning
-f *makefile*	Uses the named file instead of **Makefile** for the rules
-n	Runs in no-execute mode—only prints the commands, doesn't execute them
-s	Runs in silent mode; doesn't print any commands **make** executes

As you compile Linux freeware, you'll notice that there are a lot of conventions with **make** and **Makefile**s. For example, most **Makefiles** contain a target called **all**, which rebuilds the entire program when you execute:

```
$ make all
```

For this command to work, the **Makefile** must have a target named *all* that tells **make** what to do to rebuild everything. In addition, most **Makefiles** contain a clean target that removes all *.o* files and other files created by the compiler, and an install target that copies the built executable file to an installation directory, such as **/usr/local/bin**.

Imake

In addition to **make**, there's another tool called **imake**. **Imake** is used to generate **Makefiles** on a variety of systems. **Imake** uses an **Imakefile** for its rules. These rules then help generate a **Makefile**, which is used by **make** to build the program. Sound convoluted? It is. The main reason **imake** exists is because of radically different system configurations, especially where the X Window System is concerned.

You'll find **imake** especially popular with programs for X Window. The problem with X is that there are so many options that every UNIX platform is configured slightly differently. There's simply no way you could write a portable **Makefile** that could work on all such platforms. **Imake** uses an **Imakefile** and configuration files that are local to your system. Together, the **Imakefile** and the local configuration files generate a **Makefile** that should work on your system. (In addition to **imake**, there's an even handier package called GNU **configure**. Unfortunately, **imake** is very common among X Window programs, and **configure** is not.)

If you need to compile programs for the X Window System and you see an **Imakefile**, here's what you should do. First, run the **xmkmf** shell script. This script is merely a simple front end to **imake**:

```
$ xmkmf

mv Makefile Makefile.bak

imake -DUseInstalled -I/usr/lib/X11/config
```

These commands should make a backup of any **Makefile** you have (to **Makefile.bak**) and then create a new **Makefile** based on the commands in an **Imakefile**.

Imake isn't easy to grasp, so if you have problems with **imake**, check with your system administrator or look up **imake** in a book on the X Window System (such as *Using X*, MIS:Press, 1992; see Appendix A for a list of books on using the X Window System).

Debuggers

Because Linux remains firmly in the GNU program-development world, it provides the **gdb** debugger, as well as the X Window front end, **xxgdb**, as shown in Figure 10.1.

X Window Tools

If you're developing X Window applications, a few extra utilities may help. The **xman** program (mentioned in Chapter 5) provides a graphical front end and nice formatting for UNIX online-manual pages.

For critical X programs, you'll find **xcmap** very useful. This simple X application displays the current colormap. For color-intensive X applications, this can help you track down obscure X problems.

Similarly, the **xev** application helps you see what events the keyboard keys are really sending to the X server.

For selecting fonts, **xfd** and **xfontsel** both help you choose a good-looking font for your applications.

```
                          xxgdb 1.08

Ready for execution

XXGDB comes with ABSOLUTELY NO WARRANTY.
GDB is free software and you are welcome to distribute copies of it
 under certain conditions; type "show copying" to see the conditions.
There is absolutely no warranty for GDB; type "show warranty" for details.
GDB 4.13 (i486-slackware-linux),
Copyright 1994 Free Software Foundation, Inc...
(xxgdb) run
[tcsetpgrp failed in terminal_inferior: Not a typewriter]

Program received signal SIGSEGV, Segmentation fault.
0xe9b0 in XrmCombineDatabase ()
(xxgdb)

    Source Listing      Command Buttons      Display Window      Quit
```

```
            /home/erc/books/advx2nd/src/primary.c                  254

         * Read data from property identified in
         * SelectionNotify event.
         */
        status = XGetWindowProperty(widget->display,
                        event->requestor,
                        event->property,
                        0L,       /* offset */
                        FULL_LENGTH,
                        True,     /* Delete when read. */
                        new_target,
                        &actual_target,
                        &actual_format,
                        &number_items,
                        &bytes_remaining,
                        &data);
```

Figure 10.1 The **xxgdb** debugger.

Parsers and Lexers

If you're used to building your own parsers, you'll like the GNU **bison** (a port of UNIX **yacc**—Yet Another Compiler Compiler) and **flex** (a fast **lex**). Linux even includes **flex++** for developing C++ scanners.

Other Tools

We list some more useful tools for programmers in Table 10.5.

Table 10.5 More Useful Programming Tools

Tool	Usage
ar	Collects object files into libraries
diff	Compares differences between files
gprof	Gathers timing statistics about your programs for performance tuning
hexdump	Displays ASCII, decimal, hexadecimal, or octal dump of a file
objdump	Display information on object files
ranlib	Generates an index in an **ar**-created archive (library)
rcs	Source code Revision Control System
strace	Displays system calls from your program

There's even a tool called **ansi2knr** that converts ANSI C to old-style Kernighan and Ritchie-style C (without function prototypes). With Linux, you don't really need this, as **gcc** fully supports ANSI C.

There are more tools than what we listed in Table 10.5. Chances are that just about every UNIX freeware tool is available on Linux.

Other Programming Languages

C is by and large the programming *lingua franca* on UNIX and Linux, with C++ (an object-oriented extension to C) fast gaining in popularity. In addition to these languages, Linux provides a host of other opportunities to program.

First, the GNU C compiler also supports the Objective-C extension to the C programming language. Objective-C is very popular under the Nextstep environment. The GNU C compiler also supports a Fortran 77 front end called **g77**.

For artificial intelligence fans, there's Common Lisp (under the name **clisp**). Additional programming languages include Ada and Pascal.

 None of the programming tools or languages get installed on a Slackware Linux system unless you specifically ask for them by running the **setup** program.

Java the Hut

One of the hottest new languages, especially for World Wide Web applications, is Sun's Java. Java programs get compiled to a portable set of byte codes, which can execute on any system that supports the Java Virtual Machine. There's a version of Java for Linux; on the second CD-ROM: the Java Development Kit, or JDK.. As of this writing, this software is in a very preliminary format, but it's worth checking out.

Linux Scripting Languages

In addition to the programming languages discussed earlier, Linux offers even more, including a number of scripting languages. A scripting language is a lot like the language that comes with the UNIX shell. The main difference between a programming language and a scripting language is that *scripting languages* are usually interpreted instead of compiled, and scripting languages usually make it easier to launch Linux commands from within your programs—called *scripts* when you use a scripting language. As you can tell, the line between programming languages and scripting languages is blurry.

Of the scripting languages available on Linux, the two hottest languages are Tcl and Perl, while **gawk** continues to attract a lot of attention.

Tcl

Tcl, short for the Tool Command Language, is a very handy scripting language that runs on most UNIX platforms and Windows NT.

Combined with Tcl's X Window toolkit, called Tk, you can build a lot of neat X Window graphical programs without a lot of coding.

In addition, Tcl is made to be embedded in C programs, so you can use Tcl as a standard extension language for your spreadsheet, game, or other software you write.

We mostly use Tcl to create programs that have a friendly user interface, that look like Motif programs, and that can run on a wide number of systems. Tcl and the Tk toolkit present something akin to the Motif look and feel—not close enough for purists, but close enough for most users. This is a great benefit because the Motif libraries don't ship with Linux, but Tcl does.

Tcl is a scripting language, much like the languages built into **sh** and **ksh**, the most common UNIX command shells. The language has some nice features for handling strings and lists (of strings—just about *everything* is a string in a Tcl program).

The Tk toolkit then acts as an add-on to Tcl, allowing you to easily build widgets and create an X Window user interface. The whole concept of widgets, though, is likely to be daunting unless you've programmed with one of the many X toolkits, such as Motif. Each widget acts as a part of your user interface, for example, a list of files, a push button to exit the program, and so on. If you have worked with Motif or the Athena widgets, you'll catch on to the concepts of Tk pretty fast. Even if you haven't worked with the Motif or Athena libraries, we found the basics of Tcl very easy to grasp. (There are some frustrating parts to Tcl, though.)

The Tk add-on to Tcl provides most of the standard set of widgets you'd expect. These widgets mirror most of the main widgets in the Motif toolkit, except for the handy option-menu, combo-box, and notebook widgets. Tcl exceeds Motif in a number of areas, too, especially with the canvas widget, which allows you to place graphic "objects" such as lines, rectangles, Béziér curves, and even other widgets inside the canvas.

Scripting with Tcl

Like most scripting languages, Tcl uses a dollar sign, $, to get the value of a variable. Everything in Tcl is a text string, so it needs a special character to differentiate a string from the value held within a variable. Thus:

```
variable
```

is just the literal string *variable*, while

```
$variable
```

returns the value stored in the variable named, appropriately enough, *variable*. This is the same as most shell scripting languages. (There are some tricky aspects to this, though. We found that simple typos—such as forgetting the $—were responsible for most of our Tcl errors.)

For example, if you have a directory name in the variable *dir* and you want to use the **cd** command to change to that directory, you issue the following Tcl command:

```
cd $dir
```

The basic syntax for Tcl seems like a cross between Lisp and C. The basic function, called proc, looks much like a C function, for example:

```
proc add_one { value } {

    return [expr $value+1]
}
```

The braces give it a definite C feeling. The Lispishness comes from the use of the **set** command, instead of assignment. That is, instead of a C statement like:

```
a = b;
```

in Tcl you code this as:

```
set a $b
```

(Remembering all the while that the $ can trip you up at first.)

One nice thing about Tcl is its ability to use variables at any time, without predeclaring them—except for arrays, which you need to indicate are arrays before using them with widget commands.

Working with Tcl

To try out some Tcl programs, you should run the Tcl interpreter, called **wish**, which allows you to enter Tcl commands as if you were in a Tcl-based shell, which is what **wish** is.

The most interesting use of Tcl is to create graphical programs including widgets such as push buttons. To create a push button in Tcl, use the **button** command:

```
button .b1 \
  -text "My first button" \
  -command { exit }
```

Because Tcl is a scripting language, you can use the backslash character, \, to extend a command on one line over many lines. This makes your programs easier to read.

The preceding command creates a button widget named **.b1** (the leading period is important). Just like Linux uses the / character to mark the root directory, Tcl uses the period (.) to mark the root widget (your application's main window). We're then creating a button widget that sits like a subdirectory beneath the root widget.

The *-command* sets the Tcl command that will run when the button gets pushed. In our case, the **exit** command exits **wish** and our Tcl script.

It's important to note that the code for the *-command* gets evaluated only when the button is pushed, usually sometime after the button is created and usually when the Tcl program is in another procedure. Because of this, local variables no longer have their values at execution time.

This can be very difficult to debug. We will show some workarounds in the sample code.

To get a widget to appear, we must pack it. The **pack** command takes a lot of parameters, including the name of the widget or widgets to pack:

```
pack .b1
```

Tcl widgets don't appear until you pack them.

Making Script Files for Tcl

You can put together a set of Tcl commands into a script file, just like C and Bourne shell scripts. The program to execute the script is again **wish**. The following script assumes that **wish** is located in **/usr/bin** (as it is for Linux).

To turn our first example into a working script, we do the following:

```
#!/usr/bin/wish
#
# example1.tcl
#
# Create a button.
button .b1 \
  -text "My first button" \
  -command { exit }

pack .b1

# example1.tcl
```

To show you more of a flavor of Tcl scripting, we put together the following file. In it, Tcl commands create a set of buttons that allow you to launch useful Linux programs like **xman** and **xterm**. The toolbar appears at the bottom of the screen and uses the override-redirect mode that prevents a window manager from placing a title bar around the window. Also, in honor of Windows 95, we place the current time at the end of the toolbar.

In our script, we create a number of procedures, called *procs* in Tcl. The *exec_cmd* procedure executes a text string as a UNIX command. We use the *eval* statement to deal with text-string issues and evaluate any Tcl variables within the command. Try this Tcl script without the *eval* in the *exec_cmd* procedure and you'll see why we need it. (It has to do with evaluating the arguments as one string or as a command line; this is one area where Tcl is not intuitive.)

The *update_time* procedure gets the current time, using the UNIX **date** command, and then changes the text displayed in a widget (you pass *update_time* the widget name) and uses the **after** command to set up a callback, the *update_time* procedure, to get called after a particular amount of time. With Tcl 7.5, you can use the built-in **clock** command instead of calling the Linux program **date**.

The main part of the Tcl script creates a frame widget to hold all the buttons and then creates a set of buttons. The **logo** button quits the script when it's pressed. We use the words *Linux* and your machine's hostname for the text in the **logo** button.

The whole point of this Tcl script is to launch commonly used applications, particularly graphical ones. The buttons set up are listed in Table 10.6.

Table 10.6 Applications Launched from the toolbar.tcl Script

Button	Launches
Manuals	**xman** to view Linux online manuals
Mail	**elm** (inside **xterm** window) to read mail
Shell	**xterm** for a command-line shell
File Manager	**xfm**, a Linux file manager
Images	**xv**, an image-viewing and file-browsing program
Mahjongg	Our favorite game on X

The Tcl script that makes all this happen appears here:

```
#!/usr/bin/wish
#
# toolbar.tcl
# Tcl script that puts a toolbar to launch
# programs at the bottom of the screen.
```

```
#
# Executes a command as a UNIX process.
#
proc exec_cmd { command } {

    # Execute as a UNIX process in the background.
    # We use eval to handle the messy details of
    # separating the command into its elements.
    # (Try it without eval and you'll see why.)
    #
    eval exec $command &
}


#
# Tcl/Tk procedure to place the
# current time in a widget. With Tcl 7.5,
# you can also use the clock command.
#
set title_interval  40000
set time_command    "/bin/date \"+%I:%M %p\" "

global title_interval time_command

proc update_time { butn } {
    global  title_interval time_command

    # Get current time.
    set timestr [ eval exec $time_command ]

    $butn config -text $timestr

    # Set up command to run again.
    after $title_interval " update_time $butn"
}


#
# Global commands to execute when
```

```
# toolbar buttons get pushed.
#
set cmds(man)    "/usr/bin/X11/xman -notopbox -bothshown"
set cmds(mail)   "/usr/bin/X11/xterm -ls -e elm"
set cmds(term)   "/usr/bin/X11/xterm -ls"
set cmds(file)   "/usr/bin/X11/xfm"
set cmds(xv)     "/usr/bin/X11/xv"
set cmds(xmah)   "/usr/bin/X11/xmahjongg"

# Make cmds array global.
global cmds

#
# Main program.
#
#   Set window manager values.
wm geometry          .   +0-0
wm overrideredirect . true

#
# Frame to hold everything.
#
set back lightgray

frame .frame -relief raised -bd 2 -bg $back
.frame config -cursor top_left_arrow

#
# Logo/Name widget.
#
set title [format "Linux: %s" [ exec hostname ] ]

button .frame.logo -text $title \
  -command { exit } -bg $back \
  -relief flat -padx 8

pack .frame.logo -side left -fill y
```

```
#
# Create other widgets
# that make up our toolbar.
#
button .frame.man -text "Manuals" \
 -command { exec_cmd $cmds(man) } \
 -relief flat -padx 8 -bg $back

button .frame.mail -text "Mail" \
 -command { exec_cmd $cmds(mail) } \
 -relief flat -padx 8 -bg $back

button .frame.term -text "Shell" \
 -command { exec_cmd $cmds(term) } \
 -relief flat -padx 8 -bg $back

button .frame.file -text "File Manager" \
 -command { exec_cmd $cmds(file) } \
 -relief flat -padx 8 -bg $back

button .frame.xv -text "Images" \
 -command { exec_cmd $cmds(xv) } \
 -relief flat -padx 8 -bg $back

button .frame.xmah -text "Mahjongg" \
 -command { exec_cmd $cmds(xmah) } \
 -relief flat -padx 8 -bg $back

# Pack all the buttons, in order.
pack .frame.man .frame.mail \
   .frame.term .frame.file \
   .frame.xv .frame.xmah \
   -side left -fill y

# Set up timer label.
label .frame.time -bg $back
```

```
update_time .frame.time
pack .frame.time -side left -fill y

pack .frame

# toolbar.tcl
```

You can easily add your own commands, with three easy steps:

1. At the `set` *cmds area*, add your new UNIX command.
2. At the *button* area, copy one of the button commands to create your own. You need to change the button's name to *frame.yourname* or something like that. Also, ensure that it uses your command from the *set cmds* area.
3. At the **pack** command right after the button area, add the name of your new button.

You can use these two scripts as examples to get you started scripting Tcl applications. One of the handiest parts of Tcl is that it's supported on Windows and Macintosh systems. There's a number of books available on Tcl, including *Graphical Applications with Tcl and Tk*; see Appendix A for details.

Perl

Perl is a freeware scripting language developed to handle a number of system administration tasks. *Perl* stands for Practical Extraction and Report Language. The whole point of the language is to make it easier for you to extract data from UNIX and output reports on things such as Usenet news disk usage and a list of all users on your systems, sorted in order of largest disk usage. (Perl tends to excel at tasks that revolve around reporting system information.)

To make sure you've installed perl when you install Linux, type in the following:

```
gilbert:/$ perl -v
```

If you have perl on your system, you should see the version number for perl. If not, you need to run the **setup** program again. (The **setup** program installs Perl 5.002.)

A First Perl Script

Perl, like most Tcl and other UNIX scripting languages, uses the # as a comment marker. Any line with # is ignored from the # onward. To print data in a perl script, use the *print* statement:

```
#! /usr/bin/perl
print "Linux runs perl!\n";
print "Oh, joy!\n";
```

When you run this script, you'll see the following output, as you'd expect:

```
Linux runs perl!
Oh, joy!
```

The \n stands for a new line, or linefeed character, and is typical UNIX parlance as we described in the section on C programming.

You can also prompt for data in Perl, using the following odd syntax:

```
#! /usr/bin/perl
# Prompting for input in perl.

print "What is your first name: ";

# <STDIN> stands for standard input: the keyboard.
$first_name = <STDIN>;

# Remove trailing linefeed.
chomp($first_name);

printf "What is your last name: ";
```

```
$last_name = <STDIN>;

chomp($last_name);

print "Your name is $first_name $last_name.\n";
```

When you run this script, you'll see the following prompts:

```
What is your first name: Eric
What is your last name: Johnson
Your name is Eric Johnson.
```

Perl provides a lot of support for arrays, UNIX process control, and string handling. Perl offers a string set of array operations, which allow you to have a set of data treated as one unit, for example:

```
(1,2,3,4,5,6)
```

This array has the values 1 through 6. You can also mix text and numeric values, as shown here:

```
(1, 2, 3, 4, "Linux is out the door")
```

You can assign this array to a variable and then access any element in the array. A great strength of perl is its associative arrays, where you can use a key value for an array index and associate this with a data value. For example, you can have a perl array for a first name, last name, and street address. You could then access the street address as shown here:

```
#! /usr/bin/perl
# Associative arrays in perl.

# zippy is an associative array.

$zippy{"firstname"} = "Zippy";
$zippy{"address"} = "1600 Pennsylvania Ave.";

# Print the data.
print $zippy{"firstname"};
```

```
print "'s address is ";
print $zippy{"address"};

# End with a carriage return.
print "\n";
```

This example stores a first name and an address in the associative array named *zippy*. Associative arrays form a very powerful feature and can be used effectively in a lot of system administration tasks.

The output of the preceding script looks something like the following (and predicts the results of the next election):

```
Zippy's address is 1600 Pennsylvania Av.
```

In addition to associative arrays, perl has a lot of commands to format text to allow you to create reports (the original reason for perl's existence). perl is intimately tied in with UNIX and provides a number of shortcuts for common UNIX activities, like accessing the **password** file, as we show here:

```
#! /usr/bin/perl
# Accessing the password file.

# Get Eric's password entry and print it.

@erc_entry = getpwnam("erc");

($username, $realname, $homedir) = @erc_entry[0,6,7];

print "User $realname has";
print " a home directory of $homedir";
print " and a username of $username.\n";
```

When you run this script, you'll see output like the following:

```
User Eric F. Johnson has a home directory of /home/erc
and a username of erc.
```

Naturally, you'll want to use a username available on your system.

There's a lot more to perl, which fills more than one book on the subject. If you're interested in learning more about perl, see Appendix A.

Gawk

Developed by three Bell Labs researchers (Alfred Aho, Peter Weinberger, and Brian Kernighan—hence the acronym *awk*), **awk** is a programming language (with some strong similarities to the C programming language, discussed earlier in this chapter) but is used in much the same manner as other UNIX scripting tools. Hence its inclusion in this chapter.

Technically speaking, **awk** doesn't ship with Linux; instead, the GNU version, **gawk**, ships with Linux. (By now you shouldn't be surprised that Linux features software from the GNU Project.) Because **gawk** is virtually identical to other implementations of **awk** (there are a few extensions to **awk** in **gawk**, but you can ignore them if you choose), most users with experience with **awk** will have no problems with **awk**.

Gawk's primary value is in the manipulation of structured text files, where information is stored in columnar form and is separated by consistent characters (such as tabs or spaces). **Gawk** takes these structured files and manipulates them through editing, sorting, and searching.

Let's use a data file named **workers** as an example:

```
Eric      286    555-6674    erc       8
Geisha    280    555-4221    geisha    10
Kevin     279    555-1112    kevin     2
Tom       284    555-2121    spike     12
```

Let's sink into the trap of abstraction for a minute and compare our example file output to a two-dimensional graph. Each row across is called a *record*, which in turn is made up of vertical fields or columns, almost like a database. **Gawk** allows us to manipulate the data in the file by either row or column. Using the **gawk** command is not a complicated process. The structure of the **gawk** command looks like:

```
$ gawk [option] 'pattern {action}'
```

(The only options available with **gawk** are *-F*, which allows you to specify a field separator other than the default of white space; *-f*, which allows you to specify a filename full of **gawk** commands instead of placing a complex pattern and action on the Linux command line, and *-W*, which runs **gawk** in total compatibility with **awk**.) Here we should define our terms. A *pattern* can be an ASCII string (which **gawk** treats numerically; instead of seeing the character *e* as an *e*, it sees it as the ASCII equivalent), a numeral, a combination of numerals, or a wildcard, while *action* refers to an instruction we provide. Essentially, **gawk** works by having us tell it to search for a particular pattern; when it has found that pattern, **gawk** is to do something with it, such as printing the pattern to another file.

The simplest **gawk** program merely prints out all lines in the file:

```
gilbert:/$ gawk '{ print }' workers
Eric     286    555-6674       erc      8
Geisha   280    555-4221       geisha   10
Kevin    279    555-1112       kevin    2
Tom      284    555-2121       spike    12
```

Continuing our example, let's say we wanted to pull all records that began with the string *geisha*. We'd use the following:

```
gilbert:/$ gawk '$1 ~ /Geisha/ {print $0}' workers
```

Here's what the command means, part by part:

- *$1:* Tells **gawk** to use the first column for the basis of further action. **gawk** will perform some action on a file based on either records or fields; a number beginning with a $ tells **gawk** to work on a specific field. In this case, $1 refers to the first field.
- ~: Tells **gawk** to match the following string.
- /**Geisha**/: The string to search for.
- {**print $0**}: Tells **gawk** to print out the entire record containing the matched string. A special use of the $ sign is with the character *0*, which tells **gawk** to use all the fields possible.
- **workers**: The file to use.

In our case, **gawk** would print the following to the screen:

```
Geisha    280    555-4221    geisha    10
```

Not every action has to be the result of matching a specific pattern, of course. In **gawk**, the tilde (~) acts as a relational operator, which sets forth a condition for **gawk** to use. There are a number of other relational operators available to **gawk** users that allow **gawk** to compare two patterns. (The relational operators are based on algebraic notation.) **Gawk** supports the same relational operators found in the C programming language; they are listed in Table 10.7.

Table 10.7 Gawk Relational Operators

Operator	Meaning	Usage
<	Less than	$1 < "Eric" returns every pattern with an ASCII value less than "Eric".
<=	Less than or equal to	$1 <= "Eric".
==	Equals	$1 == "Eric" returns every instance of "Eric".
!=	Does not equal	$1 != "Eric" returns every field not containing the string "Eric".
>=	Greater than or equal to	$1 >= "Eric" returns every field equal to or greater than "Eric".
>	Greater than	$1 > "Eric" returns every field greater than "Eric."

We could increase the sophistication of **gawk** searches in a number of ways. Firstly, we could incorporate the use of compound searches, which use three logical operators:

- &&, which works the same as the logical AND
- | |, which works the same as the logical OR
- !, which returns anything NOT equaling the original

For example, let's say we wanted to know how many workers had a value in the fifth field that is greater than or equal to 10:

```
gilbert:/$ gawk '$5 >= 10 { print $0 } ' workers
Geisha   280      555-4221        geisha  10
Tom      284      555-2121        spike   12
```

We can also combine tests, to print out, for example, all workers who have the fifth field less than 10 and the second field greater than 280:

```
gilbert:/$ gawk '$5 < 10 && $2 > 280 { print $0 } ' workers
Eric     286      555-6674        erc     8
```

While these examples are obviously contrived, you can use **gawk** to help pull out all entries that share certain postal (ZIP) codes or all employees who have a salary in a certain range. We're just scratching the surface with **gawk**.

gawk can also be used to return entire sections of data, as long as you can specify patterns that begin and end the section. To return the records of Eric and Kevin and all between, use the following:

```
gilbert:/$ gawk '$1 ~ /Eric/,/Kevin/ {print $0}' workers
Eric     286   555-6674   erc      8
Geisha   280   555-4221   geisha   10
Kevin    279   555-1112   kevin    2
```

If we don't want to print the whole record, we can print just a few of the fields, as in the following example, which prints out fields 2 and 1:

```
gilbert:/$ gawk '$1 ~ /Eric/,/Kevin/ {print $2, $1}' workers
286 Eric
280 Geisha
279 Kevin
```

As with other UNIX commands, **gawk** can be used in pipes, and its output can be directed to other files or directly to the printer. For example, if we were looking through a large file and expecting many matches to a particular string (such as salary ranges or employment starting dates), we might want to direct that output to a file or to a printer.

To use **gawk** with the Linux **sort** utility, we can sort the output of the last example:

```
gilbert:/$ gawk '$1 ~ /Eric/,/Kevin/ {print $2, $1}' workers |
sort
279 Kevin
280 Geisha
286 Eric
```

(Please note that this is sorting on the leading number.)

Gawk also provides some summary abilities. The *NR* symbol in a **gawk** command returns the number of records, for example.

We can combine this with **gawk**'s ability to total fields in an **gawk** program.

Gawk Programs

You're not limited to what fits on the command line with **gawk**. You can also store a series of **gawk** commands in a file and then use **gawk** to execute the file.

For example, we can store our simplest **gawk** command, {**print**}, in a separate file and use the following **gawk** command:

```
gilbert:/$ gawk -f gawk.1 workers
Eric    286    555-6674    erc      8
Geisha  280    555-4221    geisha  10
Kevin   279    555-1112    kevin    2
Tom     284    555-2121    spike   12
```

In this case, we're assuming that the file **gawk.1** contains our very simple **gawk** program:

```
{ print }
```

You can combine this with the **gawk BEGIN**, **END**, and **NR** commands to make a more complex **gawk** program. When working with this, it's good to remember that **gawk** applies each **gawk** command to every record, that is, every line of text, in the input file. A commandlike {**print**} says that each line in the input file should be printed.

The **gawk BEGIN** command lists what to do before reading each line of text. For example:

```
BEGIN { print "Workers for Spacely Sprockets"; print "" }
{ print }
```

The preceding **gawk** program will print out the text *"Workers for Spacely Sprockets"* before printing each line in the **workers** file. One the command line, this will look like the following (if we stored the preceding **gawk** program in a file named **gawk.2**):

```
gilbert:/$ gawk -f gawk.2 workers
Workers for Spacely Sprockets

Eric    286    555-6674    erc     8
Geisha  280    555-4221    geisha  10
Kevin   279    555-1112    kevin   2
Tom     284    555-2121    spike   12
```

The print "" prints a blank line.

The *END* statement similarly lists commands to execute after all data is read. Here's where the **NR** command, number of records (or lines), comes in handy, as in the following example:

```
BEGIN { print "Workers for Spacely Sprockets"; print "" }

{ print }

END { print "There are ",
      NR,
      " employees left after the latest wave of layoffs." }
```

This example uses cleaner formatting for the END statements. It would make no difference in the output if we had instead placed the entire

END command on one line. We can name this file **gawk.3** and then execute the following command:

```
gilbert:/$ gawk -f gawk.3 workers
Workers for Spacely Sprockets

Eric    286    555-6674     erc      8
Geisha  280    555-4221     geisha   10
Kevin   279    555-1112     kevin    2
Tom     284    555-2121     spike    12
There are  4  employees left after the latest wave of layoffs.
```

This brief explanation covers **gawk** in the simplest terms. For example, **gawk** includes most of the trappings of a full programming language, including loops, variables, string operations, numeric operations, and the creation and manipulation of arrays. If you're interested in a useful programming language that can be mastered relatively quickly, we recommend further reading on **gawk**; our recommendations can be found in Appendix A.

Summary

We realize that many of you are potential and practicing programmers, so we spent a great deal of space on the many programming tools available with Linux. Even so, we've barely touched the surface of the Linux programming environment, for both traditional character-based programs and those running under the X Window System.

The chapter began with a discussion of the GNU C compiler, **gcc**, which ships with Linux. With **gcc**, you can create and compile C, C++, and Objective-C programs, as explained in this chapter. You learned about compiling the long way and the short way, using the **make** command.

The chapter then discussed programming under the X Window System and the programming libraries you'll need. A freeware library called LessTif acts as a substitute for the commercial Motif programming libraries. While LessTif is clearly a work in progress, it's interesting enough for us to include on the second accompanying CD-ROM—and it should be interesting enough for you to look at if you're at all interested in Motif programming.

In addition, you learned about the **imake** command, which is used by many X Window applications for compiling on various operating systems.

The Tcl/Tk combination allows you to create Motif-like interfaces through the use of a relatively easy-to-master scripting language. We provided an example script that throws a toolbar on the screen.

Perl is a hot scripting language, made hotter by its widespread use on the Internet. But you should be able to take advantage of its many uses, even if you never go near the Internet.

In what should come as a shock to no one, Linux features yet another command from the GNU Project, **gawk**, which is the functional equivalent of the **awk** programming language. **Gawk** works best on structured commands, although it does have extended programming capabilities.

For More Information

In all likelihood, this book will only be the beginning of your Linux voyage. You'll find that there's a sea of Linux information available—both on the Internet and in the print world. Your job will be to keep your head above water as you dive into these resources. Our emphasis here will be on Internet resources, because they are the ones you'll find most useful.

Internet Resources

Linux is a big topic on the Internet; a recent search on the Alta Vista search engine yielded 200,000 Web pages that mention Linux somewhere. Even when discarding the Web pages created by undergraduates who tinker a little with Linux, you're left with an amazing number of Web pages that cover Linux in some depth.

We've done a little editing for you and compiled this assortment of interesting Linux-related Web pages. Naturally—this being the World Wide Web and all—most of these pages spend a lot of time pointing you to other Web pages, which in turn point you to even more Web pages. Still, by beginning with these pages, you can significantly expand your Linux expertise.

The Linux Documentation Project

http://sunsite.unc.edu/mdw/linux.html

The home page of the Linux Documentation Project is an important source of Linux information and archived software; virtually any aspect of Linux usage and configuration can be found here. This is a page to be placed prominently in your Web browser's bookmarks list. You can search through the Linux Documentation Archives by connecting to *http://sunsite.unc.edu/architext/AT-Linuxquery.html* or *http://amelia.db.erau.edu/Harvest/brokers/LDP/query.html*.

Linux.Org

http://www.Linux.org/

Linux.org is a user-driven group dedicated to—surprise!—Linux.

Walnut Creek CD-ROM

http://www.cdrom.com

This is the online repository of Slackware; you can grab updated versions of Slackware from here.

The Linux Applications and Utilities Page

http://www.xnet.com/~blatura/linapps.shtml

Bill Latura maintains this excellent list of Linux applications and utilities. Unlike the Linux Software Map (see below), the applications are listed by category, making it much easier for browsing.

The Linux Software Map

http://www.boutell.com/lsm/

This site attempts to match your software needs with what's available in the Linux world.

The Linux FAQ

http://www.cl.cam.ac.uk/users/iwj10/linux-faq/

This site contains the most up-to-date version of the Linux Frequently Asked Questions (FAQ).

The Linux Configuration Page

http://www.hal-pc.org/~davidl/linux/linux.config.html

This page combines installation and configuration tips from a wide variety of users. These are the folks who have successfully installed and configured Linux on a vast assortment of PCs, and if you're having trouble with Linux on your no-name clone, you may want to check to see if someone else hasn't already invented that wheel.

The Linux Laptop Page

http://www.cs.utexas.edu/users/kharker/linux-laptop/

This page is similar to the Linux Configuration Page; it takes the experiences of many users and condenses them into a very useful guide to installing Linux on a wide variety of machines. Because it's a little harder to get hardware information about a laptop (i.e., what chipset is used for graphics) and some of the laptop components can be, well, a little fussy (check out the following Web listing), this page is essential for anyone wanting to run Linux on their laptop. Of similar interest is the Linux and X Window on Notebook Computers home page (*http://www.castle.net/X-notebook/index_linux.html*).

Linux PCMCIA Information

http://hyper.stanford.edu/~dhinds/pcmcia/pcmcia.html

Dave Hinds is a virtual god in the Linux community. Why? Because he's taken on the topic of making Linux work with PCMCIA ports, which are found mostly on laptops. PCMCIA ports are for those credit-card-type adapters (such as Ethernet and modem), and even in the mainstream community PCMCIA support isn't all it should be. Still, thanks to Hinds' Card Services for Linux, you can generally make a PCMCIA port work. We've included Card Services for Linux on the accompanying slackware CD-ROM; here's where you can go for more information.

The XFree86 Project

http://www.XFree86.org/

When you installed X Window on your Linux installation, you were really using XFree86, a version of X Window optimized specifically for the Intel architecture. This is the home page of the effort.

If there's one thing about the Web, it's always changing. If you want to generate a more current list of Linux-related home pages, check out the Alta Vista Home Page (*http://alta.vista.com*). Alta Vista is a searchable database of Web pages across the world.

Slackware Mirrors

The Slackware distribution of Linux is maintained at the *ftp.cdrom.com* site, in **/pub/linux/slackware**. At this site, you can grab the latest version of Slackware (although you shouldn't do this too often; you should upgrade in response to specific needs, not just as a general practice).

This is a busy site, however, so you may want to check out a mirror site. A *mirror site* contains the same Linux files as does the *ftp.cdrom.com* site, and they're updated regularly. In addition, as a good Internet citizen you should use the FTP site closest to you, keeping in mind that most of these sites are maintained for the use of local users, not global Internet users. (By the way, *ftp.cdrom.com* is in California.)

Table A.1 lists the sites known to mirror the Slackware Linux release.

Table A.1 Slackware Linux Mirrors

Country	Site	Directory
United States	*ftp.cdrom.com*	**/pub/linux/slackware**
	uiarchive.cso.uiuc.edu	**/pub/systems/linux/distributions/slackware**
	tsx-11.mit.edu	**/pub/linux/distributions/slackware**
	ftp.cps.cmich.edu	**/pub/linux/packages/slackware**
	sunsite.unc.edu	**/pub/Linux/distributions/slackware**
	ftp.rge.com	**/pub/systems/linux/slackware/**
	ftp.cs.columbia.edu	**/archives/linux/Slackware**
	ftp.ccs.neu.edu	**/pub/os/linux/slackware**
Australia	*ftp.monash.edu.au*	**/pub/linux/distributions/slackware**
Brazil	*farofa.ime.usp.br*	**/pub/linux/slackware**

Continued...

Country	Site	Directory
Canada	ftp.ECE.Concordia.CA	/pub/os/linux/dist/slackware
	pcdepot.uwaterloo.ca	/linux/slackware
Chile	ftp.ing.puc.cl	/pub/linux/slackware
	ftp.dcc.uchile.cl	/linux/slackware
	ftp.inf.utfsm.cl	/pub/Linux/Slackware
Czech Republic	vcdec.cvut.cz	/pub/linux/local
Denmark	ftp.dd.dk	/pub/linux/dist/slackware
Finland	ftp.funet.fi	/pub/OS/Linux/images/Slackware
France	ftp.ibp.fr	/pub/linux/distributions/slackware
	ftp.irisa.fr	/pub/mirrors/linux
Germany	ftp.uni-trier.de	/pub/unix/systems/linux/slackware
Hong Kong	ftp.cs.cuhk.hk	/pub/linux/slackware
Hungary	ftp.kfki.hu	/pub/linux/distributions/slackware
Japan	ftp.cs.titech.ac.jp	/pub/os/linux/slackware
Mexico	ftp.nuclecu.unam.mx	/linux/slackware
The Netherlands	ftp.leidenuniv.nl	/pub/linux/slackware
	ftp.twi.tudelft.nl	/pub/Linux/slackware
Norway	ftp.nvg.unit.no	/pub/linux/slackware
Portugal	ftp.di.fc.ul.pt	/pub/Linux/Slackware
	ftp.ncc.up.pt	/pub/Linux/slackware
South Africa	ftp.sun.ac.za	/pub/linux/distributions/Slackware
Spain	luna.gui.uva.es	/pub/linux.new/slackware
	ftp.uniovi.es	/pub/slackware
Switzerland	nic.switch.ch	/mirror/linux/sunsite/distributions/slackware
Taiwan	NCTUCCCA.edu.tw	/Operating-Systems/Linux/Slackware
United Kingdom	src.doc.ic.ac.uk	/packages/linux/slackware-mirror

Usenet Newsgroups

The Usenet newsgroups listed in Table A.2 are devoted to the Linux operating system.

Table A.2 Usenet Newsgroups Related to Linux

Newsgroup	Topic
comp.os.linux.advocacy	Linux is the greatest thing since sliced bread.
comp.os.linux.announce	News deemed to be of importance to the Linux community.
comp.os.linux.answers	Various "official" documents about Linux (FAQs, HOWTOs, READMEs, etc.).
comp.os.linux.development.apps	Developing Linux applications.
comp.os.linux.development.system	Discussion of developing modules and components specifically for Linux.
comp.os.linux.hardware	How to make Linux work with your NoName Inc. clone.
comp.os.linux.m68k	Porting Linux to Motorola-based computers (Amiga, Atari, et al.).
comp.os.linux.misc	Topics that don't fit within the other Linux newsgroups.
comp.os.linux.networking	Linux networking.
comp.os.linux.setup	Installing and configuring Linux.
comp.os.linux.x	Making XFree86 and X Window work under Linux.

Other Linux Implementations

Most Linux users work on a PC—after all, that's one of the big appeals of Linux. However, Linux has been ported to several other computer architectures, and more efforts are underway. In Table A.3, we list the port and the home page where you can find more information.

Table A.3 Linux Implementations on Non-PC Architectures

Project	Home Page
Alpha	*http://www.azstarnet.com/~axplinux/*
Acorn	*http://www.ph.kcl.ac.uk/~amb/linux.html*
ARM Linux	*http://whirligig.ecs.soton.ac.uk/~rmk92/armlinux.html*
Fujitsu AP1000+	*http://cap.anu.edu.au/cap/projects/linux/*
Linux/68k	*http://www-users.informatik.rwth-aachen.de/~hn/linux68k.html*
Linux/8086	*http://www.linux.org.uk/Linux8086.html*
Linux/PowerPC	*http://www.linuxppc.org/*
MkLinux	*http://nucleus.ibg.uu.se/macunix/*
MIPS	*http://lena.fnet.fr/*
SPARC Linux	*http://www.geog.ubc.ca/sparclinux.html*

Books

This book focused on the Slackware distribution of Linux on the accompanying CD-ROM. Should you wander away from this distribution, you may want to check out alternative sources of Linux information. Also, because this book doesn't cover the UNIX operating system or the X Window System in any depth (it takes entire forests to cover these topics in any depth), you may want to look for another UNIX/X book or two. The following list should fill most of your needs.

Other Linux Books

Running Linux, Matt Welsh and Lar Kaufman, O'Reilly & Assoc., 1995. This nonspecific Linux primer covers both Linux and some general UNIX commands. It's not tied to any specific distribution of Linux, so some of the information won't apply to the accompanying CD-ROMs. Welsh deals with some advanced topics not covered in this book.

Linux Network Administrator's Guide, Olaf Kirch, SSC, 1994. This technical overview of Linux networking should cover whatever you need to know about Linux on a network. Although this book is written from the viewpoint of a technically sophisticated user, it's useful for anyone who needs to deal with Linux on the network.

The *MIS:Press Slackware Series* features other books on Linux topics including: *The Linux Database* (by Fred Butzen and Dorothy Forbes); *The Linux Internet Server* (by Kevin Reichard); *Linux Programming* (by Volkerding, Foster-Johnson, and Reichard); and *Linux in Plain English* (by Volkerding and Reichard).

UNIX Books

teach yourself . . . UNIX, Third Edition, Kevin Reichard and Eric F. Johnson, MIS:Press, 1995. OK, so we're biased. This book provides an overview of the UNIX operating system, with topics ranging from system configurations and shell scripts to the Internet. Some computer experience is assumed.

UNIX in Plain English, Second Edition, Kevin Reichard and Eric F. Johnson, MIS:Press, 1994. This book covers the major commands in the UNIX command set—and most of the information should be directly applicable to Linux.

UNIX Fundamentals: The Basics, Kevin Reichard, MIS:Press, 1994. This book is for the true UNIX neophyte, who knows little or nothing about UNIX—or computing, for that matter. It's part of a four-book series covering UNIX fundamentals (the other titles are *UNIX Fundamentals: UNIX for DOS and Windows Users*; *UNIX Fundamentals: Communications and Networking*; and *UNIX Fundamentals: Shareware and Freeware*).

Programming Books

Al Stevens Teaches C, Al Stevens, MIS:Press, 1994. Provides a beginner's introduction to C programming and goes far beyond the brief introduction found in Chapter 10.

Graphical Applications with Tcl and Tk, Eric F. Johnson, M&T Books, 1996. This book covers Tcl scripting on UNIX, Linux,. and Windows. You can create a lot of neat applications with very little effort using Tcl.

Cross-Platform Perl, Eric F. Johnson, M&T Books, 1996. While the syntax may appear to have come from someone who's possessed, Perl provides many useful capabilities for system administrators and Web page developers.

X Window Books

The UNIX System Administrator's Guide to X, Eric F. Johnson and Kevin Reichard, M&T Books, 1994. This books focuses on topics related to UNIX and X, including configuration and usage. There's also some information about XFree86. An accompanying CD-ROM contains all the UNIX/X freeware detailed in the book.

Using X, Eric F. Johnson and Kevin Reichard, MIS:Press, 1992. This book covers X from the user's point of view, covering both usage and configuration issues.

Motif Books

Power Programming Motif, Eric F. Johnson and Kevin Reichard, M&T Books, 1994. This second edition covers OSF/Motif programming through version 1.2.

PC Configuration Books

IRQ, DMA & I/O: Resolving and Preventing PC System Conflicts, Jim Aspinwall, MIS:Press, 1995 (second edition in preparation).

Magazines

If you're at all serious about your Linux usage, you'll want to check out *Linux Journal* (SSC, 8618 Roosevelt Way NE, Seattle, WA 98115-3097; (206) 782-7733; $19 per year; *http://www.ssc.com*; *subs@ssc.com*). This monthly magazine covers the Linux scene, offering practical tips and profiles of the many interesting people in the Linux community.

The number of UNIX-specific magazines has fallen in recent years (a trend, admittedly, that baffles us). *UNIX Review* is our favorite, if only because two-thirds of the writing team contribute a monthly X Window column.

OSF/Motif and Linux

OSF/Motif, as licensed from the Open Software Foundation, is commercial software. OSF/Motif is actually many things, including a style guide, a window manager, and a set of programming libraries.

Because OSF/Motif is licensed commercial software, it's not included on the accompanying CD-ROMs. (Because OSF/Motif is beginning to be a prerequisite for any serious commercial UNIX development, you may at some time need to find OSF/Motif for your Linux system, if you're looking at any professional installations).

MetroLink (4711 N. Powerline Rd., Fort Lauderdale, FL 33309; (305) 938-0283; *http://www.metrolink.com*; *sales@metrolink.com*) offers OSF/Motif for Linux.

Linux HOWTO

The collective wisdom of the Linux community has been distilled into a series of text documents, called *HOWTO*, that describe various portions of the Linux operating system. We've included the latest version of these documents on the first accompanying CD-ROM (in the **/docs** directory), but if they don't answer your questions, you may want to see if a more recent version is available via the Internet. You can find them in many sites, but the official repository of these documents is at *sunsite.unc.edu*, in the **/pub/Linux/docs/HOWTO** directory.

XFree86 and Extensions

This appendix covers a frequently asked question about X on Linux: Linux doesn't support an X program that requires a specific X extension, so how do you get an X installation to run these programs? For example, XFree86 does not come configured to run three-dimensional graphics programs requiring the PEX extension.

We'll show you how to reconfigure your X server, extending it for these new needs. We'll show you how to do this and we'll discuss memory and performance trade-offs. We'll focus on the 3-D PEX extension, because it's the most-requested X extension that XFree86 doesn't support by default on Linux. However, the principles described here can apply to any X extension not directly supported by default in Linux.

What Is an X Extension?

An X *extension* is a piece of program code that extends the X server by adding some significant new functionality missing from the core X protocol, such as direct support for 3-D graphics.

Each extension needs to modify the X server and come with a programmer's library so that programs can use the extension. Some of these extensions, such as Shape, are so standard that it's hard to view them as add-ons. The Shape extension, for example, allows you to have round (and other odd-shaped) windows. The **oclock** program takes advantage of this, as we show in Figure B.1.

Figure B.1 Oclock using the Shape extension.

We list the most common X extensions in Table B.1.

Table B.1 Common Extensions to X

Extension	Usage
LBX	Low-bandwidth (serial-line) X, removed from X11R6.1
MIT-SCREEN-SAVER	Allows you to create your own screen savers
MIT-SHM	MIT shared-memory Ximage extension
Shape	Nonrectangular windows
X3D-PEX	PHIGS 3-D extension to X
XTestExtension1	Testing
XIE	X Image Extension
XInputExtension	Adds new input devices, like digitizing tablets
XVideo	Video extension

To see what X extensions your system supports, run the **xdpyinfo** program from within an **xterm** window (you must be running X, of course). When you run **xdpyinfo**, you'll see a lot of output describing your X server. Part of that output will include a list of extensions, probably something like the following:

```
number of extensions:    10
    BIG-REQUESTS
    MIT-SCREEN-SAVER
    MIT-SHM
    MIT-SUNDRY-NONSTANDARD
    Multi-Buffering
    SHAPE
    SYNC
    XC-MISC
    XFree86-VidModeExtension
    XTEST
```

Our X server doesn't support a lot of fun extensions, such as PEX.

What You Need to Extend X on Linux

Most of the time, you'll install XFree86 (the implementation of X for Linux) in binary format (meaning that you won't compile a special version designed for your unique needs). Because of this, you need a special package, called the *X link kit*, to extend the Linux X server. The link kit allows you to compile and link a new X server. The version of XFree86 that ships with this book contains the link kit; to install it, you'll need to run the **setup** program again. One of the menu choices should cover the link kit.

If you don't have this, you can get it over the Internet. Usually the file is called **X312lkit.tgz** or something like that.

The link kit allows you to rebuild the X server, adding something new: the X extension you'd like to add. You'll also need the **gcc** C compiler (which comes with Linux if you choose to install it) and **libgcc.a**, **gcc**'s standard C library. You should have installed both when you installed Linux. To see which version of **gcc** you have, try entering the following command line:

```
$ gcc -v
Reading specs from /usr/lib/gcc-lib/i486-linux/2.7.2/specs
gcc version 2.7.2
```

To really use PEX, you'll need to load the PEX libraries, include files, and fonts at install time. The PEX fonts, in **/usr/lib/X11/fonts/PEX**, are required to run most PEX programs.

In the next section, we'll show how to use the link kit to rebuild the X server for PEX, the X extension that supports three-dimensional graphics. These steps are basically the same for adding other X extensions, such as XIE, the massive imaging extension. We chose PEX because we've seen quite a lot of questions regarding this particular X extension. Three-dimensional graphics are becoming more and more popular. The basic techniques, though, apply to any X extension you need to add.

Once again, Linux can provide a nifty short cut here. Instead of rebuilding the X server, PEX support can be loaded from a module. The main page for XF86Config has more information about how to set this up.

Configuring the Server Build

Before you can build a new X server, you must edit a configuration file, **xf86site.def**, in the **/usr/X11R6/lib/Server/config/cf** directory. In this directory, edit the **xf86site.def** file (always make a backup first). In this file, you need to specify a number of things, including which X extensions to build (e.g., PEX), and which X server to build, such as SuperVGA, XF86_SVGA, or S3 XF86_S3.

In Table B.2, we list the settings we've used successfully. Note that we disable the creation of most of the X servers, because we only need the S3 and SVGA X servers. Because of this, you'll likely want to change our settings.

With any X release, these settings may change and there may be many new ones. Use Table B.2 as a guide, not as gospel. At this time, because you're rebuilding the X server anyway, you may also want to build in one of the other X extensions, such as LBX or XIE.

Most of the servers are turned on automatically. You can turn off what you don't want. For each X server, especially the SuperVGA ones, there is a list of drivers you can set. We always pick the defaults and leave the settings (XF86SvgaDrivers, XF86Vga16Drivers, XF86Vga2Drivers, and XF86MonoDrivers) alone.

If you build more than one X server, you need to uncomment the *ServerToInstall* line and put in the X server you want installed with the symbolic link from X. Otherwise, the *XF86_SVGA* gets set up as the default X server, X.

Comment out the *XF86Contrib* line to build all the contributed software.

Table B.2 Settings in the xf86site.def File

Setting	Value	Meaning
HasGcc	YES	Linux uses the **gcc** C compiler
HasGcc2	YES	Linux uses **gcc** version 2.x
XF86SVGAServer	YES	Builds 256-color SVGA X server
XF86VGA16Server	NO	Builds 16-color VGA X server
XF86MonoServer	NO	Builds monochrome VGA X server
XF86S3Server	YES	Builds S3 X server
XF86Mach8Server	NO	Builds the Mach8 X server
XF86Mach32Server	NO	Builds the Mach32 X server
XF86Mach64Server	NO	Builds the Mach64 X server
XF86P9000Server	NO	Builds the P9000 X server
XF86AGXServer	NO	Builds the AGX X server
XF86W32Server	NO	Builds the ET4000/W32 X server
XF86I8514Server	NO	Builds the IBM 8514/A X server
XnestServer	NO	Builds the Xnest server
BuildPexExt	YES	Builds the PEX extension
BuildXIE	NO	Builds the XIE extension
BuildLBX	NO	Builds the Low Bandwidth X extension
BuildScreenSaverExt	YES	Builds screen saver extension

Once you've set up the **xf86site.def** file, you're ready to starting building a new X server.

Building a New X Server

As the root user, you should perform the following steps to build your new X server:

1. Back up your current X server.
2. Build all the **Makefile**s.
3. Make the new X servers.
4. Quit X.
5. Install the new X servers.
6. Ensure that **/usr/X11R6/bin/X** links to the proper X server.
7. Start X to verify that the new X server works.
8. Run **xdpyinfo** to see if the new X extensions are available.
9. Clean the /usr/X11R6/lib/Server directory with make clean.

Before you start, always back up your current X server. This is to allow you to continue processing in case the new build fails. Then change back to the **/usr/X11R6/lib/Server** directory and build all the **Makefile**s by running the following command:

```
$ ./mkmf
```

All these commands must be run in the **/usr/X11R6/lib/Server** directory as the root user. This process will take a while, as it runs **makedepend** on a number of files.

Once **mkmf** finishes successfully, run **make**:

```
$ make
```

This builds the new X servers and will take even longer than the last step. Once you've built the new X servers, you must ensure that X is stopped. It's very convenient to **su** to the root user in one **xterm** window and build the new X servers while you have all the other windows on your screen available for your work—that's what multitasking is all about. When you need to install the new X server, however, you must ensure that X is stopped. So quit X in the usual way.

Then change back to the **/usr/X11R6/lib/Server** directory and run (again as root):

```
$ make install
```

This will copy the new X servers to **/usr/X11R6/bin** and set up **/usr/X11R6/bin/X** as a link to the default X server (the one you configured for this earlier). Double-check this essential link anyway and ensure that **/usr/X11R6/bin**/X links to the proper X server (see Chapter 3 for more on this).

Now comes the fun part. Try to run X as a normal user (as yourself, not the root user), using **startx**. This step is to ensure that X still works (presuming X worked before you did all this).

If you get X up and running (it came right up for us, so if it compiled and linked with no problems, this step should be easy), then run **xdpyinfo** in an **xterm** window to see if the new X extensions are available. The list should look something like the following:

```
number of extensions:      11
    BIG-REQUESTS
    LBX
    MIT-SCREEN-SAVER
    MIT-SHM
    MIT-SUNDRY-NONSTANDARD
    Multi-Buffering
    SHAPE
    SYNC
    X3D-PEX
    XC-MISC
    XFree86-VidModeExtension
    XTEST
```

(Yes, we cheated and built the LBX extension at the same time we built PEX.)

Once you're confident that everything is built up properly, run **make clean** in the **/usr/X11R6/lib/Server** directory (again as **root**):

```
$ make clean
```

This will get rid of all the **.o** files created when you built the X servers and free up a lot of wasted disk space.

As a final test, you may want to run one of the PEX demo programs that comes with X (you may not have loaded these programs, though), such as **beach_ball**.

Performance and Memory Issues

PEX consumes a lot of system resources, so don't load this extension if you're short on physical memory. When we built PEX and LBX into a new X server, it grew quite a lot, from 1,351,712 bytes to 1,509,550 bytes on disk.

Because of this, you may not want to compile in PEX or XIE, two of the largest X servers. If you have a low-memory system, then PEX or other large extensions like XIE (the X Image Extension) are simply not for you.

Index

About the CD-ROMs

There are two CD-ROMs accompanying this book. These disks are formatted under ISO-9660 standards, with Rock Ridge extensions. You can read the contents from both PCs and UNIX workstations. However, long UNIX filenames

The second CD-ROM contains useful source code (and in some cases, precompiled binaries) for Linux/UNIX applications and utilities mentioned in the book, as well as selected archives from two of the most popular Linux FTP sites.

communications

Communications utilities: diald (a daemon that provides a PPP connection on demand) and slirp (a SLIP/ PPP emulator that runs in a UNIX shell account)

email

Email-related utilities: MH (a mail-handling system), EXMH (an X front-end to MH), procmail (a local mail delivery/filtering utility), tkMail (a mail client built with the Tk toolkit), uudeview (a smart decoder for extracting binaries from news or email that are coded in any of the popular encoding formats), and xfmail (an XForms-based mail reader for X).

experimental

Nonsupported projects still in development: WINE (Windows Emulator for X, capable of running some Windows 3.1 programs directly under Linux) and NTFS (a kernel patch to provide read-only access to Windows NT partitions).

graphics

Graphics programs: POV-ray for Linux (a ray-tracing program).

multimedia

Multimedia and graphics programs: ImageMagick (an image-processing package), gimp (an image-editing package), mpeg_play (plays MPEG animations under X or on the Linux console), pixmap (a pixmap [xpm] editor), xpcd (a PhotoCD viewer), and xpdf (a viewer for PDF files, also known as Acrobat files, from the name of Adobe's PDF software).

networking

Networking applications: NIST (network time synchronizer), apache (World Wide Web [HTTP] server), ipfwadm (utility for setting up firewalls or IP masquerading under Linux), knews (threaded newsreader with an X interface), samba (a server for filesystem/printer access from Windows 95, NT, or other operating systems using SMB), surfit (a web browser written in Tcl/Tk/TclX), tkNet (a network configuration utility written in Tcl/ Tk), tkWWW (a Tk interface to the World Wide Web, allowing editing of HTML files), and wn (an easy-to-configure WWW server).

office

General usage items: OFFiX (drag-and-drop tools for the X desktop), TkDesk (a filemanager written in Tcl/Tk), addressbook (an address-book utility), cbb (checkbook balancer), groupkit (a library for building real-time groupware applications, such as drawing programs or editors that multiple users can use simultaneously), ical (calendar/date book), nedit (Motif-based editor for X), and teapot (spreadsheet program).

programming

Programming tools and utilities: LessTif (an X programming library compatible with Motif 1.2), Mesa (freely distributable version of OpenGL), java (the Java Developer's Toolkit for Linux), perl-5.002 (source code for the Perl language [binaries are included with Slackware on the first disk] as well as CGI—a perl add-on used for WWW programming), perl-tk (a perl extension to use the Tk toolkit), wxWindows (a C++ framework for developing multiplatform, graphical applications from the same body of C++ code), and xforms (a graphical user interface toolkit for X).

scientific

High-end applications: GRASS (a complex system developed by the Army for managing land use).

sunsite

Hundreds of programs from the sunsite.unc.edu Linux FTP site. This directory in turn contains four subdirectories: apps (applications like communications tools, text editors, math programs, TeX tools, and video programs), devel (developer tools), system (a host of system-level programs and utilities), and X11 (X Window tools and programs).

sysadmin

System-administration tools: xwatch (a program to keep an eye on system logs under X).

tsx-11

Hundreds of programs from the tsx-11.mit.edu Linux FTP site. This directory in turn contains subdirectories: doc (the contents of the Linux Documentation Project, as well as other relevant documents) and packages. which contain programs files for the likes of Epoch, Modula-2, Modula-3, Scilab, Eiffel, DSP processing, sound management, graphics, and other development tools and utility programs.

window-managers

Alternative window managers: bowman (a window manager for X with a NextStep look) and fvwm95 (a window manager for X with a Windows 95 look).

LINUX
JOURNAL

Every month *Linux Journal* brings you the most complete information
on what this powerful system can do for you and your work.
Linux Journal tells you what you need to know to make Linux work for you:

- Stay informed about current trends in Linux technologies
- Interviews with Linux developers and other personalities
- Keep up with the latest release in Linux software
- Avoid common mistakes by reading our tutorials
- Reviews of Linux-related products
- Columns on GNU, programming, technical support and more
- *LJ* Annual Buyer's Guide free with subscription (13th issue)

Questions?	FAX:	URL:
Call (206) 782-7733	+1 (206) 782-7191	http://www.ssc.com/
or (888) 66 LINUX		

For a free catalog of other SSC publications, e-mail info@ssc.com

*Just by returning this card I will
automatically receive a free issue of
Linux Journal, compliments of*

MIS:Press
Linux: Configuration
and Installation,
Third Edition

I also want to subscribe.

By subscribing
today, I will save
over
50% of the
newsstand price.

1 YEAR
❏ $22 US
❏ $27(USD) Canada
❏ $32(USD) Other countries

2 YEARS
❏ $39 US
❏ $49(USD) Canada
❏ $54(USD) Other countries

Please allow 6-8 weeks for processing

NAME _____

COMPANY _____

ADDRESS _____

CITY	STATE	POSTAL CODE

COUNTRY _____ TELEPHONE _____

FAX _____ E-MAIL _____

❏ Visa   ❏ MasterCard   ❏ American Express   ❏ Check Enclosed

CREDIT CARD # _____ EXP. DATE _____

SIGNATURE _____